the new
Northern Gardener

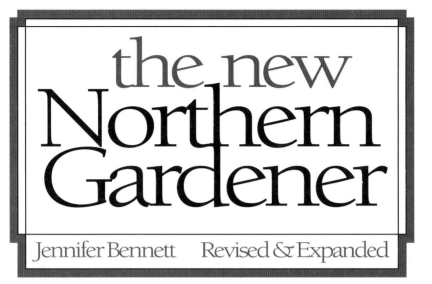

the new Northern Gardener

Jennifer Bennett   Revised & Expanded

FIREFLY BOOKS

BOOKMAKERS PRESS

First published as *The Harrowsmith Northern Gardener* in 1982 by Camden House Publishing (a division of Telemedia Communications Inc.)

Cataloguing-in-Publication Data

Bennett, Jennifer
  The new northern gardener

Rev. & expanded.
Previous ed. published under title: The Harrowsmith northern gardener.
Includes index.
ISBN 1-55209-012-4

1. Vegetable gardening – Canada.   2. Organic gardening – Canada.   3. Vegetable gardening – Northeastern States.   4. Organic gardening – Northeastern States.   5. Vegetable gardening – Northwestern States.   6. Organic gardening – Northwestern States. I. Title.   II. Title: The Harrowsmith northern gardener.

SB321.B47   1996   635'.0971   C95-933247-2

A Firefly Book

Published by
Firefly Books Ltd.
3680 Victoria Park Avenue
Willowdale, Ontario
Canada M2H 3K1

Published in the U.S. by
Firefly Books (U.S.) Inc.
P.O. Box 1338, Ellicott Station
Buffalo, New York 14205

Produced by
Bookmakers Press Inc.
12 Pine Street
Kingston, Ontario
K7K 1W1

Design by
Linda J. Menyes
Q Kumquat Designs

Color separations by
Friesens
Altona, Manitoba

Printed and bound in Canada by
Friesens
Altona, Manitoba

Cover illustration by
Heather Cooper

Printed on acid-free paper

Many of the people who worked at the Canadian magazine called *Harrowsmith* in 1982 helped create *The Harrowsmith Northern Gardener*, originally published by Camden House Publishing. Much of that book reappears within these covers. The book's new shape and appearance can be credited to former Camden House staff members Tracy Read and Susan Dickinson, now partners in Bookmakers Press Inc., and to Linda Menyes, now head of Q Kumquat Designs. Also instrumental in its production this time around were contributors Catherine DeLury and Mary Patton. And a special thanks to the ongoing support of publisher Lionel Koffler of Firefly Books.

Closer to home, I would have found the book very difficult to revise were it not for the beautiful office prepared for me by my husband John Ruskay and stepson Chris Ruskay. This room of my own has space for my computer, files, bookshelves and fax machine. I am fortunate, too, to have many gardening friends and many channels of information that provide me with much greater horticultural experience than I could possibly gain on my own.

To all the northern gardeners past and present who love discovering what will grow here.

Contents

11 Introduction

15 **Chapter One**
   Strategies & Speculations

15 Start Small

16 The Best Site

17 Vegetable Space Efficiency

19 Climatic Zones

20 Garden Plans

20 Vegetable-Garden Design

23 Flower-Garden Design

23 Exceptionally Long-Blooming Perennials

24 Using Space Efficiently

25 Fencing

25 Paper Plans

26 Tools

27 Quick Reference for Vegetable Yields

29 **Chapter Two**
   Digging & Delving

29 Breaking New Ground

32 Fertility

34 Analysis of Organic Fertilizers

35 Composition of Fresh Manure

38 Common Garden Plant Families

40 Compost, That Old Black Magic

43 Sources of Soil Tests

45 Chapter Three
A Movable Spring

46 Indoor & Outdoor Planting

46 Indoor Planting Schedule

46 Outdoor Planting Schedule

47 Light Requirements

47 Average Date of Last Spring Frost

48 Containers

50 Soil Mixes

50 Flowers for Cool Greenhouses

51 Sowing Seeds

52 Pre-germination

53 Transplanting

53 Cold Treatment

53 Hardening Off

54 Transplanting Outdoors

54 Seeding Outdoors

54 Gardening Under Glass

61 Chapter Four
Alphabetical Vegetables

62 From Artichoke to Watermelon

105 Chapter Five
Alphabetical Flowers

106 From Ageratum to Zinnia

157 Chapter Six
A Northern Bouquet Garni

157 Herb Gardens

159 Overwintering

159 The Harvest

160 Herbal Chemistry

160 From Angelica to Thyme

179 Chapter Seven
The Blooming of Summer

179 Watering

180 Mulching

182 Weeding

182 Insects: Friendly & Unfriendly

184 Companion Planting

185 Pesticides

Contents

187 Know These Bugs

190 Plant Diseases & Disorders

192 Disease Resistance

192 The Bedside Companion:
Vegetable Pollination

195 **Chapter Eight**
As You Reap, So Shall You Sow

196 Hybrid vs. Standard

197 Plant Selection

198 Seed Storage

199 Vegetative Reproduction

199 Division

199 Layering

200 Cuttings

200 The Best Vegetables for Seed-Saving

202 Seed-Sharing

203 Pollination of Vegetable Crops

205 **Chapter Nine**
Of Balconies, Bins & Boxes

207 Choosing Containers

208 Soil Mixes & Fertility

208 Seasonal Routines

210 Overwintering

210 Suspended Animation

213 **Chapter Ten**
Harvest Days, Frosty Nights

213 Frost Hardiness

215 Average Date of the Last Fall Frost

217 Vegetable-Garden Cleanup

217 Flower-Garden Cleanup

219 Vegetable Storage

219 Home Canning

220 Jams, Jellies & Pickles

221 Vegetables on Ice

223 Dried Produce

223 Root Storage

225 Flower-Bulb Storage

225 Bulb Hardiness

226 Climatic Zone Map

227 Glossary

232 Sources

240 Index

256 Credits

Introduction

"Odd as it may seem, a gardener does not grow from seed, shoot, bulb, rhizome or cutting, but from experience, surroundings and natural conditions."

—Karel Čapek, *The Gardener's Year*, 1931

It has been almost a decade and a half since *The Harrowsmith Northern Gardener* was first published. In terms of gardening information in Canada, 1982 seems a very long time ago. At that time, there were no Canadian gardening magazines, books about vegetable gardening in cooler climates were scarce and a generation of back-to-the-landers were in need of coaching. Measuring was still done mostly in inches, pounds and degrees Fahrenheit; I worked on a manual typewriter. *The Harrowsmith Northern Gardener* was an immediate best-seller, and H. Fred Dale, garden editor of *The Toronto Star*, called it "the leading choice for Canadian vegetable gardeners."

Now there is, if anything, an information overload. At least five Canadian magazines are dedicated to gardening, *Harrowsmith* has become *Harrowsmith Country Life*, and every season, there are several new gardening books on the market. Those of us who were once dedicated to the single goal of producing food at home organically find ourselves overwhelmed by information and new products. But we are eager to learn more, because we have come to want not just a utilitarian garden but a beautiful one too. It is ages old, this desire for bread and roses. As Canadian pioneer Catharine Parr Traill wrote in 1854: "Do not allow the lusty teams and the broad acres, the grass, the grain and the trees to occupy all your time, but give a thought and an eye occasionally to the beautiful."

This new edition, then, input on my Macintosh 6100/60, has been expanded not only to include the metric system of measurement but also to share information about growing the best ornamental annuals and perennials for northern gardens. And just where is North? *Harrowsmith* magazine's hard-pressed readers living north of 60 occasionally commented about what seemed to them a cavalier use of the adjective. As I wrote in the original *Harrowsmith Northern Gardener*, the word "north" is relative. The most specific I can be for my own purposes is to state that northern gardeners have a summer twilight long enough to allow all the carrots to be thinned after the sun sets but before dark. Northern gardeners have at least one trick up their horticultural sleeves for protecting the tomatoes

Flowers such as heliopsis and globe thistle, above, as well as bleeding heart, right, nourish northern spirits.

from fall frosts, and northern gardeners have lost most of their topsoil to Pleistocene glaciers that pushed it somewhere down around the corn belt. Northern gardeners may find their gardening endeavors squeezed into a growing season that some Southerners would consider little more than wishful thinking, but it is long enough to thaw their spirits and produce an abundance of fresh homegrown food and beautiful flowers for indoors and out. My own garden, a different one from my garden of a decade and a half ago, is north of Lake Ontario, with a frost-free season from about mid-May till mid-September, hot, dry summers, and winter lows around minus 31 degrees F (–35°C), sometimes without a protective snow cover.

This book is written for beginners and seasoned gardeners alike. It makes no presumption that you need a green thumb to be successful. A green thumb, after all, is little more than the experience, confidence and intuitive understanding of weather, plants and the earth that eventually come to everyone after a few seasons of observing and working in the garden.

The aim of this completely revised version of *The Harrowsmith Northern Gardener* is, as it has always been, to inspire the reader to grow a garden that is both economical and enjoyable, a garden that is a personal expression of your own likes and dislikes, climate and environment. Your garden can supply you with food and beauty without harming its surroundings, biologically or aesthetically. A lovingly tended garden is a living work of art that will repay you in ways too diverse to count.

—*Jennifer Bennett*

Chapter One

Strategies & Speculations

"Show me your garden, and I shall tell you what you are like."
—Alfred Austin, 19th-century English poet

Neat or disorderly, energetic or relaxed, practical or fanciful, brightly colored or quietly dressed in shades of green, a garden does indeed tell much about its owner. But a garden is also a reflection of climate and environment, answering questions not only about who you are but about where you are—what your soil is like, your winters and summers, your sun and shade, your rocks and trees, your rain and drought.

Every garden is a singular, distinct bit of land that must be understood gradually. You can't expect to have an immediate grasp of all the elements of a very complex ecosystem.

If you are fortunate enough to have fallen heir to an existing garden, you already have a head start. But perhaps you have a suburban plot whose topsoil was removed by the building contractors and replaced with an instant carpet of lawn over subsoil, or maybe you have a windswept apartment balcony, a shady, root-bound city backyard, an acre of impenetrable bush or a country field choked with weeds and old tires. If you are starting from scratch, the ground must be brought into condi-tion, and some hard manual work is unavoidable.

Take heart. Begin by setting your priorities.

Start Small

Great expectations may be inspiring, but they can also be intimidating. To expect that your first garden will look just like the one Aunt Minnie has been tending since you were knee-high to a Colorado potato beetle is an invitation to disappointment. A horticulturist at the University of Michigan puts it this way: "First-time gardeners, particularly, tend to take on larger gardens than they can handle. A workable rule of thumb is to decide how large a garden you think you can manage and then cut that roughly by half."

During your first year, then, limit what you do so that you can keep your garden manageable and enjoyable. What seems easy in spring can become overwhelming with the onset of summer weeds and droughts. Begin by buying transplants rather than growing your own, and when you do start growing from seed, step in at the shallow end by trying a few plants that are easy, such as tomatoes

Consideration of light exposure is critical; few plants are as shade-tolerant as begonias.

and marigolds. Every year, grow at least one plant just for fun, a leafy "pet" whose survival will not be critical to the home food supply but whose progress will be a matter of interest: perhaps sunflowers, bottle gourds or tomatillos. And, even if your aim is to grow useful plants, include a flower or two in odd garden corners—marigolds, nasturtiums or gladiolus are three favorites for vegetable gardens. They will cheer you up and may also act as pest-deterring companion plants.

On the other hand, if you think you want nothing but flowers, expand your horizons with a few vegetables or herbs pretty enough for an ornamental garden, such as basil, parsley, rosemary, Swiss chard, cherry tomatoes and chile peppers.

This is going to be *your* garden, a very personal, living extension of your property, your soil, your climate and your tastes, experiences and way of life. It won't be quite like anybody else's garden, and like any living thing, it will not be truly mature

for some time. Have patience. Many organic farmers estimate that it takes at least four years to make a real impression on the soil and crops. If you are planting shrubs and trees, they will not look really settled for 10 years. Traditional Japanese gardeners measure garden maturity not in decades but in centuries.

Remember, too, that gardening becomes easier as it goes along. Not only will your garden progress as you acquire skills and knowledge, but well-tended soil becomes progressively more free of weeds, more fertile and easier to work. One of the ironies of gardening is that it is the beginner, with the fewest gardening skills, who is often faced with the worst gardening conditions. But the gardener and the garden grow together, a process that can last a lifetime.

The Best Site

Whether you are establishing a new garden or enlarging an old one, begin by taking stock of your particular situation—its possibilities and shortcomings—so that you can make the most of it. There are plants that will suit any garden. You may not always be able to grow what you had hoped—roses will not thrive in wet ground, for instance, nor peppers in shade or azaleas in alkaline soil—but when you learn to work with your garden, you will discover exciting plants you did not know about. Those cherished plants of your dreams can be visited elsewhere.

Light: The garden's most pressing necessity is light. Unlike houseplants, most of which are tropical natives adapted to the rainforest floor, most vegetables, herbs and flowers need at least six potential hours of sunshine a day. Many plants will do better with even more. In the North, where the growing season is short, most vegetables and many flowers cannot receive too much light. Indeed, it is because of the longer days of the northern summer that gardens in these latitudes survive as well as they do. Plants exposed to less light than they require become weak and spindly, are slow to mature and are susceptible to pests and diseases.

The best orientation for the vegetable and herb garden is south or, almost as good, southeast or southwest. A garden that slopes slightly toward one of these directions is ideal. If you are able to remove or avoid overshadowing objects, you should do so, although many gardeners simply have to make the best of a plot surrounded by buildings and trees. Unfortunately, nearby trees not only shade the garden but also tap soil nutrients at the expense of smaller plants. If possible, situate the garden beyond the trees' drip line. If shade is unavoidable, plan to use that area for shade-tolerant plants, such as bunching onions or leafy vegetables like lettuce, spinach and Chinese cabbage. These crops actually do better in shade during hot weather. Foil reflectors and mulches can help by increasing light in shady areas.

Vegetable-garden rows are usually planted in a north-south orientation for equalization of light, but even if the rows are oriented differently, situate tall plants toward the north side of the garden, where they will not overshadow shorter plants. Corn, asparagus, sunflowers, Jerusalem artichokes

Vegetable Space Efficiency

The National Garden Bureau, a nonprofit American organization, has estimated the space efficiency of common garden vegetables. The theoretical maximum rating is 10, but no vegetable reaches 10, because no single item performs well under all soil conditions. In preparing these results, three dozen researchers across the United States considered total yield per square foot, average value per pound harvested and seed-to-harvest time; some plants may produce more than one crop in a year.

Space efficiency will change as one moves farther north. Hardier plants, such as onions and peas, will move upward on the scale, while tender selections, such as tomatoes and summer squashes, decline in productivity, until finally, in the shortest-season gardens, they become totally unproductive unless grown under cover.

This chart is most useful for gardeners whose growing space is very limited. The highest-rated vegetables listed are those which, all things considered, such gardeners will find most productive or valuable.

Vegetable	Rating
Tomato, grown on supports	9.0
Green bunching onions	8.2
Leaf lettuce	7.4
Summer squash: zucchini, scallop & yellow	7.2
Onion bulbs for storage	6.9
Edible-podded (snow or snap) peas	6.9
Bean, pole or runner (green or wax)	6.8
Beet, grown for greens and roots	6.6
Bean, bush (green or wax, snap)	6.5
Carrot	6.5
Cucumber (not bush types), grown on supports	6.5
Pepper, sweet green or yellow	6.4
Broccoli	6.3
Kohlrabi	6.3
Swiss chard	6.3
Mustard greens	6.2
Spinach	6.2
Radish	6.1
Cabbage	6.0
Leeks	5.9
Collards	5.8
Kale	5.6
Cauliflower	5.3
Eggplant	5.3
Pea, green shelled	5.2
Brussels sprouts	4.3
Celery	4.3
Corn, sweet	4.1
Melon: musk, honeydew and water	3.8
Winter squash (not bush types)	3.8
Pumpkin	1.9

Raising the beds not only prolongs the season but also promotes soil warmth and drainage.

and staked plants, such as tomatoes, cucumbers, peas and pole beans, are tall enough for the north end of the garden. Leafy crops, root crops and onions are among the shortest vegetables, while bushy plants—beans, potatoes, broccoli and such—fill in the midrange.

Flower gardens are more forgiving. There are ornamental plants which will tolerate spots that receive little or no direct sun. Virtually nothing except a few weeds will grow in the constant, deep shade in a tunnel or right against a north-facing wall, but provided there is reflected light, dappled light or direct exposure for part of the day, you can have an ornamental garden. In general, foliage plants are more shade-tolerant than flowering ones. Ferns, bergenia, hostas and houseplants moved outdoors for the summer are good shade dwellers. Among flowering plants, consider fuchsia, impatiens, browallia, lobelia and several others described in Chapter Five. In the shadiest spots, the most attractive options may be paving stones or bricks or a ground cover of bark chips or rounded pebbles.

Wind: In exposed gardens, especially on the prairies and the plains and in the Far North, harsh winds can dry out and damage garden plants. A row of trees or shrubs, called a shelterbelt, should be planted on the windward side of the garden and could even extend around the north, east and west sides, at a sufficient distance to prevent shading but close enough to be effective; it has been demonstrated that for every 1 foot (30 cm) of tree height, a distance of 50 feet (15 m) on the leeward side of the shelterbelt is somewhat protected from wind damage. Berries such as currants, gooseberries, highbush cranberries or saskatoons can be both protective and productive. The flowering shrubs caragana and potentilla are also tough enough for the job. Where trees or shrubs are impractical, Agriculture Canada suggests the substitution of a 4-to-6-foot (1.2-2 m) fence. At the lowest topographical point in the shelterbelt, leave a space between the trees or in the fence to allow cold air to pass out of the garden.

Warmth: Keeping the plants warm is the gardener's next priority, especially in spring and fall. Not only will seeds germinate slowly—if at all—in very cool soil, but throughout the season, plants are extremely dependent on a suitable temperature range for health and growth. Some plants, those termed "tender" because they can be killed very quickly by a frosty night, may die a slow death even at temperatures slightly above freezing. For instance, in an experiment at the University of California, 5 day old tomato plants were killed by 7 days' exposure to a temperature of 34 degrees F (1°C).

The average base temperature, the point below which plants cease growing, is 41 degrees F (5°C). The base temperature of spinach is 36 degrees (2°C), peas 42 degrees (5.5°C), corn and beans 50 degrees (10°C) and tomatoes and pumpkins 55 degrees (13°C). What this means is that if the average temperature does not rise above 50 degrees (10°C) during July, the corn, beans, tomatoes and pumpkins will either deteriorate or simply rest in suspended animation until August, provided the weather improves then. Pests and diseases, however, will not be so dormant and may finish off the stunted plants before they can progress.

Even if little can be done about the weather in such situations, the temperature around the plants can still be raised. Decreasing wind velocity is important, and for warmth as well as light, shade on plants should be kept to a minimum. Where there is sun, of course, there is probably warmth, and many of the northern gardener's schemes for increasing warmth depend on solar power.

Clear plastic and glass are the gardener's best allies in making the most of the sun's heat in any unshaded location. Just as in a greenhouse, the sun's warmth is held and concentrated beneath a transparent cover. The uses of transparent or translucent materials as crop covers are discussed in greater detail in "Gardening Under Glass" in Chapter Three.

Because cold air moves downward, any device that will raise plants above the surrounding soil surface will also help increase and prolong the warming power of the sun; raising the beds, gardening on a slightly sloping site and avoiding low

spots, or "frost pockets," can all make quite a difference. According to Alberta Agriculture: "On a small scale, the effects of cold-air drainage may be visible in the widely variable frost damage observed within a medium-sized garden. The lowest areas are hardest-hit, while higher portions may escape all frost damage."

One of the most reliable ways to suit the garden to the available warmth is to grow only plants which are frost-hardy or which will mature before the first fall frost. Sweet potatoes and okra, both frost-tender and slow to mature, will not mature in most northern gardens unless they have special mulches or covers. Many more gardens will not see watermelons, bell peppers or eggplants through to fruition, even if the plants are protected on frosty nights. You can discover the approximate length of your growing season by calling the closest horticultural society, state Cooperative Extension Service or office of the provincial Ministry of Agriculture and Food. As well, a climatic zone map is included at the end of this book. Taking into consideration the microclimate of your own garden and annual variation, you can expect that the duration of warm weather will vary from the norm by 2 to 3 weeks every year.

Climatic Zones

The North American continent has been divided several times into a system of zones determined by climate. The map most often used by Canadians is based on data collected during the 1960s and uses a complex formula to assess the information and divide the country into 10 zones, numbered 0 to 9. The U.S. map, revised by the United States Department of Agriculture during the 1980s, divides each climatic zone from the next by a difference of 10 Fahrenheit degrees (5.5C°) in the average minimum winter temperature. The U.S. system includes 10 zones. The lower the number, the lower the minimum winter temperature.

The reference you will find on page 226 is a simplified version of the U.S. Department of Agriculture's latest climatic-zone map, created to indicate general temperature trends that occur throughout the United States and the 10 Canadian provinces.

Climatic zones are most useful for determining

which shrubs and trees are likely to be successful in your garden. Most nurseries that sell woody plants indicate which map they use, labeling their plants appropriately. Whatever your zone, chances are that you can grow plants rated for your own or a lower zone number, but you may be taking your chances growing anything rated for a higher number. Also, climate does not follow precisely demarcated borders. As the scientists involved in the Agriculture Canada map project noted in the *Canadian Journal of Plant Science* in 1967: "Some plants recommended for a given zone may not survive every winter near the northern limit of that zone. Conversely, the southern limits may be more comparable to areas in the adjacent zone."

For vegetables and annual and perennial flowers, climatic-zone notations may be given by a nursery or seed house, but they are only general guidelines. The important climatic consideration with annuals is the length of the growing season. For herbaceous perennials—the standard flower-garden perennials that die back to the ground in winter—many factors influence winter survival. Snow cover and the soil water content during any particular year are as important as climatic zone.

Garden Plans

Unless you are planning to do all your gardening in containers, you are going to need a cleared patch of ground. How large an area you prepare depends not only on the amount you wish to grow but also on the way you garden; some gardeners make far more efficient use of space than others. In Chapter Two, the best methods of clearing and improving soil are discussed, but before any clearing begins, you should have a good idea of your space requirements. And remember, start small.

Vegetable-Garden Design

There are four basic vegetable-garden types: the single-row garden, the temporary wide-row garden, the permanent wide-row garden and the container garden. You might use only one type. Probably, you will combine two or more types, because each has advantages and drawbacks.

The Single-Row Garden: This has been the traditional Western garden plan for years, a small-scale version of large-scale farming that calls for planting vegetables in single rows, like lines of soldiers, with a pathway beside every row. Gardening this way requires a lot of space: Paths are usually about 2 to 3 feet (0.6-1 m) wide, while the crop may be only a few inches wide.

The single-row system is best suited to extensive use of mechanization, so it is popular with market gardeners and others who tend very large plots that would otherwise demand an overwhelming amount of mulching or hand-weeding. If the paths are wide enough to accommodate a tiller that is run down the paths every couple of weeks, weeds will appear only in the spaces directly around and between each plant, so hand-weeding might not be necessary at all. After the harvest, the entire garden can be cultivated, and next season's pathways may or may not fall where this season's vegetables grew.

Some crops are ideal for the single-row system. Asparagus, raspberries, corn and potatoes, for instance, need at least 1 foot (30 cm) between rows, and ease of picking or digging necessitates wider spacing. With other crops, such as leaf and root vegetables, however, the single-row system may be only one-thirtieth as space-efficient as a permanent wide-row garden. There are other disadvantages to the single-row system:
• It usually requires a monetary investment in mechanized (or horse-drawn) garden equipment, such as a tiller or cultivator.
• Because mulches cannot be used, the garden is vulnerable to drought and does not receive the additional organic matter a mulch provides.
• Despite cultivation, soil in growing areas becomes somewhat compacted, because pathways change from year to year. This year's trampled pathway may support next year's plants.

The Temporary Wide-Row Garden: In this system, plants grow not in widely separated single-file rows but in beds, usually about 3 to 4 feet (1 m) wide, narrow enough that the center of each bed can be reached comfortably from the pathway on either side. Such plantings are far more space-efficient than single rows, but they also may be more labor-intensive: Once a bed has been sown, it must be mulched or hand-weeded. Pathways should be wide enough—at least 18 inches (45

In a temporary wide-row garden, a mixture of annuals grows in beds until early autumn.

cm)—to allow you easy passage. Unless the paths are wide enough for a tiller, they, too, must be hand-weeded or mulched.

After the harvest, all or part of the temporary wide-row garden is cultivated—both beds and pathways—so the position of the pathways changes from year to year. Because this system, like the single-row garden, usually involves tiller use, it is most suitable for gardeners who must grow a great deal of food or who simply prefer mechanical over manual tending.

The Permanent Wide-Row Garden: In this case, pathways are permanent. The same beds are used from year to year and may be either mechanically tilled or hand-spaded between crops. As with the temporary wide-row garden, space is used far more efficiently than with single rows. Plants can

be spaced much more closely, not only because there are fewer paths but because the system encourages the gradual improvement of soil in the beds. Since pathways are permanent, they can be mulched or made attractive with some sort of paving. At the same time, all fertilizing and cultivation goes where it is most needed—in the beds—and no soil compaction need occur, since beds are never trampled.

Because the permanent wide-row garden is usually the most appealing in appearance and the most intensive in its use of space, it is often the choice of city gardeners, gardeners who are short of space or fertilizing materials and gardeners who simply prefer its aesthetic attributes. The beds need not be straight; they can follow the land's contours or the whims of the garden designer.

Annuals such as cosmos, calendula and gaillardia can be grown in special beds for cutting.

On the down side, making the beds and laying the paths demand a lot of time. If the gardener opts for buying materials such as framing lumber and paving stones, this permanent system can be expensive. In succeeding years, however, the garden should be fairly easy and inexpensive to maintain, although a certain amount of hand labor will always be required in sowing, weeding, cultivating and probably mulching.

The growing beds of the permanent wide-row garden may or may not be raised, although elevation of the soil level in the beds is usually a natural part of establishing this type of garden. Remove topsoil from the pathways, where it will not be needed, and add it to the growing beds, which will effectively lower the paths and raise the beds. Wide beds that are level with the paths are less susceptible to erosion than raised beds, which is a boon in very dry or windy areas, but raised beds are somewhat easier to tend, since the soil surface is closer to the gardener's working level. This characteristic makes raised beds especially useful for elderly and handicapped gardeners: beds can be made high enough for easy working from a wheelchair. There is yet another advantage to raised beds. A report from the University of Wisconsin notes: "Raising the soil level of the garden bed should be the first step taken to improve growing conditions on heavy soils. Better drainage can speed drying, which in turn increases soil temperature and allows earlier working in the spring." Conversely, in dry areas, and particularly where soil is sandy, raising the beds will worsen the effects of drought. Under these conditions, the beds should be at, or close to, path level and should be well mulched.

Whether raised or level, the beds will usually be about 3 to 4 feet (1 m) wide and can extend for any length the gardener finds convenient, usually the width or length of the garden. Paths should be at least 18 inches (45 cm) wide to allow passage with a wheelbarrow. Leave a wider area where a path turns a corner. A narrow path may look fine on paper but will not even be visible when bordered with full-grown bean and broccoli plants.

If beds are raised, the soil may or may not be contained within a framework. Raised, unframed beds are common in the Orient. These beds work well in areas that receive heavy rains, such as on the Pacific Coast, because they drain well. Unframed beds usually have a flat surface about 6 inches (15 cm) above the surrounding pathways, and their edges slope gradually to the path.

Alternatively, raised beds can be framed with such materials as brick, stone or, most commonly, wood, in which case you should opt for a decay-resistant wood such as cedar, buy wood that is pressure-treated or treat the wood with copper naphthenate, a preservative which is not toxic to plants when it dries. Frames can be made quite simply from 2x4s, 2x6s, 2x8s or rough lumber and can be constructed either outside the garden or *in situ*, after the soil has first been mounded into the approximate shape of the bed. Surround the raised soil with the frame, then level the bed soil and fertilize it as described in Chapter Two. Before the beds are constructed, deep digging, also described in Chapter Two, will help ensure that the soil is in good condition. The ground immediately around a framed bed should be free of grasses and weeds, because these plants will creep up under the frame and make for difficult weeding and an eventual invasion of the bed.

Framed beds are admittedly attractive, but they can be expensive, and they need construction and maintenance. Frost may cause frames to heave, and wooden frames must eventually be replaced.

The Container Garden: Container growing is described in detail in Chapter Nine. At this point, suffice it to say that while all gardeners may choose to grow a few plants in containers, taking advantage of the compactness, attractiveness and portability of the system, it is of the greatest value to gardeners with no real garden at all. If you have only an apartment balcony or a rooftop, for instance, you may have little alternative but to confine your horticultural adventures within the boundaries of a few pots and apple crates.

Flower-Garden Design

Flower gardens exist for beauty, not practicality. Only if you are growing flowers for indoor rather than outdoor beauty might you grow them in rows, in the manner of vegetables, specifically for cutting. Quantities of good cutting annuals such as gladiolus, zinnias, sweet peas and marigolds, as well as everlastings like strawflowers and globe amaranth, can be grown just like carrots or peas, so you can harvest the flowers without worrying about leaving empty spaces in the garden design.

Generally, however, the flower garden is a more permanent place inspired by your favorite color scheme and your preference for formality or in-

Exceptionally Long-Blooming Perennials

This selection is taken from a longer list compiled by Darrel Apps, who owns a plant nursery in Chadds Ford, Pennsylvania. The complete list was published in the Spring 1990 issue of *Perennial Plants* (Perennial Plant Association, 3383 Shirtzinger Road, Columbus, Ohio 43026).

20 weeks	*Corydalis lutea*, April-October
20 weeks	*Dicentra* x 'Luxuriant,' April-October
18 weeks	*Hemerocallis* x 'Happy Returns,' 'Stella de Oro,' June-October
18 weeks	*Scabiosa caucasica* 'Butterfly Blue Beauty,' May-October
16 weeks	*Verbena bonariensis*, June-October
15 weeks	*Achillea millefolium* 'Fire King,' June-October
15 weeks	*Coreopsis verticillata* 'Moonbeam,' June-October
14 weeks	*Coreopsis verticillata* 'Zagreb,' June-October
14 weeks	*Gaillardia* x *grandiflora* 'Baby Cole,' May-September
14 weeks	*Aster* x *frikartii* 'Monch' and 'Wonder of Stafa,' July-October
14 weeks	*Stokesia laevis* 'Bluestone,' June-September
14 weeks	*Veronica* x 'Sunny Border Blue,' June-October
12 weeks	*Chrysanthemum zawadskii* 'Clara Curtis,' July-September
12 weeks	*Geranium sanguineum* 'Striatum,' June-September
12 weeks	*Phlox paniculata* 'Eva Cullum,' July-October
12 weeks	*Phlox paniculata* 'Franz Schubert,' July-September
12 weeks	*Platycodon grandiflorus*, July-September
12 weeks	*Salvia* x *superba* 'Lubeca,' June-September
12 weeks	*Salvia* x *sylvestris* 'May Night,' June-September
12 weeks	*Sedum* x 'Autumn Joy,' August-October
11 weeks	*Rudbeckia laciniata* 'Goldquelle,' July-October
11 weeks	*Malva alcea* 'Fastigiata,' June-September
10 weeks	*Nepeta* x *faassenii* 'Dropmore,' May-September
10 weeks	*Phlox paniculata* 'Sandra,' July-September
10 weeks	*Rudbeckia nitida* 'Autumn Glory,' July-September

Easily outdistancing angelica flowers, honeysuckle exhibits the vertical prowess of vines.

formality. Your beds may be geometric or free-flowing. They may be island beds, entirely surrounded by lawn or paving, or they may themselves surround or edge a tree or wall. They may consist of only perennials or may be devoted to flowering annuals, remaining as empty as an unpainted canvas during winter.

In any case, there are a couple of design principles that almost always hold true: tall flowers go behind shorter flowers, with low ground covers in front, and you will probably want to have something in bloom from spring till fall or at least have attractive foliage. One nice thing is that modifications can always be made to improve your design. Most plants can be moved. This is best done in spring, when the plants are small. If that isn't possible, try to move them when they are not in full bloom. Always take as big a rootball as possible, replant immediately and water thoroughly.

Using Space Efficiently

Vertical Gardening: This is not really a system unto itself but, rather, a space-saving enhancement of any of the methods already described. Vertical gardening takes advantage of the fact that some plants will grow upward if offered support, thereby occupying less of your precious cultivated area. It also keeps fruit, foliage and flowers clean, relatively free of pests and high enough to facilitate easy picking, while contributing to the visual appeal of the garden. Vertical gardening, then, is likely to play a part in all but the most spacious gardens.

Among plants that grow upward on supports are twiners, clingers and climbers. Twiners include pole or runner beans, asparagus beans (related to peas, not asparagus), morning glories and many more flowering vines—plants that will wind around a stake or string. Clingers are plants that support themselves with holdfasts, like climbing hydrangea. Climbers hold on with tendrils or petioles. They include clematis, gourds, climbing cucumbers and all sorts of tall peas—shelling, snow, snap and sweet. Vining vegetables with heavy fruit, such as most cantaloupes, watermelons, winter squashes and pumpkins, have few tendrils to support their large fruit, so buttressing is necessary to prevent the fruit from pulling the vine down or breaking off and falling. Encourage these plants to grow upward by draping their vines over the trellis, and support their fruit with slings made of fabric tied at each end to the trellis so that the fabric and trellis, not the vine, take the weight of the growing melons or squashes. Bush or dwarf varieties of cucumber, melon, squashes and pumpkin will not climb but are ideal for gardens where vertical growing is not needed or not convenient.

In the flower garden, the usual vertical supports are trellises, walls and fences. Some vigorous climbing plants, such as clematis and morning glory, will also reach into deciduous shrubs and trees, providing flowers in unexpected places. In the vegetable garden, good vertical supports include sturdy stakes, wire fencing, a lean-to or wooden arch 6 to 7 feet (2 m) high and tripods or quadripods shaped like tepees. For these, make the legs about 8 feet (2.5 m) long, using 1x2 lumber or fairly straight poles. Paint the bottom 2 feet (60 cm) of the legs, push the painted ends securely into the soil, then tie the tops together.

Climbing or twining plants can also be encouraged to climb a trellis, guy wires, vertical strings, apartment-balcony railings or fish netting fastened against the sunny wall of a house, garage or outbuilding. Among edible plants, try cucumbers, gourds, melons, scarlet runner beans and climbing nasturtiums, whose flowers and leaves can be added to salads.

Although tomatoes do not climb naturally, they are the most popular vegetables for vertical gardening. Again, this method saves space, keeps fruit clean and allows for easy picking. Tomato plants can be tied to 5-foot (1.5 m) stakes, trained to twine around vertical strings hanging from a supported cross-member or held up in cylindrical cages, either purchased or handmade from wire fencing. Roses, too, need assistance. The tall-growing type, called climbing roses, can be tied up and coaxed to drape over a fence or pergola. Curved thorns hold them in place.

Fencing

A garden fence can serve many functions. It can be used to support climbers, vines and roses, and if it is on the windward side of the garden, it can lessen wind damage. Moreover, as Thomas McCulloch wrote in *The Stepsure Letters*: "Good fences make good friends and safe crops." One's "friends," in this case, may be chickens, cows, a raccoon eyeing the ripening corn or a neighbor's child who wants to gather the tulips. Although even the best fence will not keep all unwanted visitors away—squirrels and crows find their way through, over or around almost anything—a good fence is certainly one of the best defenses a gardener has.

Fencing materials include hedge plants, rocks, bricks, chicken wire and neat rows of white pickets, each material having its own expense and degree of usefulness and attractiveness. A single line of electric fencing around the perimeter of a vegetable garden, at least during corn-ripening season, is a fairly effective defense against raccoons. Bush-country gardeners whose gardens are grazed by deer may want to try sloping a tall fence inward—deer are unwilling to make the long jump necessary to clear such a barrier. When designing a fence around a garden, don't forget to leave a gate wide enough to accommodate a wheelbarrow or, if necessary, cultivation equipment.

Paper Plans

All the elements already described—the fence, the growing beds or rows, the vertical plantings, the pathways—should be plotted on paper as you, the prospective gardener, formulate your plans, taking into consideration the climate, your needs, your skill and willingness to work, your tastes and the space to which you must confine your garden.

Refer to the table "Quick Reference for Vegetable

Yields," on the facing page, to find out approximately how large a crop to expect from 100 feet (30 m) of row and how much to plant in order to harvest an entire year's supply of that vegetable. More specific details can be found in the vegetable descriptions in Chapter Four.

The table "Exceptionally Long-Blooming Perennials," on page 23, may help you choose perennial flowers. When selecting annual flowers, consider the following stalwarts that can be sown directly in the garden in fall or early spring: alyssum, calendula, calliopsis, callistephus, candytuft, cleome, cornflower, cosmos, dianthus, forget-me-not, larkspur, nicotiana, annual poppy, portulaca, rudbeckia, snapdragon, sunflower, sweet pea and Virginia stocks. If a few flowers are left in the garden to produce seed, these annuals are likely to reappear next year, free of charge and in even greater numbers than before.

Tools

With the garden planned, you will need tools to put your ideas into action. The tools you require may be as expensive as a rotary tiller or as inexpensive as a spade or a trowel, often available for next to nothing at country auctions and garage sales. Tillers can be rented from garden stores or tool-rental outlets, while lumber, poles, fencing and pathway-paving materials may be available secondhand. Rustic materials such as bark chips, tree branches and stones can help create a very attractive garden.

A good spade, one with the blade nailed to the handle, will be necessary for digging beds and pathways, mixing compost and preparing hills for squashes and melons. Stainless steel is expensive but esteemed, because it keeps a sharp edge and is long-lasting. A small trowel is almost indispensable, from spring seeding through summer weeding and fall digging of carrots and planting of tulips. A hoe is a wonderful leveling and weeding device. Scraped over the soil surface every few days, it easily keeps weeds in check.

A soil thermometer is not a necessity, but it is a help to the beginner and to anyone with a scientific curiosity. Soil temperatures will be noted frequently in this book, particularly the ideal soil tem-perature for seed germination of individual vegetables listed in Chapter Four. Good-quality soil thermometers are available from several mail-order seed houses, such as Johnny's Select Seeds or Stokes (see Sources), as well as from some nurseries. A standard metal thermometer can also be used, inserted 2 to 3 inches (5-7.5 cm) into the soil.

Buckets are useful for carting transplants to the garden, for watering, for bringing produce indoors, for preparing manure teas and as temporary resting places for perennial weeds. A bucket, in fact, performs many of the duties of a wheelbarrow, but on a smaller scale. A wheelbarrow or, better yet for those who can afford one, a garden cart is good for transporting mulching materials, compost, soil and harvested vegetables.

A manure fork, which has five tines (a pitchfork has only three), is useful for turning compost, especially when the pile is newly made, and can also be used for digging potatoes, Jerusalem artichokes and parsnips, although a potato fork, which has rounded tines, will do a better job with underground crops.

Some watering equipment is needed for most gardens. The system may consist of a cleaned oil drum to catch rainwater dripping from the eavestroughs, a hose and sprinkler, a system of underground pipes and pop-up sprinklers, a drip or soaker system involving perforated hoses or even an irrigation network. Take into consideration your water pressure, the distance from the water source to the garden, the water quality (fluoride and chlorine can harm plants), the water's financial and environmental value and how much time you are willing to devote to watering. The best water you can give your plants is rainwater; it is soft, relatively pure and comes naturally warmed to the ambient temperature. If you have a way to collect and distribute rainwater during times of drought, your garden will be all the better for it.

As you progress, you will probably add to your collection of tools and equipment, but do so gradually. Later, you may want to buy containers for homegrown transplants, row markers, a rake (useful for gathering compost and mulch materials), pruning shears, a watering can, spraying equipment, a gardening fork (for searching out weedy grass roots), plant pots, plastic mulches and hot caps (see Chapter Three). Keep all equipment and tools under cover when not in use, and clean rusted metal blades with steel wool or sandpaper, wiping the blades with an oily rag at the end of the season. For best storage, hang tools on a wall.

The old saying "It's a poor workman who blames his tools" still has the ring of truth, but while good tools cannot make a good gardener, they certainly help.

Quick Reference for Vegetable Yields

The following chart lists "typical crop yields in northern home gardens of average fertility," according to estimates by Johnny's Select Seeds of Maine; in other words, the yields are typical of the northeastern United States, about zone 5 (see "Climatic Zone Map" on page 226). Gardeners with higher zone numbers may experience greater average yields (especially with fruiting crops), just as those with lower zone numbers may have lower yields. But, whatever the climatic zone, yields can vary greatly. The planting recommendations apply to gardeners who wish to grow a full year's supply of that vegetable for fresh use, storage, canning or freezing.

Vegetable	Average crop per 100 feet (30 m)	Recommended planting per person
Bean, bush snap	120 lb (55 kg)	20-30 ft (6-9 m)
Bean, pole snap	150 lb (68 kg)	20-25 ft (6-7.5 m)
Bean, dry	10 lb (45 kg)	100 ft (30 m)
Beet, greens	40 lb (18 kg)	15 ft (4.5 m)
Beet, roots	100 lb (45 kg)	10-20 ft (3-6 m)
Broccoli	75 lb (34 kg)	10-15 plants
Brussels sprouts	60 lb (27 kg)	10-15 plants
Cabbage	150 lb (68 kg)	10-20 plants
Carrot	100 lb (45 kg)	25-30 ft (7.5-9 m)
Cauliflower	100 lb (45 kg)	10-15 plants
Celery	75 heads	5-10 plants
Corn, sweet	10 dozen ears	50-100 ft (15-30 m)
Cucumber	120 lb (55 kg)	15-25 ft (4.5-7.5 m)
Jerusalem artichoke	150 lb (68 kg)	10-20 ft (3-6 m)
Kale	75 lb (34 kg)	10-20 ft (3-6 m)
Kohlrabi	50 lb (23 kg)	10-15 ft (3-4.5 m)
Leeks	150 leeks	10 ft (3 m)
Lettuce, head	80 heads	10-15 plants
Lettuce, leaf	50 lb (23 kg)	10-15 ft (3-4.5 m)
Muskmelon	75 fruits	10-15 ft (3-4.5 m)
Onion, bulb	80 lb (36 kg)	50-100 ft (15-30 m)
Parsley	30 lb (13.5 kg)	5-10 ft (1.5-3 m)
Parsnip	100 lb (45 kg)	10 ft (3 m)
Pea, shelled	15 lb (6.8 kg)	50-100 ft (15-30 m)
Pepper, bell	50 lb (23 kg)	5-10 plants
Potato	100 lb (45 kg)	30-50 ft (9-15 m)
Pumpkin	200 lb (90 kg)	5-10 ft (1.5-3 m)
Radish	100 bunches	15-25 ft (4.5-7.5 m)
Rutabaga	150 lb (68 kg)	10-20 ft (3-6 m)
Spinach	30 lb (13.5 kg)	30-50 ft (9-15 m)
Squash, summer	150 lb (68 kg)	5-10 ft (1.5-3 m)
Squash, winter	125 lb (56.5 kg)	25-30 ft (7.5-9 m)
Tomato	100 lb (45 kg)	10-20 plants
Watermelon	50 fruits	10-15 ft (3-4.5 m)

Chapter Two

Digging & Delving

"... this fertility must be maintained by rational, judicious cultural
methods, or the excellent results obtained when
these soils are first tilled will more or less rapidly disappear."

—Frank T. Shutt

Central Experimental Farm, Ottawa, 1908

Ever since we could crawl through it, we've been warned to keep out of the mud, to keep clean. Reputations, we've since learned, can be "soiled," thoughts and books can be "dirty." No wonder the most fastidious gardeners don rubber boots and gardening gloves before tackling the stuff that has suffered so much bad press.

But any gardener who wants a successful, satisfying garden will have to get used to working hands-on with the fingernail-clogging salmagundi that supports all vegetables and flowers, a goodly number of earthworms, countless underground microorganisms and, less directly, all the land-bound life of the planet. Gardening gloves have their uses—when pulling stinging nettles and pruning roses and junipers, for instance—but most times, they get in the way of that vital handshake between gardener and garden.

Breaking New Ground

Will the garden soil be sandy, loamy or principally clay or silt? Little will be known until the land is cleared, a sometimes backbreaking task that should take place as far as possible in advance of the first gardening season. That way, soil conditioning will have a few months' head start and the plot will be warm and ready for planting as early as possible in spring. No matter what the time of year, however, the gardener should not work very wet soil—soil that oozes water if a handful of it is squeezed—the situation which prevails immediately following a heavy rain or a spring thaw. After being worked, wet soil hardens into unmanageable clumps. Wait until the soil is slightly dry and crumbly.

Before any new garden plot can be worked, it must be cleared of stones, trash, shrubs and trees. While debris can be removed right away, clearing bushland is so time-consuming that it generally calls for a gradual expansion of the garden plot. If your budget allows, hire professionals to do the job. They can clear land relatively quickly and efficiently.

Most plots are far too small for a tractor and plow, even if the gardener has access to them, and a tiller will make little headway in sod. Sod can be smothered if it is blanketed for several months

Trenching prepares a new garden bed so that the area is free of weeds and large stones and the soil is more fertile and porous. Each trench is dug, amended and shoveled into the previous trench.

under a light-excluding cover such as black plastic or a deep mulch of compost or straw over several layers of newspaper. Otherwise, sod is best removed by hand, a fairly slow job but one that leaves the ground ready for gardening almost immediately and makes a long-lasting dent in weed growth. The sod can be removed and the soil underneath deeply improved.

If the soil under the sod is in fairly good condition, trenching may not be necessary. Simply pry up the sod a chunk at a time—a task that is a lot easier in spring or just after a rain or watering, when the sod is soft and wet. Shake free and scrape off as much soil as possible, then pile the sods upside down at one end of the garden, where they will slowly compost. In about a year, the soil at the bottom of the sod pile can be returned to the garden.

Once the surface is clear, work through it with a spade or pitchfork, removing stones, trash and weed roots as deeply as you can easily dig. After that, simply dig or till weeds as they appear. Twitch grass, or quack grass, is especially persistent, spreading both by seed and by underground rhizomes, so it must be combated with diligence. Dig up all the rhizomes, if you can, and toss them where they cannot take root again. The failure to remove all twitch-grass roots and not to keep up with its reemergence is one of the most common mistakes beginning gardeners make.

Bring the soil surface back up to at least its for-mer level by adding topsoil, compost or rotted manure. The planting of a green-manure crop, described later in this chapter, will also help get the new plot off to a good start and is an ideal way for city gardeners with no ready supply of animal manure or compost to add similar nutrients and organic matter to their soil.

Trenching: This is a thorough method of soil preparation where quality is paramount—for vegetables and roses, for instance—but trenching is so laborious that it is usually confined to places where the soil is very poor or where cultivation will be intensive. Proceed as follows:

• Remove the sod from a patch about 2 feet (60 cm) wide and the width or length of the garden, or whatever you can manage, shaking free as much soil as possible, then pile the sod at one end of the garden.

• Dig at least 6 inches (15 cm) of soil from the cleared rectangle, piling it beside the sod and tossing any stones or trash into a different pile or into path areas.

• Remove the sod from a 2-foot-wide (60 cm) strip parallel to and bordering the first trench, placing these chunks upside down on the bottom of the first trench and breaking them up with the spade.

• Remove 6 inches (15 cm) of soil from the second trench, and spread it over the sods you have just placed in the first.

• Proceed along the garden in this fashion, digging

Prepare a new garden by removing weeds and sod in chunks and shaking off the soil.

the last trench and then placing the sod and soil from the first trench in the last one.

• Fertilize the entire plot with compost or manure at the rate of 1 pound per square foot (5 kg/m²).

Deep Digging: Where sod is not involved, the soil can be rejuvenated or conditioned by the same process, in this case known as deep digging. Deep digging allows plant roots, many of which descend very deep into well-worked soil, to grow unimpeded. Dig a long, narrow trench about 6 inches (15 cm) deep, and pile the soil alongside the trench, removing stones, trash and weed roots. Break up the bottom of the trench with a spade, and mix in 1 pound of manure per square foot (5 kg/m²). Then replace the topsoil, incorporating the topsoil from pathways as well, if you are building raised beds (described on page 22).

Once the soil has been cleared, future cultivation can be done by hand or with machinery as large as a tractor or horse-drawn cultivator or as small as a rotary tiller, depending on the gardener's prefer-

ence and scale of operation. However, horticulturist Bob Fleming of the Ontario Ministry of Agriculture and Food points out that the overuse of a rotary tiller can damage soil structure, since it reaches to a depth of only about 4 inches (10 cm) in heavy soils, which ideally should be cultivated to a depth of 8 to 10 inches (20-25 cm). Fleming encourages trenching followed by hand-spading: "An easy way to make sure that you incorporate an even amount of organic material is to spread it evenly over the garden surface before you begin the spading process."

Organic Material: By "organic material," Fleming means animal or vegetable materials that raise the soil's content of fiber and humus. The usual organic materials are composts and livestock manures. All soil contains organic matter, formed by the decomposition of animal and plant cells. Organic matter supports the life of the soil, binding its particles together, providing a spongy texture that protects soil from erosion and drought, holding moisture for plant roots, feeding earthworms and containing more than half the nutrients needed by plants. A report from the University of Wisconsin illustrates this point. In a test plot provided with organic material (peat moss and sawdust) but no fertilizer, "the yield of beets and onions on heavy soils was increased 47 percent and 77 percent, respectively, and petunias produced 32 percent more blooms where soil drainage and tilth were improved." Also, adding organic matter is one of the best ways of improving saline soils, most often found on the prairies or where excessive amounts of fertilizers have been used and rainfall is not sufficient to wash out the excess.

The best gardening practices focus on maintaining or, better still, increasing the levels of organic matter in the soil, thus automatically helping sustain soil fertility and quality as well. By returning all crop, livestock and even human wastes to the soil, some Eastern cultures have managed to grow intensively planted crops on the same land for thousands of years without deterioration of soil quality or diminished harvests.

Whatever the constitution of the soil, it will benefit from the addition of organic material. Garden soil may be sandy or loamy or principally composed of clay or silt. If *sandy*, it will feel gritty and will allow water and nutrients to percolate through easily. Because sandy soil is well aerated, many crops appreciate it, but it does dry out quickly and thus requires mulching in most circumstances. Soils with a high *clay* or *silt* content have particles so fine that the soil may feel slippery or gluey. Rain stands in puddles, and as the soil dries, it becomes hard and cracks. Such soils need a great deal of organic matter in the form of mulches or composts to become really workable and porous. *Loam* is a mixture described by Agriculture Canada as "soil material that contains 7 to 27 percent clay, 28 to 50 percent silt and less than 52 percent sand." More to the point, gardeners blessed with loamy soil are already well on their way to success, but even loam can be further improved with organic matter.

Fertility

If organic material is so essential for plant growth, what, then, is the role of fertilizer? The word "fer-

Compost is the best soil builder for a new plot, providing organic matter and gentle fertilizer.

tility" suggests the soil's nutrient content, which makes it capable of supporting plants. Just as people require various vitamins and minerals to remain healthy, plants require a diet containing many elements: macronutrients (substances needed in fairly large quantities), such as carbon, hydrogen, oxygen, nitrogen, phosphorus, potassium, calcium, magnesium and sulfur; and micronutrients, such as boron, copper, iron, manganese, molybdenum, zinc and chlorine. Hydrogen and oxygen are supplied by the air and water, but the remainder must be in the soil—and available to plants—if the garden is to be productive.

Fortunately, providing such a complex diet is not as difficult as it might appear. Plants, like people, can obtain all the nutrients they require from a very simple menu. Unfortunately, encouraged by the agricultural chemical industry, home gardeners sometimes wrongly take their cues from commercial growers, most of whom rely on synthetic fertilizers, because of the scale of their operations, their monocropping—growth of just one type of plant on its own—and their use of methods that deplete soil organic matter and certain nutrients. Home gardeners, on the other hand, grow a great variety of plants on a relatively small plot of soil, an ideal situation for the use of soil-amending measures, such as crop rotations, mulching and composting. Also, because home growers are much more willing to accept misshapen or blemished produce than are commercial growers, nutrient levels need not be precisely the best for each plant, an extravagant ambition under any circumstances.

Chemical Fertilizers: There are a few situations in which chemical fertilizers are valuable: for indoor seedlings and houseplants; for quickly correcting a severe soil deficiency, as indicated by a soil test; for starting compost (described on page 40); for providing sufficient nutrients to a small garden that must produce a very large crop; and as all-round fertilizers for gardeners who cannot devote the time or labor necessary for collecting organic fertilizers and adding them to the soil. In all cases, however, the use of chemical fertilizers should be balanced by the use of some organic fertilizers. No gardener should depend entirely on synthetic or chemical fertilizers for several reasons:

• They are expensive and nonrenewable, some mined and some petroleum-based. The procedures involved in collecting, processing and shipping synthetic fertilizers are environmentally damaging.

• Most synthetic fertilizers are fast-acting and powerful. They can be easily overapplied, in which case they will do more harm than good—killing plants, upsetting the soil balance and contributing to water pollution.

• Synthetic fertilizers add nothing to the tilth or quality of the soil, the lack of which may be the basis for the presumed fertilizer requirement.

• Synthetic fertilizers are never the only answer to a garden problem. Gardeners often become involved in a routine of using fertilizers every year, encouraged by advertisements and their own lack of experience. Soil that is too cool, too hot, too shady, too wet, too acidic or too alkaline can produce plants that seem to need fertilizer, although there are plenty of nutrients in the soil—the plants

Pile compost until the surface is higher than the surrounding ground. Level, firm, water, and plant.

simply cannot make use of what is already there.

Gardeners who do buy fertilizers should know that the numbers on the package, called the analysis, refer to the percentage (by weight) of nitrate, phosphate and potassium, in that order. So superphosphate, 11-48-0, for example, contains 11 percent nitrate, 48 percent phosphate and no potassium; the remaining 41 percent is composed of other chemicals or inert fillers. Compared with organic fertilizers, the analysis looks impressive. If poultry manure were sold in the same fashion, for instance (and if such a low analysis were legal), it would be labeled something like 0.9-0.7-0.4. But that doesn't tell the whole story. The other 98 percent of poultry manure is all nutrients, water and organic matter; it is 100 percent useful.

Acidic or Alkaline: Whether fertilizers are organic or synthetic, they have the greatest effect on plants when the soil is close to neutral, the midpoint between acidic and alkaline. Chemists ex-

Analysis of Organic Fertilizers

Organic Materials	Analysis	Applications
Livestock manure & bedding	0.5 to 2–0.1 to 0.8–0.4 to 1.0	Excellent fertilizer and soil conditioner. See chart on facing page. Apply rotted manure to good soil at 5 pounds per square yard (2.8 kg/m^2), or 12 tons per acre; double that as an initial application on poor soil. Use as manure tea throughout the season.
Sewage sludge (dry) (i.e., Milorganite)	0.7 to 5.1–1.1 to 6.1–0.2 to 1.1	Human wastes treated to kill pathogens and commercially prepared sewage sludge may still contain harmful amounts of heavy metals. If certified safe in this respect, use in place of any high-nitrogen fertilizer. Otherwise, use only on lawns and flowers.
Compost	0.5 to 3.5–0.5 to 1–1 to 2	Apply freely where most needed, year-round.
Bonemeal (steamed)	0 to 4–11 to 26–0	Apply sparingly to compost pile or as side-dressing if soil test indicates lack of phosphorus. One pound (500 g) of bonemeal per 100 square feet (9.3 m^2) is usually adequate.
Cottonseed meal (dry)	6–2.5–1.7	Expensive; seldom available in Canada. Apply sparingly as side-dressing.
Dried blood	12–1.5–0.57	Expensive and very rich in nitrogen. Use sparingly in compost or as side-dressing.
Fish emulsion	5–2–2	Rich in micronutrients. Dilute and apply as foliar (leaf) spray or fertilizer throughout the season according to need.
Sawdust & wood shavings	0.4–0.3–0.7	Use in garden pathways or sparingly in the compost pile.
Straw	0.5–0.2–0.1	Use as mulch or as an ingredient in the compost pile.

Natural Deposits

Wood ashes	0–1 to 2–3 to 7	Use only if soil test indicates acidic soil, lack of calcium. Substitute double the rate recommended for crushed limestone.
Colloidal phosphate	0–25–0	Use only if soil test indicates lack of phosphorus.
Rock phosphate	0–20 to 30–0	Use only if soil test indicates lack of phosphorus.
Granite meal or dust	0–0–3.5	Apply only where soil test indicates lack of potassium. Also contains trace minerals.
Greensand	0–1.35–4 to 9.5	Seafloor deposit containing many trace minerals. Mix with high-nitrogen fertilizer as compost additive.

press acidity or alkalinity in terms of pH, a scale that varies from 0 to 14, with 7 indicating neutral. Values below 7 indicate increasing acidity; values between 7 and 14, increasing alkalinity. Values between 6 and 7, slightly acidic, are the best for most garden plants. (Other plants, however, may have quite different pH preferences.) The pH scale is logarithmic, so a pH of 6 is 10 times as acidic as pH 7, a pH of 5 is 10 times as acidic as pH 6, and so on.

As the soil pH approaches neutral, more nutrients become available to plants. Thus soil may be rich in nutrients, but if it is too acidic or alkaline, the plants will nevertheless exhibit the same symptoms of nutrient deficiency that they would if the nutrients were not there at all. This also happens in cold soil, a frequent problem in the North, where unhealthy-looking plants often grow vigorously as soon as the soil warms. Adding chemical fertilizer is no help in either situation, because it simply upsets the soil balance. If the problem is an incorrect pH, however, adding organic matter may help, because it tends to urge the soil toward neutral. There are a number of additives that have a dramatic effect on pH, but they should be avoided until the pH of the garden soil is known.

The precise soil pH is easily determined by doing a soil test using a purchased kit or by having one done by a professional laboratory (see "Sources of Soil Tests" at the end of this chapter). The soil-test report will indicate both the soil pH and what should be done to adjust it.

Lime is usually recommended for raising pH in acidic soil. There are two types of agricultural limestone available for this purpose: calcitic and dolomitic. Calcitic, the most common, is primarily calcium carbonate ($CaCO_3$), while dolomitic limestone contains a high proportion of magnesium carbonate ($MgCO_3$) and should be used if the soil test also indicates a magnesium deficiency. If the report calls for the application of lime, twice the amount of wood ashes may be substituted.

If the soil is really off balance, correcting its pH may have a dramatic effect on yields. A report from the University of Pennsylvania notes: "Using sweet corn, snap beans, tomatoes and cabbage, when the best lime and fertilizer treatments were compared, the lime had nearly as great an effect on the total yield, in tons per acre, as the fertilizer treatment." The effect of liming is most dramatic on finely textured (clay or silt) soils.

Most acidic soils are found on the east and west coasts and, to a lesser degree, throughout the mid-

Composition of Fresh Manure

All figures are for the total combination of feces, urine and ample bedding, and all values are approximate. Information comes from Agriculture Canada, *Manures and Compost*, Publication 868, revised 1974.

Animal	Amount of manure produced annually in tons	Percentage of Nitrogen (as N)	Percentage of Phosphorus (as P_2O_5)	Percentage of Potassium (as K_2O)
Horse	10	0.66	0.23	0.68
Cow	14	0.57	0.15	0.53
Pig	2	0.56	0.32	0.52
Sheep	1	0.90	0.34	1.00
Chicken	0.05 (100 lb/45 kg)	0.97	0.77	0.41

A young green-manure crop of fall rye is ready to be dug into the soil to condition and fertilize it.

eastern and northern regions, generally in areas that experience heavy rainfall.

Sulfur compounds are the usual prescription for helping to neutralize alkaline soils, those usually found in areas of low rainfall, such as on the prairies or in the interior of British Columbia and in the North, as well as where the bedrock is composed of calcitic rocks, especially limestone. Peat, which is somewhat acidic, will also help neutralize alkaline soils.

The Soil-Building Program: It is not really necessary for most gardeners to pay for a soil test, nor is it necessary to follow the soil test's recommendations. Since these recommendations are based on only one tiny soil sample, they may be inconsistent with the big picture of the garden. Still, a soil test is better than ignorance. Do not use pH-altering soil amendments, such as limestone, sulfur and even wood ashes, if you are not sure whether—or to what degree—your soil is acidic or alkaline. The soil and plants can be badly dam-

aged by the improper use of such amendments.

Ultimately, the best proof of the quality of the soil will be the health of your garden. If it is reasonably productive, be patient and continue using organic soil-building techniques. If, despite adequate weeding and watering, plants in midsummer are stunted, leaves are discolored or splotchy and vegetables are discolored or misshapen, have a soil test done.

Green Manures: Whatever the soil condition, mulches, composts and green manures can be used freely and safely. Green manures are crops that are not harvested but are turned back into the soil, usually when they are green and succulent. They can be used to increase soil quality in garden areas not under cultivation during summer, they can be used as part of the crop-rotation plan, or they can be used in the off-season by gardeners who find organic matter, especially compost and livestock manure, expensive or hard to come by.

Green-manure plants bring nutrients from deep in the soil to the topsoil, convert sunlight and rainfall into organic matter and may even incorporate, or fix, atmospheric nitrogen into the soil. Most plants that can fix nitrogen are members of the family Leguminosae and are called legumes; they include alfalfa, clover, peas, beans and vetch. In an experiment in Charlottetown, Prince Edward Island, the yield of potatoes was 248 bushels per acre after fallow (no crop) and 294 bushels per acre after a green-manure crop of clover was plowed under.

Legumes are a uniquely valuable plant family because of their ability to fix nitrogen, some of which remains in the soil for the use of following plants. This ability comes from a symbiotic relationship between the legume and soil organisms of the genus *Rhizobium*. Different species of legume work with different species of *Rhizobium*. If the correct microorganisms are not present in the garden, there will be little or no fixation, so some gardeners inoculate the seeds with bacteria before planting them. Since bacteria differ slightly with soil conditions and area, however, inoculated seeds are not a guarantee that fixation will occur; those who wish to make fixation more likely can order an all-purpose garden-inoculant mix from a garden seed house. The inoculant comes with directions for application. Once an area of the garden has been treated, it should not require any further inoculation. While thinning leguminous plants or during harvesting, the gardener can check the roots for tiny nodules, evidence that fixation has occurred.

Unfortunately, legume seed is expensive, and legumes take some time to become established. While they are best when sown in spring or fall and left at least a year before being plowed under—often a forage crop is taken off in the meantime—legumes are not as hardy as some grasses. The gardener who has just cleared a new piece of ground might be better off planting a hardy over-wintering crop such as fall rye, which germinates in fall, remains dormant over the winter and, if conditions are favorable, grows again the next spring.

Fall rye will survive the winter in most northern gardens, while winter wheat, a more tender alternative, can be planted where temperatures are not likely to go much lower than 19 degrees F (–7°C). Broadcast fall rye or wheat seed about 2 weeks before the first fall frost at the rate of 2 to 3 pounds per 100 square yards (1-1.4 kg/92m²). Seeds can be lightly raked to cover them. In spring, as soon as the soil is dry enough to work, spade or plow the crop under, then wait 2 weeks before planting, allowing the green manure time to begin decomposing.

In the case of grains, harvest them before they go to seed, or volunteer seedlings will sprout in the garden. The object is to turn the crop under when it is young and juicy—just 4 to 5 inches (10-13 cm) tall—not mature and dry. (You may, however, elect to let a patch of grain mature to harvest for bread, cereal or bird feed.)

Hardier green-manure crops without culinary value include timothy, Russian wild ryegrass, crested wheatgrass, creeping red fescue and smooth bromegrass. Green-manure crops suitable for your area will be stocked by local feed and grain stores. In the Far North, where green-manure crops are not hardy enough to survive the winter, sow part of the garden each spring to field peas, fall rye, barley or buckwheat, to be plowed or turned under in fall.

Crop Rotation: In the vegetable garden, green manuring can form part of a crop-rotation routine. The gardener who has plenty of space may be able to grow a legume on one side of the garden and vegetables on the other, rotating every year. Or the green-manure crop may temporarily fill a bed or a section of the garden.

With or without green manures, the best crop-rotation plans take into consideration the types of plants grown in the garden. Each plant is affected by different pests and diseases, reaches to different depths in pursuit of nutrients and requires different nutrients, with the legumes contributing to soil nitrogen levels. Anyone who has grown potatoes in one spot for several years will notice a rise in the number of Colorado potato beetles. Moving the potato patch to the other end of the garden will result in a sudden if temporary drop in the beetle population. Clubroot can be kept in check if brassicas such as cabbage and turnip, which are vulnerable to the disease, are rotated with other less susceptible plants.

In crop rotation, the gardener must consider not only the plant itself but also its family. Plant families are divided in turn into genera, species and varieties. Beets, for example, belong to the family Chenopodiaceae. Their botanical name (which can be likened to the Chinese system of listing the surname first) is *Beta vulgaris*; *Beta* is the genus, *vulgaris* the species. Swiss chard has the same botanical name but includes the variety *cicla*; it is *Beta vulgaris cicla*. There is little benefit, then, in rotating beets with Swiss chard, as they are botanically virtually identical. Replacing any crop with another in its family is far less valuable than replacing it with one in another family. The table below indicates which rotation will be of the greatest benefit.

Livestock Manures: Besides legumes, another common source of soil nitrogen is livestock manure. While all livestock manure is valuable, it varies in nutrient content according to the type of livestock and the age of the manure. Allow it to compost at least a year before using. Agriculture Canada notes that "weight for weight, rotted manure is more valuable than fresh manure, because it contains a larger percentage of plant-food elements in more readily available form." For instance, there are approximately 12 pounds (5.5 kg) of nitrogen in a ton of fresh cow manure and 17 pounds (7.7 kg) in a ton of well-rotted manure.

Gardeners who happen to keep livestock or who live in a farming area are fortunate to have a ready supply of manure, but it can also be bought packaged from garden-supply stores. Dig manure into newly cleared soil at the rate of 1 pound per square foot (5 kg/m^2).

A small supply of manure can go a long way if you prepare manure tea: Place an amount of manure about the size of two fists in a bucket or watering can, fill it with water, and let the mixture sit for a day or overnight. Use the liquid to water any plants, especially those that appreciate a high-nitrogen diet, following about the same schedule as that for side-dressing. (Side-dressing is done by applying a line of fertilizer evenly under the edge of the foliage of plants every couple of weeks in spring and early summer; this conserves fertilizer and, at the same time, ensures that the plants are not overfed.) Use the same manure for three refills of water, then add the manure to the compost pile or put it straight on the garden.

Earthworms: No discussion of fertilizers would be complete without mentioning the humblest of manure-producing livestock: the earthworm, literally worth its weight in fertilizer every day. Earthworms may be the plainest of creatures, but they aerate the soil, perforate it with their tunnels, bring up nutrients from deep in the soil and digest organic matter to produce nutrient-rich castings. Tests at the Connecticut Agricultural Experiment Station have indicated that earthworm castings

Common Garden Plant Families

Plant rotation is essential only in the food garden, but because herbs and flowers might be grown there too, some are included in this table. Some perennials are included in the table. These do not rotate, but you may want to choose neighboring plants, annual or perennial, that belong to a different family.

Family Name	Family Members	Rotation
Amaryllidaceae (amaryllis family)	Vegetables: garlic, leeks, onion, shallot Flowers: allium Herbs: chives	Ornamental onions and chives are perennial and so do not rotate, but as is the case with annuals, they are valuable in interplantings with all other families (so long as the onions are not overly shaded). They attract few pests and may help repel pests from other plants.

Family Name	Family Members	Rotation
Chenopodiaceae (beet family)	Vegetables: beet, Swiss chard, spinach Flowers: kochia	Of medium height, these plants will rotate with others in the garden's midrange: Cruciferae, Leguminosae, Liliaceae, Solanaceae.
Compositae (sunflower family)	Vegetables: globe and Jerusalem artichokes, cardoon, chicory, dandelion, endive, escarole, lettuce, salsify Flowers: ageratum, aster, calendula, chrysanthemum, coreopsis, cornflower, cosmos, dahlia, daisy, gaillardia, gazania, gerbera, globe thistle, leopard's bane, liatris, marigold, purple coneflower, rudbeckia, sanvitalia, stokesia, strawflower, sunflower Herbs: chamomile, tarragon, yarrow	Jerusalem artichokes are perennial and so will not be rotated. Rotate sunflowers with staked peas or pole beans. Leafy Compositae are best rotated with Cucurbitaceae, Leguminosae, Liliaceae, Solanaceae, Umbelliferae. Interplant and rotate marigolds with tomatoes.
Cruciferae (mustard family)	Vegetables: broccoli, Brussels sprouts, cabbage, Chinese cabbage, cauliflower, cress, kale, kohlrabi, mustard greens, radish, rutabaga, turnip, watercress Flowers: alyssum, aubrieta, candytuft, flowering cabbage and kale, stocks, wallflower Herbs: horseradish	Watercress needs a very wet spot where it will grow every year. Rotate all others with members of other families that grow to about the same size (midrange)—bush beans and onions, for example.
Cucurbitaceae (gourd family)	Vegetables: cucumber, gourd, melon, pumpkin, summer and winter squashes	If staked, rotate with staked tomatoes, pole beans, sunflowers, peas. If allowed to sprawl, rotate with other space-demanding crops, such as potatoes, or other low-growing crops, such as leafy Compositae.
Gramineae (corn family)	Vegetables: corn Flowers: ornamental grasses	One of the garden's hungriest crops, corn should be rotated with legumes.
Leguminosae (pea family)	Vegetables: bean, lentils, pea, peanut Flowers: hyacinth bean, lupin, sweet pea	Although they will grow happily in the same spot for several years in succession, their nitrogen-adding properties make them valuable in rotation with all other families.
Solanaceae (nightshade family)	Vegetables: eggplant, garden huckleberry, ground cherry, pepper, potato, tomatillo, tomato Flowers: browallia, Chinese lantern, datura, nicotiana, painted tongue, petunia	Quite susceptible to fungus diseases and nematodes, members should not be next-door neighbors and should follow other families of similar midrange height in rotations.
Umbelliferae (parsley family)	Vegetables: carrot, celeriac, celery, parsnip Herbs: anise, caraway, chervil, coriander, dill, fennel, lovage, parsley	Deep-rooted plants that help break up soil; interplant and rotate with leafy or fruiting crops of other families, such as lettuce and tomatoes.

contain 5 times the nitrogen, 7 times the available phosphorus, 3 times the magnesium, 11 times the potash and 1½ times the calcium of the surrounding soil. And earthworms excrete their weight in castings every day.

Unfortunately, not every garden has earthworms; most are pioneer species in North America, and it takes some time for them to invade newly cleared land. They can be introduced, however, and will thrive if they are given the same soil conditions that promote healthy plants: a pH near neutral, plenty of organic matter and adequate moisture. Under an organic garden mulch, earthworms thrive. On the other hand, soil that is very low in organic matter, especially if fine in texture, seems to suffer from the presence of earthworms, and their tunnels dry rock-hard. Gardeners have been known to apply pesticides to the soil to kill earthworms, compounding their problems. The best answer to this sticky situation is organic matter. What keeps the worms happy keeps plants, soil-building microorganisms and gardeners happy too.

Compost, That Old Black Magic

Compost, a stable humus material that promotes healthy soil and, by extension, healthy plants, is the most valuable free soil conditioner available to the gardener. Agriculture Canada's booklet *Manures and Compost* puts it succinctly: "[Compost] improves the physical and biological condition of the soil and supplies major and minor plant nutrients." Could a gardener ask for more?

Compost also happens to be very easy to prepare. In fact, it practically makes itself, given only a little cooperation from a gardener who has plenty of patience and organic refuse. The patience is required while the organic matter is piled up and kept moist. Provided the weather is not too cold, the pile heats spontaneously and decomposes, with the help of air and microorganisms, to produce a crumbly, rich humus.

Some common compost ingredients include kitchen scraps, grass clippings (but not from a lawn recently sprayed with a herbicide), fallen leaves (avoid those of walnut and butternut trees), livestock manures, spoiled hay, straw and seaweed. Avoid ingredients that are not biodegradable, such as plastic wrappings, foil and glass. Do not add weeds that might take root. The gardener should also steer away from using meat scraps and bones, which will attract cats, dogs and raccoons, seemingly from miles around—undesirable for both the compost pile and the garden. Do not use pet or human feces, because they can contain parasites and pathogens. Human urine, however, is nitrogen-rich (about 2.5 percent) and is safe for the compost pile, provided the donor does not have a bladder or kidney infection.

City gardeners may be worried about the unsightliness and smell of a compost pile. In some cities, there is also the danger of attracting rats. To guard against that, small amounts of compost can be made quickly and easily if the gardener simply pours kitchen garbage and other moist biodegradable materials into black plastic bags which are then tied and placed in a sunny spot. The bags can be turned every week, and composting should be complete after a month or so of warm weather.

Larger amounts of compost can be prepared inoffensively in any of a variety of purchased or home-made compost bins. Situate the pile at the edge of the garden and, if possible, in full sun, where composting will take place as rapidly as ambient temperatures permit. Turn the pile occasionally to keep it well aerated—that "rotten egg" smell comes from oxygen-free (anaerobic) decomposition, which results when a pile is overly wet or compacted.

Containers: All a compost bin needs to do is keep the compost together and allow you to turn it, keep it wet, add new material and, finally, remove it. Simplest is a pile exposed on all sides. Albert Howard, a British agronomist who first systematized the composting procedures he observed in India, recommended a compost pile about 6 to 7 feet (2 m) wide, 3 to 5 feet (1-1.5 m) high and 7 to 30 feet (2-9 m) long—a massive farm-scale construction that required a great deal of biodegradable matter all at once. Ingredients were layered, and the completed

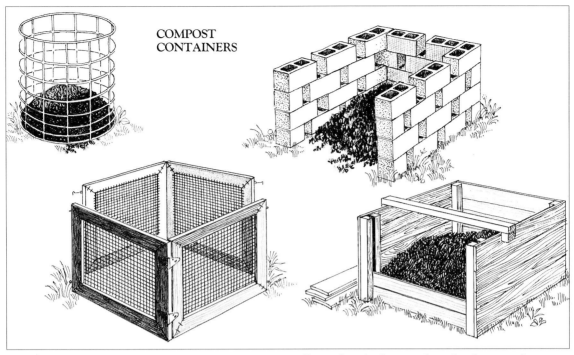

COMPOST CONTAINERS

Any large container open to the air can hold compost effectively, whether purchased or homemade.

pile was watered, then covered with a layer of soil, hay or burlap to help hold in moisture.

Such a gargantuan project is fine for gardeners or farmers with plenty of manure, straw and space, but most gardeners work on a far smaller scale. As ingredients become available, place them in a pile or an enclosure. Include a sprinkling of garden soil now and then to help introduce biodegrading organisms. Soil can also be used to cover the pile and prevent lightweight ingredients such as fallen leaves from blowing away. If the container is big enough to keep about 1 cubic yard (0.8 m³) of material moist and well aerated, composting can be as satisfactory as Howard found it.

The container should be rot-resistant, fairly large and permeable

to air, at least on top. There are many on the market, some easier to work with than others. Homemade equivalents include a perforated oil drum or barrel and cylinders made of chicken wire or snow fence; they are lifted off when it is time to turn the pile, which is then shoveled or forked back into the cylinder. Three-sided boxes of rough or used lumber are permanent, attractive and easy to use. Boxes about 3 feet (1 m) long on each of three sides will hold enough compost for an average garden and can be constructed in rows of two to four boxes, each holding a pile in a different stage of decomposition. In 1940, J.J. Woods, an agronomist working at the federal agricultural experimental station in Agassiz, British Columbia, reported his success using this type of box, which

he installed under the downspout of an eavestrough. Lacking an eavestrough, I use two bins side by side against the garage wall.

Inner Workings: The size of the compost pile determines the amount of "fuel" available for composting as well as the amount of insulation available to contain the heat, since both fuel and insulation are provided by the organic matter. Optimally, a temperature of 158 degrees F (70°C) is reached in the center of the pile, killing pathogens and weed seeds. This high temperature can be attained only if conditions are just right, which is not likely to be the case with a compost pile smaller than a cubic yard (0.8 m³). The more modest the pile, the lower the temperature and, therefore, the more important it is that weed seeds and potentially pathogenic matter, such as human or pet feces and diseased plant material, be avoided.

In any pile, occasional turning is necessary so that cooler outside material is incorporated into the warm interior for composting. The frequency of turning depends on how quickly the pile works, and that, in turn, depends on the size of the pile, the type and coarseness of ingredients and the ambient temperature. Most northern compost piles stop working in fall, freeze solid in winter and begin working again after thawing in spring. Covering the pile with a sheet of clear polyethylene will slow cooling in fall and speed up warming in spring. But a summer pile can be thoroughly composted in less than a month if the ingredients are finely ground, damp and fairly high in nitrogen.

The efficiency with which the material composts depends on its average carbon-to-nitrogen (C:N) ratio. Nitrogen speeds decomposition. Carbon slows decomposition but provides food for the microorganisms. High-nitrogen materials include urine, livestock manures, grass clippings, seaweed, hay, kitchen wastes (especially coffee grounds and eggshells) and commercial compost starters. High-carbon materials include straw, paper and sawdust. A very carbonaceous pile—a truckload of sawdust, for instance—will eventually compost, but it could take years. A nitrogen-rich pile, on the other hand, will probably smell of ammonia, a sign that precious nitrogen is being lost to the air. Ingredients that fall into the middle range, such as

Biodegradable kitchen scraps and garden refuse take as long as a year to become good compost.

grass clippings and fallen leaves, can compost quite efficiently on their own. A gardener with little else to add can pile these ingredients alone, layering them with about an inch (2.5 cm) of garden soil on every foot (30 cm) or so of leaves or grass, and turning the pile occasionally.

Chopped or shredded materials decompose faster than those left whole. Thus a small amount of sawdust can be added to a compost pile, but wood chips or twigs will likely still be in their original condition when the rest of the pile is ready to use. Bonemeal can go on the pile, but not discarded meat bones. Shredded paper will compost better than whole sheets, although both should be used sparingly, if at all, because paper is very low in nitrogen. For the same reason, cardboard is a poor compost ingredient. To speed the process, run composting materials through a lawn mower or a specially designed compost shredder. These shredders can turn tree

roots, branches, leaves, leather, bones, whole fish and seashells into a meal so pervious to air, moisture and microbes that it decomposes quickly, even under adverse conditions. The Berkeley compost method, devised in California, uses shredded material for a process that takes just 14 days.

The Berkeley method calls for turning the moistened pile of at least a cubic yard (0.8 m³) of shredded material on the 4th, 7th and 10th days. Albert Howard's method, on the other hand, called for turning those huge compost piles 2 or 3 weeks after piling and again 2 or 3 weeks later. His compost was ready for use about 3 months after piling—this was in India, where the weather was warm. A garden compost pile requires turning whenever the pile shrinks noticeably in size—by the end of composting, the pile should be about one-third its original size—but no more frequently than twice a week. When the composted material is cool and fairly dark and crumbly but some shape of the original matter is still evident, it is ready to use.

Where summers are short or when you want compost in a hurry, the use of a chemical starter will help speed heating and decomposition. Starters can be purchased from some garden-supply outlets or can be concocted at home. Agriculture Canada offers the following recipe:
• 4 pounds (1.8 kg) sulfate of ammonia (21-0-0)
• 2 pounds (1 kg) superphosphate (11-48-0)
• 1 pound (500 g) muriate of potash (0-0-60)

• 2 pounds (1 kg) ground lime-stone *or* 4 pounds (1.8 kg) wood ashes

Thoroughly mix the ingredients, and spread ½ pound (230 g) over each 10 pounds (4.5 kg) of organic matter, then mix it in.

One shovelful of fresh livestock manure, where it is available, per 100 pounds (45 kg) of organic matter is a good organic starter.

Compost Applications: Compost is an all-round soil conditioner and mild fertilizer that can be used wherever it is most needed: for houseplants, when potting vegetable transplants, in containers, in hills for squash and melons and as a side-dressing or mulch for all vegetables, flowers and fruits in summer. It is almost impossible to overuse, because it is a gentle, slow-acting fertilizer. In fact, when seeds germinate in the compost pile itself, the plants that grow there are often the healthiest you will see.

Sources of Soil Tests

Do-it-yourself soil-test kits and pH testers are available from some garden stores and seed catalogs (see Sources). There are also commercial and government soil tests available. Write to the appropriate address for prices and instructions on gathering soil for testing. The least expensive test generally measures phosphorus (P), potassium (K), magnesium (Mg) and pH; additional elements cost more. The returned report will include recommendations, in terms of synthetic fertilizers. A few places will also test composts and manures.

British Columbia & Yukon Territory
Griffin Laboratories
1873 Spall Road
Kelowna, British Columbia V1Y 4R2

Alberta
Norwest Soil Research Ltd.
9938–67 Avenue
Edmonton, Alberta T6E 0P5

Saskatchewan
Plains Innovative Laboratory
  Services
107–111 Research Drive
Saskatoon, Saskatchewan
S7N 3R2

Manitoba
Norwest Labs
Agricultural Services Complex
203–545 University Crescent
Winnipeg, Manitoba R3T 5S6

Ontario
Analytical Services
Department of Land Resource
  Science
University of Guelph
Guelph, Ontario N1G 2W1

Quebec
Tests available to farmers only.

New Brunswick
Plant Industry Branch
Department of Agriculture
P.O. Box 6000
Fredericton, New Brunswick
E3B 5H1

Nova Scotia
Department of Agriculture
  and Marketing
P.O. Box 190
1690 Hollis Street, 7th Floor
Halifax, Nova Scotia
B3J 2M4

Prince Edward Island
Soil and Feed Testing Laboratory
P.O. Box 1600
Charlottetown, Prince Edward
  Island C1A 7N3

Newfoundland & Labrador
Soil and Land Management
  Division
Provincial Agriculture Building
P.O. Box 8700
St. John's, Newfoundland A1B 4J6

United States
Contact the local Cooperative Extension Service, which may be listed in the telephone book under USDA, or call the closest state university. For a modest sum, the Extension Service of your own or a nearby state will conduct and interpret a garden-soil test.

Wood's End Laboratory, Inc.
Old Rome Road
Route 2, Box 1850
Mount Vernon, Maine 04352
Specializing in services for organic farmers and gardeners, Wood's End offers a detailed analysis of the soil as well as recommendations for nonsynthetic additives. They also sell compostable bags for the collection of household scraps. Write for prices and Customs information if you are ordering from Canada.

Chapter Three

A Movable Spring

"Snow lingers in secluded corners and frost is still in the ground,
but spring is awaiting a welcome."
—Samuel Thomas Wood
Rambles of a Canadian Naturalist, 1916

Spring comes earliest to gardeners. Long before the possibility of another blizzard has disappeared with the last snowy owl, gardeners are ordering seeds, mapping out their paper gardens and sowing seeds indoors. For gardeners, the tail end of winter is immeasurably cheered by a windowsill full of tiny flowers and vegetables.

Growing your own transplants—that is, sowing seeds indoors or in a greenhouse for plants that will grow outdoors—can be both more economical and more rewarding than buying commercial transplants. Seeds come in far greater variety than purchased transplants, and growing your own gives you the satisfying feeling of being involved in the entire life cycle of your plants, from germination to blooming or harvest.

But homegrown transplants may not be for everyone. They require space, care and light. If you want fewer than half a dozen of a common type of plant, you will find it easier to buy bedding plants in spring. The beginning gardener is wise to delay growing transplants for at least a season; your first garden is usually challenging enough.

Then again, some seeds are easy, but don't overdo it. Most gardeners will need only one packet of seeds for any flower or vegetable that would normally be started indoors. Because the plants that must be started early are apt to have small seeds, a packet contains plenty. You might want to buy larger quantities of big seeds, such as corn, beans, peas, morning glories, nasturtiums and sunflowers, but these can all be sown directly in the garden.

Of course, the one-packet rule does not take into consideration the gardener's preference for more than one variety. One packet of tomato seeds will be more than enough, but if you'd like to grow cherry, paste and beefsteak tomatoes, you'll need three packets. Also, some expensive hybrid varieties are sold in very small amounts. (When there are just a few seeds in a packet, it is usually mentioned in the seed catalog or on the packet.)

As you scan the seed catalogs, you may also notice that there are both "treated" and "untreated" vegetable seeds. Companies such as Stokes and Vesey's offer the gardener a choice. A few others that specialize in hybrids sell only treated seeds, while more organically oriented companies sell only untreated seeds. Treated seeds are brightly colored, evidence that they have been coated with a fungicide, such as captan or thiram, to help prevent two fungal ailments: seed decay and damping-off. Because the safety of these chemicals is questionable, many gardeners avoid them. Both fungal diseases can be minimized, in any case, if you use sterile potting mix, avoid sowing seeds outdoors in soil too cool for the crop and ensure that the soil is well drained, perhaps in raised beds. Flower seeds are untreated.

Indoor & Outdoor Planting

Once the seed order arrives in the mail or is bought at the store, usually between the beginning of January and the end of March, you should separate the seeds into indoor and outdoor seeders. Then divide them again according to planting dates, writing the best sowing date on the packet or on a divider in a seed file box to ensure that all seeds are sown on time. If the packet contains more than enough seeds for this year, write the year of purchase on it for reference in following years.

Certain plants are started indoors for three reasons: (1) these plants, such as onions and globe artichokes, have a longer maturation season than most northern gardens can provide; (2) they are frost-tender and must mature while the weather is still warm (tomatoes, petunias); (3) the gardener would prefer an early harvest or early flowers (cabbage, lettuce, morning glories, zinnias).

Indoor Planting Schedule

In most areas, indoor seeding begins in late February or early March. If it is earlier than that, you will need electric lights to supplement the limited sunlight available during short winter days.

Practically every planting calculation from now on depends on the estimated date of your last spring frost. Check with a local horticultural society or department of agriculture office for the approximate date of the last spring frost in your area. Because local conditions may vary, it is wise to double-check with neighboring gardeners. Record this date in your garden notebook along with the approximate date of the first fall frost. Using the

spring frost date as a reference, you can estimate spring indoor planting dates by subtracting the following numbers of weeks from the last spring frost date. For example, Calgary's last spring frost usually occurs around May 20, so the first indoor seeding of onions and such will occur 10 weeks earlier, about March 11. See the list on the facing page for a few more locations.

10 weeks: early celery, eggplants, eustoma, impatiens, leeks, onions, peppers, violas
9 weeks: globe artichokes, begonias, nicotiana, parsley, petunias
8 weeks: early lettuce, most perennial flowers
6-8 weeks: early basil, early brassicas, tomatoes
5-6 weeks: late cabbage, cauliflower, late celery, early leaf lettuce, most small-seeded annual flowers
4-5 weeks: basil, cucumbers, gourds, melons, pumpkins, squashes, large-seeded annual flowers

It is usually unwise to start plants much earlier. Unless they are moved into progressively larger pots, overly mature transplants become root-bound and stunted. They wilt easily and may display symptoms of nutrient deficiencies. When they are transplanted outdoors, they take longer to recover than younger transplants. They may never reach full size or productivity.

Outdoor Planting Schedule

Outdoor planting times are also calculated around the usual date of the last spring frost. As is apparent from the following list, many of the plants noted above can be sown outdoors *or* indoors.

5-7 weeks before last spring frost: seeds of broad beans, carrots, leaf lettuce, peas, spinach, turnips; onion sets or transplants; parsley seeds or transplants; seeds of candytuft, cornflowers, pansies, poppies, annual rudbeckia, snapdragons, annual stocks, violas; sweet pea seeds or transplants
3-4 weeks before last spring frost: all items mentioned above; lettuce seeds; seeds or transplants of asparagus, beets, broccoli, Brussels sprouts, cabbage, collards, kale, potato eyes, radishes; transplants of frost-tolerant annuals such as violas, pansies, cornflowers, snapdragons
2-3 weeks before last spring frost: all items mentioned above; lettuce transplants; corn seeds, summer bulbs, sunflower seeds

Around last spring frost: all items mentioned above; seeds of beans, peanuts; seeds or transplants of cauliflower, cucumbers, summer squashes; transplants of globe artichokes, peppers, tomatoes; seeds of marigolds, zinnias, lavatera and other fast-growing annuals; all annual and perennial flower transplants; cover all tender plants on cold nights

1-2 weeks after last spring frost: all items mentioned above; seeds of lima beans, soy beans; seeds or transplants of winter squashes, pumpkins; transplants of celery, muskmelon, watermelon; sweet potato roots

Sometimes, sowing or transplanting earlier than these dates will be successful, especially if hot caps or row covers are used. It all depends on the garden site, the weather in any particular season and your willingness to watch over your plants. Experimentation is definitely worthwhile, as long as some seeds or transplants are saved for insurance in case of early crop failure.

Light Requirements

Seedlings that will grow indoors need a dependable supply of bright light. Leaf and root crops require at least 4 hours of direct sunlight daily, while annual and perennial flowers and fruiting crops such as tomatoes need a minimum of 8, preferably more in all cases. A greenhouse or a south-facing window ledge, therefore, is required by any plants that will not receive artificial light. Alternatively, the plants must be moved from window to window with the sunlight or, even better, taken outdoors on warm days to a sheltered place or a cold frame.

Besides providing natural light, attached greenhouses and window ledges allow plants to use household heat and keep them within easy reach. Unfortunately, space on window ledges is severely

Average Date of Last Spring Frost

The following are the average dates of the last light frost, 32 degrees F (0°C), in spring. There is a 50 percent chance of a frost occurring after these dates. Canadian information comes from Environment Canada, U.S. information from the National Climate Center.

Alberta	Calgary	May 28
Alberta	Edmonton	May 15
British Columbia	Kamloops	May 2
British Columbia	Vancouver	March 31
British Columbia	Victoria	April 13
Colorado	Denver	May 3
Maine	Portland	May 10
Manitoba	Winnipeg	May 25
Michigan	Lansing	May 13
New Brunswick	Fredericton	May 18
Newfoundland	St. John's	June 12
Northwest Territories	Yellowknife	May 30
Nova Scotia	Halifax	May 15
Ontario	Ottawa	May 15
Ontario	Thunder Bay	May 31
Ontario	Toronto	April 20
Pennsylvania	Carlisle	April 10
Prince Edward Island	Charlottetown	May 16
Quebec	Gaspé	May 26
Quebec	Montreal	May 5
Quebec	Sherbrooke	May 12
Saskatchewan	Saskatoon	May 27
Washington	Seattle	March 24
Yukon Territory	Whitehorse	June 5

Recycled cups suit many annual flower seedlings.

limited in most homes, and houses that are kept warm can mean patches of sunshine which are too hot for plants. By the time all the seedlings have been transplanted into larger containers, some are far from the glass. Attached or freestanding growing shelters work better (see "Gardening Under Glass" on page 54), or fluorescent or incandescent fixtures can boost the light supply.

If you decide to grow your plants under lights, refer to the plant requirements stated above and supply 2 hours of artificial light for every hour of natural light missed. This artificial light may be provided in any of several ways:

• Commercial grow-light fluorescents, used according to the manufacturer's directions.

• Household incandescent bulbs and cool white fluorescents, at the rate of 1 watt of the former to 3 to 5 of the latter. Keep incandescent bulbs about a foot above plant tops, as they produce enough heat to burn foliage. Fluorescents may virtually touch the plants.

• 40-watt fluorescents, in a one-to-one ratio of cool white to warm white tubes. Two tubes supply an area about 4 feet (1.2 m) by 6 feet (2 m).

• Where there is a good supply of natural light, cool white fluorescents can be used alone.

In all cases, fluorescent and incandescent bulbs should be set in reflectors that will direct the light downward, and all units should be installed by a window if possible. Turn the lights off at night so that the plants have a rest period of about 8 hours.

If you use window ledges for seedlings, remember that the night temperature by the glazing may be so low that the plants are slowed or damaged. Prepare to move all the plants to a warmer spot at night, putting them by the window again in the morning. Every morning, give the containers a quarter-turn to keep the stems growing straight.

Seedlings that grow weak and leggy are suffering from too little light, sometimes accompanied by temperatures which are too high and by too much water and fertilizer. Certain plants, usually quick growers, are very susceptible to legginess, which can result in plants that are too weak to survive the move outdoors. Cooler, drier, brighter conditions can make sturdier transplants, but such an environment can be difficult to find indoors. If seedlings become hopelessly leggy, discard them and sow the seeds again when the days are longer; soon after germination, allow seedlings to spend at least part of most days outdoors.

Containers

Gardeners who have been starting seeds indoors for a few seasons become ingenious at recycling containers suitable for seedlings. As long as a container is reasonably sturdy, 2 to 3 inches (5-7.5 cm) deep, will drain water and can be expected to release the rootball easily, it should be adequate. Egg-carton indentations are too small to be really useful, while large plant pots take up too much space and soil to be practical. Plastic 4-packs, 6-packs or other containers that once held purchased plants are ideal. Paper, plastic or polystyrene beverage cups or dairy containers, their bottoms perforated, allow the gardener to write the variety name on the rim—use crayon on plastic containers, ballpoint on others. Quart-sized milk cartons cut off partway down are good for large transplants such as melons and tomatoes. Soil blocks, peat pots, peat pellets and paper pots (made by rolling newspaper around a purchased form) are biodegradable containers intended to be planted directly in the garden. Since no root disturbance occurs, these

Common seedling containers include peat pots, peat pellets, soil blocks, plastic pots and 6-packs.

containers are best reserved for plants that resent transplanting, such as poppies and cucumbers.

A flat can be filled with growing medium and used directly for growing seedlings, or it can hold several smaller containers. A standard plastic flat holds 10 plastic 6-packs and can be moved about easily. To make a wooden flat, cut end pieces of ⅝-inch (15 mm) lumber about 12 inches (30 cm) long and side and bottom pieces of ¼-inch (6 mm) wood 22 inches (56 cm) long. Nail the side and end pieces into a rectangle, then nail on the bottom board or boards, leaving narrow spaces between them for drainage. Using containers with large drainage holes, line each with a single sheet of newspaper before filling it with growing medium. By the time the paper biodegrades, the soil will stay in place.

The container that is best for any particular seed or seedling depends in part on the sensitivity of that plant to transplanting. Some seeds must be sown in the pots in which they will remain until

they are planted in the garden; others are transplanted once or even twice, each time receiving more growing room.

Beets, Swiss chard, spinach, broccoli, Brussels sprouts, cabbage, lettuce, tomatoes and most fibrous-rooted flowers are easy to transplant and so can first be sown thickly in rows or broadcast evenly in flats. Later, they can be transplanted into larger containers before finally being moved into the garden.

Cauliflower, celery, eggplants, onions and peppers need more care when transplanted. Either plant them initially in the containers that will hold them until they are moved into the garden, or try to retain as much of the rootball as possible when transplanting.

Cucumbers, melons, squashes, gourds and certain flowers, such as annual poppies and members of the dill family, are sensitive to root disturbance. Those which cannot be sown directly in the garden should be sown in containers large enough to hold them until they are transplanted into the garden. The container should be either a biodegradable type that can be planted or one that will easily release the entire rootball intact. Cardboard or polystyrene containers are also suitable, because they can be carefully torn away from the rootball.

Soil Mixes

From germination until the true leaves begin to grow, seeds live on nutrients stored within. For this reason, commercial growers often start seedlings in an infertile growing medium, moving the plants to a more fertile medium at greater spacing only when the true leaves form. The true leaves are the second set the young plant produces—and all the leaves from then on. The first set of leaves are called seedling leaves, or cotyledons. They are relatively simple-looking, either elongated or rounded, and lack the indentations and wrinkles of the true leaves that follow. Germination can take place on something as seemingly inhospitable as a damp paper towel, or a medium for germination can be provided by any of the following ingredients, usually in a mixture containing some peat:

Perlite: volcanic rock that has been heated to about 1,800 degrees F (990°C), causing it to expand and turn white and porous. Although perlite is nonnutritive and unable to hold water as well as vermiculite, it is lightweight and sterile.

Vermiculite: a mica compound heated to about 1,400 degrees F (765°C), which causes it to expand and become porous. It holds water well, contains some potassium and magnesium and is lightweight and sterile. Zonalite—vermiculite packaged for use as insulation—costs less than horticultural vermiculite.

Sand: builder's sand (not ocean-beach sand, which is salty) is heavier but less expensive than perlite or vermiculite. It, too, promotes drainage and aeration. It is not sterile, so it may contain weed seeds or soil pathogens.

Peat Moss: partially decomposed sphagnum moss can hold a large quantity of water when damp but will shed water if allowed to dry out

Flowers for Cool Greenhouses

Greenhouses or sunrooms that stay at about 50 degrees F (10°C) or cooler in fall, winter and spring are a good environment for certain potted plants and flowers.

Antirrhinum spp	snapdragon
Aster spp	aster; Michaelmas daisy
Aubrieta spp	rock cress
Bellis perennis	English daisy
Brassica oleracea acephala	ornamental cabbage
Calceolaria spp	calceolaria; slipperwort
Calendula spp	calendula; pot marigold
Cineraria x *hybridus*	cineraria
Delphinium spp	larkspur
Dianthus spp	sweet William; pink
Freesia spp	freesia
Gerbera spp	gerbera
Lobelia spp	lobelia
Matthiola spp	stocks
Moluccella laevis	bells of Ireland
Petunia spp	petunia
Primula malacoides	fairy primrose
Primula vulgaris	common primrose
Tagetes spp	marigold
Torenia spp	torenia; wishbone flower
Viola spp	pansy; viola; violet

thoroughly. Stir or knead water into it to begin, and do not let it dry out. Peat has little or no nutritive value but is often acidic. Gardeners who have compost shredders can substitute shredded pine cones for peat.

Sphagnum Moss: sold both milled and un-milled. Milled is easier to handle but more expensive than unmilled. Both have water-holding properties similar to those of peat moss. Because sphagnum is slightly antiseptic, it helps the gardener avoid soil-borne diseases. Spreading ¼ inch (6 mm) of sphagnum on top of any other soil mix will help prevent damping-off, a common fungus disease.

Several other growing media composed of paper, polystyrene and minerals are similarly sterile and low or absent in nutrients.

Mixtures of these ingredients are sold by garden suppliers specifically for seedlings. It is most convenient to use the same growing mix throughout the indoor growing schedule, but as soon as the first true leaves begin to grow, start fertilizing.

Topsoil & Compost: Topsoil alone becomes too compact indoors for best root growth. However, if sterilized, as described below, and combined with one of the above ingredients so that the mix is aerated and drains well, topsoil and compost can be used for seedlings. If compost or garden soil is to be used in the mix, it should be brought indoors in fall before freeze-up. Left in bags on the porch or in the basement, it may freeze before use, so it should be moved into a warm room about a week before it is needed.

Compost or garden soil should be sterilized before it is used for seeding indoors. In its natural state, it contains weed seeds, fungi, bacteria and viruses that can compete with or harm seedlings, but these can be destroyed easily. Put the soil into a bucket or bowl, and cover with boiling water, while stirring. Allow the mixture to cool, drain off the excess water, and the soil is ready to use.

Tender young roots can make their way best through a lightweight medium. Suitable mixes can be purchased or made at home. Some good mixes that can take the gardener right from seed germination to outdoor planting include:

• 1 part potting soil, compost or topsoil/1 part peat/1 part perlite, vermiculite or sand;

Some seeds are covered, others left on the surface.

• 7 parts by weight of fertile soil or compost/3 parts peat/2 parts sand.

Sowing Seeds

Sort the containers, deciding which are appropriate for which plants according to their tolerance to transplanting. Mix the soil with the other ingredients, make sure the mixture is thoroughly wet and no cooler than room temperature, then fill the containers to within ¼ inch (6 mm) of the rim, lightly tamping down the soil.

As a general rule, plant seeds indoors or outdoors at a depth of one to three times their diameter. Dust-fine seeds, such as those of begonias and some herbs, are lightly pressed into the soil surface. In any case, do not allow the soil to dry out before the seeds sprout. Spray the surface regularly, or cover the containers with plastic, or place the flats or containers in a bath of lukewarm water ½ inch (1 cm) deep until the seedlings emerge. Seeds germinating in sunlight under glass or by a window should *not* be covered with plastic, because the resulting double greenhouse effect can bake the soil and kill the seedlings.

Some seeds can go immediately into the container that will hold them until they are transplanted outdoors. In this case, after the true leaves have formed, pinch off all but the strongest seedling at soil level.

Other seeds can be planted quite thickly in rows or evenly broadcast over the soil surface and then covered to the proper depth. After germination, transplant all the healthiest seedlings into larger, perhaps even individual containers. This is the case with lettuce, spinach, beets, chard, the cabbage family and virtually all bedding annuals except poppies, members of the mallow family and anything with a taproot. Onions are exceptions among vegetables. They, too, are sown thickly—seeds can touch one another—but they can be left in the original flats, looking like a patch of grass, until they are separated and planted in the garden.

Pre-germination

Since seeds germinate best at temperatures higher than those preferred by the plants themselves, gardeners face a problem in logistics. Newly sown flats or containers should be placed in a spot warm enough to promote fairly speedy germination—60 to 90 degrees F (15-32°C) for most seeds. A few suitable locations include a flat surface under a heat lamp, the warm top of a refrigerator or the floor under a wood stove. In a cooler spot, seeds may germinate very slowly or might simply die and rot. Fortunately, most seeds do not require light for germination, so the seeded container can be placed in a warm spot away from windows or lights until the seeds begin to sprout; at that point, they must be moved into the light immediately.

The germination problem can be further circumvented if the gardener allows the seeds to sprout before sowing them. This simplifies the provision of ideal germination conditions and also ensures that only viable seeds are planted—wasteful thinning of healthy seedlings is avoided.

Pre-germination should be done only with large seeds, as the handling of tiny germinated seeds would be too difficult. Pre-germination is most useful for vegetables. The smallest seed candidates for pre-germination are those of eggplants and tomatoes. Other seeds that can be handled this way are those of beans, cucumbers, melons, okra, peas, peppers and squashes. Pre-germination can precede either indoor or outdoor planting. The seeds

Transplant most seedlings at the same depth.

of balloon vines, morning glories, sunflowers and sweet peas are also sometimes pre-germinated.

To pre-germinate seeds, use a container that can be securely lidded. Container size will depend on the quantity of seeds used—dairy containers are usually suitable. Place a paper towel or a piece of finely woven cloth on the bottom, wet it with lukewarm water, and cover with a single layer of seeds. To allow for germination failures, use about 25 percent more seeds than you want plants. Several cultivars can be put in a single larger container: Simply draw sections on the towel with a ballpoint pen, then record the variety name on each section before wetting the towel.

Place lids on the containers, and put them in a warm spot, preferably 80 to 90 degrees F (27-32°C), no hotter. Check every day to ensure that the towel is still wet. Germination will take anywhere from a couple of days to 3 weeks, depending on the type of seed, its freshness and the temperature. As soon as its tiny root, or radicle, appears, the seed is ready for planting at the usual depth—one to three times the diameter of the seed. Plant it very carefully so that the radicle is not damaged and either lies sideways or points downward. Cover the seed, and gently tamp down the soil. Pre-germinated seeds may be placed at the final transplant spacing best for that vegetable. Water with room-temperature water, place the seeded containers in a warm spot, and keep the soil damp until the sprouts appear.

One of the most common disorders of seedlings is damping-off, a fungus disease that may attack the tiny shoots before or after they emerge from the soil. Damping-off is usually manifest either as "germination failure" or as a pinching of the stem at the soil line, which causes the seedling to bend over and die. The gardener can best avoid damping-off by using clean containers and sterilized soil, keeping the seedlings warm and ensuring that the soil is well drained and never sodden. If you are using containers that previously held soil, wash them in hot water before reusing. The use of peat in the mix or sprinkled on the soil surface also helps discourage the disease. Do not sow seeds too thickly or too deep. If damping-off does infect plants, apply a spray of crushed garlic cloves and water.

Transplanting

From the time the seedlings appear, they must be allowed sufficient light and enough water so that the soil never dries out entirely. Always use water that is close to room temperature—never hot or icy cold. As soon as the true leaves form, plants that have been sown in rows or broadcast in flats should be transplanted into larger containers. Use the tip of a knife to obtain as large a rootball as possible, and holding the seedling by its cotyledon (first leaf), plant it at about the same depth in the new container, allowing 1 to $1\frac{1}{2}$ inches (2.5-3.8 cm) around each seedling. Onions and celery can be left in their original flats; members of the carrot, mallow, melon and poppy families should not be transplanted.

Every week, water the transplants with manure tea (see page 38) or a dilute solution of fish fertilizer or a balanced liquid fertilizer, used as directed on the bottle. If plants become pale or discolored or stop growing, they should be transplanted into larger containers. Tomatoes may need a further transplanting about 2 weeks before they go into the garden. Each time they are transplanted, tomatoes should be planted more deeply; new roots will emerge from the stem. During *any* transplanting operation, however, the roots should be disturbed as little as possible.

Cold Treatment

The early yield of tomatoes and peppers may be increased by a cold treatment, a sort of premature hardening-off process that may be included as a matter of course by gardeners who cannot avoid the low temperatures involved. In the treatment, tomatoes are grown at a minimum night temperature of 50 to 55 degrees F (10-13°C) for 3 weeks from the time the first true leaves appear. After 3 weeks, the temperature is maintained at 60 to 65 degrees (15-18°C) day and night. Similarly, when the third true leaves of peppers appear, they are subjected to a night-temperature range of 53 to 55 degrees (11.5-13°C) for 4 weeks, after which they are kept at around 70 degrees (21°C) day and night. Although cold treatment will not increase overall yield in most cases, it will encourage the development of those important first fruits.

Hardening Off

About a week before plants are ready to go into the garden, they must be hardened off, or made ready for the comparatively harsh environment that awaits them outdoors. Hardening off involves dropping the air temperature or withholding moisture, or both. For home gardeners, the best way to harden off plants is to take them outdoors for the first time on a calm, warm day, at least 60 degrees F (15°C), about a week before the planting-out date. Leave them in a shady spot for an hour, then bring them in again. The next day, leave them in the shade for 2 hours, and the next day, give them an hour in full sun and a couple of hours in the shade. If you are away all day, leave them out in a shady, sheltered spot. If the weather is very cold or windy, wait until it improves before putting out the plants. By the end of the week, provided the weather has remained fairly stable, the plants should be able to stay outdoors all day and, if there is no danger of frost, all night as well. Be sure that the plants do not dry out enough to wilt, but do not keep them constantly moist. Hardening off can also be done in a cold frame (see pages 56 and 57).

Transplanting Outdoors

As we have seen, some plants are sown or transplanted into the garden before the last frost in spring, some around the time of the last frost and the most tender plants after the soil is warm and the nights are mild. Before the garden is ready to receive seeds or transplants, however, you should weed and rake the bed flat and work the soil to a crumblike texture as you remove stones and break up clods. The ground should be thoroughly damp before you plant.

Set out transplants on a calm, overcast day. Laying down plastic mulch or protecting transplants under shelters will help get them off to a good start (see "Gardening Under Glass" below).

Seeding Outdoors

To sow seeds directly outdoors, follow the same rule that applied indoors: plant at a depth about one to three times the diameter of the seed. Pre-germinated seeds sprout faster. For most seeds, dig a furrow in the soil with the point of a stick or a trowel to the correct depth for planting each seed, spaced at the rate recommended in this book or on the packet. Fine seeds such as lettuce, however, may be broadcast on the soil surface and lightly pressed down. Later, all seedlings are thinned so that they are far enough apart for healthy growth; plants should never be closer than just touching.

After all the seeds are sown or the transplants are in place, water again. Identify the seeds in each row or bed with a seed packet or with plastic or wooden markers that can be purchased from garden stores. Or you may prefer to identify them only in the appropriate spaces of the paper garden plan in your gardener's notebook. You should also mark down the date of planting. If you have a soil thermometer, note the soil temperature at seeding time and the length of time it takes for sprouts to appear.

Now, you are on your way to a beautiful, bountiful summer.

Gardening Under Glass

Fashions in gardening are often influenced by changes in technology. A couple of generations ago, many gardeners used a greenhouse device heated with composting horse manure. Known as a hot bed, it was judged by a Canadian horticulturist as "desirable wherever vegetables or flowers are grown in Canada.... With a hot bed, it is possible to mature certain vegetables in parts of Canada where, if started in the open, they would not ripen before being killed by frost."

Since then, a shortage of horse manure along with a plentiful supply of new plastics and electric grow lights have eclipsed the use of the hot bed. Now, rather than being "started in the open," the seeds of long-season or tender plants are sown indoors under lights or inside any of several types of plant shelter.

All plant shelters fall into one of two general categories: attached shelters and detached, or freestanding, shelters. While hot beds are included in the freestanding category, attached shelters such as sunrooms and window greenhouses are directly connected to the house or another building. Both attached and detached shelters extend indoor growing space and increase the amount of light available to plants, but the two types vary greatly in cost, spaciousness and accessibility.

When the sun shines through glass or plastic into an enclosed space, heat is absorbed by objects in the shelter but does not pass out easily through the glazing. Instead, it collects, causing the temperature in the shelter to rise, a gain that may be spectacular and even deadly to plants. In hot, sunny weather, any type of glazed shelter requires ventilation to allow excess heat to escape while supplying plants with fresh air. With detached structures, this heat is vented to the outdoors. With attached shelters, it can enter the neighboring building. On clear days, spring through fall, for instance, a northern home can receive free heat from an attached greenhouse. Attached structures have another big advantage: They are easily accessible from indoors, which is a real boon at all times, since plants in shelters require daily and sometimes even hourly maintenance. But they are especially convenient when icy weather makes the trip outdoors an unpleasant ritual.

Attached structures are, however, less versatile in their location than detached ones. Also, they usually demand more sophisticated carpentry and thus a greater initial investment of time and money than freestanding shelters, many of which are easy to build and can be placed in almost any sunny spot.

Passive Solar Greenhouse: If changing technology has taken the hot bed almost into obscurity, it has likewise brought the sunroom and the passive solar greenhouse to the forefront of today's gardening scene. Modern insulation and glazing materials have made these large, energy-efficient indoor spaces practical for many gardeners.

Preferably extending from the south, southwest or southeast side of a building, a passive solar greenhouse or a sunroom is a permanent structure large enough to allow the gardener to stand. The solar greenhouse has growing beds or benches along the outer wall and, above them, glazing that slopes upward to meet either the greenhouse roof or the house wall. The sunroom may have plants only in pots. A doorway leads from the greenhouse into the house, and another may lead outdoors.

Although a solar greenhouse requires a suitable location, often a building permit and usually the

A window greenhouse provides solar warmth and natural light.

expenditure of considerable time and money, it is very useful for anyone who wishes to garden beyond the growing season and whose home can accommodate it. It will likely be large enough for all the garden transplants in spring and even some cold-tolerant vegetables, herbs and flowers in winter. A sunroom is a variant, whose primary purpose is the comfort of human beings, not plants. It is big enough to take chairs and perhaps a table but can also have benches along the windows for seedlings and larger plants.

Window Greenhouse: A window greenhouse is a small version of an attached solar greenhouse. As such, it shares many of its advantages—easy access for the gardener, air exchange between

house and greenhouse—but it has a few unique qualities of its own. Compared with a full-sized greenhouse, it requires less time and money, can be built onto almost any home and needs little maintenance. Its growing space is, however, limited to the width of the window and to the extent of your arm's reach outside.

This addition is built on the outside of any sunny window that slides open or can be opened inward. Its floor, which extends to the outside from the bottom of the window frame, is a shelf, often insulated, that may go beyond the window on both sides but is small enough so that all corners can easily be reached from inside the house. Plastic or glass is supported and attached to the shelf and to the outside of the window frame in such a way that a tentlike shelter is formed. Window greenhouses can be temporary, made of plastic stapled to the growing shelf and window frame, or permanent. Commercial models are available from window suppliers, or you can design and build your own. If you are using a ground-floor window, consider supporting the structure on a foundation with footings below the frost line. Opening the window provides enough ventilation in cool weather, but any unit used in summer will require ventilation to the outdoors as well.

Detached Growing Space:

A freestanding greenhouse might cover acres of ground or might be just big enough to accommodate the gardener and a row of growing benches. Built of plastic stapled to a wooden frame with an A-frame or Quonset (semicircular) shape, a little greenhouse can be constructed quickly and quite inexpensively. Double-glazed, metal-framed commercial units, on the other hand, can be very expensive, but they are correspondingly longer-lasting.

A detached unit has the disadvantages of being separate from the house (and therefore relatively inaccessible) and of requiring supplementary heating if it is to be used in winter, spring or fall —otherwise, temperatures in the greenhouse will be as cold as outdoors at night or on cold, windy or overcast days.

Hot Beds & Cold Frames:

Hot beds and cold frames are small versions of the detached greenhouse: big enough for plants but not for the gardener. Because

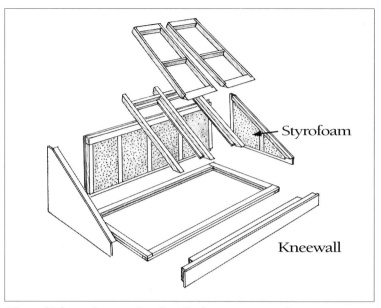

This cold frame has insulated walls for extra warmth.

hot beds are heated, they can receive plants earlier in the season than can cold frames. Hot beds are usually put to work as soon as seedlings started indoors develop their first true leaves. The units can even be used for germination, but in the North, that is risky and demands frequent temperature checking and insulation adjustments. The cold frame, however, usually receives tender plants only in time for hardening off. While frost-hardy plants may be sown there, they are more often transplanted into the bed after the first true leaves have developed. A cold frame is, after all, as cold as the outdoors at night and on overcast days. As the weather warms, the top of the frame is left open for increasingly longer periods so that the plants in the frame gradually become acclimatized, or hardened off, and ready to face life outdoors.

Both the hot bed and the cold frame are enclosed by a ground-level frame, with the southernmost wall about 8 inches (20 cm) high and the back wall roughly 13 inches (33 cm) high. The frame is made of logs, stones, concrete blocks or corner-braced lumber treated with copper naphthenate. If the structure is heavy and permanent, the footing must extend below the frost line to prevent damage from soil heaving. The frame must be big enough to support whatever glazing will be used, perhaps recycled 3-by-6-foot (1 x 2 m) storm windows. Two such windows, supplying 36 square feet (3.3 m²) of growing space, are sufficient for most home gardens. The windows rest on the frame, angled toward the south. The glazing can be hinged to the frame, but that is not essential; instead, it can just rest on the frame so that it can be turned slightly when ventilation is required. The outside of the frame can be bermed to the rim with soil.

Both structures can overheat

Storm windows provide effective glazing for a cold frame made from recycled materials.

quickly on sunny days because of the relatively limited amount of contained air space. The temperature in the bed should always be between 50 and 85 degrees F (10-29°C). Leave a thermometer inside where it can be seen through the glazing. On frosty nights, both structures should be covered with insulation such as straw, old carpets, blankets or burlap bags.

Venting is necessary when the outdoor temperature rises above 45 degrees F (7°C) on sunny days, but take care that icy winds do not blow on the young plants—a narrow crack is often all the venting that is needed. The proper care and maintenance of a hot bed or a cold frame are skills that come with practice and are certainly easier if the gardener is home most of the day. Try to check it at least twice a day.

To harden off plants before transplanting into the garden, open the glazing for a few hours when the air is warm and the sky is overcast, and continue to leave it open a bit longer each day until the frame is open all day and, if possible, all night just before transplanting. A few plants can be left in the open frame to mature. In fact, frames with very high walls can be covered on frosty nights until tender plants are full-grown—a good idea where summer frosts are possible.

Cold Frame Installation: In autumn, choose a sunny, well-sheltered spot, clear the sod and make a 6-inch-deep (15 cm) pile of light, fertile topsoil, slightly wider all around than the frame. Mulch the pile with 2 feet (60 cm) of fallen leaves or straw. About a week before the frame is to be used in spring, remove the mulch and place the frame and glazing over the soil, allowing it a few days to warm. Hardy seeds can then be sown directly into the soil in the frame, or transplants can be set at the spacing recommended for transplanting into containers. Even better, leave the seedlings in their individual containers, which are buried to the rim in soil or surrounded with mulch. If you do this, be sure to water *inside* the containers.

Hot Bed Creation: In the days of horse-drawn wagons, hot beds were warmed with decomposing horse manure, which creates heat in the same manner as compost. A deep layer of fresh manure under the potted plants produces enough heat to keep plants warm and also supplies them with carbon dioxide, which encourages growth.

Heating a cold frame with an electric cable gives gardeners the same extended season. One system, described in the booklet *The Home Vegetable Garden*, produced by the British Columbia Ministry of Agriculture and Food, calls for a waterproof electric cable, available from any hardware or build-

Clear plastic row covers keep out frost and wind but must be slitted to vent excess heat on sunny days.

ing-supply store, with a thermostat set at 65 degrees F (18°C). To contain the cable, the frame—14 inches (35 cm) deep in front and 19 inches (48 cm) deep at the back—must be buried 6 inches (15 cm) in the ground. An electrically heated bed dries out quickly, so check it every day.

Electric heating can also be provided by a cable hung around the inside of the frame walls above the ground or, for a 3-by-6-foot (1 x 2 m) unit, by eight 25-watt incandescent bulbs in porcelain sockets mounted on a board that is attached under the glazing or to the back wall. Use a weatherproof extension cord between the house and the shelter.

Row Covers & Plant Protectors: These are the smallest greenhouses of all—portable structures that are built or set directly over the seeds or plants in the garden. They are left in place over tender plants for a couple of weeks in spring to speed soil warming and plant development, often encouraging maturation 1 to 3 weeks sooner than would otherwise occur. They also provide some protection against frost: a single layer of plastic will protect plants from very light frost, while a double layer will keep plants from harm to about 27 degrees F (–2.8°C). If you expect the temperature to drop lower than that, cover the plastic with blankets.

The original cloche (French for "bell") was just that—a glass bell jar used by French market gardeners as a plant protector. Now, however, there are almost as many sizes and shapes of plant cover as there are sizes and shapes of gardener. The covers may blanket entire rows or individual plants. All are designed to shed water. As is the case with other plant shelters, they should include some provision for ventilation if they are used during the daytime.

For individual plants, several styles of cover are available commercially, including plastic rings that can be filled with water for solar-heat storage. Clear plastic or glass jars turned upside down or plastic bottles cut in half are possible recycled substitutes.

Bonded row-cover fabrics such as Reemay are chiefly meant to keep insects off plants, although they also retain heat and resist light frost. These fabrics have enabled gardeners to mature tender crops in marginal areas and to raise vegetables free of damage from pests that resist other organic methods of control.

Plastic row covers can be left in the vegetable garden for weeks of inclement weather. Stretch 1½-to-2-mil clear plastic sheets over a row of wire hoops high enough to accommodate the plants, especially tomatoes, peppers or eggplants. Lengths of wire 63 inches (160 cm) long are best for 5-foot-wide (1.5 m) plastic sheets. The plastic is split for aeration and anchored against the wind on both sides and each end.

Some of these shelters are designed only to get the young plants off to a good start. Others may see a crop of tender vegetables through to maturity, but in gardens where summers are quite dependably frost-free, this is not recommended, as temperatures in the shelters will rise too high. For instance, tomato blossoms can burn if they contact the inside of a plastic row cover on a sunny day. Remove the covers when the plants outgrow them or as soon as all danger of frost has passed.

Easy to situate, a freestanding greenhouse can be expensive to heat.

Plastic Mulch: Although plastic mulch covers the soil, not the plants, it is included in this chapter because it also makes use of the greenhouse effect to encourage plant growth. Black plastic mulch is best for weed control and is thus recommended under plastic row covers. Clear plastic is better for warming the soil, often by as much as 12 Fahrenheit degrees (6.7C°). To help the growth of early crops, spread 2-mil clear plastic sheets along the rows or on the beds after a rain and about a week before sowing seeds or setting out transplants, weighing down the edges of the plastic with soil to keep it in place. Cut slits or X's into the plastic where the seeds or transplants will go. (Or remove the plastic, sow the seeds—pregerminated or not—replace the plastic, and slit it as soon as the seeds sprout. Leaving the plastic unslit after sprouting will eventually kill the seedlings.)

Plastic mulches also allow the soil to retain moisture, one of the reasons that a 47 percent increase in carrot yields was charted by Canadian scientist Gerard H. Gubbels in the experiments he carried out in the Yukon Territory with mulched and unmulched beds. Cabbage growth, too, was enhanced by plastic mulch. In the *Canadian Journal of Plant Science*, Gubbels noted: "The important point demonstrated is that clear poly can be used to increase soil temperature while making maximum use of water in northern latitudes, where low soil temperature and moisture often limit plant growth."

Black plastic is less effective than clear plastic in providing warmth, but because it excludes light, it controls weed growth better. Among dark plastics are photodegradable plastic mulches that decompose in sunlight, an advantage because after a season in the sun, regular plastic mulch is usually a tattered mess. However, a drawback to photodegradable mulch is that it does not decompose in the shade of plant foliage.

Chapter Four

Alphabetical Vegetables

"In these pages will be found some hints that will help
the Canadian farmer to an acquaintance with requisites essential
to success in the cultivation of the garden."

—D.W. Beadle, *The Canadian Fruit, Flower and Kitchen Gardener*, 1872

What is a vegetable? What is a fruit? These questions seem easy to answer. Vegetables are those edible plants, often annuals, that are usually eaten raw in salads or cooked with the main course at dinner, perhaps *au gratin* or lightly buttered. Savory foods high in vitamins, vegetables may be stems, leaves, roots, seeds, flowers or tubers, but all have an aura of culinary respectability, of dependable, even dowdy wholesomeness. Fruit, on the other hand, is that sweet stuff which hangs on trees and shrubs and is regularly eaten as a snack or dessert. A chef finds little problem with the fruit-or-vegetable question, being as unlikely to serve an entrée of grapes with cheese sauce as to present guests with a dessert of tomatoes *belle Hélène*.

For the botanist, the answer is equally clear, though different. Again, a vegetable is any edible plant that is not a fruit, but in botanical terms, fruit has a more precise definition. It is the ripened ovary and accessory parts of a plant, usually containing seeds. Corn is an aggregate fruit. Peppers, tomatoes, cucumbers, squashes and eggplants are all botanical fruits, as are the foods we usually consider fruit, except rhubarb, which is a vegetable. Beans and peas are fruits until they are shelled; then they are seeds.

This chapter uses the customary, not the botanical, definitions of fruits and vegetables, so it focuses on plants that might be grown in a vegetable garden, including muskmelon, watermelon, garden huckleberry and ground cherry.

Specific cultivars of these vegetables are seldom mentioned—both because new and often faster-maturing cultivars appear every year and because each seed company includes only a limited selection. Search the garden-store seed racks and the seed catalogs every year to keep up to date on the best selections available to Northerners.

Directions indicating that a vegetable can or must be started indoors do not mean you have to grow your own transplants. Greenhouses, nurseries, even grocery and convenience stores carry a selection of popular transplants in spring. When buying these plants, you can ignore the indoor planting directions and pick up the instructions with outdoor timing and spacing. However, be sure to harden off commercial transplants in the same way as homegrown transplants by following the instructions on page 53.

Artichoke, Globe

(Compositae, *Cynara scolymus*)
French Artichoke

C. scolymus was described in 1754 as "very like the thistle but hath large, scaly heads, which are shaped somewhat like the cone of the pine-tree. The bottom of each scale, as also at the bottom of the florets, is a thick, fleshy, eatable substance." Two and a half centuries later, this "fleshy, eatable substance" still inspires us to navigate the prickly landscape of this close relative of the common thistle. The globe artichoke is a native of the humid, warm climes of the southern Mediterranean so is not usually considered suitable for the northern garden, but where the season is 100 days long, it will produce a crop if started early indoors. The bushy, prickly plant grows about 3 feet (1 m) tall, though heights three times as great have been reported in very mild areas, so it should be planted where it will not shade other vegetables but will itself receive full sun. Commercial growers plant roots, but only seeds are available to most Northerners. Grown from seed, some plants may not be productive, but others may produce three or four heads.

Culture: Sow seeds 9 weeks before the last spring frost date. Seeds germinate in 10 to 15 days at a soil temperature of 70 to 75 degrees F (21-24°C). After the first true leaves form, thin to one plant per container. Four weeks before the last frost, transplant individually into 5-inch (13 cm) pots of compost. Harden off for a week before planting outdoors in fertile, well-drained soil, allowing at least 3 feet (1 m) around each plant.

Harvest: Cut the central head while it is still compact and almost entirely edible—as the flower head opens, it becomes tough. Cut through the stem about 1 inch (2.5 cm) below the head, then remove and discard the rest of the stem. Smaller lateral

heads will form later in a manner similar to broccoli. The plant will survive light fall frost. Before the soil freezes, cut the plant to the ground. In mild areas, the roots may overwinter successfully in the garden if they are hilled over and heavily mulched. Roots that stand in water will not survive. In spring, dig down to the roots and remove suckers to use for propagating the plants. In colder areas, dig the roots after the first fall frost and store them indoors in soil, keeping them cool and watered. Set outdoors the following spring around the last frost date. Plants should be renewed by seed or sucker every four years.

Pests & Diseases: Grown beyond its usual range, the plant suffers little infestation. If flea beetles are troublesome, use rotenone or diatomaceous earth regularly. The artichoke plume moth can be combated with plant rotations and garden cleanliness.

Artichoke, Jerusalem

(Compositae, *Helianthus tuberosus*)
Sunchoke

A perennial sunflower grown for its sweet, tender tubers, *H. tuberosus* is one of very few vegetables native to the northern part of North America. Samuel de Champlain wrote in 1603 that the Algonquin Indians served cultivated roots that tasted like artichokes. The misnomer "Jerusalem" probably originates from an English version of its Italian name, *girasole*, which refers to the flower's supposed habit of facing the sun. Tall enough, at 6 to 8 feet (2-2.5 m), to form an effective windbreak, Jerusalem artichoke must be planted where it will not shade or crowd out other vegetables. It should, in fact, be allotted a permanent, well-chosen spot, because it is very persistent and difficult to eradicate.

Culture: Because Jerusalem artichoke is a native plant, it is exceedingly hardy and easy to grow, to the point of weediness. *H. tuberosus* does not breed true from seed but is propagated by tubers that should be planted as soon as possible after they are received—they must not be allowed to dry out. Plant as soon as the soil can be worked in spring or

Started early, globe artichokes mature in a season.

anytime thereafter until fall, cutting tubers to one or two eyes per piece and planting them 4 inches (10 cm) deep and at 12-to-14-inch (30-35 cm) intervals in rows 24 to 40 inches (60-100 cm) apart.
Harvest: Tubers are ready to dig from late summer until the soil freezes. In fall, cut the stems down to the ground and mulch the roots heavily to prolong the harvest. The tubers are thin-skinned, so they do not store well unless kept moist in a root cellar or bagged in the refrigerator. Tubers are eaten raw or cooked like potatoes.
Pests & Diseases: None of note.

Arugula
(Cruciferae, *Eruca sativa*)
Rocket; Roquette; Ruchetta
Among Europeans, *E. sativa* has been a favorite for generations, but it has only recently begun to develop a following in North America, where its radishlike leaves with their horseradish flavor are quite different from the usual salad and sandwich fare. The plant grows about 12 inches (30 cm) wide and equally tall.
Culture: Arugula is similar to spinach in its affinity for cool weather. It goes to seed rapidly in summer. Sow the seeds outdoors at ¼-inch (6 mm) intervals about 2 weeks before the last spring frost

date, thinning the plants gradually until they stand 12 inches (30 cm) apart. A steady supply of water will ensure that tender, fairly mild-tasting leaves develop. As soon as the plants bolt to seed in summer, they should be removed from the garden and replaced with seeds or seedlings of a heat-tolerant vegetable. Or arugula seeds may be allowed to mature for collection and sowing next season.
Harvest: Use thinnings in salads and sandwiches. From 6 to 8 weeks after seeding, the entire plant may be cut and eaten fresh or frozen to store.
Pests & Diseases: None of note.

Asparagus
(Liliaceae, *Asparagus officinalis*)
One of the earliest vegetables to appear in the spring is asparagus, a perennial native of Europe and North Africa that is hardy enough to overwinter almost everywhere south of the permafrost. The plants need a well-fertilized, well-drained permanent plot with a pH of about 6.6, where their 5-foot (1.5 m) height and 4-foot (1.2 m) root spread can be accommodated. They are dioecious (some plants are male and some female, producing berries). If your soil has a high salt content, asparagus will be one of your most successful vegetables.
Culture: Asparagus can be grown from seeds or transplants; the former is considerably less expensive but does delay the first harvest by a year. If using seeds, soak them in lukewarm water for 48 hours before planting, then sow at ½-inch (1 cm) intervals in ½-inch-deep (1 cm) drills 1 foot (30 cm) apart as soon as the soil can be worked in spring. As the seeds are slow to sprout, rows can be marked with radish seeds. Alternatively, seeds can be sown indoors and transplanted outdoors at 2-inch (5 cm) intervals in early spring. A year later, plant them in their permanent location in the same manner as purchased transplants. It is very important that perennial weeds, especially twitch or couch grass, be eliminated from the bed. Prepare the asparagus bed by turning the soil and incorporating well-rotted manure and compost. Dig

Freshly cut homegrown asparagus is a springtime delicacy that can be garnished with edible violas.

trenches 6 inches (15 cm) deep and 2 to 4 feet (0.6-1.2 m) apart. Lay a low ridge of manure along the center of each trench, then spread the roots of each plant over the ridge at 18-inch (45 cm) intervals. Cover the roots, and gradually fill in the trench as the shoots grow. When the trenches are filled, mulch the entire bed deeply with grass clippings, partly composted leaves, straw or hay to discourage weeds and retain moisture. Diligent weeding is otherwise mandatory. Manure and mulch should be reapplied every spring. In marginal growing areas, mulch the roots heavily over the winter. Although asparagus ferns are frost-hardy, new shoots are harmed by frost. Harvest or cover the young shoots if there is a frost warning.

Harvest: No picking at all is done either the year of transplanting or the following spring. The next year, spears may be picked for about 5 weeks; the following year and thereafter, they may be picked for 6 to 8 weeks. Cut the spears with a knife, or break off just below soil level. Shoots are best cut when 6 to 8 inches (15-20 cm) long and before the tips begin to open—harvest may be daily in warm weather, twice weekly in cool. Do not cut spears less than $\frac{1}{4}$ inch (6 mm) thick, but allow these ferns to reach their full height in order to produce nutrients for the next crop. Asparagus loses its quality quickly after picking—eat or preserve by freezing as soon as possible.

Pests & Diseases: The most common pest is the black-and-white asparagus beetle and its small, grayish larva, which can be dusted with lime or rotenone. Rust and fusarium wilt are easily combated by choosing a resistant variety—check the seed catalog or nursery listing. Removing dead ferns in early spring will help limit pest and disease infestations.

Bean, Broad
(Leguminosae, *Vicia faba*)

Fava Bean; Horse Bean; Windsor Bean; Tick Bean

A Eurasian bean, *V. faba* is far hardier than its New World relatives. It is, in fact, a blessing to gardeners of the high latitudes, bringing homegrown beans to their dinner plates, despite frosty spring or cool summer weather, and leaving a bonus of nitrogen in the garden. The bean itself varies in size according to cultivar, but most, when mature, are larger than any other common bean. Five to eight beans are produced in each pod, which may be up to 7 inches (18 cm) long and is borne singly or in a cluster in the leaf axil. The pod, whose interior is white and fuzzy, is not usually eaten. The plants are upright, about 3 feet (1 m) tall, and slender, with heavy stems. There are two types of broad bean: field beans and garden beans, the former smaller and rounder than the latter. Broad beans were the only garden beans known to Europeans before the discovery of the New World and were a common silage crop. They are sometimes substituted for soy beans in livestock feed.

Culture: Consider *V. faba* more like a pea than a bean in its cold tolerance. It can be sown directly outdoors as soon as the soil can be worked in spring—light frost will not harm the young plants—but can be given a boost in a cold frame or a cool, sunny window, sown 4 weeks before the last spring frost date and planted outdoors a week after sprouting. In very mild areas, it may be planted in late summer for a fall crop—allow the plant 2 to 3 months to mature before frost, which will damage the pods. As the bean requires cool, moist weather for best growth, spring planting should not be delayed past the last frost date. Plant seeds 1 inch (2.5 cm) deep at 4-to-6-inch (10-15 cm) intervals in rows or beds. If seeds are planted in beds, leave about 1 foot (30 cm) between cross-

wise rows to allow for cultivation with a hoe. Plants may require staking.

Harvest: The beans should be ready to pick 65 to 90 days after planting. Immature beans may be bitter; pick the pods when they are almost full-grown but not ripe; the beans inside will be slightly visible as bumps. Shell them, then cook or preserve them like green peas. Or allow the mature beans to dry on the plant or indoors and use as baking beans. The plants do not continue bearing for long. Some people, especially of Mediterranean descent, are very allergic to fava beans, a disorder known as favism. Try a little before eating a lot.

Pests & Diseases: Plants are fairly pest- and disease-resistant. Aphids are common but can be controlled with insecticidal soap used according to the manufacturer's directions. Pinching off plant tops as soon as pods have formed will also help control aphids.

Bean, Hyacinth
See page 130.

Bean, Kidney
(*Phaseolus vulgaris*)

One of many variations on the theme of the string bean, the kidney bean is well named to suggest both the color and the shape of its fruit. At the turn of the century, any kidney-shaped bean, whatever its color, used the same name. Best known as the bean in chili and succotash—an adaptation of the native *msickquatash*, a stew originally made from kidney beans, maize and bear grease—the red kidney bean is a relative rarity in northern gardens because it requires a fairly long frost-free season (about 100 days) and produces its biggest crops where killing frosts come after late September.

Culture: Plant kidney beans at the same time and in the same way as bush snap beans. The plant produces large, flat green pods filled with red kidney-shaped beans.

Harvest: Kidney beans may be picked fresh and shelled or left to dry on the vine, but do not let

The scarlet runner bean is decorative and edible.

them freeze or become moldy. If left too long, the pods will split and beans will be lost. If they are shelled when mature but not dry, the beans should be roasted in a warm oven until dry and hard. Store in jars or paper bags in a cool, dry place.

Pests & Diseases: See Snap Bean.

Bean, Lima
(*Phaseolus limensis; P. lunatus*)

Available in bush or pole varieties, limas need a warmer soil than do snap beans, and they also take longer to mature: 70 to 80 days for bush varieties, 85 to 100 for pole limas. All in all, limas are an unpredictable crop in most of Canada and the northern United States. Choose the earliest varieties available, or for a better harvest, select one of the

early lima-like beans, such as 'Limelight' or its predecessor, 'Princess of Artois.' Although these beans are *P. vulgaris* cultivars, lacking the lima bean flavor, they do have the lima bean's color and shape but are ready to harvest at the green-shell stage about 70 days after sowing.

Culture: Plant as snap beans, but not until 2 weeks after the last spring frost. The seeds will not germinate in cool soil and may take 17 days to germinate even at a soil temperature of 68 degrees F (20°C)—the coolest recommended. Seeds germinate in about 6 days at 77 degrees (25°C). To extend the season, start them indoors 4 weeks ahead of the planting-out date.

Harvest: Pick beans before the pod shows any yellowing; it should be green and succulent, the beans swollen inside. Shell and serve fresh, or preserve by freezing or drying.

Pests & Diseases: See Snap Bean.

Bean, Scarlet Runner
See below.

Bean, Snap
(Leguminosae, *Phaseolus vulgaris*)
String Bean

Thanks to the work of seed breeders, string beans are now snap beans, the fibers or strings having been bred out of the pods of all but the old heirloom varieties, some of which were observed by Jacques Cartier in 1535 growing in native gardens of the St. Lawrence Valley. Snap beans, whether of vining or bush-forming habit, whether green-, yellow- or purple-podded, whether considered Italian romanos or French filets, are the only beans routinely eaten with pods intact. Bush beans will grow about 18 inches (45 cm) tall on sturdy plants, while pole beans, such as scarlet runner (*P. coccineus*) need support and will grow to heights of 6 to 9 feet (2-2.7 m). All are tender plants that cannot withstand frost and require warm soil to germinate and grow, ceasing growth if temperatures dip to 50 degrees F (10°C). On the other hand, the blossoms may drop off if prevailing daytime temperatures are over 90 degrees (32°C). Given suitable growing conditions, however, snap beans are prolific, easy and dependable.

Culture: Snap beans are usually seeded directly outdoors around the last frost date and at 2- or 3-week intervals until midsummer; allow the plants at least 2 months to mature before frost. Seeds can be soaked for half an hour or even pre-germinated before planting for speedier emergence. If they are to be sown where beans have not grown before, treat with nitrogen-fixing inoculant (see page 37). Seeds will germinate in 16 days at the coolest recommended soil temperature of 60 degrees F (15°C), in 11 days at 68 degrees (20°C) and in 8 days at 77 degrees (25°C) but will not germinate in very hot soil. Seed treated with fungicides will be less likely to rot at cool soil temperatures, but treatment is not needed at 68 degrees (20°C) or warmer. If using untreated seeds, either delay planting or warm the soil with clear plastic before sowing. Plant seeds of bush beans 1 inch (2.5 cm) deep and 2 inches (5 cm) apart in rows or in beds. If in beds, plant in crosswise rows about 1 foot (30 cm) apart, far enough that weeding can be done with a hoe. Thin plants to stand 4 inches (10 cm) apart. The plants need full sun and well-drained, friable soil. Plant pole beans at 2-inch (5 cm) intervals along a fence, thinning later to 6 inches (15 cm) apart, or plant four seeds around a 6-foot (2 m) pole. Cover plants if frost threatens. Surrounding the plants with plastic mulch or growing bush beans under a row cover will help ensure maturation in cool-season areas.

Harvest: Bush beans mature 45 to 60 days from planting, pole beans about 10 days later. Pick pods before the beans inside swell noticeably and the pods discolor. Continual picking every 3 or 4 days will prolong the harvest of tender, young beans for about 3 weeks. To prepare, remove the blossom end, pull off strings if any are present, then snap into pieces and cook or preserve. Left to mature further, the beans can be shelled and served in the manner of lima beans, or they may be left to dry on the vine or brought indoors to dry for use in soups and baking. Horticultural beans, navy beans, pinto beans, black turtle beans and hundreds more in a spectrum of colors, from white, beige, pink and red to gold, brown and black, plain, striped and speckled, are chiefly *P. vulgaris* cultivars meant primarily for shelling.

Pests & Diseases: Do not tend wet plants, as this can spread disease. Remove plant debris at the end of the season and compost it. The Mexican bean beetle, a problem in some southern areas of Canada, can be controlled with a tea of cedar chips brewed in warm water or with pyrethrum or rotenone. As this beetle looks much like the beneficial lady beetle, check with an expert or an identification book before harming it. Deformed or curled bean pods may result from lack of moisture, drought or insect damage during blossoming. Fungus diseases such as rust are common on pods, especially in damp weather. Discard discolored pods and beans.

Bean, Soy

(Leguminosae, *Glycine max*)
Soya Bean; Vegetable Soy Bean; Mao Du
Cultivated in the Far East for centuries, strains of *G. max* are now among North America's most important forage crops, and their value as a food crop is also increasing. Soy beans are exceedingly high in protein—about 40 percent on a dry-weight basis—double that of lima beans. The soy bean's range is moving steadily northward as breeders pare days from its maturation requirements. Now, most Northerners can grow early cultivars and may even have sufficient time before frost to allow the beans to dry on the plant. Select early-maturing cultivars carried by companies catering to Northerners. The sturdy plants grow about 14 inches (35 cm) tall; 3-inch (7.5 cm) fuzzy pods each enclose two or three beans.

Culture: Sow soy beans directly in the garden at about the same time as limas, 2 weeks after the last frost date—the seeds germinate best at 86 degrees F (30°C)—or start them indoors 4 weeks before the planting-out date. Pre-germination of seeds indoors will also speed emergence. Plant seeds 1 inch (2.5 cm) deep and 2 inches (5 cm) apart in rows or in beds. If in beds, leave 1 foot (30 cm) between crosswise rows so that they can be cultivated with a hoe. Do not tend plants when they are wet.

Harvest: Each plant produces about 50 pods, ready to be harvested 70 to 120 days after planting, depending on variety and soil temperature. For fresh beans, pick the pods when they are just beginning to change color from green to yellow. Boil for 1 minute, then cool in ice water and shell by squeezing out beans. Serve or preserve as for green peas. Beans can be dried on the plants or roasted in a warm oven until hard. Store in jars or in paper bags in a cool, dry cupboard, and use as baking beans.

Pests & Diseases: Seeds will rot if they are planted in soil that is too cool. The bean leaf beetle may attack plants in eastern Canada. It is ¼-inch (6 mm) long, reddish orange and shiny, with a black head and sometimes black spots. The larva is a small white grub. Hand-picking is usually a sufficient control, but rotenone or pyrethrum can be used for severe outbreaks. Groundhogs and other rodents are fond of young soy beans. Plants may need to be caged or surrounded by electric fencing.

Unusual Beans

As a look through the catalog of a seed saver's exchange will confirm, there are hundreds of varieties of beans. Most are cultivars of string beans, snap beans or shelled beans, meant to be eaten fresh or dried for later use. They appear in almost the full spectrum of colors and in a myriad of shapes and sizes. Unfortunately, many of these heirloom cultivars and some of the more unusual beans, such as the adzuki bean (*Phaseolus angularis*), asparagus bean (*Vigna unguiculata*), garbanzo bean (*Cicer arietinum*), mung bean (*Vigna radiata*) and winged bean (*Psophocarpus tetragonolobus*), either produce so few beans per pod or require such a long season that they are impractical in the northern garden as anything but novelties.

Beet
(Chenopodiaceae, *Beta vulgaris*)
Beetroot
Although the beet was originally more prized for its spinachlike greens than its swollen root—con-

sidered little better than livestock feed—its priorities have been more or less reversed by North Americans. The plant, a biennial, produces a sweet, tender root that may be purple, white, golden or variegated and ranges in shape from the usual globe, big or small, to cylindrical. A variation, the sugar beet, is grown mostly for sugar production in temperate climates, while another, the mangel, is chiefly a forage crop. Both can also be used for the table if harvested while young and tender. Beets love cool, moist conditions and are thus ideal plants for Northerners, producing crops even where the season is as short as 80 days.

Culture: A beet "seed" is actually a dried fruit composed of several seeds, so early thinning is usually necessary. Beet seeds can be sown as early as the soil can be worked in spring, then every 2 weeks until early summer. A late-storage cultivar such as 'Winter Keeper' should be sown about 10 weeks before the first fall frost. Give beets deeply worked, loose soil high in organic matter. The seed germinates in 4 to 10 days within its preferred soil-temperature range of 45 to 70 degrees F (7-21°C). Sow seeds about 1 inch (2.5 cm) apart and ½-inch (1 cm) deep. Thinnings may be eaten whole, either cooked or raw. Keep the plants thinned sufficiently to maintain about 1 inch (2.5 cm) between each root. Plants need a steady supply of water and will tolerate light frost but may bolt to seed in areas where the days are very long. In the Far North, choose quick-maturing, small-rooted varieties. Bolting reduces leaf and root quality. Mulch plants or keep them well weeded, because weed competition can produce tough roots.

Harvest: The greens, high in vitamins and iron, are at their best until roots are 1 to 1½ inches (2.5-3.8 cm) in diameter. Pull only a few outer leaves at a time so that the roots continue to grow. Use greens fresh or cooked like spinach. Except for the large storage varieties, roots are best when 2½ to 3 inches (6.3-7.5 cm) across and become woody when overmature. For winter storage, however, large, fully mature roots keep best. Pull them on a dry day after the first fall frost, cut tops to within ½ inch (1 cm) of the root, and leave the roots outdoors on newspaper one sunny day to cure, turning occasionally and rubbing off loose soil. Store in moist sand, peat or perforated plastic bags at 32 to 40 degrees F (0-4.5°C) and high humidity. Roots may also overwinter in the garden if heavily mulched before the soil freezes. Harvest before plants fulfill their biennial destiny by going to seed in spring.

Pests & Diseases: White rings in the root (except in variegated varieties) are caused by growth checks; the best roots develop quickly and steadily. Internal browning of the root, often a problem in alkaline soil after a long hot period, is caused by soil low in boron. Apply boron according to soil-test recommendations. Scab—raised brown spots —is also common in alkaline soil. However, none of these conditions make roots inedible, and all can be countered with a high proportion of organic matter in the soil.

The green caterpillar of the beet armyworm can be controlled by hand-picking or with *Bacillus thuringiensis*. The beet leafhopper, a tiny, greenish insect, can be controlled with diatomaceous earth.

'*Premium Crop*' *broccoli ready for first harvest.*

Broccoli
(Cruciferae, *Brassica oleracea italica*)

A cabbage mutant but, unlike cabbage, an annual, broccoli was first described in the Middle East in the 12th century. The part eaten is actually a cluster of inflorescences, immature flowers harvested before they bloom. The word "broccoli" is Italian and means tender stalks—an apt description of broccoli raab, or sprouting broccoli, a European strain that does not form a central head but produces small shoots throughout the season. Guy lon—Chinese broccoli, or Chinese kale—is similar to raab, producing no large central head. Broccoli plants grow about 2 feet (60 cm) tall and equally wide. They do best in very fertile soil mulched with straw, grass clippings or leaf mold.

Culture: Broccoli needs about 2 months without a succession of hard frosts. Start seeds indoors 6 or 7 weeks before the last spring frost date to ensure an early harvest, although in most areas, seeds of early varieties may be sown directly in the garden from 2 weeks before until 2 weeks after the last spring frost. Seeds germinate in about 7 days in soil 45 to 90 degrees F (7-32°C). As very young plants are more frost-hardy than mature ones, early planting is recommended in short-season areas. Plants mature 60 to 70 days from transplanting, 80 to 90 days from direct seeding. Sow seeds ½ inch (1 cm) deep in clusters of three or four seeds spaced 18 inches (45 cm) apart or in rows at 2-inch (5 cm) intervals. Gradually thin plants to stand 18 inches (45 cm) apart, or plant transplants at 18-inch (45 cm) intervals, deeply enough that the first true leaves are just above the soil level. Mulch with about 4 inches (10 cm) of organic material when the soil is warm and plants are growing well. Throughout the season, ensure that plants receive adequate moisture—about 1 inch (2.5 cm) a week. Roots are close to the surface, so do not cultivate deeply. Watering with manure tea or fish fertilizer every 2 weeks will help maintain suitable soil-nutrient levels.

Harvest: When the flower buds are full but before they begin to open, cut the large central head at the stem. Smaller lateral heads form later and should be harvested in the same manner. Serve fresh, or freeze heads to preserve.

Pests & Diseases: Flea beetles, root maggots and cutworms are the worst pests when plants are young. Control flea beetles with rotenone. Since root maggots crawl down plant stems to the roots, circle the stem with a tarpaper or cardboard disk flat against the soil. Control cutworms as described on page 188. Later, various cabbage-moth larvae are troublesome and best controlled with *Bacillus thuringiensis*, used according to the manufacturer's directions. Light infestations can be managed with hand-picking, a soap spray or rotenone, but do not use rotenone within a week of harvesting. Clubroot, a fungus disease, is best prevented by cleanliness, crop rotation, the use of resistant cultivars and ensuring that the soil is well drained and near neutral in pH. Destroy any infected plants.

Brussels Sprouts

(Cruciferae, *Brassica oleracea gemmifera*)
Closely related to cabbage and broccoli, Brussels sprouts originated in Belgium, where *sprossenkohl* were grown for about 400 years before they made their way into France in the 18th century and Britain in the 19th. The sprouts are tiny cabbage heads that form from the ground upward, in leaf axils along the main stem. The plant is among the hardiest of the brassicas. It is an easy plant for Northerners to grow and, like all brassicas, thrives in very fertile soil during cool, moist weather. Most sprouts are green, but there are purple varieties as well.

Culture: Plant and tend as for broccoli. Brussels sprouts take approximately 3 months to mature. Time their planting so that the first sprouts are mature when fall frosts begin. As the sprouts form, pull out the lower leaves, gradually removing them to roughly halfway up the stalk. To encourage sprout growth, pinch off the top of the plant about 2 weeks before the first fall frost date or when the lowest sprouts are 1 inch (2.5 cm) wide.

Harvest: Start to harvest the lowest sprouts when they are the size of golf balls. Moving up the stem, continue to harvest them gradually until all are picked or until the plant is killed by frost. Light frost, however, improves the flavor. Each plant produces about 1 pound (500 g) of sprouts. Before the soil freezes, the entire plant can be pulled from the garden and hung upside down in a cool, moist cellar to prolong the harvest.

Pests & Diseases: As for broccoli, but pest problems are less severe with Brussels sprouts, because they mature after the worst pest infestations.

Cabbage

(Cruciferae, *Brassica oleracea capitata*)
Cabbage, introduced to the North by Jacques Cartier, is a native of the northern Mediterranean. An easy crop to grow and one that thrives in the cool northern growing season, cabbage may have smooth leaves or curly leaves (savoy) and may be purple or green. While some plants may produce heads more than 12 inches (30 cm) wide, there are "mini" varieties with heads only half that size. Like other leafy crops, cabbage is at its best when it grows steadily and quickly, which happens when the soil is moist, fertile and high in organic matter. A Canadian scientist noted in 1917: "We have never heard of anyone using too much manure for cabbage."

Culture: Plant and tend as for broccoli. If properly hardened before being set out in the garden, transplants can withstand a heavy frost of 20 degrees F (–6°C) but otherwise will be quickly killed by such cold. (Seeds sown outdoors harden themselves.) Early varieties mature about 70 days after transplanting, main-crop varieties in 75 to 80 days, storage varieties in 90 to 100 days. Add 10 to 20 days for direct seeding in the garden. Since heads may crack when overmature or after heavy rains, gardeners who wish to delay harvesting mature heads should twist the head slightly or push a spade into the soil on one side of the plant to break some of the roots. Time fall plantings so that heads are mature just before the first frost. Light frost will not harm cabbage but will slow or stop its growth.

Harvest: Cut through the stem just below the head, leaving the surrounding leaves on the plant.

A nutritious staple of the northern garden, cabbage can be comely, too, if a savoy or ornamental variety.

If the first head is harvested fairly early, three to five small heads will grow on the central stem and will be ready for harvest a month or two later. Cabbage can be made into sauerkraut or preserved by slicing and freezing, or entire heads can be stored for several weeks in a damp root cellar at a temperature near freezing. To store this way, harvest entire plants, complete with roots, remove damaged leaves and hang the plants by the roots, or harvest the heads only and store in perforated plastic bags in a root cellar or refrigerator.

Pests & Diseases: See Broccoli.

Carrot
(Umbelliferae, *Daucus carota*)

The carrot is a highly refined version of a common weed, Queen Anne's lace, which hails from the Middle East. There are many sizes and shapes of carrot. Very small ones, either round or cylindrical, are the best choices for shallow soil or where quick maturation (about 55 days) is desired. Fat types, such as 'Chantenay' and 'Oxheart,' are the best choices for heavy soils and for storage. The long, thin commercial types need very loose, deeply worked soil and a steady water supply.

Culture: Like all root crops, the best carrots of any type will grow in deeply worked, well-drained and aerated soil without clumps or stones. If the soil is heavy or compact, grow carrots in raised beds in which the soil has been mixed with peat, compost and sand. Carrot growth and color develop best at moderate soil temperatures of 60 to 70 degrees F (15-21°C). Because they prefer cool soil, carrots will mature in almost every northern garden. Seeds can be sown outdoors any time after the soil can be worked in spring, although faster growth will occur with seeds planted around the last frost date. Plant carrots for winter storage about

To blanch older varieties of cauliflower, tie the leaves.

yellow or white larvae of the carrot rust fly chew holes in roots and are best controlled by crop rotation or the use of a spunbonded crop cover such as Reemay. The carrot rust fly lays eggs at the base of the plant, and the small white larvae tunnel into the roots. There may be a second or even third generation. Adults overwinter in crop remains, so clean out the garden after the harvest. Where the fly is a common problem, late planting—from the end of May till early June—avoids damage from the first generation. The parsleyworm, which is the larva of the black swallowtail butterfly, chews foliage but seldom requires more control than hand-picking. Hairy carrots are caused by overfertilization with nitrogen or by irregular weather conditions during early root formation. Splitting can be caused by heavy rain just as the roots are maturing. Forked carrots are the result of compact heavy soil or stones.

100 days before the first fall frost date. Sow a continuous line of seeds in a furrow about ½ inch (1 cm) deep. Lightly cover with moist, finely textured soil, pat firmly, and water again. The seeds are slow to germinate: 6 to 21 days at 45 to 86 degrees (7-30°C). Adequate watering is important from the time seeds are sown until root swelling begins a couple of weeks after emergence; be sure that the soil never dries out during this critical period. In very dry, windy places, cover the seeded beds with boards or plastic until the seeds sprout. As they grow, thin carrots regularly so that the roots are never closer together than ½ inch (1 cm). Hill the soil over the crowns to prevent greening of roots, which causes bitterness. Keep the bed clear of weeds by mulching or diligent weeding.

Harvest: Harvest and store as for beets. Eat the thinnings raw or cooked. Carrot tops may be used fresh or dried as a potherb, fed to livestock or used as compost or mulch.

Pests & Diseases: Few present a real risk to garden carrots, most doing cosmetic damage only. The bluish white 1-inch (2.5 cm) larvae of the carrot beetle, wireworms and the ½-inch-long (1 cm)

Cauliflower
(Cruciferae, *Brassica oleracea botrytis*)

The first part of this vegetable's common name comes from the Latin *caulis*, meaning "stem"; the ending identifies the part of the plant eaten, the flower. Cauliflower is the most temperamental of the brassicas, the least frost-hardy and the most likely to suffer damping-off, to bolt to seed or to be attacked by root maggots; in short, it is the most likely to produce no crop. From seeding to harvest, cauliflower does best with little fluctuation in temperature or moisture, preferring cool, damp weather and fertile, moist soil high in organic matter. Purple-headed cauliflower is less demanding, but its heads do not have the delicate flavor of the common white curds. Mini varieties, which produce a central head only 4 inches (10 cm) across, are best where quicker maturation is required—about 50 days, compared with 55 to 85 for others. All plants grow roughly 14 inches (35 cm) tall.

Culture: Sow and transplant as for broccoli, but start the seeds indoors later (5 or 6 weeks before the last spring frost date), and do not move outdoors until the last spring frost. The plants will not stand as much cold as other brassicas but are just as frost-hardy when very young, so planting should not be left so late that maturation is checked by fall frost. Since overgrown transplants are likely to bolt to seed or become stunted, select the youngest available if purchasing them. Applying about 4 inches (10 cm) of mulch to plants at least that tall will help maintain adequate soil moisture. Most new varieties are self-blanching—the inner leaves fold over the head, keeping it white (check the seed catalog or packet descriptions). Older varieties must be blanched by hand. As soon as the heads are teacup-sized, gather the leaves up over the head and tie them with string. Unblanched heads become greenish or purplish and may have a bitter flavor, but their vitamin content is higher. Do not tie up the leaves of purple-headed varieties.

Harvest: Heads are ready to cut when they are full and frothy but the flowers have not yet begun to open. Cut the stem just below the head, which may be cooked, served raw or frozen to preserve. (Purple heads turn light green when blanched or cooked.) After the heads have been harvested, the rest of the plant should be removed from the garden and composted, as it will produce no more heads.

Pests & Diseases: As for broccoli. Leafy curds are caused by high temperatures, great fluctuations in temperature or too much high-nitrogen fertilizer, such as manure. This degree of overfertilization is uncommon, however, where only organic fertilizers are used. Buttoning, the production of tiny curds rather than a large head, is caused by drought or too much cold or damp. Browning of the heads may be caused by a boron deficiency. Apply boron at the rate recommended by a soil-test report.

Celeriac
(Umbelliferae, *Apium graveolens rapaceum*)
Turnip-Rooted Celery
This relative of celery produces a turniplike root that has the flavor of celery. Roots are mature in about

4 months, and the plants are as cold-hardy as celery.
Culture: Celeriac benefits from the same soil and planting schedule as celery, although the plants do not need blanching. Set them outdoors at 9-inch (23 cm) intervals.
Harvest: Pull before the soil freezes. Roots may be stored as beets if they are at least 2 inches (5 cm) across. They may attain weights of 2 to 4 pounds (1-1.8 kg). Serve raw or cooked.
Pests & Diseases: See Celery.

Celery
(Umbelliferae, *Apium graveolens dulce*)
The common name for celery comes from the Greek *selinon*, meaning "parsley," to which this plant is related. Although few gardeners will produce stalks as long, succulent and blemish-free as those sold in grocery stores, celery's reputation for being a difficult crop to grow is undeserved. It is simply slow to germinate and grow and must be nursed along in very fertile, moist soil if the stalks are to be tender. Celery can withstand light frost but is likely to bolt to seed if the young transplants are exposed to temperatures below 55 degrees F (13°C) for 10 days or longer. As well as the standard green varieties, there are golden and self-blanching strains of celery.
Culture: Celery is so slow to germinate that it is best started indoors or purchased as transplants. At a soil temperature of 60 to 70 degrees F (15-21°C), it germinates in 10 to 21 days. Seeds should be lightly covered and kept moist throughout, with day temperatures around 75 degrees (24°C) and night temperatures of 65 degrees (18°C) until germination. When seedlings are 2 inches (5 cm) tall, they can be transplanted, 2 inches (5 cm) apart, into new containers. If they become spindly, cut off the top half. Harden off seedlings by letting the soil dry slightly, but do not expose them to cold. Set them outside about a week after the last frost date in a well-worked, sunny or partially sunny spot where manure or compost has been worked into the soil. Blanching of the spears is not necessary

but will produce a milder flavor. To blanch, dig trenches 1 foot (30 cm) deep and equally wide and fill with 8 inches (20 cm) of topsoil mixed with 25 percent manure or compost. Set transplants in this mixture 6 inches (15 cm) apart along the trench. As the plants grow, fill the trench with soil or a soil/manure mixture, holding the stalks together as the mixture is placed around them. If you do not want to blanch the celery, set plants 6 inches (15 cm) apart in the garden, in double rows or staggered in beds. Keep plants well watered. In places where frost may come in summer, celery can be left in cold frames to mature.

Harvest: Stalks can be pulled singly from the outside of the plant while it continues to grow, or entire heads can be pulled, trimmed and stored in plastic bags in a cool, damp place—the refrigerator or a cold room. After the first fall frost, pull heads with roots, remove one-quarter of the tops and replant in damp sand in the root cellar. At a temperature of about 45 degrees F (7°C) with high humidity, the heads will keep for several weeks. Celery leaves may be used fresh or dried as a potherb, like parsley.

Pests & Diseases: The parsleyworm—the larva of the black swallowtail butterfly—can be handpicked from foliage. Carrot rust fly may attack roots (see Carrot). Stem cracking may be caused by a boron deficiency; apply boron according to recommendations in a soil-test report. Blackheart can result from too little calcium, aggravated by dry soil and sometimes by too high a content of potassium in the soil.

Chicory
(Compositae, *Cichorium intybus*)
Witloof; Magdeburg; Italian Dandelion; Radichetta
Like its wild blue-flowered counterpart, cultivated chicory is a very hardy, vigorous plant whose foliage has a bitter taste unless it is blanched. There are several types. Asparagus chicory is grown for its thick, leafy stems. Heading types may be used for summer greens. Magdeburg produces large

Chicory is a hardy leaf and root vegetable.

parsniplike roots usually used as a coffee substitute or extender. Witloof, or leaf chicory, which may be eaten as a summer salad green, has long been cherished in Europe for its ability to produce fresh greens in winter. Radichetta is a looseleaf type whose foliage becomes sweeter and more tender in winter. Chicory is sometimes called French or Belgian endive, names that confuse it with true endive, *C. endivia*.

Culture: Plant all varieties after the last spring frost, sowing seeds about 1 inch (2.5 cm) apart and ½ inch (1 cm) deep in rows or in groups of three or four seeds spaced at 6-inch (15 cm) intervals. Thin later so that the plants stand 1 foot (30 cm) apart.

Harvest: Foliage of all types can be eaten in summer, though it will be bitter unless blanched under inverted flowerpots or boxes, in the manner of endive. After the first fall frost, all types are harvested. Magdeburg is dug up, the tops trimmed off and the long roots washed, ground or cut into small pieces, then roasted in a warm oven until coffee-brown.

Use alone for brewing, or blend with coffee. Wild chicory roots can be prepared in the same manner. For witloof, cut stems and foliage back to within 1 inch (2.5 cm) of the soil, dig up the root and replant it upright in a box of wet sand. Place the box in a cool—50 to 65 degrees F (10-18°C)—cupboard or root cellar that provides total darkness. Any light will cause bitterness in the heads, or *chicons*, which are cut at soil level when they are 4 to 5 inches (10-13 cm) long, usually in 2 to 3 weeks. As with beets, roots can be stored horizontally until they are needed throughout the winter. One set of roots will produce two or three crops of *chicons*, but crops are successively smaller. Spent roots can be used as livestock feed. Radichetta, available in both green and red cultivars, is used only as a leaf vegetable. Again, the plants are dug in fall, transplanted into boxes or pots of wet sand and placed in a cold frame or greenhouse where they can be kept at a temperature around freezing. The plant produces new, mild-tasting, tender foliage until it freezes or goes to seed in spring. In very mild areas, radichetta will overwinter in the garden under mulch.

Pests & Diseases: See Dandelion.

Chinese Cabbage

(Cruciferae, *Brassica pekinensis*)
Celery Cabbage; Michihli; Wong Bok;
Suey Choy; Pe Tsai

Orientals grow a variety of leafy brassicas, but the one usually called Chinese cabbage in North America is *B. pekinensis*, which produces loose upright heads of somewhat wrinkled leaves that are closer in texture to lettuce than cabbage. A cool-weather crop, Chinese cabbage withstands light frost but will bolt to seed very quickly, even before heading, in hot weather or when days are long. In variety trials in Alaska in 1980, all cultivars bolted to seed before harvest. Chinese cabbage is thus not recommended for Far Northerners, and other gardeners must plant it in early spring or late summer. The plant thrives in constantly moist, fertile soil high in organic matter and in a temperature range of 60 to 68 degrees F (15-20°C), though it will withstand light frost in spring and fall.

Culture: Sow as cabbage, but do not transplant

unless a short season demands it, since the change can cause bolting. Seeds germinate best at a soil temperature between 68 and 77 degrees F (20-25°C), but the plant will grow at temperatures as low as 40 degrees (4.5°C). Apply mulch when the plants are a few inches high to protect them from drought.

Harvest: Use like lettuce or cabbage, pulling leaves as needed or harvesting the entire head. The plant is especially suited to light cooking in stir-fry dishes. Trimmed and wrapped in newspaper or perforated plastic, the heads can be stored for several weeks in a root cellar or refrigerator at a temperature just above freezing and in high relative humidity.

Pests & Diseases: See Broccoli.

Corn

(Gramineae, *Zea mays*)

Bred into scores of varieties by the indigenous peoples of North and South America long before Europeans arrived, this annual member of the grass family has since been hybridized to produce ever sweeter, larger kernels for gardeners ever farther north. Because sweet corn grows 5 to 8 feet (1.5-2.5 m) tall and is wind-pollinated, it tends to dominate the garden. Several rows of each variety must be planted to ensure full ears. Pollen is produced on the tassels that form at the tops of the plants; the female receptacles for the pollen are the silks at the top of each ear. Each strand of silk pollinates one kernel, so incomplete pollination results in poorly filled ears. Sweet corn is available with yellow, white or bicolor kernels. The best home-garden hybrids are described as sugar-enhanced, supersweet or eversweet, all types that have been bred to stay sweet after harvesting. There are several classes of these supersweet types, which vary in sweetness. The sweetest full-sized varieties require a fairly lengthy frost-free season. Very early hybrids (53 to 60 days) produce cobs just 4 to 6 inches (10-15 cm) long, best for short-season areas. Buy them from companies specializing in seeds for Northerners. Mature corn plants will withstand light frost, but the kernel flavor will deteriorate.

Culture: Corn may be started in flats 4 weeks before planting out, but because it germinates and grows quickly in warm soil, corn is best sown directly in the garden. Plastic mulch will help warm the soil in marginal areas and was found to speed maturation by 10 to 12 days in experiments in Atlantic Canada. Corn needs a great deal of nitrogen to grow well. Incorporating manure or compost into the corn bed before planting will help it along. Sow the seeds around the last frost date or early enough to allow the corn to mature at least 2 weeks before the first fall frost, spacing seeds at 2-inch (5 cm) intervals in rows about 2 feet (60 cm) apart, later thinning plants to stand 6 inches (15 cm) apart. Or sow in groups of two or three seeds, each hill a foot (30 cm) from the next in the row, with rows 2 feet (60 cm) or more apart. Seeds germinate in 4 to 7 days at 60 to 90 degrees F (15-32°C). Allow a minimum of four rows of each variety. Hybrids that mature at the same time should be separated by a tall crop such as sunflowers or kept at least 10 feet (3 m) apart to limit cross-pollination, which can drastically reduce kernel quality, especially with the new supersweets. Keep the bed well weeded until plants are tall enough to compete. Thereafter, a mulch will help control weeds. Do not cultivate deeply, because roots are shallow.

Harvest: Most varieties ripen about two ears per plant. When corn is ripe, the silks appear dry and the cobs full. To check for ripeness, pull back the husk on one ear; the top kernels should be full. Standard sweet corn loses its sweetness quickly after being picked. Serve or preserve as soon as possible, or put it into cold storage immediately—conversion of sugar to starch is five times faster at 80 degrees F (27°C) than at 30 degrees (–1°C).

Pests & Diseases: Incomplete filling of ears is usually the result of too few plants in a patch but may also be caused by poor weather during pollination. Corn smut, which produces a grotesque swelling of kernels, comes from a wind-borne fungus. Cut off affected cobs, and eat them if you like—they taste like mushrooms and are considered a delicacy by some cultures—or burn them, because if the kernels burst, spores will spread throughout the garden and can survive for 4 to 5 years. To combat corn earworms, squirt mineral oil down into the silks 4 or 5 days after they wilt. Corn borers overwinter on stubble left in the garden; discourage them by removing corn refuse after the harvest. Earwigs may eat corn silks to the base. Larger predators must be fended off with larger means. Catharine Parr Traill wrote that corn "has many enemies—bears, raccoons, squirrels, mice and birds—and is a great temptation to breachy cattle who, to come at it, will even toss down a fence." An electric fence will discourage many predators, while birds and squirrels can be foiled with paper bags placed over the ears after pollination. Planting vining crops such as pumpkins around the patch is something of a deterrent to small animals, as is cayenne pepper applied to the ears after every rain.

Ornamental Corn; Indian Corn; Squaw Corn

Culture & Harvest: These are long-season (around 100 days) types of corn that usually grow about 8 feet (2.5 m) tall. The kernels, which are starchy in flavor, are white, yellow, orange, blue, red, brown, black or bicolored. Plant like sweet corn. Harvest ornamental corn as for popcorn, but leave the kernels on the cobs. Standard types have ears about 8 inches (20 cm) long. There are miniature types, with ears about half that long, but they take as long to mature as the standards. All are enjoyable crops for children to grow. To prevent cross pollination, be sure to separate ornamental corn from other cultivars that mature at the same time. Varieties of ornamental corn suitable for grinding into meal are available from a few seed companies. Harvest as for popcorn, and grind as needed.

Popcorn

Culture & Harvest: Available with large or small white, yellow, blue, red or black kernels, popcorn is planted and grown like sweet corn but harvested when the stalks and leaves are completely dry, even if this means waiting past the first few light frosts. Choose early varieties, however, because some require a long, hot season of more than 100 days. Bring the ears indoors, husk them and hang in a warm, dry place to dry further, popping a sample from time to time to test it. As soon as they pop well, remove the kernels by twisting them off the cobs, and store in airtight containers so that they do not dry further. The best popcorn is hull-less, such as 'White Cloud.'

Pests & Diseases: See Corn.

Corn Salad

(Valerianaceae, *Valerianella locusta*)
Lamb's Lettuce; Feldsalat; Doucette; Mache
Corn salad matures quickly, producing its spoon-shaped leaves during cool spring or fall weather. Plants are easy to grow in cool, moist soil, and flavor improves with frost. Because plants are small—roughly 3½ inches (9 cm) tall at maturity—they are useful in interplantings in containers, herb gardens and other small gardens.

Culture: Sow 2 weeks before the last spring frost, and continue into late summer, thinning seedlings to 6 inches (15 cm) apart when they are about 2 inches (5 cm) tall. In very mild areas, late plantings will bear all winter and go to seed in spring or will remain dormant during the winter and produce early greens in spring. Heavy mulching will enable crops to overwinter in cooler areas.

Harvest: As leaf lettuce. Begin harvesting the outer leaves after three or four true leaves have developed and until the plant bolts in summer or freezes in winter.

Pests & Diseases: See Dandelion.

Cress

(Cruciferae, *Lepidium sativum*)
Peppergrass
A native of the Middle East, cress is the garden's fastest-maturing crop, ready to harvest only 10 days after sowing in damp, cool soil. Familiar as the mossy vegetable that grows on terra-cotta lambs and pigs from specialty stores, cress does equally well outdoors in spring or indoors on a sunny windowsill all winter. Although the tiny plants are too small to make a salad on their own, they are an excellent homegrown addition to winter salads. Plants go to seed quickly in hot weather, producing small white flowers.

Culture: Sow seeds outdoors or indoors in pots or even on a wet brick, sponge or piece of cloth set in a bowl of water by a window. Broadcast the seeds evenly over the surface; if on soil, press them in and water with a fine spray. The seeds germinate in 2 days at room temperature. Resow every 2 to 3 weeks. During hot, dry weather, sow outdoors in a moist, shaded place for the tenderest leaves.

Harvest: Begin to harvest cress with scissors or a knife when the stems are 1 to 1½ inches (2.5-3.8 cm) long. Use fresh in salads or sandwiches. Cress has a pungent, peppery flavor similar to that of watercress.

Pests & Diseases: See Dandelion.

Cucumber

(Cucurbitaceae, *Cucumis sativus*)
The cucumber is an old-world plant popular with North America's early settlers, who found that it suited their new situation well. One, Thomas Mc-Grath, wrote from Toronto in 1832: "Melons, cucumbers and pumpkins grow freely and very abundantly in the open air and require less attention than any crop we have." Had McGrath been living farther north, he'd have given his cucumbers more thought. The plant is very sensitive to frost, so in most Far Northern gardens, it must be protected for at least part of the season. As the cucumber is monoecious, producing separate male and female flowers, it must be pollinated by insects or by hand. Some varieties produce mostly female flowers, the type that bear fruit. Dyed male seeds are included in the packet; plant one for every one to six females. Seedless all-female varieties, called gynoecious, are principally for greenhouse culture, because accidental pollination will lower the fruit quality. There are also lemon-shaped cucumbers, low-acid "burpless" fruits and Oriental types that are long, thin and snakelike. Pickling varieties pro-

duce a large crop of 3-to-4-inch (7.5-10 cm) fruit almost simultaneously, some varieties in as few as 48 days after planting. Slicing varieties produce longer fruits a few at a time over a longer period.

Culture: All the cucurbits have very delicate roots that must not be damaged in transplanting. Sow cucumbers directly in the garden around the last frost date or transplant in peat pots, peat pellets or containers that can be removed without disturbing the roots. Seeds germinate in 3 to 7 days in the preferred soil-temperature range of 68 to 95 degrees F (20-35°C) but will not germinate below 50 degrees (10°C). Choose a sunny, sheltered place for cucumbers—excessive winds will damage plants and slow growth. Vining cucumber varieties can be allowed to sprawl in the garden or can be planted at 6-inch (15 cm) intervals against a trellis, slender poles or vertical strings about 5 feet (1.5 m) tall, which they will climb readily. Bush varieties do not climb but take less garden space than do unsupported vining cucumbers—some require as little as 18 to 20 square inches (115-130 cm²). Vining or bush varieties may be planted in hills of two or three plants (six to nine seeds, thinned later), the hills 3 feet (1 m) apart—or closer for small bush varieties. Covering plants with commercial or homemade shelters such as glass jars will help get them off to a good start, as will a black or clear plastic mulch. Hand pollination is necessary if the plants are unlikely to be visited by bees (see the instructions on page 192). If pollination does not take place, no fruit will form. Be careful not to handle wet plants, because doing so may spread fungal diseases.

Harvest: Continual picking will prolong the harvest. If the fruits are allowed to remain on the vine, a typical plant will produce only 10 to 12, but if the fruits are picked while young, the plant may produce up to 50. Pinch or cut the fruits off with a knife, because pulling hard may damage the plant. Pick all fruits before they turn yellow.

Pests & Diseases: Cucumbers suffer from a variety of ailments, although many gardeners have no pest or disease problems, in part because most new varieties have inbred resistance to some diseases; check the catalog or packet. Squash bugs can be controlled with a tea of cedar-bark chips or by placing boards on the ground around the plant. At night, the bugs congregate under the boards and can be killed in the morning. Earlier in the season, destroy their clusters of yellow to brown eggs, which are usually laid between two main veins on the underside of the leaf. Striped cucumber beetles and aphids do little damage themselves but may spread bacterial wilt and mosaic virus. Control them with pyrethrum or rotenone. If a single vine suddenly wilts, the culprit is likely the squash vine borer. Search along the vine to find a hole. Slit the stem, remove the borer, hill soil over the damaged vine, and water. If bacterial or fungal diseases occur, most common in hot, wet weather, destroy all plant refuse at the end of the season, and choose a resistant variety next spring, rotating the planting.

Dandelion
(Compositae, *Taraxacum officinale*)

Culture & Harvest: This plant needs little introduction, so thoroughly has it become adapted to life in North America. The dandelion is, however, not only a weed but also a salad vegetable or potherb, with vitamin-rich leaves, flowers that can be used to make wine, and roots that can be roasted and used as a coffee substitute in the same manner as chicory. While any field dandelion is edible, the selected strain carried by some seed houses (usually listed under herbs) has milder-tasting foliage. Even the commercial strains have foliage more bitter than that preferred by the average North American palate and are best used young or blanched like endive. In *Roughing It in the Bush*, Susanna Moodie's 19th-century journal of life in rural Canada, she wrote: "The dandelion planted in trenches and blanched to a beautiful cream color with straw makes an excellent salad, quite equal to endive, and is more hardy and requires less care." Sow seeds in spring for a fall crop, or sow later for harvest the following season, mulching the roots over winter. Allow each plant 1 foot (30 cm) all around. Dig roots in fall to force like chicory.

Pests & Diseases: Slugs can be troublesome, especially during damp weather or in deeply mulched gardens. Dust plants and the surrounding soil with diatomaceous earth, reapplying it after every rain. Flea beetles may attack young plants, and although they seldom kill the plants, the beetles can be controlled with rotenone or diatomaceous earth.

Eggplant
(Solanaceae, *Solanum melongena*)

Eggplant, a native of Asia and India, is a luxury crop for Northerners. It loves heat and is so sensitive to cold weather that growing it outdoors in the North has moved beyond the realm of fantasy only since the development of quick-maturing cultivars. Eggplant fruits may be elongated or globe-shaped, the former tending to be the short-season varieties, maturing in about 60 days of hot weather as opposed to 70 to 75 days for the largest globe fruits. There are purple-, lilac-, striped- and white-fruited varieties. The latter, which best suit the name eggplant, are sometimes promoted as "egg trees."

Culture: Eggplants must be started indoors at least 10 weeks before the last spring frost date, as they grow very slowly at first. Seeds will not germinate below 60 degrees F (15°C) and prefer 85 degrees (29°C). The plant grows best at 70 to 75 degrees (21-24°C). Transplant outdoors about 2 weeks after the last frost date or when night temperatures are consistently warmer than 45 degrees (7°C). Choose a sunny, sheltered place where the soil is well worked and perhaps prewarmed with plastic mulch, setting plants 18 inches (45 cm) apart. In most northern gardens, hot caps or glass jar covers are recommended for at least the first 2 weeks. When the weather is consistently warm, remove the covers to prevent overheating.

Harvest: With a knife or pruning shears, cut fruit off when it is firm and glossy. Each plant should produce 1 to 10 fruits. Eggplant does not store well, so it should be cooked soon after picking.

Pests & Diseases: Eggplant transplants are very attractive to flea beetles, which can be controlled with rotenone or pyrethrum. Colorado potato beetles and their larvae can be hand-picked or dusted with rotenone. To avoid verticillium wilt, do not plant eggplants where relatives (see page 203) or strawberries grew the previous season. Protect transplants from cutworms by encircling them with paper collars that extend 1½ inches (3.8 cm) above and below the soil surface.

Endive & Escarole
(Compositae, *Cichorium endivia*)

Endive and escarole are closely related to chicory, so the three are sometimes confused. Endive and escarole are less cold-tolerant than chicory, and the foliage is more like lettuce, but like chicory, both may be bitter if not blanched or grown in optimal conditions. The large, bright heads go to seed in hot weather, but they are more frost-hardy than lettuce and thus stand longer in the garden in fall. Endive has deeply serrated, curly, sometimes feathery leaves, while escarole or Batavian endive has broad, upright leaves and a self-blanched heart.

Culture: Both plants may be sown in a partially shady spot in furrows ½ inch (1 cm) deep with the seeds ½ inch (1 cm) apart and rows 18 inches (45 cm) apart. Thin plants to stand 12 inches (30 cm) apart. For a fall crop, sow in midseason, early enough to allow the crop to mature around the first fall frost date, 90 to 100 days after sowing. To blanch, tie the outer leaves around the head, and invert a flowerpot or box over each head or cover rows with blankets for about 3 weeks before harvesting. Plants grown in a cold frame or under cover are less bitter than those grown in the open. Prolonged hot weather increases bitterness, while cool fall weather produces the sweetest greens.

Harvest: Cut the entire head, and use as lettuce.

Pests & Diseases: See Dandelion.

Garden Huckleberry
(Solanaceae, *Solanum nigrum*; *S. melanocerasum*)
Wonderberry; Sunberry

Unrelated to the sweet, red, wild huckleberry (*Vaccinium ovatum*), *S. nigrum* is also quite unlike it in appearance and flavor. The shrubby plants resemble their cousins, the peppers and eggplants, but are larger and more spreading, about 30 inches

(75 cm) tall. The plants are prolific enough that most families will want only two to six plants. The fruits are bitter when green and bland when ripe, but their flavor is pleasant and fruity when they are sufficiently sweetened in puddings or pies.

Culture: Start plants indoors about 6 weeks before the last spring frost, in flats or individual containers, allowing each seedling 1 inch (2.5 cm) of space all around. A week after the last spring frost date, plant 2 feet (60 cm) apart. In cool-season areas, grow this frost-tender plant under cover or cover it when frost threatens. It requires about 3 months of frost-free growing.

Harvest: Pick berries when they are very black and ripe, and either use fresh, freeze to preserve or store sweetened as jam or pie filling.

Pests & Diseases: Garden huckleberries are remarkably vigorous and have few problems as long as the soil is sufficiently warm, although flea beetles may attack the young seedlings. If necessary, control with pyrethrum or rotenone. Colorado potato beetles and their larvae can be hand-picked. Remove leaves bearing their bright orange egg clusters.

Remove husks to reveal sweet ground cherries.

Garlic

(Amaryllidaceae, *Allium sativum*)

For thousands of years, garlic has been respected as both seasoning and medicine. It is very easy to grow, although large bulbs do not always result from home plantings. Garlic does not reproduce true from seed, so it is grown from cloves, the divisions into which the bulb easily separates. Supermarket garlic can be used for planting, but northern seed companies sell varieties with proven success in cooler climates. Elephant garlic, which is milder and larger, is somewhat less winter-hardy and requires a longer season. Rocambole is a hardy type that forms a twisted seed stalk. There are additional varieties carried by specialist seed companies.

Culture: Garlic cloves may be planted in very early spring for fall harvest, but as they require 3 to 4 months to mature and respond to increasing daylight, they are better planted in fall for harvest the following year. This also ensures that the bulbs' dormancy is broken; plants never exposed to temperatures below 64 degrees F (18°C) may fail to form bulbs. Break the bulb into cloves, discarding the long, slender ones at the middle of the bulb, and plant in fertile soil high in organic matter, each clove with its pointed end up and about 1/2 inch (1 cm) below the soil surface. Allow each clove 3 to 6 inches (7.5-15 cm) all around. Cloves may also be interplanted with other crops as long as they are not crowded out or overshadowed. Garlic is shallow-rooted, so avoid deep cultivation. In the Far North, mulch the cloves over the winter or plant in early spring in a cold frame, leaving them there till harvest or moving them into the garden when the soil can be worked.

Harvest: Bulbs are ready to pull when the tops die back. Cure and store as onions.

Pests & Diseases: None in most areas, which makes garlic an ideal companion plant in the vegetable garden.

Ground Cherry

(Solanaceae, *Physalis peruviana*)

This bushy plant, about 1 foot (30 cm) tall, produces round, golden ³/₄-inch (2 cm) berries enclosed in papery husks similar to the Chinese lanterns and tomatillos to which they are related. The fruit is used for desserts and preserves, although it is sweet enough to be eaten out of hand. **Culture:** Sow the seeds indoors in flats or individual containers about 6 weeks before the last frost date, allowing each seedling 1 inch (2.5 cm) all around. About a week after the last frost, plant outdoors in the manner of garden huckleberries. Gardeners in very mild areas can seed directly outdoors around the last frost date. Volunteer plants are likely to appear the following year if some mature fruit has been allowed to remain in the garden. **Harvest:** The berries are ready to pick when the husks are straw-colored and the fruits golden, about 70 days after transplanting. The papery lantern, which is easy to remove, should be left on if the fruit is to be stored. It will keep for a few weeks in a single layer in a box in any cool, dry place. The fruit may be eaten fresh, made into preserves or frozen. **Pests & Diseases:** Flea beetles may be attracted to young transplants, while the striped blister beetle may attack ripe fruit in some gardens. Neither is likely to inflict severe damage, but rotenone or pyrethrum can be applied if infestations are severe. Hand-pick tomato hornworms, Colorado potato beetles and their larvae. Ground cherries are not the first dietary choice of these pests, but they will spread onto most members of the family Solanaceae in a year of severe outbreaks. Rotate ground cherries with other families, and do not plant next to other Solanaceae.

Kale
(Cruciferae, *Brassica oleracea acephala*)
Borecole
Kale is a standby in short-season gardens because it is nutritious, productive, versatile in the kitchen, easy to grow and capable of maturing even on permafrost. In fact, kale does not grow well in hot weather, preferring cool, damp days for the best development of its curly, dark green leaves, which

are rich in iron and vitamins A and C. Kale is grown primarily as a fall green, because it is very frost-resistant, usually the last leafy green standing in the garden as winter approaches. All types of kale grow about 2 feet (60 cm) tall and almost as wide. Siberian kale has fairly smooth leaves, while Scotch kale has curly leaves. Ornamental kale, described on page 124, is also edible. Chinese kale, or Chinese broccoli (guy lon), is also frost-hardy, yielding smooth kale-like leaves and small broccoli-like buds.
Culture: In short-season areas, kale can be started indoors 6 weeks before the last frost date and grown in a cold frame, but it is generally seeded directly in the garden about 2 weeks before the last frost. Sow seeds $\frac{1}{4}$ inch (6 mm) deep and at $\frac{1}{2}$-inch (1 cm) intervals or in groups of three or four seeds, each group 1 foot (30 cm) from its neighbors. Thin seedlings or set transplants so that each plant has at least 1 foot (30 cm) all around. Seeding may continue until midsummer, as long as the plant has about 2 months to mature before the first fall frost, although leaves may be harvested before then. If the garden is very hot, plant kale in a shady spot and keep it watered. Watering with manure tea once a week will help produce large leaves.
Harvest: The most tender leaves grow at the center of the plant. Pull leaves singly as needed, using them fresh or cooked in the same manner as cabbage. Kale leaves can be frozen to preserve them.
Pests & Diseases: See Broccoli.

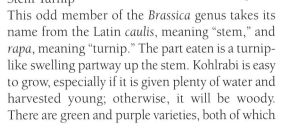

Kohlrabi
(Cruciferae, *Brassica oleracea caulorapa*)
Stem Turnip
This odd member of the *Brassica* genus takes its name from the Latin *caulis*, meaning "stem," and *rapa*, meaning "turnip." The part eaten is a turnip-like swelling partway up the stem. Kohlrabi is easy to grow, especially if it is given plenty of water and harvested young; otherwise, it will be woody. There are green and purple varieties, both of which

are white under the skin. Kohlrabi will withstand light frost throughout the season.

Culture: Plant like kale, with a final spacing of 8 inches (20 cm) all around. Kohlrabi does best in well-worked, fertile soil that is kept moist.

Harvest: Pull the entire plant when the swelling is the size of a tennis ball, about 50 days after seeding or 40 days after transplanting. Peel the vegetable, and use fresh or cooked, as cabbage. Kohlrabi can be stored for a few weeks in a cool, damp root cellar. Cut off the leaves, stem and root, and spread the vegetables between layers of straw or newspaper.

Pests & Diseases: As for broccoli. Because kohlrabi is planted early in the season and harvested early and because the stem is not easily damaged, kohlrabi seldom needs to be protected from pests.

Leeks

(Amaryllidaceae, *Allium porrum*)

The leek, a thick, sweet, nonbulbing onion, was one of the most popular medieval European vegetables and has retained a favored position among cordon bleu chefs. The best part is the stalk, not the leaves, and the best leeks are blanched; unblanched leeks are stronger in flavor and darker in color. Leeks do best in very fertile, finely worked soil and will not tolerate weed competition. Although frost-tolerant, they require about a 3-month growing season and so should be started indoors or purchased as transplants.

Culture: Sow seeds thickly indoors in flats or containers, as for onions. Keep seedlings clipped to a 4-inch (10 cm) height until planting outdoors some time from 4 weeks before until 2 weeks after the last spring frost date, allowing each plant 6 inches (15 cm) all around. To blanch, set transplants in a 6-inch-deep (15 cm) trench at 6-inch (15 cm) intervals, in the same manner as asparagus, filling the trench with rich soil, compost or a

soil/manure mixture as the leeks grow. Then mulch with organic matter.

Harvest: Pull plants as needed until the soil freezes. In mild areas, leeks may overwinter successfully in the garden, especially if trenched and mulched; the harvest then resumes in spring until the plants go to seed. Slice leeks to use fresh or cooked, or preserve them by drying or freezing.

Pests & Diseases: Most gardeners will have none, but root maggots may be troublesome in some areas. See Onion.

Lentil

(Leguminosae, *Lens culinaris*)

The lentil, attractive enough to take its place in any flower garden, is a shrubby plant about 12 inches (30 cm) tall that produces dark green leaves and small white or pale blue flowers like sweet peas. Hardy, easy to grow and a source of soil nitrogen, the lentil has recently become an important specialty crop in western Canada, but unfortunately, it is less practical to grow on a small scale, as each pod produces only two or three lentils. Shelling is so time-consuming that most gardeners choose to buy their lentils already bagged.

Culture: Plant any time in early spring, sowing seeds ½ inch (1 cm) deep and 4 inches (10 cm) apart. Like peas, lentils do best in loose, cool, moist soil.

Harvest: Leave the pods on the plants until they are dry, about 2 months after planting. Then harvest pods and shell them. Store lentils in a jar or paper bag in a cool, dry cupboard.

Pests & Diseases: None of note.

Lettuce, Head

(Compositae, *Lactuca sativa*)

The lettuce with which North Americans are most familiar is head lettuce or, more specifically, crisp-

Head lettuce need not always be green or iceberg, as the variegated butterhead 'Pirat' shows.

head lettuce. There are two other common types of head lettuce as well: butterhead, or Bibb, which produces loose heads of tender, rounded leaves; and cos, or romaine, with elongated, crisp leaves that are sometimes wrinkled. Either type may have green, red or variegated leaves. Some lettuces cross the class boundaries. All head types are more difficult to grow and more demanding of space than leaf types. The young seedlings or transplants can withstand temperatures of 20 degrees F (–6°C) if properly hardened off, while the mature heads will not bear frost and must be covered if frost threatens before they are ready to harvest. Lettuce will germinate and continue to grow as long as the soil temperature is at least 40 degrees (4.5°C).

Culture: Head lettuce is often started indoors in flats or containers 6 to 7 weeks before the last frost date so that it will mature before the hottest summer weather causes it to bolt to seed prematurely. But it may also be seeded directly outdoors 2 to 3 weeks before the last frost or until early summer, as long as the plants are allowed about 3 months to mature before the first fall frost. Germination is fastest around 75 degrees F (24°C); growth is best from 60 to 65 degrees (15-18°C). Sow seeds thinly in very shallow furrows 1 foot (30 cm) apart, or broadcast seeds over the soil surface, pressing them down and watering with a fine spray. When the plants have two or three true leaves, thin them to stand 1 foot (30 cm) apart. Keep plants watered until they are about 4 inches (10 cm) tall. Then they can be mulched with organic matter, such as straw, grass clippings or compost, to retain moisture. Water every 2 weeks with manure tea or fish fertilizer.

Harvest: Thinnings may be eaten. The head is ready to harvest when it feels firm under light pressure or when it has attained full size for the cultivar.

Pests & Diseases: Slugs are a problem in wet gardens. Press saucers or jar lids of beer into the soil around the plants, or dust plants and surrounding soil with diatomaceous earth after every rainfall. Fungal diseases are also most likely to strike lettuce in wet gardens, causing leaves to wilt or discolor. Choose fungus-resistant or quick-maturing leaf varieties, and rotate crops every year. Tipburn may result when temperatures vary widely from day to night. Counter with resistant varieties and a limited nitrogen supply. Lettuce is also susceptible to a virus infection called mosaic. Resistant cultivars may be described as such or labeled MI, mosaic-indexed. Lettuce is, of course, a favorite of rabbits and other rodents. As a deterrent, sprinkle plants with chile pepper flakes after every rainfall.

Lettuce, Leaf

If head lettuce can be a demanding crop, looseleaf lettuce is among the easiest, and the final product is just as tender and sweet as the foliage of the heading cultivars. Some types have broad leaves; some have curly leaves. Leaves may be green or reddish, a color that develops best in direct sunlight. Leaf lettuce is fully mature about 2 months after seeding, with some varieties more resistant to bolting to seed than others. Check the seed-catalog descriptions for long-standing types (often, unfortunately, not the sweetest). The plants will bear light frost both early and late in the season. Row covers or a cold frame can extend the season by more than a month in spring and fall.

Culture: Sow indoors 5 to 6 weeks before the last spring frost date, transplanting seedlings outdoors 3 to 4 weeks later. Successive sowings can be transplanted outdoors all season, with midsummer transplants going into a spot overshadowed by a crop that will be harvested in late summer. Or sowing may be done directly in the garden, as for head lettuce. When there are two or three true leaves, thin plants to stand 6 to 8 inches (15-20 cm) apart. Water regularly, and fertilize with manure tea or fish fertilizer every 2 weeks. An organic mulch will help retain soil moisture. Choose heat-tolerant (bolt-resistant) cultivars for late planting.

Harvest: Thinnings can be eaten. Single outer leaves can be pulled from several plants, or the entire head can be pulled, trimmed and served. Store in plastic bags in the refrigerator.

Pests & Diseases: See Head Lettuce.

Luffa

(Cucurbitaceae, *Luffa cylindrica*)

A Far Eastern gourd of many uses, the luffa is a conversation piece for Northerners. Some years, it may produce a crop; many times, it will not. Luffa is extremely frost-tender. It needs a warm season of at least 115 days, a very sunny location and fertile soil. It takes one common name, Chinese okra, from the shape and edibility of the fruits, which may be eaten young. Allowed to mature, the fruits can be used as sponges. Made of the inner fibers of the gourds, luffa sponges are expensive items in bath shops.

Culture: Plant seeds 4 weeks before the last spring frost date, two or three seeds to a peat pot or 4-inch (10 cm) container, pinching off all but the strongest seedling. Like other cucurbits, luffas will not tolerate much root disturbance, so they must be sown in containers which can be planted (peat pellets or peat pots) or which can be torn away from the rootball. If the plant outgrows a peat pellet indoors, the entire pellet must be planted in a larger container. Plant outdoors 2 weeks after the last frost in a sunny, sheltered location, with plants 1 foot (30 cm) apart. The luffa likes to climb and may extend 10 to 30 feet (3-9 m) in a very good year—so plant it by a fence or a trellis or a south-facing wall where netting has been hung. Plastic mulch and hot caps will help get the plants started, and the mulch should be left in place all season.

Harvest: For culinary use, pick the gourds when they are less than 6 inches (15 cm) long. Pare off the ridges with a potato peeler, and cook or serve raw like zucchini. To make sponges, the mature gourds, which may weigh up to 5 pounds (2.3 kg), are harvested after the vine has been killed by frost, then soaked in warm water to remove the skin. The husk is dried and the seeds emptied out, leaving a spongelike framework.

Pests & Diseases: See Cucumber.

Malabar Spinach

(Basellaceae, *Basella alba*)
Perpetual Spinach; Malabar Nightshade; Basella
An Asian biennial treated as an annual in the North, *B. alba* produces glossy, spinachlike greens (red leaves on *B. rubra*) that are very frost-tender but will not bolt to seed with summer's heat and long days; in fact, the higher the temperature, the better it grows. Leaves are mature about 2 months after sowing but may be harvested sooner.

Culture: Seed is more commonly available from seed houses in the United States than in Canada, because this is a favorite in hot southern gardens. Start seeds indoors about 2 weeks before the last spring frost date, and transplant outdoors 3 weeks later, or sow directly outdoors in a sunny place around the last frost date. Sow seeds about ¼ inch (6 mm) deep at 2-inch (5 cm) intervals, later thinning or transplanting to stand 9 inches (23 cm) apart. The plant produces a long, creeping stem that can be supported on a fence or trellis. Cover plants if frost threatens.

Harvest: Use raw or cooked throughout the season, like spinach.

Pests & Diseases: See Dandelion.

Mesclun

Not a vegetable but, rather, a term for a blend of salad vegetables and herbs, mesclun combines any cut-and-come-again green, such as cress, lettuce, arugula, spinach, beet greens, chervil, mustard greens, chives and rocket. Harvest greens when young by snipping them at the base with scissors. Repeat harvests can be taken from the same plants every 2 to 3 weeks until the leaves become tough or bitter. Some seed houses offer a ready-made mesclun blend.

Mushroom, Field

(Fungi, *Agaricus bisporus*)
There are many edible mushrooms growing wild in the North, and armed with a suitable manual, even a beginner can safely identify a few of them. For those who prefer the standard supermarket variety, *A. bisporus*, several seed companies stock the spawn, or "seed." It requires a cool, damp, dark place either indoors or outdoors. Conditions being somewhat easier to control indoors, however, mushrooms are usually raised on composted manure in boxes in a basement.

Culture: For outdoor sowing, select a shady spot in spring, roll back the sod and spread the spawn evenly over the soil; water if necessary, then replace the sod. Mushrooms should appear in about 7 weeks and continue for several "flushes" thereafter. Indoors, the spawn is sown in a box of thoroughly composted livestock manure—avoid manure that has been contaminated with disinfectants. Compost the manure outdoors by composting about 1 cubic yard (0.8 m³) horse manure, ½ to 1 bale hay, ½ bushel (18 L) poultry manure, 10 pounds (4.5 kg) gypsum and 1 pound (500 g) ammonium nitrate. This should fill a bed 10 feet (3 m) long, 3 feet (1 m) wide and 8 inches (20 cm) deep. Some home gardeners have reported success using only composted horse manure (including bedding).

When the manure is thoroughly composted, pile it into boxes and apply the spawn according to package directions. Throughout the growing process, the compost must be kept moist and within the temperature range of 52 to 70 degrees F (11-21°C). It must also be kept in the dark. In 2 to 3 weeks, a cottony layer of mycelia, the working part of the mushrooms, will appear on the top of the compost. Cover it with 1½ inches (3.8 cm) of a wetted mixture of equal parts by weight of peat moss and calcitic limestone. Cover this with a layer of plastic or with newspaper that is sprinkled daily with water. In 10 days, remove the plastic or paper. Mushrooms should begin to appear within a week. **Harvest:** Once a mushroom begins to open, it will not become any larger. Snap it at the soil level when it reaches the preferred stage of maturity, usually about a week after emergence. New flushes should continue for 2 to 5 months, with each harvest less abundant than the previous one. Total yields of 3 pounds per square foot (14.6 kg/m^2) are possible. Mushrooms may be used raw or cooked, or they can be preserved by drying or freezing.

Pests & Diseases: The growing bed is prey to many insects and diseases, including unwanted fungi; all are best controlled in a very clean growing area with a well-composted growing mixture that is never sodden.

Muskmelon

(Cucurbitaceae, *Cucumis melo*)
Cantaloupe; Honeydew

The small orange or whitish melons grown in northern gardens are mostly muskmelons, fruits of Asian origin that are much better known than their name. They have netted skin, unlike cantaloupes, which are smooth. More than a century ago, Sir John A. Macdonald wrote to his daughter Mary: "The garden looks fine now…there are some fine melons….You must pick them for dinner and feed the chickens with the rind." Melons were possible then, but they are even easier now. Although melons are extremely frost-tender, quick-maturing varieties have been bred that, when grown under cover and hand-pollinated, will take advantage of the long days to produce a crop even north of the 60th parallel. By starting them indoors and coddling them along, almost any gardener can produce one of the most delicious and exotic of the garden's offerings: vine-ripened, sun-warmed melons. Nothing in the grocery store can even come close.

Culture: Start melon seeds indoors 4 to 5 weeks before the last spring frost date. Sow two or three seeds per container, choosing fairly large ones, such as disposable milk-shake cups or milk cartons, that can be torn away in transplanting. Or use peat pots—peat pellets are too small. The roots will not stand any disturbance in transplanting. Germination takes place in 4 to 14 days at 68 to 86 degrees F (20-30°C) and is best at 72 degrees (22°C). Seeds will not germinate below 60 degrees (15°C). Thin seedlings to one per container by pinching off the weaker ones. Transplant outdoors into warm, fertile soil 2 weeks after the last spring frost, allowing 3 feet (1 m) all around each hill of two or three plants. Vining (not bush) varieties can be encouraged to climb. Plant them 1 foot (30 cm) apart along a fence or trellis, training the vines upward and supporting the fruit as it develops. Mulching young plants will help discourage weeds and will keep the fruit of sprawling plants clean. In experiments at the University of New Hampshire, fruit maturity was as much as 13 days earlier for plants grown with black plastic mulch under a slitted clear plastic row cover than with the black mulch alone. Daytime temperatures under the row covers averaged 39 to 41 Fahrenheit degrees (22-23C°) above outside air temperatures. Provided there is a warm, frost-free season of about 90 days, muskmelons will also do fine outdoors, though ripening will be slower. An early hot cap or a season-long plastic mulch will provide a boost. Select the earliest varieties available of either the orange-fleshed muskmelon or the green-fleshed honeydew. The use of hot caps or plant shelters will help the plants during their first 2 to 3 weeks outdoors, but later, insects must be allowed to visit the flowers or else they must be hand-pollinated (see page 192). Adequate moisture is especially important directly after transplanting and again when the fruit begins to form. Do not move vines while cultivating.

Harvest: The fruit is ready to pick 70 to 100 days after transplanting, when muskmelon skin color changes from green to slightly orange and honeydew skin becomes paler. The fruit is fragrant and will "slip" easily off the stem—do not force it. Fruit picked slightly prematurely, however, will ripen indoors if the skin is not cut. It can be eaten fresh or cubed and frozen to preserve.

Pests & Diseases: As for cucumbers. Also,

wireworms may penetrate fruit lying on the ground or mulch; rest each fruit on a squat tin can that has had its top and bottom removed. The main problem that confronts northern gardeners when raising muskmelon is cool soil. Cold weather late in the season may cause the plant to wilt; in cool-season areas, use plastic mulch or crop covers and ensure that the soil is moist and fertile.

Mustard Cabbage

(Cruciferae, *Brassica chinensis*)
Chinese Mustard Cabbage; Bok Choy;
Looseleaf Chinese Cabbage
This staple of Oriental cuisine most closely resembles Swiss chard, with very pronounced white ribs and stems and dark green leaves. A cool-weather plant, it survives light frost but will bolt to seed quickly in warm weather. It matures from seed in about 8 weeks but may be harvested much sooner. Wild mustards that are members of the genus *Brassica* are also edible.

Culture: Sow indoors 8 weeks before the last spring frost date, transplanting outdoors 4 weeks later, or sow directly in the garden from that time until about 10 weeks before the first fall frost date. Sow seeds ¼ inch (6 mm) deep and about 1 inch (2.5 cm) apart. Thin to stand 4 to 6 inches (10-15 cm) apart. Mustard cabbage requires a steady supply of moisture and fertile soil. Water every 2 weeks with manure tea or fish fertilizer.

Harvest: Pull single leaves or entire plants. Leaves are used raw or cooked, like spinach, while the stems may be chopped and used like celery or asparagus. This vegetable is a popular ingredient in stir-fry dishes.

Pests & Diseases: See Dandelion.

Mustard Greens

(Cruciferae, *Brassica juncea*)
This tall, hardy plant produces peppery leaves that do not, in fact, taste like mustard, though its seeds may be used for home preparation of the condiment. Mustard greens are available in both broad- and curly-leaved cultivars. The vegetable matures from seed in about 45 days, though thinnings may be eaten 2 weeks earlier. It is frost-resistant, but it bolts to seed quickly in hot weather.

New Zealand spinach is a frost-tolerant, heat-sensitive vine that resembles spinach in flavor only.

Culture: As for mustard cabbage.
Harvest: Harvest and use like spinach.
Pests & Diseases: See Dandelion.

New Zealand Spinach

(Tetragoniaceae, *Tetragonia expansa*)
T. expansa, like Malabar spinach, is a spinachlike green that will not bolt to seed in hot weather. It thrives in high temperatures and is sensitive to frost. It is thus commonly available from Southern seed houses, because it is most highly valued where summers are hot. Plant it in spring, after frost, to take over when spinach bolts, providing salad greens until fall. A native of New Zealand, the plant produces 2-to-3-foot (0.6-1 m) trailing branches with fairly small, fleshy leaves. New Zealand spinach is well suited to hanging baskets—one to three plants in a 10-inch-diameter (25 cm) container.

Culture: To speed germination, soak the large

Egyptian onions are decorative and hardy.

seeds in lukewarm water for 24 hours before planting. Around the last frost date, sow seeds ½ inch (1 cm) deep and 1 inch (2.5 cm) apart in a sunny place, thinning later to stand 8 inches (20 cm) apart.

Harvest: Harvesting may be done every 2 to 4 weeks throughout the summer once the plants are 8 to 10 inches (20-25 cm) long. Snap off the tips, which are used like spinach, raw or cooked.

Pests & Diseases: See Dandelion.

Okra
(Malvaceae, *Abelmoschus esculentus*)
Gumbo

An unusual vegetable to find in northern gardens, okra is usually associated with the cuisine of the Deep South, where it is a prolific plant that grows as tall as 7 feet (2 m). Yet some fairly quick-maturing, small-fruited varieties have been developed, so any gardener who can grow eggplant can also grow okra—both thrive in the same temperature range and appreciate plastic mulches and crop cov-

ers. The part eaten is the long grooved pod, which must be picked while very young and tender.

Culture: Sow indoors as for muskmelons, transplanting outdoors 1 to 2 feet (30-60 cm) apart 2 weeks after the last spring frost. One to four plants are sufficient for most families.

Harvest: The seed packet will indicate the best harvest size for that variety, usually about 4 inches (10 cm) long. Slice the pods to cook in soups, curries, stews and gumbos, where they have a thickening effect. Harvesting every few days will ensure that plants continue to bear until the first frost or until the soil becomes too cool. Freeze to preserve.

Pests & Diseases: None of note.

Onion
(Amaryllidaceae, *Allium cepa*)
Available in various shapes and sizes, some biennial, some perennial, onions should be included in every garden. Among the most popular onions:

• Globe onions come in red-, yellow- and white-skinned varieties, and some of them are especially hard and therefore long-lasting in winter storage. Check the seed catalog for this information. Sweet Spanish onions are as easy to grow as regular globe onions, but most take longer to mature. They do not store as long.

• Egyptian, tree or top onions are very hardy plants that will overwinter in most of the North. At the top of each stalk, bulblets form that can be eaten or planted for propagation or for the production of spring onions.

• Spring onions, also called scallions or bunching onions, can be grown from seeds or sets. While any onions can be harvested young for scallions, the true spring onions (*A. fistulosum*) produce clusters of greens but no bulbs. The National Garden Bureau rates scallions among the most space-efficient vegetables. Consider chives (see page 166) as an alternative.

• Pickling or pearl onions are white bulbing onions that are ready to harvest in late July, when they are still very small.

• Shallots produce garliclike bulbs that have a delicate, mild flavor. Not as frost-hardy as garlic (see page 80), they are planted in early spring and harvested in fall. Otherwise, grow and tend as garlic.

All onions are quite frost-hardy and pest- and disease-resistant. Onions may be interplanted among other crops, provided they are not overshadowed in the process. They do best in light, well-drained, fertile soil high in organic matter. Shallow-rooted, onions should be mulched or watered regularly. Do not cultivate deeply around them, but keep weeds in check. Growth interruptions caused by weeds or drought can produce unpleasantly hot onions.

Culture: Globe onions are usually started indoors in flats about 10 weeks before the last spring frost date and transplanted outdoors a month later, or anytime until the last spring frost. They are dependent upon increasing day length for bulb formation, so early seeding and planting is important. They may be clipped to 4 inches (10 cm) tall if they become overgrown before the garden is ready for planting. Allow transplants 4 inches (10 cm) in all directions—slight crowding speeds maturation. Most onions grown from sets or cloves can be given the same spacing, and all are put out at the same time. Plant the sets so that the pointed tips are even with or just under the soil surface. Sow the seeds of bunching onions by broadcasting them thickly on the soil surface from early through late spring, covering them with about ¼ inch (6 mm) of soil. Be sure that all onion seeds are covered, as germination is retarded or prevented if seeds are exposed to light. A packet of bunching onion seeds should cover about 5 to 6 square feet (0.5 m²) and provide 20 to 25 bunches of onions. To grow your own sets for next year, sow seeds of a suitable long-storage variety, such as 'Ebenezer' or 'Stuttgarter,' in early spring. Seeds are sown thickly, so the onion greens resemble grass. Harvest when the tops are dry and brittle, cure, and store in a cool, dry place until the following spring. In some mild areas, onions can be seeded in fall and mulched to overwinter, providing early greens and bulbs the next year.

Harvest: Any type of onion can be harvested young, before the bulbs swell, and used as scallions. Bulb onions are mature when the tops die down; afterward, they may rot if allowed to stand in the garden. The best storage onions do not form flower stalks. Those which do, and all others that have a thick stem after harvesting, must be used first, as they will not store well. The formation of flower stalks—bolting to seed—is often caused by the use of oversize onion sets, which should be no larger than ½ inch (1 cm) in diameter when purchased. Bolting can also be caused by prolonged cold weather or other stress early in the season. If the tops have not fallen 2 weeks before the first fall frost date, bend them to one side.

On a sunny day about a week later, pull the onions and place them on newspaper in the sun, turning them occasionally. Continue curing them in this way for several days, bringing them indoors at night or when rain or frost threatens. When the skin and tops are thoroughly dry, brush off loose soil and bring the onions indoors to store in a dry place at about 40 degrees F (4.5°C). They keep best when air circulates around them, so store onions loose in baskets, boxes, string bags or old nylon stockings or braid them together and hang.

Pests & Diseases: In most gardens, onions will suffer no damage at all and may even have a pest-repellent effect that will help protect neighboring plants. The most serious pest of onions is the onion maggot, the larva of a small fly that lays its eggs on the soil near onions. The maggots then crawl into the soil to attack the bulbs. If maggots are a problem, rotate the onion patch among plants of different families (see the chart on page 203) and cover the soil around the onions with diatomaceous earth.

Parsnip

(Umbelliferae, *Pastinaca sativa*)
The Latin *pastinaca*, "a thing dug up," is scant praise for the parsnip—a large, white root well suited to most northern gardens because its delicate flavor sweetens with fall frost. The parsnip is easy to grow but does require patience; it germinates and grows slowly, taking about 4 months to mature from seed.

Peas love cool soil, so even unusual varieties such as 'Blue Pod Capucijners' are easy to grow.

It is a biennial that often self-sows if allowed to go to seed the spring after planting.

Culture: Like all root crops, the parsnip does best in deeply worked, light-textured soil. The parsnip is longer than most garden roots, so give its bed a thorough spading before planting. As soon as the soil can be worked in spring, sow seeds 1 inch (2.5 cm) apart and ½ inch (1 cm) deep, in rows about 6 inches (15 cm) apart. The minimum germination temperature is 36 degrees F (2°C), although the seedlings may not emerge for 3 weeks. During this time, keep the seedbed weeded and watered. Gradually thin seedlings to stand 4 inches (10 cm) apart in all directions.

Harvest: Although thinnings can be eaten, roots are not mature until late fall and become sweeter with each frost. The best roots are dug in early spring after the soil thaws but before the parsnips go to seed. In most areas, they will survive winter even without a mulch, although a heavy organic mulch such as fallen leaves or bales of hay may pre-vent the soil from freezing so that roots can be harvested all winter. Parsnips can be stored like beets, sliced and frozen or dried.

Pests & Diseases: Parsnips suffer from few ailments in home gardens, as long as they are grown in moist, deep soil. Carrot rust flies are troublesome in some places (see Carrot). Cover rows with a spunbonded cover such as Reemay, or hill soil over the roots as they grow. Hand-pick parsleyworms.

Pea
(Leguminosae, *Pisum sativum*)
Snap Pea; Snow Pea; Soup Pea

Sweet and nutritious, the garden pea thrives in cool weather, preferably under 81 degrees F (27°C), and is thus a northern standby. There are two main types: those with wrinkled seeds, which are the longest-maturing, sweetest peas, and those with smooth seeds, which are earlier and more cold-tolerant but not as sweet. Peas can also be classified according to the shape and edibility of their pods. The standard shelling pea produces the smallest harvest per plant, while edible-podded snow or snap peas may double the weight of the harvest. Some seed companies sell green or yellow soup peas that are planted like other peas but harvested after about 3 months, like dry beans. Coating the seed with nitrogen-fixing inoculant, available from some seed outlets, will help ensure a vigorous crop that will enrich the soil with nitrogen. Peas will grow as long as the soil temperature is no cooler than about 41 degrees (5°C), with most varieties ready for harvest about 2 months after sowing.

Culture: Peas may be planted 4 weeks before the last spring frost date or at any time during the season, as long as the soil temperature is not much above 60 degrees F (15°C). Seeds will not germinate well later than mid-June in most areas, so a late crop should be pre-germinated indoors in a towel dampened with cool water, then sown outdoors in a spot shaded by an early-maturing crop. In calculating the planting time for a fall crop, allow sufficient time for pods to mature before the first heavy frost, and prepare to cover the plants during light frosts. The plants are quite frost-hardy, but blossoms and pea pods are not, so after the flowers have begun to bloom, the plants should be covered when frost threatens. Fall crops are less dependable than spring crops and more susceptible to powdery mildew. Although all peas will climb if given the opportunity, their need for support varies with the length of the vines, which ranges from 1 to 6 feet (0.3-2 m). Plant seeds ½ inch (1 cm) deep and 1 inch (2.5 cm) apart in a double row by a fence or trellis, or plant seeds of short-vining or leafless varieties in beds, allowing 2 inches (5 cm) around each seed. Strong twigs or tomato cages can be set upright throughout the bed to provide support. Seeds take 5 to 8 days to germinate at 39 to 75 degrees (4-24°C) and grow best between 50 and 60 degrees (10-15°C) in moist soil rich in organic matter. The application of an organic mulch when plants are about 4 inches (10 cm) tall will help retain moisture and discourage weeds.

Harvest: Shelling peas and snap peas are ready to harvest when the pods are well rounded but have not yet begun to look leathery. Snow peas are ready when the pods are full-sized and the peas inside have just begun to swell. Picking peas every 3 or 4 days will prolong the harvest. Harvest and store soup peas as for dry beans, allowing them to dry on the vine or picking the mature pods for indoor drying. With all varieties, pull the pods off the plants gently so that the plants are not damaged. Snow peas and snap peas may have strings that should be removed before they are eaten; break off the top end and pull strings downward. Peas can be eaten raw or cooked or may be frozen to preserve.

Pests & Diseases: None in most gardens, but aphids can weaken plants and spread disease. Control with insecticidal soap diluted according to the manufacturer's directions. Aphids spread a disease that causes vines to yellow and die; remove and destroy affected plants. The spotted cucumber beetle can be controlled with rotenone or pyrethrum. If powdery mildew is a problem, look for resistant varieties next year.

Peanut
(Leguminosae, *Arachis hypogaea*)

Spanish or Valencia peanuts, the types grown in the North, are very attractive plants and fun to grow, but like lentils, they may not produce much to harvest. The plant develops orange blossoms that bend and touch the soil after pollination. Peanuts then develop in clusters on "pegs" under the soil surface. Thus the plant needs a very light, preferably sandy, warm soil in which the nuts can easily expand. It also needs a long, warm season of 2 to 3 months—the longer the season, the greater the yield. Peanuts are more frost-hardy than snap beans but less so than peas.

Culture: Shell carefully, without damaging the membrane on the nuts, and sow in a sunny location about a week before the last spring frost date in rows 1½ inches (3.8 cm) deep and 3 inches (7.5 cm) apart, with rows 18 inches (45 cm) apart, or

Maturing standard bell peppers demand almost 3 months of warm, dependably sunny weather.

in a bed, allowing 8 inches (20 cm) all around each plant. Keep the bed free of weeds.

Harvest: Dig up the plants and nuts after the first fall frost. Break the pods off the pegs, and spread the nuts in a warm, dry place to cure for about 2 weeks, after which the shells should be brittle. Store peanuts in their shells in a cool, dry cupboard, or roast on cookie sheets in a 300°F (150°C) oven for an hour, stirring occasionally. Discard any moldy peanuts.

Pests & Diseases: None of note.

Pepper

(Solanaceae, *Capsicum annuum*)

Bell peppers and hot peppers, both cultivated in South America for thousands of years, are some-where between the eggplant and the tomato in their need for warmth and their likelihood of producing a crop in the North. A gardener who can grow eggplant can grow peppers in much the same way, but a gardener who can grow tomatoes will not necessarily harvest peppers as well. The plant needs a sunny, sheltered location, prefers sandy soil with regular watering and requires almost 3 months of warm weather—or the same length of time under cover—to produce a crop. If in doubt, choose the fastest-maturing varieties available. Early strains usually produce smaller fruits with thinner walls than do later ones. A poor crop may be caused by nights below 50 degrees F (10°C) in early summer. Do not rush the season, and plant more than one cultivar to hedge your bets. Green-fruiting peppers may turn red later—red-color development is best between 64 and 75 degrees (18-24°C) but stops at 55 degrees (13°C) or cooler, when the fruit begins to rot instead. In addition, cultivars are available that produce elongated or globe-shaped yellow fruit, which turns orange or red as it matures. For instructions about hot peppers, see Chile Pepper (page 165).

Culture: As for eggplant. Remove the first peppers when small if they feel delicate and thin-walled. They will not be good quality and will slow the growth of later, better fruits.

Harvest: Pick the peppers when they are glossy and the right size for the cultivar. If watery spots appear, a symptom of sunscald, pick the peppers immediately and remove the damaged sections. Peppers can be kept fresh for 8 to 10 days at 44 degrees F (6.5°C), perhaps in the vegetable bin of your refrigerator, or they can be preserved by freezing or drying. Use peppers raw or cooked.

Pests & Diseases: As for eggplant. Aphids, usually a problem with plants under cover, can be controlled with a strong jet of water or with insecticidal soap diluted according to the manufacturer's directions. Surround plants with paper collars where cutworms are a problem. The beet armyworm and corn earworm can be controlled with *Bacillus thuringiensis*. Fruit infested with pepper maggots must be removed and destroyed. Chilling injury manifests itself in surface pitting of fruit and can occur after 2 days at 32 degrees F (0°C), 7 days at 34 degrees (1°C) or 14 days at 45 degrees (7°C).

Potato

(Solanaceae, *Solanum tuberosum*)
Spud

After the potato arrived in North America from South America via Europe, it became this continent's most popular starchy vegetable. Canadian horticulturist W.T. Macoun wrote in 1918: "The potato succeeds well everywhere in this country where the season is long enough for the tubers to develop before the tops are killed by frost; hence potatoes are cultivated in practically every settlement in Canada, even up to and within the Arctic Circle." The part eaten, the tuber, is a swelling of an underground stem used by the plant for food

storage. Tubers of the most popular North American cultivars have either brown or red skin and white or golden flesh, though adventurous potato growers can find blue, purple and finger-shaped types as well. Early, midseason and main-crop strains of potato are available. Some of the most common North American potatoes include:

• 'Chieftain,' whose tubers have red skin and mature in midseason, about 3½ months after planting. The yield is high. The tubers do not store very well, but plants are resistant to scab and late blight.

• 'Irish Cobbler,' an early strain more than a century old. Its chief advantage is good flavor; its chief disadvantage is a susceptibility to scab and other diseases. The tubers are lumpy. The flesh is all-purpose.

• 'Kennebec,' a high-yielding strain that matures in midseason. The tubers are especially susceptible to greening when exposed to light, to hollow heart if widely spaced and to many diseases. The flesh is mealy and flaky, best for baking or frying.

• 'Keswick,' one of the best for Far Northerners. It is resistant to scab and fungus diseases, and its uses are similar to those of 'Kennebec.'

• 'Netted Gem,' also known as 'Russet Burbank' or 'Idaho Baker.' It produces large tubers with netted skin and mealy, flaky flesh best baked. These potatoes store very well if they are sound. This is the most demanding of popular potatoes, however, requiring optimal growing conditions and plenty of space—18 inches (45 cm) between plants and 3 feet (1 m) between rows—for top-quality tubers. Knobby, misshapen potatoes are likely to result from overcrowding or unsettled weather. The tubers are scab-resistant, but the plants are susceptible to late blight.

• 'Norland,' whose medium-sized, pink-skinned tubers are particularly well suited to early harvesting as new potatoes.

• 'Red Pontiac,' which produces heavy yields of round, red-skinned potatoes in midseason. It is most popular in the United States.

• 'Sebago,' a late-maturing potato with large, smooth tubers in great quantity. The tubers, which have firm, waxy flesh best for boiling and salads, store dependably well for only about 3 months.

• 'Superior,' an early white-skinned strain that, like 'Norland,' is especially prized for new potatoes.

'Superior' does best in well-drained soil that is neither cold nor hot.

• 'Yukon Gold,' whose medium-sized tubers have pale golden flesh. Flavor is good, but storage is not especially long.

Culture: Although the potato will produce a crop in almost any soil, it does best in light, well-drained, slightly acidic soil where a legume grew the previous season. It thrives in cool, moist growing conditions with night temperatures around 54 degrees F (12°C), but it is not frost-hardy. The greens will be killed by frost, although the tubers contain sufficient nutrients that plants usually revive when suitable conditions recur. Left in the soil over winter, tubers may sprout in spring to produce a crop by fall. In short-season areas (80 days), plants should be surrounded with plastic mulch.

Traditionally, potatoes are grown from eyes, pieces of tuber used to clone the parent plant. Seeds do not normally reproduce true and so are not used for garden propagation. If you want to grow potatoes from the true seeds, sow them indoors like tomato seeds. Certified potato eyes, disease-free and suitable for planting, are available at garden outlets and rural general stores and from some mail-order sources in spring. Each potato can be planted whole or cut the day before planting into two or three egg-sized pieces, each bearing at least one eye.

Three to five weeks before the last spring frost, when the soil has warmed to about 42 degrees F (5.5°C) or as long as a month thereafter, take a spade and dig holes 8 inches (20 cm) deep and 18 inches (45 cm) apart in rows the length of the potato patch. The day after cutting the potatoes into sections, lay one piece of potato, eye upward, in each hole, covering it with roughly 2 inches (5 cm) of soil. Water if necessary. As the plant grows, fill in the hole, but do not bury all the foliage. This hilling is done because tubers develop above the eye and must be protected from exposure to light, which causes greening. Once the holes are filled level with the soil surface, mulch with plastic (in short-season areas) or with organic matter that will keep the soil cool and retain moisture. As the plants develop, cover any exposed tubers with soil or add another layer of organic mulch.

Gardeners who have a plentiful supply of mulching materials can simply lay the potato eyes on the ground in rows, then cover the potato patch with at least 1 foot (30 cm) of organic mulch. Although animal predation is a possibility with this system, planting and harvesting are greatly simplified. But again, make sure the tubers are always covered to prevent greening.

Harvest: New potatoes can be dug as early as a month after hilling is complete. These tender, sweet tubers can be found by digging directly under a plant and carefully removing one or two or by digging up entire plants. Potatoes are fully mature when the tops die; after this, the tubers will keep in cool soil but are susceptible to damage by grubs and worms. The fall potato harvest should begin on a sunny, dry morning after the plant tops have died. Using a spade, pitchfork or potato fork, dig straight down about 1 foot (30 cm) from each plant stem and pry up the soil toward the plant. Dig carefully so that few tubers are damaged—any which are undersized or damaged should be set aside for immediate use; they will not keep well. Lay the others in the sun, and turn them several times during the day to cure. Brush off any clumps of soil while doing this. At the end of the day, put all the sound, large tubers in boxes, feed sacks or paper bags—they must be exposed to air but not light—and store them in a cool, airy, dark place at 45 to 50 degrees F (7-10°C). Remove any green parts before serving, as they contain excess glycoalkaloids, which are bitter and can cause indigestion or sickness. After about 2 months of rest, potatoes in storage will sprout. Potatoes that are not diseased can be used as next year's eyes.

Pests & Diseases: Potatoes attract pests and diseases in almost every garden, although the entire crop will seldom be lost. The worst pest is the larva of the Colorado potato beetle, which has a voracious appetite for potato foliage. Search for and destroy its egg clusters in late spring—the bright orange eggs are deposited on the undersides of leaves. Later, the orange larvae may be hand-picked or dusted with rotenone. The adults, black-and-orange-striped beetles, will appear throughout the season; knock them into a jar half full of soapy water. Other pests include wireworms and the fat, white larvae of June beetles, which tunnel into tubers and are best controlled by crop rotation. The most damaging diseases, such as early and late blight, are caused by fungi and are worse in warm, wet weather. Do not set the plants too closely, do not mulch in very damp areas, and do not tend wet plants. Blighted plants, which eventually appear burned, must be destroyed, not composted. Late blight was the disease that resulted in the Irish potato famine. Along with other fungal diseases, blight is kept under control mostly by heavy use of fungicides in the commercial production of seed potatoes. Hollow-heart of potatoes is caused by fast growth, while scab is the result of overly alkaline soil. Neither disorder affects the edibility of the tubers.

Radish

(Cruciferae, *Raphanus sativus*)
Daikon
The garden's fastest-maturing root vegetable is the common globe radish, ready about 3 weeks after sowing; winter-storage varieties take about 2 months to mature and may mature heavier than a pound (500 g). All radishes prefer cool, moist soil and do best with a fairly short day length—in the Far North, choose small-rooted and quick-maturing cultivars to discourage premature bolting to seed. Mild, tender radishes result from steady growth in cool weather; any setbacks may produce unpleasantly peppery, tough roots.

Culture: Sow from early spring through early summer and again in late summer in rich, moist, cool soil. Plant the seeds $\frac{1}{2}$ inch (1 cm) deep and $\frac{1}{2}$ inch (1 cm) apart. In hot weather, choose a spot shaded by another crop. Radishes require only 1 inch (2.5 cm) around them and so can be interplanted with other crops in the garden or in containers. As they are very quick to sprout, germinating in 4 to 6 days at 45 to 70 degrees F (7-21°C), they are often sown in the same rows as slow-emerging seeds, such as parsnip, asparagus, carrot and beet. The sprouting radishes break the soil

crust and mark the row, then the radishes are harvested before the slower crops need the space. Storage radishes, such as the Oriental types, are planted in late spring or summer, allowing time for maturity before the first frost date. Mulching or regular watering helps ensure good root quality—in too wet soil, roots may crack, while in too dry soil, they become woody, as they do when overmature.

Harvest: Pull small-rooted types from the time the root begins to swell until it is about 1 inch (2.5 cm) across, after which it becomes hot and woody. Harvest larger cultivars according to the maturation rate indicated by the seed company. Washed radishes will keep several weeks in jars, plastic containers or bags in the refrigerator or cold room. Keep the winter-storage varieties as for beets.

Pests & Diseases: Flea beetles and cabbage root maggots. See Broccoli.

Rhubarb

(Polygonaceae, *Rheum rhaponticum*)
Although rhubarb is technically a vegetable, plenty of sweetening gives it a flavor sufficiently fruity that it is treasured for use in northern desserts and preserves. Of the two types—red-stalked and green-stalked—the former is sweeter and more flavorful but less productive than the latter. Red-stalked cultivars include 'Valentine,' 'Crimson Red' and 'Canada Red'; green-stalked include 'Victoria' and 'Sutton's.' As green-stalked cultivars are better for winter forcing than red-stalked ones, rhubarb aficionados should plant a bed of each: red rhubarb for spring and fall use, green for forcing in winter, which results in stalks that are light pink and very tender.

Culture: Plants can be grown from seed, although this is a slow procedure with unpredictable results. Usually, roots are planted in early spring as soon as the soil can be worked or, if necessary, in late fall just before freeze-up. Set plants in a sunny location 2 to 4 feet apart (0.6-1.2 m), with the tips of the buds just even with the soil surface. The soil should be prepared by thorough weeding and mixed with compost or well-rotted manure. As the bed will be in place for many years, the initial preparations have long-lasting consequences. Rhubarb will grow on any well-drained soil but does best on sandy loam. Every year, add manure or compost and a layer of organic mulch to the rhubarb bed. After about 10 years, or when stalks have become spindly, divide plants in early spring as soon as the buds break through the soil. Dig up plants, and cut vertically into several pieces, each one with two or three good buds and part of the root attached. Plant these as usual. Rhubarb that is at least 2 years old can also be divided in spring for propagation or in fall for indoor forcing. For forcing, dig the roots before the soil freezes, divide them and spread on the garden, lightly mulched, where they will remain through several light frosts. Then replant the roots in boxes or pots of wet sand, soil or peat moss, allowing each one about 2 square feet (0.2 m²) of soil surface, and place them in a dark room at 50 to 60 degrees F (10-15°C). Keep the soil moist but not sodden. The most productive forced roots will be those from which stalks were not harvested the previous year.

Harvest: Do not harvest stalks the first year from roots planted outdoors. The second year, harvest the largest stalks for only 2 weeks in spring. Thereafter, stalks may be pulled in spring and fall, but allow the plants about 2 months in summer to build up strength. Removing seed stalks in spring will prolong the early harvest. Forced stalks are ready to pick about a month after they are brought indoors and for 3 to 8 weeks after that. Discard the roots after forcing. Harvest stalks by tugging or twisting them from the crown, not by cutting. Rhubarb leaves, which contain toxic levels of oxalic acid, must never be eaten or fed to livestock; put them on the compost pile. Rhubarb freezes well.

Pests & Diseases: A native of Asia that has become a welcome member of almost every Canadian garden, this hardy perennial is quite pest- and disease-free.

Rutabaga

(Cruciferae, *Brassica napus*)
Swede; Turnip
This large, gold-fleshed root is often called a turnip, a word that more properly refers to one of its ancestors, the white-fleshed root of *B. rapa*. The rutabaga, which probably derives its name from the Scandinavian *rotabagge*, meaning "round root," takes longer to mature and is frost-hardy throughout the season. Like other root crops, it requires well-worked soil, even though much of the root develops above the soil surface.

Culture: The rutabaga's main attraction is its provision of winter vitamins—it is nutritious and easy to store. It is usually sown a few weeks after the last spring frost, following an early planting of lettuce or spinach. To determine the best time for sowing, subtract its maturation time of about 3 months from the first fall frost date. In shorter-season areas, the rutabaga can be sown in the same manner as Brussels sprouts or early cabbage, either indoors or outdoors. Roots should have a final garden spacing of 1 foot (30 cm) all around in soil that is not too acidic, with a pH above 6. Water regularly or mulch, because checks in growth produce tough roots.

Harvest: Leaves of the young plant are tender and nutritious and can be used in place of turnip greens, collards or kale. Harvest roots when they are about 6 to 10 inches (15-25 cm) across or according to the maturation date suggested by the seed company. Roots can remain in the garden until just before the soil freezes. Cut off the tops and store the same way as for beets, up to 6 months. Waxing is not recommended. Roots can also be sliced and dried or frozen.

Pests & Diseases: A soft, brown interior is usually symptomatic of a boron deficiency; apply agricultural borax according to the recommendation of a soil-test report. Blackleg, black rot and turnip mosaic virus can all be combated with crop rotation and disposal of infected plants. Control flea beetles, which attack seedlings, with rotenone or pyrethrum. Clubroot may be a problem in acidic soil and in areas of high rainfall; purchase seed of resistant cultivars, such as 'Fortune' and 'York,' and lower soil acidity in the rutabaga bed with ground limestone.

Salsify

(Compositae, *Tragopogon porrifolius*)
Oyster Plant; Vegetable Oyster
Culture & Harvest: This long, white root is

thinner than a parsnip and has a distinctive flavor reminiscent of oyster. Plant, tend, harvest and serve in the manner of parsnip. A biennial, salsify is frost-hardy and matures in about 4 months.

Pests & Diseases: None of note.

Scorzonera

(Compositae, *Scorzonera hispanica*)
Black Salsify

Culture & Harvest: Scorzonera is much like salsify, but its root has dull white flesh and black skin. Like parsnip, it is frost-hardy and slow to mature. Plant, tend, harvest, and serve in the manner of parsnip.

Pests & Diseases: None of note.

Spinach

(Chenopodiaceae, *Spinacia oleracea*)
The Moorish *isfānākh* has become today's spinach, with sweet, nutritious foliage of distinctive flavor. Its ability to produce a crop in cool weather and even to resist light frosts has made it a northern favorite. Seeds will germinate and plants will grow at a soil temperature of just 36 degrees F (2°C). Spinach will, however, sprout to seed quickly in hot weather. Where spring is short and summer is hot, choose long-standing, bolt-resistant cultivars or grow a heat-tolerant substitute such as Malabar spinach. Spinach contains appreciable amounts of calcium, iron, potassium and vitamin A. Lamb's-quarters, *Chenopodium album*, a spinach relative, grows wild in many gardens and is a nutritious substitute. Its texture and flavor are best if it is harvested very young.

Culture: The best spinach grows in spring and fall in moist, well-worked, very fertile soil with a pH of 6 to 6.8. Sow spinach outdoors 6 weeks before the last spring frost and until the last spring frost date, or seed a fall crop in late summer. In mild areas, seeds can be sown in early fall and mulched to overwinter for early-spring greens next season. Alternatively, seeds may be sown in flats indoors and transplanted outdoors 4 weeks later; in

hot weather, transplant into a shady spot. Allow each plant 4 inches (10 cm) all around in fertile, well-drained soil. Water once a week with a manure tea or fish fertilizer.

Harvest: Single outer leaves can be pulled from plants as soon as they have six to eight true leaves; thereafter, harvest leaves as needed or pull entire plants. Leaves may be eaten raw or cooked and can be frozen or dried to preserve. Heads will keep for about a week in a plastic bag in a refrigerator or cold room.

Pests & Diseases: Few. Hand-pick caterpillars, and control flea beetles and aphids with insecticidal soap diluted according to the manufacturer's instructions.

Squash, Summer

(Cucurbitaceae, *Cucurbita pepo*)
Crookneck; Straightneck; Pattypan; Scallop; Vegetable Marrow; Zucchini

Summer squash cultivars are harvested while immature, when seeds and skins are still soft and edible. Such a variety of colors and shapes of summer squash fruits exists that any gardener who likes these frost-tender but quick-maturing vegetables (6 to 8 weeks) should plant more than one type. But don't overdo it—one or two plants will serve two people. Crookneck produces club-shaped crooked fruit with yellow skin that may be bumpy or smooth. Straightneck squash is, as the name suggests, a straight version. Pattypan or scallop has flat, round, scallop-edged green or white fruits. Vegetable marrow is oval with green or white skin, while zucchini is long and slender with green or yellow skin.

Culture: Plant and tend in the manner of cucumbers. There are, as yet, no seedless cultivars—all plants have both male and female flowers.

Harvest: As with cucumbers, frequent picking will encourage a greater fruit set. Most fruits are best soon after they begin to form, when 6 to 8 inches (15-20 cm) long and 1½ to 2 inches (3.8-5 cm) wide. Pick scallops when 3 inches (7.5 cm) across. Use all young fruit whole—skin, seeds and all—raw or cooked. The flowers are also edible. Fruits left to mature may be used in baking or as livestock feed. They will store for several weeks in a cool, dry room.

Pests & Diseases: As for cucumbers and winter squash. Blossom-end rot may occur in soils deficient in calcium or after a long, cool, rainy period. The disease should disappear as conditions improve.

Squash, Winter

(Cucurbitaceae, *Cucurbita maxima*: 'Atlantic Giant,' 'Blue Hubbard,' Buttercup, 'Hungarian Mammoth,' Turban; *C. moschata*: Butternut, 'Tahitian'; *C. pepo*: Acorn, Pumpkin, Spaghetti)

Unlike the summer squashes to which these are closely related, winter cultivars are left to mature until the seeds are hard and the skins are tough and unpalatable. This means they take much longer to mature, 2½ to 3 months from seed, depending on weather and cultivar. There are three species for Northerners, listed above, and some hybrids are interspecific. *C. maxima* cultivars are known for good flavor and fine texture. Most *C. moschata* cultivars are very sweet and are grown for commercial processing in tropical places. They are more likely to be damaged by frost and low temperatures than are the other species. However, butternut is successful in most of Canada and the northern United States and is one of the best for storage. It is pear-shaped and golden, weighing about 2 pounds (1 kg) at maturity, about 80 days after seeding. *C. pepo* cultivars are prolific, store well and are more cold-hardy than *C. moschata*. They are by far the most popular winter squashes in the North, led by acorn, also known as pepper squash. This heart-shaped variety with grooved green or orange skin is a convenient one-meal size of 1 to 5 pounds (0.5-2.3 kg) and matures quite speedily, in 80 to 90 days. It does not store especially well and is not as sweet and finely textured as the other species.

Pattypan summer squash is best when the fruit is only about 3 inches (7.5 cm) across.

Buttercup and turban squashes are squarish, usually with a cup-shaped indentation at the stem end. They mature in 80 to 100 days to weights of 3 to 7 pounds (1.4-3 kg) and are delicious. On the other end of the *C. maxima* scale are fruits of such size—sometimes over 500 pounds (227 kg)—that they are the subject of "pumpkin"-growing contests. Pumpkins, on the other hand, tend to weigh less than 100 pounds (45 kg), and the best pie cultivars, those with the sweetest flesh, are only about the size of bowling balls. There are, in addition, smaller decorative pumpkins and naked-seeded pumpkins, whose shell-less seeds are relatively difficult to germinate but easy to roast and eat. All winter squash seeds are 30 to 40 percent protein.

Culture: In most gardens, seeds can be sown directly outdoors, although in very short-season areas, the seeds should be started indoors (see Muskmelon). All squashes are frost-tender and grow best in warm, fertile soil with a temperature of at least 55 degrees F (13°C). Hot caps or overturned glass jars will urge all seeds or seedlings along to a good start. Seeds of naked-seeded pumpkins should be pre-germinated indoors (see page 52), since their germination is undependable because of their lack of seed coats. Squashes quickly develop a long taproot and are easily damaged by root disturbance. Two or three transplants or six to nine seeds, all the same variety or a mixture of different types of squash, may be planted in hills outdoors a week or two after the last frost date. Make a hill about 1 foot (30 cm) wide and a few inches high out of compost or rotted manure. Flatten the top and scoop it into a slight dish shape before planting seeds in groups of two or three, in three stations per hill. Thin seedlings to three per hill, and allow 6 feet (2 m) around each hill for vining varieties. Vines can also be trained onto a lawn or patio or where they will not occupy garden space. Bush types of *C. pepo* and *C. maxima* have been developed and require far less space, but of course, they tend to produce less fruit. Because there are relatively few leaves, the fruit is less sweet than that of their vining counterparts. In cool gardens, the area around the stems should be mulched with plastic; elsewhere, with organic mulch that extends as far as the vines will spread in the garden. This controls weeds and keeps the fruit clean.

The first flowers are usually male and thus do not set fruit. As the weather warms, female flowers open, characterized by immature fruit at the base. Regular watering will keep fruit growing. For larger (but less) fruit, pick off all but three or four per vine. About 3 weeks before the first fall frost, begin pinching off growing tips, flowers and new fruits, as they will not mature before the first frost and will slow the development of older fruit. Cover the plants with plastic or fabric if frost threatens before fruits are mature.

Harvest: Flowers and seeds of all types are edible. Some fruits change color when mature. All can be harvested when the skin is tough enough that it cannot be easily dented with a thumbnail. In any case, do not leave harvesting past the first light frost unless plants can be easily covered during frosty weather. The first light frost is likely to damage only foliage and to sweeten the flesh, but if the fruit itself is touched by frost, its keeping quality will deteriorate. Fruit that has begun to ripen will continue after picking. When picking, leave 4 inches (10 cm) of stem attached to each fruit, slicing through it with a knife or pruning shears. Cure fruits in a warm, dry place for about 10 days, then store them, not touching, at 50 to 55 degrees F (10-13°C) for 2 to 6 months, depending on the variety. Most squashes taste best in late fall, but then the flavor and quality begin to deteriorate. Spaghetti squash is prepared by boiling or baking the entire squash, after which the meat is scooped out and served like pasta.

Pests & Diseases: Cucumber beetles may be combated with rotenone or pyrethrum. Both insecticides will also kill squash bugs. Squash vine borers are problematic in some areas, causing sudden wilting of a stem. Search along the stem to find the hole where the borer entered, then cut the stem on the plant side. Powdery mildew may defoliate vines late in the season. There are resistant varieties. Some virus-resistant varieties have also been developed. Look for descriptions on the seed packets or in the catalogs if you have had squash-crop failures because of disease.

Sweet Potato

(Convolvulaceae, *Ipomoea batatas*)

Even though the names of the common potato and the sweet potato are both derived from the South American Indian word *batata*, the two plants are unrelated and quite different. The sweet potato is such a tender plant that it is virtually unknown as a northern-garden vegetable. Still, there are a few early varieties that will mature in about 100 days, provided they are coddled along the way and never exposed to frost. They grow best in a soil not too high in organic matter, which encourages rough or cracked roots.

Culture: Sweet potatoes carried by a seed outlet or nursery are sold as small shoots or slips. You can also grow your own shoots from a mature sweet potato, but only short-season cultivars such as 'Georgia Jet' and 'Carter' should be grown in the North. About 2 weeks before the last spring frost, place the root in a pan of warm water in a warm place. Meanwhile, heat a sunny raised bed or ridge of soil with clear plastic mulch. A week or two after the last frost date, break the shoots off the root and set them into the soil through holes in the plastic, covering the plants with hot caps or crop shelters for the first week or until the weather is dependably warm. Plants should be 18 inches (45 cm) apart in all directions. Throughout the season, plants must be covered when frost threatens, and in cool weather, crop shelters should be available for augmenting the sun's heat.

Harvest: Dig the plants before the soil temperature drops below 55 degrees F (13°C) or before the first fall frost. Cure the roots indoors by covering them with perforated plastic for 1 week at 85 degrees (29°C) or 2 weeks at 75 degrees (24°C) at high humidity. Store sweet potatoes at 55 to 60 degrees (13-15°C) in moderate humidity.

Pests & Diseases: Cold soil is the most immediate danger to sweet potatoes in the North; any other malady is insignificant by comparison.

Swiss Chard
(Chenopodiaceae, *Beta vulgaris cicla*)
Called by western Europeans "Swiss chardon," to distinguish it from the "French chardon," or cardoon (a relative of the globe artichoke), chard is one of the most practical, easy and productive plants for the northern garden. Spinachlike in flavor and nutrients, its leaves are edible throughout the season, and they are frost-resistant and do not bolt to seed in hot weather as spinach does. Swiss chard is a leafy, slim-rooted version of the garden beet that grows well in pots and satisfactorily in shade. It comes with white, red or golden leaf ribs, so it can add foliage interest to the middle of a flowerbed.

Culture: Sow seeds in the garden as soon as the soil can be worked in spring or anytime while the soil is still relatively cool; the seed germinates in 4 to 10 days within its preferred soil-temperature range of 45 to 70 degrees F (7-21°C). Sow seeds about 1 inch (2.5 cm) apart and ½ inch (1 cm) deep, gradually thinning plants until they stand

The red-veined cultivars of Swiss chard are decorative enough for a flowerbed.

6 inches (15 cm) apart. Thinnings may be eaten. Chard requires little care, although the best greens grow in soil that is quite fertile and watered once a week with manure tea or fish fertilizer.

Harvest: Single outer leaves may be pulled once the plants have developed four or five true leaves. It is best to pull the entire plants only during thinning or at the end of the season, when the leaves begin to deteriorate after the first light frost. Use leaves as you would spinach, raw or cooked. Preserve by drying or freezing. Ribs and stems can be prepared as for celery or asparagus.

Pests & Diseases: See Spinach.

Tampala
(Amaranthaceae, *Amaranthus tricolor*)
Vegetable Amaranth; Chinese Spinach
Tampala is very popular in the Far East, where several cultivars are grown. It is a highly nutritious, green leafy vegetable, closely related to grain ama-

ranth, which contains quality protein in generous amounts. Tampala shares with Swiss chard, New Zealand spinach, Malabar spinach and beet greens the ability to produce spinachlike greens in hot, dry weather, after spinach has bolted to seed. The leaves of tampala are, however, most tender and tasty when they are young. The same can be said of its wild counterpart, A. retroflexus (redroot pigweed or green amaranth), and both can be harvested as nutritious spinach substitutes.

Culture: Around the last spring frost, plant seeds about ¼ inch (6 mm) deep and 1 inch (2.5 cm) apart in rows 1 foot (30 cm) apart. As they grow, thin plants to stand 1 foot (30 cm) apart. Thinnings can be eaten.

Harvest: As for Swiss chard, but older plants become tough and less flavorful. With pigweed, pick only the young leaves for best flavor and texture.

Pests & Diseases: None of note.

Tomatillo

(Solanaceae, *Physalis ixocarpa*)

The tomatillo, a golf-ball-sized fruit in an attractive Chinese-lantern husk, is a larger version of its cousin, the ground cherry. Tomatillos are used frequently in authentic Mexican cooking but can be substituted to provide a different color (green) and mild flavor in any dish demanding whole tomatoes. The plants are shrubby, about 3 feet (1 m) tall.

Culture: Sow indoors as for tomatoes, 4 weeks before the last spring frost date. Set transplants outdoors around the last frost date, giving each one 2 feet (60 cm) of space all around. The plants require little care and are more weather-resistant than tomatoes. The fruit is ready to pick about 10 weeks after transplanting.

Harvest: Harvest fruit when it is deep green and the husks are tan-colored. Husked tomatillos can be eaten raw or cooked or preserved by freezing or canning. To store, leave fruits in the husks and spread them one layer deep in a cool, well-ventilated area. They will keep a couple of weeks this way.

Pests & Diseases: As for ground cherry. In addition, blister beetles may infest fruit. Use rotenone or pyrethrum for severe problems.

Tomato

(Solanaceae, *Lycopersicon esculentum*)

Tomatoes are the most popular garden vegetable in Canada. In the North, they are far from the easiest plants to grow, but even Far Northerners will go to almost any lengths to include in the garden a tomato plant or two…or four…or eight. Fortunately, plant breeders have responded to this desire for fresh tomatoes by producing some very fast-maturing cultivars. Others grow best under cover, extending the tomato's range to wherever there is light and heat, even if artificial. Tomatoes are available in various fruit colors and shapes and in small- and large-fruiting cultivars, the former generally earlier than the latter. There are also determinate and indeterminate cultivars. Determinates, including most of the earliest tomatoes and almost all paste tomatoes, are bushy in shape and produce a single crop of fruit, sometimes virtually simultaneously. Most seed catalogs refer to determinates as bush tomatoes. They need not be staked and should not be pruned. The indeterminates grow tall and produce tomatoes for as long as the weather permits; they are usually staked and pruned. There are also semi-determinates, cultivars that include qualities of both types.

Culture: All tomato plants are very frost-tender and should be purchased or given an early start indoors. In choosing a spot to grow tomatoes, avoid low-lying areas, shady locations or any place where water collects. The plants also do best where air circulates freely. The use of plastic mulch will promote fruit production in cool-season gardens. Elsewhere, organic mulch can be applied in early summer when the soil is warm and plants are about 1 foot (30 cm) tall. Start seeds indoors 6 to 8 weeks before the last spring frost date, pre-germinating seeds as described on page 52 and sowing sprouted seeds ¼ inch (6 mm) deep in individual containers placed in the sun. About 3 weeks later, transplant the seedlings into larger containers, burying them as deep as the seedling leaves. The plants are usually set outdoors around the last frost date—be prepared to cover them if frost threatens. In a system developed at Morden, Manitoba, transplants are set outdoors on May 15, a few days earlier than the last frost date for the area, and covered with hot caps ventilated with a slit in the peak. The opening must be enlarged when the temperature rises above 75 degrees F (24°C). If frost threatens, place a second protector over the first. Allow the plants to grow out of the protectors freely.

Set staked tomatoes 18 inches (45 cm) apart in rows and unstaked plants 2 to 3 feet (0.6-1 m) apart. For each plant, dig a hole wider and deeper than the rootball and place the rootball in the hole so that the soil will be filled in to the level of the first true leaves. Fill the hole with compost or fertile soil, and surround each stem with a cutworm-proof collar that extends above and below the soil level by 1½ inches (3.8 cm). Water deeply, with ambient-temperature water. If plants are to be staked, pound 5-foot (1.5 m) poles 1 foot (30 cm) into the earth directly behind each plant now, when there is no danger of root damage. Fasten the plant loosely to the stake with a figure eight of fabric encircling both stake and stem. Tomatoes may also be supported in wire cages, or indeterminates may be trained up strings that descend from a horizontal wire or pole supported 6 feet (2 m) above a row of plants. Every few days, twist the plant stem around the string. All staked or twining indeterminate tomatoes must be pruned, or they will become unmanageable. Regularly throughout the season, pinch out the suckers that form in branch axils. These pruned suckers can be planted in the soil and kept moist to root and grow into full-sized plants, producing late fruit.

After the first fruit has set, water the plants about every 2 weeks with manure tea or a fish-fertilizer solution. Toward the end of the season, the tips of indeterminate and semi-determinate plants should be pinched off so that the plant's energy is concentrated on developing fruit.

Harvest: Tomatoes are ready to pick when they are somewhat soft, fragrant and full-colored. If pests are a nuisance or if fall frosts threaten, fruits may be ripened indoors as soon as they have become whitish, a stage called mature green, or anytime thereafter, although the flavor will not be as good as that of vine-ripened tomatoes. Store ripe fruit indoors out of the refrigerator, preferably at about 40 degrees F (4.5°C).

Pests & Diseases: Tomato plants and fruit are susceptible to a number of disorders, pests and diseases. Blossom-end rot of fruit is caused by drought or by a soil calcium deficiency. The disorder usually affects only first fruit and disappears as the soil warms. If it persists, have a soil test done, and apply calcium according to the report's recommendations. Oddly shaped fruit may be caused by a cold snap during pollination. Tomatoes are readily damaged by some herbicides such as 2,4-D and 2,4,5-T, a problem in gardens near lawns or farm roadsides where weeds are sprayed.

Nematodes are tiny worms that can attack roots, weakening plants. Some control comes from planting French marigolds, *Tagetes patula*, around tomato plants. Resistant tomato varieties are available. Some cultivars are also resistant to the fungus diseases verticillium wilt, fusarium wilt and tobacco mosaic virus. Resistance is indicated by the initials V, F and T after the cultivar name. Early blight, most often seen on early determinate tomatoes, causes spotting of foliage and wilting of plants. All fungus diseases are best combated with resistant varieties, planting in warm soil, good air circulation and proper plant spacing. Among pests, hornworms are the largest, but they are easily hand-picked or killed with a *Bacillus thuringiensis* spray. Slugs, crickets and other insects and worms that devour fruit can be controlled somewhat by keeping the fruit off the ground. Tomatoes must not be planted within 40 to 50 feet (12-15 m) of a walnut or butternut tree, because an exudate, juglone, causes "walnut wilt," which kills tomato plants.

Turnip

(Cruciferae, *Brassica rapa*)
Summer Turnip; White Turnip
Turnips are grown like big radishes. They do best in cool weather and fertile soil with a regular wa-

ter supply that encourages quick, steady growth. Turnips are frost-hardy and ready to harvest about 2 months after seeding.

Culture: From the time the soil can be worked in spring until the last spring frost date, sow seeds outdoors ¼ inch (6 mm) deep and apart, gradually thinning or transplanting seedlings until the plants stand 4 inches (10 cm) apart. Thinnings may be eaten. Checks in growth produce tough, fibrous roots. They may also result in bolting to seed. Late sowings should be left in the soil until the ground almost freezes, because the sugar content of turnips, like parsnips, increases with frost.

Harvest: Greens may be eaten raw or cooked. The roots may be pulled any time after they have reached a diameter of about 4 inches (10 cm). Use as rutabagas. Unlike rutabagas, however, turnips do not store well, so they should be harvested gradually and kept in plastic bags in a refrigerator or cold room until needed.

Pests & Diseases: See Rutabaga.

Watercress
(Cruciferae, *Nasturtium officinale*)

Watercress, a European native, has adapted so well to the North American habitat that it grows wild along streams and in boggy meadows throughout much of the continent. Watercress can also be cultivated, but it demands cool weather and plenty of water for the best growth of its peppery, nutritious greens. Thus it is a good choice for wet garden spots or even in the shallows by cool running water, where no other vegetable grows well. Grown in suitably wet locations, watercress will self-sow annually. It is ready for harvesting about 50 days after sowing.

Culture: Six weeks before the last spring frost date, pre-germinate seeds in a cool, moist paper towel, then sow in growing medium, two seeds per peat pellet or small pot set in a shallow pan of cool water. Transplant outdoors 2 weeks later in a shady, moist spot. Alternatively, seeds can be sown directly in the wet soil of a streambed or in a wet garden.

Harvest: The leaves are best in spring and fall. Pick out the side shoots, and use raw or cooked.

Pests & Diseases: None of note.

Watermelon
(Cucurbitaceae, *Citrullus lanatus*)

Watermelons seem unlikely residents of northern gardens, so closely are they identified with the Deep South, yet they can be expected to mature anywhere muskmelons ripen. But Northerners must think small, preferably about muskmelon-sized. Small, early cultivars will mature as soon as 70 days after transplanting and are sweet and delicious, whether the flesh is red or yellow. Earliness is a priority, because watermelons are such lovers of warmth that they will not grow at all in cold weather, let alone in frost. In short-season areas, plant through a clear plastic mulch under a plastic or glass row cover and hand-pollinate as described on page 192.

Culture: As for muskmelon, but leave 4 feet (1.2 m) between hills of vining cultivars. If they are trained up a fence or trellis, the fruit must be supported. There are also bush varieties.

Harvest: Sooner or later, the question arises: How do you know when a watermelon is ripe? Some cultivars have a white or yellow belly when ripe, but others do not. There are gardeners who claim to know the difference between the "plunk" of an unripe melon, when tapped, and the "plink" of a ripe one, but a safer route is to check the maturation time noted by the seed company. Then make sure the tendril on the vine nearest the melon has dried. Finally, as the British Columbia Ministry of Agriculture and Food recommends: "If unsure about the ripeness, wait a little longer." If melons are harvested unripe, they can, nevertheless, be used for pickling or candying in the same way as citron, a melon grown exclusively for that purpose.

Pests & Diseases: See Cucumber, Squash and Muskmelon.

Alphabetical Flowers

"We must know how long they last, when and how long they
bloom, their color, their height, their texture of foliage and
their freedom of growth before we can consider them for placing.
We can gain much of this information from plant lists."
—Roy E. Biles, *The Modern Family Garden Book*, 1942

Perennial flowers are recurring delights, old friends that decorate the garden around the same time year after year. Annual flowers are paradoxically more enduring and more fleeting than perennials. Some annuals bloom from spring through fall, long-distance runners that outlast perennials by many weeks, perhaps months. On the other hand, the defining characteristic of an annual is that its life ends with the end of the growing season. In nature, an annual goes from seed in the ground, through flowering, to seed in the pod in one year. But some annuals act much like perennials: they show up again the following year, without any intercession on the part of the gardener, because they have overwintered as seeds.

Certain annual flowers are good candidates for vegetable gardens. They decorate the beds, have insect-repellent or decoy qualities and can even be used in salads. Nasturtiums, small marigolds, cornflowers, calendulas and snapdragons are a few edible flowers. This is also the place for flowers grown in quantity for indoor arrangements: everlastings, summer bulbs and cutting annuals, such as zinnias and smaller cultivars of sunflower. At the end of the season, everything can be cleaned out and tilled under in preparation for winter.

Perennials need areas of their own, where they can grow undisturbed. Since they are in place for the long term, you must prepare for them. See the directions in Chapter Two for removing sod and preparing a new bed. The soil for perennials should be as deep and as rich in organic matter as you can manage. It must be thoroughly weeded. Rhizomes of twitch grass left in the bed will come back to haunt you. When weeds do show up, pull them out right away. The perennials will gradually spread to form a continuous plant cover that weeds will have difficulty penetrating, but at the beginning, you must work to keep the bed clean.

That also means edging at least once a year. Plant nothing closer than about 1 foot (30 cm) from the edge—rambling ground covers will eventually fill the space—so you can trim around the bed with an edger or spade every spring, cutting away sod and weeds that would invade the bed. Mulching between plants with grass clippings or another organic substance during summer also helps keep weeds down and retains soil moisture.

The aesthetic rules for planting flowers are as varied as are the gardeners who plant them, but a few general guidelines apply everywhere: taller plants behind shorter ones; ground covers in front; something blooming or at least attractive all season. Some plants can grow in shade, and some need full sun. Planting in the wrong place can mean no flowers or poor plant health. Few plants will tolerate standing water for long. Most do best in well-drained humusy soil with a good rain or deep watering about twice a week.

Ageratum

(Compositae, *Ageratum houstonianum*)
Flossflower

A favorite in public parks is the 4-to-8-inch (10-20 cm) version of this frost-tender annual, which has fuzzy-looking blue flowers that are dependable and pest-free but neither graceful nor exciting. There are also pink and white types. Slow from seed, ageratum is usually bought as a bedding plant, but growing from seed brings the possibility of the more comely, taller cultivars better for vases, such as the 2½-foot (75 cm) 'Blue Horizon.'

Culture: Start ageratum seeds at least 2 months before the last spring frost date. The seeds need exposure to light to germinate and a temperature range of 70 to 75 degrees F (21-24°C). Set plants 6 inches (15 cm) apart in full sun or partial shade. Water during dry weather. Deadhead occasionally to keep plants looking neat.

Pests & Diseases: None of note.

Allium

(Amaryllidaceae, *Allium* spp)
Ornamental Onion; Purple Sensation

There are many ornamental types of onion. All are as hardy as daffodils, with slender "green onion" foliage and one vertical stem per bulb, topped by an umbel of small flowers in spring or summer, in shades of yellow, pink, white, blue or purple, depending on the species and cultivar. One of the most dramatic and dependable is *A. aflatunense*, sometimes labeled Purple Sensation. In early summer, its 3-foot (1 m) stems are topped by dark purple 3-inch (7.5 cm) umbels. *A. moly* bears its golden flowers on stems about 1 foot (30 cm) tall. *A. caeruleum* has smaller blue flower heads, while *A. giganteum* is dramatic the first year, with grapefruit-sized umbels of magenta flowers on 4-foot (1.2 m) stems, but less long-lived than most others. There are several additional species sold by bulb specialists in fall. For ornamental value, do not ignore chives or garlic chives, with purple and white flowers, respectively.

Culture: Sow allium seeds indoors in spring, in the manner of onions (see page 88), or buy bulbs to plant in fall. Alliums do best in sun. The bulbs are apt to multiply gradually where conditions suit them: reasonably fertile soil, dry or moist, in full sun or partial shade. Divide them in spring, when they sprout, or in fall, after the stems turn brown.

Pests & Diseases: None of note.

Alyssum

(Cruciferae, *Lobularia maritima*; *Aurinia saxatilis*)
Sweet Alyssum; Basket-of-Gold

Annual alyssum (*L. maritima*) is hardly noticeable when planted singly, yet when massed, it makes a lovely ground cover of almost uninterrupted color from late spring to fall. Tiny four-petaled flowers form thumb-shaped clusters at the tip of each slender stem. There are white, pink, lilac and purple cultivars.

Culture: Plants are available from greenhouses in spring, but if you want large masses, sprinkle seeds directly on the ground any time in spring till the last frost date. Do not cover the seeds; they need light to sprout, which will happen when the soil is damp and between 55 and 75 degrees F (13-24°C). Flowers begin to bloom 6 weeks after germination. Grow alyssum about 1 foot (30 cm) back from the front of the border so that it has room to spill forward. It also suits containers, either on its own or surrounding other plants. Given some sun and watered during dry weather, alyssum may flower all summer, its stems gradually lengthening

Alyssum and California poppies are both annuals.

to a recumbent 1 foot (30 cm) or so, and can be clipped back for renewed flowering. It sometimes self-sows, a prize for gardeners who do not inadvertently weed out the seedlings.

Perennial alyssum (*A. saxatilis*), sometimes called basket-of-gold, is a very hardy ground cover that looks best when it trails down a slope or over rocks in full sun. The stems are about 9 inches (23 cm) long, with soft grayish leaves and bright gold flowers in late spring. Give it well-drained soil, and cut it back after flowering.

Pests & Diseases: None of note, although all members of the family Cruciferae may be infested with flea beetles in early spring.

Amaranth

(Amaranthaceae; *Amaranthus* spp)
Joseph's-Coat; Love-Lies-Bleeding; Prince's-Feather
There are many annual-garden amaranths, but most have an unkempt look that betrays their kinship with pigweed. This peasant background promises plants that grow rapidly from seed and will put up with almost anything but frost—drought, full sun,

heat, poor soil, some shade—to give 2 months or more of summer color. Some species offer beauty as well. One of the best is Joseph's-coat (*A. tricolor*), which has 1-to-4-foot (0.3-1.2 m) stems bearing foliage brightly splashed with red and yellow. Love-lies-bleeding (*A. caudatus*) is another old-fashioned favorite. It is named for its drooping ropes of purple flowers. The upright form is prince's-feather, with feathery flower spikes in brilliant shades of pink, yellow, red and purple.

Culture: Amaranth seeds can be started early indoors in the manner of tampala (see page 100) or, more easily, sown directly in the garden in early spring. Give them full sun. All will sprout and grow with weedlike speed once the damp soil warms to 70 to 75 degrees F (21-24°C).

Pests & Diseases: None of note.

Anemone

(Ranunculaceae, *Anemone* spp)
Pasqueflower; Prairie Crocus
Small, hardy anemones are lovely additions to the spring-bulb show. Looking a little like daisies, they are nice complements to the taller narcissus and crocuses. *A. blanda* is crocus height, with 2-inch (5 cm) blue, purple, pink or white flowers. Pasqueflower (*A. pulsatilla; Pulsatilla vulgaris*) grows 1 foot (30 cm) tall, with violet, burgundy or purple flowers that resemble those of the prairie crocus (*A. patens*). Japanese anemone (*A.* x *hybrida*) is 3 to 5 feet (1-1.5 m) tall, with 2-to-3-inch (5-7.5 cm) white, rose or pink flowers, single or double. Similarly tall is grapeleaf anemone (*A. tomentosa*), which spreads quickly by runner, forming a ground cover of woolly grapelike leaves and 2-to-3-inch (5-7.5 cm) white flowers.

Showiest of all are the hybrids of poppy-flowered anemones, *A. coronaria*, with 4-inch (10 cm) flowers, sometimes double, in white, pink, blue or red. This is a 2-foot-tall (60 cm) tender perennial planted in spring and grown as an annual in the manner of summer bulbs (see page 150).

Culture: All anemones do best in rich, moist soil in partial shade. Anemones are somewhat difficult and irregular from seed, but once you have plants, you can sow the fresh seeds, and some species self-sow. *A. blanda* is easy from tubers planted in fall.

Pests & Diseases: None of note. A sudden cold snap can cause yellow edges on leaves.

Aster

(Compositae, *Aster* spp; *Callistephus chinensis*)
Michaelmas Daisy; China Aster

Asters are native North American daisies whose value in the garden comes chiefly from two attributes: later flowering than most perennials—from late July or early August till frost—and some attractive shades of blue, within a color range from white and pink through purple, all with yellow centers. The yellow varieties are less distinctive.

Among the most popular asters are the perennials often called Michaelmas daisies (*A. novae-angliae*), named in England for the festival of St. Michael on September 29, when they are at their best there. Michaelmas daisies are easy to grow, even invasive, and are easy to divide into clumps when they have spread too far. Most grow about 3 feet (1 m) tall and should be staked while young, before they topple. There are many additional perennial hybrid asters in varying heights.

Annual asters come in single and double types, some of which are available as bedding plants. Some must be staked and coddled in the garden but are impressive for arranging: spider asters have pompons of needle-slender petals; peony types are descriptively named.

China asters, another group of annuals, are properly grouped as the genus *Callistephus*. The best China asters, including the variety 'Single California,' are single, eye-catching and very easy to grow.

Culture: For seed-grown perennial asters, stratify the seeds about 3 months before the last spring frost date by sowing them as usual, then enclosing the pots in plastic bags and refrigerating for 3 weeks. Move to a sunny, warm place for sprouting. Asters appreciate full sun and decent soil. The perennials may be somewhat invasive and so need dividing every few years, which is easily done by slicing a clump into pieces. Sow the seeds of single callistephus directly in the garden. Allow a few to dry on the stem, and they will self-sow in the garden to provide late-summer color year after year, requiring only thinning to prevent overcrowding.

Pests & Diseases: Asters are vulnerable to the fungal diseases aster yellows, powdery mildew and rust. Avoid late-day watering that wets the foliage. If you have fungal problems—most prevalent in late summer, when cold nights follow warm, humid days—search next year for species and cultivars that are disease-resistant.

Astilbe

(Saxifragaceae, *Astilbe* x *arendsii*)

Feathery spires of tiny flowers in shades of purple and red through pink to white rise above beautiful fernlike foliage. Astilbe is appreciated as a hardy perennial for shade and dampness, though it will put up with a considerable amount of sun, provided the soil is fertile and not too dry. Flower stems rise 2 to 3 feet (0.6-1 m) tall on standard varieties, about half that height on the dwarfs.

Culture: Obtain plants in spring. Astilbe is not long-lived. It should be divided every 3 years or so for rejuvenation. Lift the crown in early spring before new growth unfolds. With a sharp knife, cut it into sections, each with several growing points. Replant the sections with the eyes about ½ inch (1 cm) below the soil surface.

Pests & Diseases: None of note.

Aubrieta

(Cruciferae, *Aubrieta deltoidea*)
Rock Cress; Arabis

Pretty foliage and an eye-catching show of ground-hugging color in late spring make this hardy perennial, sometimes called rock cress, a valued plant for the front of a border—a good companion for creeping phlox. Aubrieta has lilac or pink flowers; the closely related arabis is the white version.

Astilbe, a hardy perennial, tolerates some shade and dampness and blooms in several colors.

Culture: Buy plants in spring or grow aubrieta from seeds sown in the garden or indoors several weeks before the last frost. Seeds are sown on the soil surface and sprout in about a week at a temperature of 65 to 75 degrees F (18-24°C). Seed-grown plants bloom the following year. Aubrieta will bloom in full sun or light shade, doubles its spread every year if happy and can be easily divided. Shear off the flower stems after blooming.

Pests & Diseases: None of note, although all members of the family Cruciferae may be infested with flea beetles in early spring.

Baby's-Breath
(Caryophyllaceae, *Gypsophila* spp)
There are two types of baby's-breath: annual and perennial. Both are valued for clouds of tiny flowers, white or pink, that act as fillers for the flower garden and the vase, fresh or dried. The usual hardy perennial (*G. paniculata*) grows 2 to 3 feet (0.6-1 m) tall, with long, graceful sprays of flow-

ers. At just 4 inches (10 cm) tall, creeping baby's-breath (*G. repens*) is better for border edges, and its foliage remains attractive all season. The annual (*G. elegans*) grows less than 2 feet (60 cm) tall.

Culture: Sow *G. elegans* directly outdoors in mid-spring, or start the seeds indoors any time after December for early blooms. Seeds, just covered, sprout in about a week at 70 degrees F (21°C). Plants bloom 3 months after seeding. *G. paniculata* is difficult to divide successfully. Obtain as many plants as you require, and leave them in place. In areas with severe winters (zone 4 or cooler), mulch for the winter. Both types do best in full sun, preferably in alkaline soil; hence the genus name suggests a love of gypsum.

Pests & Diseases: None of note.

Balloon Flower
(Campanulaceae, *Platycodon grandiflorus*)
Strange but lovely, balloon flower is named for buds that resemble hot-air balloons. Throughout summer, they open into 2-inch (5 cm) stars reminiscent of campanulas, in shades of blue through violet, pink and white, sometimes double. Stems are as tall as 3 feet (1 m), though there are smaller forms, such as the 6-inch (15 cm) 'Baby Blue.'

Culture: Obtain plants in spring. Give balloon flower a position in the sun. Ordinary soil is fine, but regular watering is needed. It resents division and transplanting and is late to sprout in spring, so mark its spot to avoid damage. Once settled, it is long-lasting and dependable. Balloon flower is easy to grow from seed, though it may not bloom for a couple of years. Seeds need light to germinate, so they are sown on the surface. They will germinate at a temperature of about 70 degrees F (21°C).

Pests & Diseases: None of note.

Begonia
(Begoniaceae, *Begonia* spp)
Begonias are tender perennials often grown as annuals in the North, though they can overwinter indoors. The tuberous types (*B. x tuberhybrida*) produce big, bright, showy flowers that light up containers and window boxes. There are cultivars with green and bronze foliage, as well as the pendula types for hanging baskets.

The wax, or fibrous, begonia (*B. x semperflorens-cultorum*) has smaller, waxy-looking foliage and single or double flowers in shades of red, pink and white or bicolors. Stems are about 8 inches (20 cm) long. The leaves may be green, bronze or variegated. There are upright and hanging-basket types. Alternatively, you can use wax begonias as edging plants—they grow into roundish mounds about 10 inches (25 cm) high.

Culture: The usual way to start with begonias is to buy plants in spring. Begonias have extremely tiny seeds: about 66,000 per gram. Sow the seeds on the surface, and keep them moist, exposed to light and at 70 to 80 degrees F (21-27°C) till germination. Thereafter, plants do best with at least 14 hours of light a day, but not direct sunlight. If you are using natural light, adjust your sowing schedule accordingly. To take advantage of the perennial nature of the wax begonia, grow it in a pot, shear it back almost to the ground in fall, then bring it indoors and put it in a sunny window for the winter. Before moving it outdoors in spring, shear it back again and top-dress with compost. You can also root cuttings in fall. The tubers of tuberous begonia can be dug up and brought indoors to overwinter. Prevent the tubers from drying out by packing in vermiculite or storing in paper bags in a cool, dry place. Plant the tubers in pots about two months before the last spring frost date.

Both types of begonia bloom best in dappled or partial shade, but they will tolerate full sun if the weather is not too hot, provided they are watered regularly and kept out of strong winds.

Pests & Diseases: Begonia tubers may dry out or become infected with fungus while in storage. In gardens in some areas, tuberous begonias are vulnerable to black root rot, prevalent in unsterilized potting soil or compost. Plants wilt and die, and roots are blackened. Cinnamon has been shown to be effective against mildew on begonias.

Bells of Ireland
(Labiatae, *Moluccella laevis*)
A green-flowered annual may not seem an appealing proposition, but bells of Ireland has a reputation as an everlasting. In fact, it is fragile when

Blue is the usual color of browallia, which lights up a shady garden during summer.

dried and does not keep its color, but the spires of green bells, somewhat like green gladiolus, can be attractive and unusual as living flowers in vases or garden beds. Stems grow about 2 feet (60 cm) tall.
Culture: Sow seeds 2 inches (5 cm) apart directly in the garden in late spring, in sun or partial shade, thinning plants to stand 6 inches (15 cm) apart.
Pests & Diseases: None of note.

Bergenia
(Saxifragaceae, *Bergenia cordifolia*)
Heartleaf Bergenia
A hardy perennial valued for its ability to tolerate shade, bergenia, like hosta, is better known for its large, decorative leaves than for its flowers. Bergenia grows a rosette of thick, waxy green leaves directly from the ground, the standard types reaching about 18 inches (45 cm) tall; these turn reddish or bronze later in the season. The usual flower color is pink, but there are also purples and whites,

borne in showy clusters just above the leaves in spring. Bergenia is a good ground cover best suited to the front of a border or under leafy trees.

Culture: Obtain plants or rhizomes in spring and set 1 foot (30 cm) apart in fertile soil in partial or full shade. Bergenia will tolerate full sun if the soil is not too dry. Water deeply in dry weather. Divide in spring or fall.

Pests & Diseases: Bergenia is a favored food of slugs, snails and rodents. Spray with cayenne pepper if infested. Fungal infection of the young leaves can cause them to become severely distorted. Use baking-soda spray (see page 192).

Black-Eyed-Susan Vine

(Acanthaceae, *Thunbergia alata*)

A rampant climber of tree trunks and hillsides in the Central American sunshine, this vine is modest and eager to please in northern hanging baskets and window boxes, where it blooms from mid-summer to frost on a vine that eventually grows about 3 feet (1 m) long. Most common is the yellow-flowered version with a black throat, but there is also a white one.

Culture: Sow the seeds, just covered, directly in pots or baskets outdoors after the last frost, or start the seeds indoors 2 months earlier in peat pots.

Pests & Diseases: None of note.

Bleeding Heart

(Fumariaceae, *Dicentra spectabilis*)

A favorite farmhouse perennial, bleeding heart grows into an attractive shrub in spring as tall as 3 feet (1 m) and dies back to the ground in winter. It has unique dangling heart-shaped flowers, usually light pink, which, when opened up, reveal what has been dubbed a "lady in the bath," one common name for the plant. The cultivar 'Luxuriant' has deep pink flowers; 'Bountiful' is almost red. There is also a white form.

Culture: The customary way to grow bleeding

heart is to obtain plants in spring. It is easy to grow in shade or partial sun and can spread beyond bounds if not checked and divided every couple of years. The beautiful grayish leaves with undulating edges become shabby in summer, so bleeding heart should be hidden behind plants that are at their best later in the season.

Pests & Diseases: None of note.

Brachycome

(Compositae, *Brachycome iberidifolia*)

Swan River Daisy

This Australian native is a frost-tender annual that forms a 10-inch (25 cm) bush covered in summer with fragrant 2-inch (5 cm) white, pink, blue or purple daisies. Brachycome is ideal for growing in window boxes and containers or when placed near the front of a sunny bed.

Culture: Buy plants in spring, or sow the seeds, barely covered, indoors 6 weeks before the last spring frost. Set plants in groups of three to five, 6 inches (15 cm) apart, in rich soil in sun.

Pests & Diseases: None of note.

Browallia

(Solanaceae, *Browallia speciosa*)

Sapphire Flower; Amethyst Flower

Browallia is a petunia cousin grown for its contribution of beautiful clear blue to the shady garden. Less valued are the white versions. Browallia cannot take frost, but it is heat-tolerant as long as it has some shade and the soil does not dry out. It creates a low mound about 1 foot (30 cm) tall, covered with starry trumpet flowers 1 to 2 inches (2.5-5 cm) wide. Browallia is excellent for a shady window box, container or pathway edging.

Culture: Most greenhouses sell small plants in spring, though gardeners who are experienced can grow browallia from seeds, provided they are started indoors at least 3 months before the last spring frost date. Sow the seeds on the surface, and expose them to light and a temperature range of 60 to 65 degrees F (15-18°C). After frost, set plants 8 inches (20 cm) apart in pots or the garden bed. Give them steady watering, and fertilize every 2 weeks. In fall, before frost, browallia can be sheared back and potted up to continue blooming

indoors in a bright, cool window or under lights.
Pests & Diseases: None of note.

Calendula
(Compositae, *Calendula officinalis*)
Pot Marigold
The best-known garden calendula is called pot marigold in England, because it is edible and thus fit for the soup pot. The species grows 2 feet (60 cm) tall and bears golden flowers, but there are shorter cultivars, and the flowers may be cream or orange. Calendula petals can be used like saffron.
Culture: Sow seeds indoors ¼ inch (6 mm) deep, 6 weeks before the last spring frost date. Plant out 6 inches (15 cm) apart. Deadhead calendula frequently to prolong blooming. Like all daisies, calendula thrives in full sun and will even put up with poor, dry soil and high heat. It also tolerates cool weather better than regular marigolds. It is a long-lasting cut flower.
Pests & Diseases: None of note.

Campanula
(Campanulaceae, *Campanula* spp)
Bellflower; Bluebell; Harebell
There are many garden species and cultivars in this genus, including biennials and perennials, all with bell or cup flowers, mostly blue and purple. Popular among the perennials are Carpathian bellflower (*C. carpatica*), with 2-inch (5 cm) flowers on stems about 1 foot (30 cm) tall, and peach-leaved bellflower (*C. persicifolia*), 2 to 3 feet (0.6-1 m) tall with 1-inch-wide (2.5 cm) flowers. Canterbury bells (*C. medium*) is a biennial with 2-inch (5 cm) rose, white or blue flowers on 2½-foot (75 cm) stems. Canterbury bells takes 2 years to bloom from seed. It spends the first year producing a ground cover of leaves and the second year growing its stems and flowers. You must sow the seeds 2 years in a row to have bells every year. *C. carpatica* cultivars, such as 'Blue Clips' and 'White Clips,' less than 8 inches (20 cm) tall, are excellent near

the front of a border that is not too hot and dry.
All bellflowers tend to be somewhat invasive, both by underground root and by seed, but the pushiest may be *C. rapunculoides*, which beguiles unwary gardeners with its pretty, small bluebells on stems about 3 to 4 feet (1 m) tall. It is even more persistent and invasive than twitch grass.
Culture: The usual way to grow a variety of bellflowers is from plants purchased in spring. However, Canterbury bells is a good candidate for sowing, as described above, either directly in the garden in early spring or indoors about 6 weeks before the last spring frost date. Sow seeds of all campanulas on the soil surface, and expose to light and a temperature range of 60 to 70 degrees F (15-21°C) until germination. Tall stems can be staked or allowed to relax among other flowers.
Pests & Diseases: Watch for slugs.

Canary Creeper
(Tropaeolaceae, *Tropaeolum peregrinum*)
This nasturtium cousin has bright canary-yellow flowers and a twining habit. Although canary creeper is well suited to trailing from hanging baskets and window boxes, it can also be given a trellis to climb, which it does in the manner of the climbing nasturtium, holding itself up with its leaf stalks, or petioles, to a height of about 4 feet (1.2 m). The attractive foliage is blue-green and indented. Canary creeper is a frost-tender annual, but it does best in coolish weather and fades when conditions are hot and dry.
Culture: As spring bedding plants are seldom available, grow from seed in the manner of nasturtiums. Steady watering and fertilizing every 2 weeks will help keep the plant green and growing.
Pests & Diseases: None of note.

Candytuft
(Cruciferae, *Iberis* spp)
There are both annual and perennial types of candytuft, but the annual (*I. umbellata*) is best known.

Flat clusters of starry, fragrant flowers, in pink, lilac, purple or white, bloom in early summer atop 10-to-15-inch (25-38 cm) stems, then go to seed.

Perennial candytuft (*I. sempervirens*) is a hardy evergreen rambler with spring clusters of white flowers that may continue blooming for weeks if the weather stays cool. It grows about 9 inches (23 cm) tall. 'Snowflake' is an improved form, with larger flowers.

Culture: Around the last spring frost date, sow the seeds of annual candytuft directly where they will grow, in sun or light shade, covering them lightly. Thin to 6 inches (15 cm) apart. Perennial candytuft needs some sun. Shearing it back encourages more flowers. Propagate from cuttings. Candytuft grows in any soil in sun or light shade and, if happy, will self-sow to reappear next year.

Pests & Diseases: None of note.

Catharanthus

(Apocynaceae, *Catharanthus* hybrids; *Vinca rosea*)
Vinca; Madagascar Periwinkle

Unrelated to the genus *Vinca*, though it often goes by the same name, this tender perennial arrived on the horticultural scene during the 1980s, when it won several All-America awards. Catharanthus resembles impatiens not only in flower shape and plant size but also in nonstop blooming, despite little maintenance and no deadheading. Unlike impatiens, however, catharanthus has leathery leaves and will take full sun and drought. Frost kills it.

Culture: Catharanthus is slow from seed, which must be sown about 3 months before the last spring frost date, but transplants have become widely available in spring. Set them 1 foot (30 cm) apart in sun. Plants fare best on the dry side and will die in standing water.

Pests & Diseases: None of note.

Catmint

(Labiatae, *Nepeta* spp)
There are many types of nepeta for the perennial garden. The best known is catmint (*N.* x *faassenii*;

N. mussinii), which grows 1 to 3 feet (0.3-1 m) tall, depending on the cultivar, and makes an attractive mound for carpeting or midborder. Above the blue-gray leaves, spikes of blue flowers bloom in early summer and sometimes again later if they are sheared back after blooming. There are also pink, purple and white cultivars. When crushed, a spicy odor is released, similar to that of two related perennials: catnip (*N. cataria*, a culinary herb described on page 164) and creeping Charlie (*N. hederacea*; *Glechoma hederacea*), a lovely blue-flowered creeper which is, unfortunately, so aggressive that it is a weed.

Culture: Grow catmint in well-drained soil in sun or partial shade. It tolerates heat and drought. Catmint must be grown vegetatively. Obtain plants in spring, and when plants become large, they can be divided in spring.

Pests & Diseases: None of note.

Celosia

(Amaranthaceae, *Celosia* spp)
Celosia is an annual that continues to bloom despite anything nature or passersby throw at it, so it is a reliable summer brightener of public parks. The flowers on the upright plumed species, *C. plumosa*, have a dry, feathery look, in neon shades of yellow, red and orange. Its *C. cristata* cousin, cockscomb, is similarly colored but is a top-heavy oddity that is more appreciated by adventurous flower arrangers than by garden designers. Plumed celosia cultivars are about 1 foot (30 cm) tall; cristatas range from 6-inch (15 cm) dwarfs to 40-inch (100 cm) monstrosities. Wheat celosia (*C. spicata*) looks like a pale, wispy 2-foot (60 cm) version of *C. plumosa*.

Culture: Buy bedding plants in spring, or grow celosia from seeds sown indoors, just covered, 4 weeks early or directly in a sunny part of the garden around the last frost date. They will germinate when the soil warms to 70 to 75 degrees F (21-24°C). Set plants 6 inches (15 cm) apart. The stiffness of the plant suits geometric designs and formal rows. It is also good in dry, sunny containers or window boxes.

Pests & Diseases: None of note.

Chrysanthemum

(Compositae, *Chrysanthemum* spp)
Pyrethrum; Shasta Daisy; Crown Daisy

For summer and fall color, a gardener could get by with chrysanthemums alone, so varied is the genus. All are daisies, and all make good cut flowers, but there, the similarities end. Among hardy perennials, the genus includes pyrethrum, or painted daisy (*C. coccineum*; *Pyrethrum roseum*), with fernlike foliage and white, pink or rose flowers on 2-foot (60 cm) stems, and Shasta daisies (*C.* x *superbum*), restrained versions of the white oxeye daisies that bloom along country roadsides in summer. There are single and double chrysanthemums and cultivars which grow so tall that they will require staking. The more practical dwarfs are about 1 foot (30 cm) tall.

Most of us associate the word chrysanthemum with "mums," the plants florists force into bloom for Mothers' Day or Easter. The hardy versions, labeled garden chrysanthemums, are grown for their fall daisies, in a range of flower colors, sizes and shapes. Most varieties of chrysanthemum sold as pot plants die after the flowers fade, but chrysanthemums sold for the garden may be so hardy, they will bloom every fall and need frequent dividing. A few dependable cultivars are 'Baby Tears,' 'Small Wonder' and 'Daisy Royal.'

Among annual chrysanthemums are some that are as bright as Mexican skirts. Tricolor chrysanthemum (*C. carinatum*) has brilliant three-colored petals and carries descriptive cultivar names like 'Court Jesters.' The crown daisy (*C. coronarium*) forms a 2-foot (60 cm) mound with double white

The woody stems of cleome hold its unusual flowers high above 'Nicki' hybrid nicotiana.

or yellow flowers. The ground-hugging *C. multicaule* bears yellow daisies.

Culture: All the annuals can be sown in late spring in a sunny spot directly where they will grow. Pyrethrum and Shasta daisies will take full sun or some shade and are normally obtained as plants in spring, although they are easy from seeds. They grow in any ordinary soil, forming a gradually widening clump that can be divided in about 3 years. Cut stems back after flowering. Pinch hardy chrysanthemums back at least once in spring. In late fall, after they have bloomed, cut them back to 4 inches (10 cm) high and mulch untested varieties for insurance.

Pests & Diseases: Birds, slugs and snails can be problems early in the season. Chrysanthemums are also favorites of earwigs and aphids. Combat both with insecticidal soap spray. Tender types of chrysanthemum are vulnerable to fungal diseases, such as mildew and gray mold. Use a baking-soda spray (see page 192). The worst viruses are aspermy, stunt and mosaic, all spread by aphids or by contact with infected plants. The first disease causes flowers to become distorted, the second causes dwarfing and the third causes a greenish yellow mottling. Remove and destroy infected plants, and spray remaining plants to kill aphids.

Clarkia
(Onagraceae, *Clarkia* spp)
C. elegans, a native of western North America, resembles a miniature hollyhock in flower color and shape, though it grows only 2 to 4 feet (0.6-1.2 m) tall. *C. pulchella* is half that height. Both species prefer a maritime climate. Hot, dry summers shorten their season, but they thrive in prolonged cool, moist weather in sun or partial shade.

Culture: Sow seeds outdoors from late spring through early summer, as clarkia produces just one crop of flowers. Thin to 6 inches (15 cm) apart. Successive sowings prolong its season. The flowers are good for cutting, and the seed pods are ideal in dried arrangements. Where it is content, clarkia readily self-sows.

Pests & Diseases: Clarkia stems are sometimes infected by gray mold. Remove infected plants.

Clematis
(Ranunculaceae, *Clematis* spp)
The most popular flowering perennial vine for northern gardens, clematis is available in a bewildering number of species and cultivars, some tough enough for prairie gardens, some so tender that they scarcely grow beyond the Deep South. As a rule, the smaller-flowered vines are hardier and more vigorous. Hardy clematis generally flowers for most of the summer and is deciduous or dies back to the ground in winter. Very hardy types include the white *C. vitalba* 'Traveler's Joy,' *C. paniculata* and *C. tangutica*. Among the large-flowered, hardy types are *C.* x *jackmanii*, a purple-flowering species whose hybrids include the pink 'Hagley,' crimson 'Mme. André,' lavender 'Mrs. Cholmondeley' and ruby 'Niobe,' all hardy to zone 5. *C. florida* is less hardy but has bigger flowers, some 6 inches (15 cm) wide. Fluffy seed heads add to the late-season interest.

There are shrubby species and some that are trailing but will not hold themselves up, so if it is a vine you want, be sure to check the fine print when ordering a new species.

Culture: Obtain plants in spring. All of the climbing species need a trellis or fence to climb, unless you want them to ramble. The old rule of thumb recommends planting their roots in shade and their heads in sun. A few well-placed rocks can shade the root area. Encourage climbing by twining the soft new shoots through the support. Pruning schedules vary with species and cultivar. *C.* x *jackmanii* blooms only on new growth, so it can be pruned back in fall. Many others bloom in spring on last year's growth and again in summer on new growth. Check the catalog or nursery for details.

Pests & Diseases: A common fungus disease produces brown leaf spots. The larger-flowering types, including *C.* x *jackmanii*, are especially susceptible to clematis wilt, a fungus disease that causes shoots to wilt and rapidly die. Remove wilted shoots back to the healthy base, even if this means cutting under the soil level, and apply baking-soda spray (see page 192).

Cleome
(Capparaceae, *Cleome hasslerana*)
Spider Flower
Cleome is the only garden member of the caper family, so it looks different from anything else you are likely to grow. The flower is large, loose and showy, with paddle-shaped petals and long, hairy stamens. Narrow, curving seed pods suggest spider legs. Woody stems 3 to 6 feet (1-2 m) tall make this annual suitable for the back of a border, where it looks best in groups. Cleome is unusual enough to

The best hybrid columbines resemble wild ones.

established its reputation for dependability in low light. Its flowers are insignificant, but the foliage, which grows in a clump directly from the ground in variegated patterns of green, pink, cream, yellow and maroon, can be as beautiful as any flower. Leaf edges may be smooth, pinked or lacy. The leaves of some varieties are as long as 10 inches (25 cm) and half as wide, but leaves of coleus for hanging baskets, such as the 'Poncho' series, are small with deeply indented edges.

Culture: Plant coleus outdoors after the last spring frost in partial shade. They can be set 6 inches (15 cm) apart at the front of a flower border, along a path or in containers. In good soil and in a place where they do not severely dry out, coleus may grow 1 foot (30 cm) tall and wide or even larger, forming a beautiful, if temporary, ground cover. To encourage bushiness, pinch out flower stems and pinch back plants. In fall, before frost, take cuttings or pot up favorite plants and bring indoors to double as houseplants. Coleus is also easy from seeds, which are sown on the soil surface and exposed to light and a temperature range of 65 to 75 degrees F (18-24°C). Packages of mixed seeds yield a fascinating variety of leaf colors.

Pests & Diseases: None of note.

attract attention if grown close to a house wall or near a porch or door, where it can be easily seen, but keep it downwind, because its smell is unpleasant. It can also be the tall focal point in the middle of an island bed of annuals. In a windy place, it may need staking.

Culture: Cleome is easy from seeds sown directly in a sunny spot in the garden any time in spring. Germination will take place once the soil warms to 70 to 75 degrees F (21-24°C). Thin plants to stand 2 feet (60 cm) apart. Flowers bloom about 8 weeks after seeding. Cleome usually self-sows to reappear the next year.

Pests & Diseases: None of note, although aphids may infest young plants. Spray with insecticidal soap.

Coleus

(Labiatae, *Coleus* x *hybridus*)
This tender perennial was known as a houseplant before it became popular outdoors. Indoors, coleus

Columbine

(Ranunculaceae, *Aquilegia* spp)
These North American natives bear graceful, uniquely shaped flowers in late spring. The sculptured, finely textured leaves are also beautiful. Wild species, such as the crimson *A. canadensis*, are showy, but for a greater color range, look for the hybrids, some of which are as tall as 3 feet (1 m) and have larger flowers. The doubles have lost their wildflower charm.

Culture: Plants are widely available in spring. Columbines will bloom in shade but will also take some sun, provided the soil is humusy and does not stay dry for long. They are perennial but tend to be short-lived, only 2 or 3 years, so prepare to replace plants. Some self-sow, and others are easy from seeds sown indoors or outdoors in early spring.

Pests & Diseases: Alternaria, a fungus disease, causes black spots with yellow halos on the leaves. Remove affected foliage, and apply baking-soda spray (see page 192).

Coral Bells
(Saxifragaceae, *Heuchera* spp)
Reminiscent of Victorian cottage gardens, though it is a North American native, coral bells is named for its summer spires of tiny, jewel-bright magenta, pink or white flowers. The foliage is leathery and dark green. The *H. micrantha* cultivar 'Palace Purple' is valued for beautiful, reddish foliage in a 1-foot-tall (30 cm) mound that looks best at the front of a border or in a mass planting. A new cultivar, the 2-foot-tall (60 cm) 'Ruby Mist,' from Morden, Manitoba, is hardy to minus 31 degrees F (–35°C) with minimal snow cover.

Culture: Coral bells does best in loamy soil in partial shade, though it can tolerate sun if it is not too hot. Plants can be obtained in spring or multiplied from cuttings or divisions. Set them 1 foot (30 cm) apart. Sow seeds indoors about 8 weeks before the last spring frost date, or sow in pots in fall and leave outdoors all winter. Seeds need light for germination, so they are scattered on the soil surface. They germinate at a soil temperature of about 50 degrees F (10°C).

Pests & Diseases: Fungi can produce purple or brown leaf spots. Remove affected foliage, and apply baking-soda spray (see page 192).

Coreopsis
(Compositae, *Coreopsis* spp)
Coreopsis has recently gained new popularity in the perennial garden because of the introduction of *C. verticillata* 'Moonbeam,' a hardy, cream-colored cultivar widely available as a spring bed-ding plant. The color is refreshing in a daisy, and 'Moonbeam' blooms for as long as 15 weeks on 16-inch (40 cm) stems.

Sunny yellow is the usual color associated with coreopsis, which is generally easy and hardy, demanding little but well-drained soil and plenty of sun. Other than 'Moonbeam,' the most popular are *C. lanceolata* cultivars, as tall as 2 feet (60 cm), with flowers in the cream, pink, orange and mahogany range.

Annual coreopsis, sometimes called calliopsis or tickseed (*C. tinctoria*), is a windblown daisy sometimes included in wildflower mixtures and best in that kind of planting.

Culture: Seeds can be sown directly in the garden on the soil surface any time in spring. Thin plants to stand 1 foot (30 cm) apart. Annual and perennial coreopsis often self-sow. 'Moonbeam' cannot be grown from seeds, but once established, plants can be divided in spring. Cuttings can be taken from new growth. Like balloon flower, 'Moonbeam' is late to sprout in the spring garden. All coreopsis needs well-drained soil to the point of dryness.

Pests & Diseases: None of note.

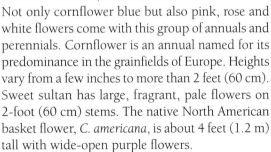

Cornflower
(Compositae, *Centaurea* spp)
Bachelor's-Button; Sweet Sultan
Not only cornflower blue but also pink, rose and white flowers come with this group of annuals and perennials. Cornflower is an annual named for its predominance in the grainfields of Europe. Heights vary from a few inches to more than 2 feet (60 cm). Sweet sultan has large, fragrant, pale flowers on 2-foot (60 cm) stems. The native North American basket flower, *C. americana*, is about 4 feet (1.2 m) tall with wide-open purple flowers.

The most common perennial, *C. montana*, is hardy to zone 3. It has 3-inch (7.5 cm) purple flowers on 2-foot (60 cm) stems in early summer. It spreads quickly if it is happy, so it should be divided every few years.

Culture: Buy bedding plants, or sow the seeds directly in the garden in late spring or early summer. Centaureas prefer sun and well-drained, even dry soil. Cornflowers self-sow modestly in most gardens. They can be put outdoors as soon as the soil begins to warm in spring; plants tolerate light frosts. The flowers are edible.

Pests & Diseases: None of note, although plants may fade and die back in hot, dry weather.

Corydalis

(Fumariaceae, *Corydalis lutea*)
Fumitory
With its blue-green, delicately indented foliage and creamy yellow flowers spring through summer, corydalis deserves to be better known. It is a hardy perennial that forms a shrub 1 foot (30 cm) tall.

Culture: This species can be grown from seeds only if they are fresh but is easy to grow from cuttings or divisions. It self-sows to the point of invasiveness, so remove unwanted seedlings. Give it a protected position in good, well-drained soil near a wall or along a walkway. It thrives in partial sun or dappled shade.

Pests & Diseases: None of note.

Cosmos

(Compositae, *Cosmos* spp)
Cosmos is so easy that some gardeners dismiss it, yet the 3-inch (7.5 cm) daisy flowers are graceful and can be as lovely as large single roses. *C. bipinnatus* is the white and pink through rose species. The central stalk, which is woody, grows about 4 feet (1.2 m) tall in the standard varieties. Staking may be needed in windy places. There are also shorter cultivars, such as the 2-foot (60 cm) 'Sonata.' The long, slender flower stems are good for cutting. There are many cultivars, some bicolored and some with oddly shaped petals. 'Sensation Mixed,' colored white, pink, rose and magenta, is an older, dependable variety that will self-sow

if some flowers are allowed to go to seed. The next spring, seedlings are easily weeded out or transplanted if you wish.

C. sulphureus has flowers in the yellow and orange through mahogany palette, and stems are usually shorter, though there are a few as tall as 3 feet (1 m), such as 'Bright Lights' and 'Sunset.'

Culture: Cosmos is easily grown from seeds sown in a sunny place as soon as the soil can be worked in spring. Seeds sprout when the soil warms to about 68 to 86 degrees F (20-30°C), and seedlings grow quickly. You can also buy transplants in spring. Plants bloom from midsummer until they are killed by the first frost.

Pests & Diseases: None of note.

Crocus

(Liliaceae, *Crocus* spp; *Colchicum* spp)
Even the largest, most exaggerated hybrids from the Dutch bulb mills retain the innocence of species crocuses. All are winter-hardy and should reappear year after year, gradually increasing in number until you can dig the corms carefully and plant a few elsewhere. Plant crocuses along a path, in a rock garden or in pots—anywhere their small size will be an asset. Crocuses are among the few hardy bulbs that look fine even when planted in a mixture of different colors, because all of them blend well.

Aside from the standard pink, blue and white Dutch crocuses, there are several lovely crocus species. *Crocus ancyrensis* is smaller, earlier and brilliant yellow. *C. chrysanthus* is also earlier.

The fall-blooming crocuses and colchicums are anachronisms suited to naturalizing in lawns in the places where they are hardy, around zone 5. Colchicums are somewhat larger than crocuses.

The so-called prairie crocus is actually an anemone, *Anemone patens wolfgangiana*.

Culture: In fall, plant spring-blooming crocus

Cosmos 'Sensation Mixed' is a tall cultivar that often self-sows to bloom year after year.

corms, pointed side up, in groups about 4 inches (10 cm) deep in well-drained soil in sun. If they are happy, they will gradually form widening clumps. Plant colchicums in August or early September, 4 inches (10 cm) deep and 6 inches (15 cm) apart. The foliage and seed pods appear in spring, then die back. The flowers bloom in fall without leaves.
Pests & Diseases: None of note. Birds occasionally pick off crocus flowers, especially yellows.

Cup-and-Saucer Vine
(Polemoniaceae, *Cobaea scandens*)
Purple Climber; Cathedral Bells
This rampant tropical vine may start slowly, but it grows swiftly in warm weather, easily reaching 10 feet (3 m) if it has a couple of months of heat. With a longer season, it grows even higher, but it cannot take heavy frost. The flowers are large and interesting, resembling a cup hanging below a wider saucer. They open green and gradually turn purple. There is also a cream-flowered version.

Culture: Sow the big seeds indoors in peat pots 8 weeks early. One vine is enough for a trellis or each side of an archway. Give cup-and-saucer vine rich soil in full sun.
Pests & Diseases: None of note.

Daffodil, Narcissus
(Amaryllidaceae, *Narcissus* spp)
All daffodils and narcissus are members of the genus *Narcissus* and are thus variations on the same theme. The former are best known for stems taller than 1 foot (30 cm) and large, brilliant yellow trumpet flowers, though there are also white and bicolored daffodils and some that are just a few inches tall. Narcissus are smaller, with white petals

and cup-shaped centers that may be white, pink-ish, yellow or orange. Some are sweetly fragrant, such as 'Peridot' and 'Thalia.'

Culture: Plant all of them 3 to 6 inches (7.5-15 cm) deep, depending on the bulb size, well before the first fall frost; they need plenty of time in cool soil to develop their roots. Give them well-drained soil in sun or light shade. Narcissus can be naturalized to grow in grass that is not mowed till the foliage dies. Pry up a clump of grass, and bury the bulb under it. Certain cultivars are well suited for this and are recommended as such in bulb catalogs. Narcissus generally form a clump in several years and look best that way. When you want more, dig up the clump in late summer and pull away some of the bulbs to plant elsewhere.

Pests & Diseases: In some places, the narcissus bulb fly is troublesome. It can be combated with a beneficial nematode sold under the brand name Biosafe.

Dahlia
(Compositae, *Dahlia* spp)

Summer-long flowering in a rich palette of colors comes from dahlias, sleek-petaled, frost-tender daisies that may be as small as pennies or as big as dinner plates. The flowers have many forms, from the singles, resembling wild daisies, to pompons, anemone-flowers and cactus-flowers. Plants range in height from 1 to 6 feet (0.3-2 m). The tall types require staking.

Culture: Some dahlias will bloom in about 3 months from seed, an inexpensive way to grow a quantity; check the catalogs. Others are grown from roots or plants obtained in spring. In any case, after the tops have been killed by the first fall frost, dig up the entire plant to expose the tuber-like roots, which can be stored in peat moss or vermiculite or covered with gladiolus corms in a paper bag in any cool, dry place. When you break the roots apart, ensure that each piece has an eye, or

bud. Plant the roots indoors in pots just under the soil surface about a month before the last spring frost, and set them out in the garden or in pots after the last frost. Given sun and sufficient water, they will bloom all summer. Remove spent flowers.

Pests & Diseases: Slugs and snails can be a problem on young plants. Aphids and earwigs can be combated with insecticidal soap spray. Aphids can carry virus diseases to dahlias. Cold, wet summers can cause petal blight—petals look water-soaked, then turn brown. Remove affected flowers until the weather improves.

Datura
(Solanaceae, *Datura* spp)

Angel's-Trumpet; Thorn Apple

There are several species of datura grown in gardens. Some winter as houseplants. All are frost-tender and have tubular flowers, usually white or cream, and dull green leaves. Flowers may be rather small, as in thorn apple (*D. stramonium*), a weedy annual that is a rampant self-sower, or they may be large and sweetly perfumed, as in the 3-to-5-foot-tall (1-1.5 m) *D. meteloides*, *D. suaveolens* and *D. sanguinea*.

Culture: Search the specialist catalogs for seeds, which are easily sprouted when sown directly in a pot indoors about 8 weeks before the last spring frost for blooms that summer. Some perennials are available as bedding plants in spring. Set outdoors in sun after the last spring frost date.

Pests & Diseases: None of note, although flea beetles may perforate young plants.

Day Lily
(Liliaceae, *Hemerocallis fulva*)

Dependable and beautiful in almost any situation, even on roadsides—evidence of their tenacity—day lilies are such rampant hybridizers that there are now more than 13,000 types in cultivation, a nightmare for botanists but a generous resource for gardeners. Colors vary from white to yellow, orange, plum, lavender, green and pink, almost all with an underlying hint of yellow. Flower size varies from small and self-supporting to huge and needing staking for some of the tetraploids. There are doubles, some with fragrance, and some unusual flower shapes. The longest stems, 6 feet (2 m) or so, may require staking. All day lilies have sword-shaped leaves that keep the garden looking attractive until late summer. Some of the more tender cultivars are evergreen.

Day lilies are named for the one-day blooming period of each flower. Stems have many buds, however, so flowering usually lasts about 3 weeks, starting in early summer. An unusually long flowering time comes from the 1-foot-tall (30 cm) golden 'Stella de Oro,' yellow 'Happy Returns' and golden-and-red 'Black-Eyed Stella.'

Culture: Day lilies are commonly available in spring as bedding plants. For the best variety, shop from specialist nurseries, most of whom offer mail-order service (see Sources). Day lilies spread quickly enough that in 3 years, you should be able to divide them in fall by digging up clumps and pulling individual plants away from one another. Day lily flowers are edible.

Pests & Diseases: None of note.

Delphinium
(Ranunculaceae, *Delphinium* spp)
Larkspur

These are the signature plants of English cottage gardens, lovely at the back of a border, with their spires of pink, blue, lilac, cherry and white. The English climate is the one that suits them: damp, cloudy, warm. Delphiniums are the perennial version, larkspurs the annual.

Culture: The difficulty with the tall delphiniums—the 'Pacific Giants' reach about 5 feet (1.5 m)—is that without staking, they will flop over in a strong wind or heavy rain. They thrive in rich soil with fertilization, but it encourages even taller, lankier growth. Cut the flower spikes back to the ground after blooming. A fall crop may emerge. For delphinium flowers without bother, consider one of the small cultivars, such as *D. chinensis* 'Dwarf Blue Butterfly,' which forms a charming mound of sky-blue flowers only 1 foot (30 cm) tall.

It is easily grown from seeds sown 8 weeks early indoors. Seeds germinate in darkness at 50 to 55 degrees F (10-13°C). Then the flats or pots must be moved into cool sun. Plants will bloom the first year and may self-sow.

Buy taller delphiniums as plants in spring, or start them indoors or in the garden from seed. They will bloom the second year. Although they are perennials, they seldom last more than 3 or 4 years in areas where summers are hot and dry. Delphiniums are difficult to divide but easy to propagate from cuttings taken in spring. Half-bury pencil-thick 3-inch (7.5 cm) shoots in damp seeding mix, and cover with glass or plastic. When rooted, pot individually.

The larkspur (*D. ajacis*; *Consolida ambigua*) looks similar, though just 1 to 3 feet (0.3-1 m) tall. Sow seeds in the garden as soon as the soil can be worked, or start indoors 8 weeks before the last spring frost. Plants should be about 1 foot (30 cm) apart in full sun and rich soil.

Pests & Diseases: Slugs and snails may dine on young plants. Tall types of delphinium are especially prone to fungal diseases such as powdery mildew, which turns foliage white, usually in dry weather. Spray with baking-soda solution (see page 192), starting when plants are small, or after infection, cut stems back to a few inches high, for a second bloom later in summer. A bacterial disease causes black spots with yellow halos, and black rot can hollow out stems at ground level. Remove infected plants, and grow delphiniums in a new spot next year.

Dianthus
(Caryophyllaceae, *Dianthus* spp)
Carnation; Pink; Sweet William

Carnations and pinks—tall, short, annual and perennial—belong to the genus *Dianthus*. Some are sweetly perfumed, some lack scent. Some are very tall, while *D. deltoides* 'Microchip' is a beautiful hardy spreading perennial that hugs the ground. All need well-drained soil, preferably neutral or somewhat alkaline, in an open site not under trees,

Everlastings include golden ageratum, pink strawflowers, rose statice and white acroclinium.

and all bloom in the warm-color range of pink, rose and magenta, along with white and bicolors. The descriptive term "pink" describes not only the color but also the "pinked" edges of some petals. Pinks are edible.

New hybrids of *D. barbatus* x *chinensis*, sometimes called hybrid dwarf sweet William, are winter-hardy biennials or perennials that form mounds of glossy foliage less than 1 foot (30 cm) high topped by brilliant flowers in late spring; the 'Telstar' series, 'Festival' series and 'Ideal' series fit this description. Sweet William itself (*D. barbatus*) comes in both annual and biennial types. Check before you buy seeds or plants.

Culture: Dianthus tolerates full sun, though it does best in good soil watered whenever it dries out. The tall-stemmed carnations may need staking, but small ones can be used along border edges. Most are easy from seeds, which offer a far greater range of possibilities than what is usually available as bedding plants in spring. Sow seeds 8 weeks be-fore the last spring frost date, with seeds just covered. Germination takes place at 60 to 70 degrees F (15-21°C). Set outdoors around the last frost date. Most cultivars go about 6 inches (15 cm) apart.

The carnations sold by florists are greenhouse varieties that bloom continuously. Few are fragrant. If you want something similar, look for annual carnations in seed catalogs or among the bedding plants sold in spring. Remove seed pods to encourage continued flowering.

Pests & Diseases: Fungal diseases can produce spots on leaves or stems or may cause plants to wilt even in moist soil. Remove affected foliage, or if the entire plant is infected, destroy it.

Dimorphotheca

(Compositae, *Dimorphotheca* spp)
Cape Marigold; Star of the Veldt; Osteospermum
This frost-tender South African daisy has flat flowers of white, cream, orange, yellow or unusual pastel shades of pink to salmon, all with yellow cen-

ters. It tolerates full sun and fairly dry, sandy soil but prefers coolish nights and fades when night temperatures rise past 70 degrees F (21°C). Plants grow about 1 foot (30 cm) tall and spread equally wide, forming mats that look best in borders, in pots and at the edge of a patio.

Culture: Sow the seeds directly in the garden after the last spring frost. Seeds germinate at a soil temperature of 60 to 70 degrees F (15-21°C).

Pests & Diseases: None of note.

Edible Flowers

Included in this category are calendula, cornflower, day lily, hollyhock, impatiens, mallow, nasturtium, snapdragon, viola and the flowers of many herbs. Edible flowers are generally used as garnishes in salads or on desserts. Use only perfect flowers, and make sure they are scrupulously clean. Never use flowers that have been sprayed.

Evening Primrose

(Onagraceae, *Oenothera* spp)

There are some lovely evening primroses for gardens, but the best known, though a member of the genus, is not an evening bloomer and so has the common name sundrops (*O. tetragona*; *O. fruticosa*). This easy spreading perennial grows about 2 feet (60 cm) high, with brilliant yellow 2-inch (5 cm) flowers in early summer. Ozark sundrops (*O. missourensis*) is an evening bloomer, also with yellow flowers, though stems are just 1 foot (30 cm) tall. Showy primrose (*O. speciosa*) is the same height, with white or pink day-blooming flowers and a spreading habit.

Culture: All evening primroses tolerate poor soil and can be used in areas where little else will grow. In fertile ground, most will spread quite rapidly, though they are easy to dig out. Evening primroses grow readily from seed, which affords a wider selection than what can be purchased as bedding plants. Barely cover the seeds, which germinate at 70 to 85 degrees F (21-29°C). Plants can be set in

the garden about 2 weeks before the last spring frost date.

Pests & Diseases: None of note.

Everlastings

This term describes a score or so of flowers that maintain their shape and some color after air-drying. A few actually dry on the stem in the garden, while others dry better after picking, often hung in bunches upside down in a dry, airy place out of the sun. In the garden, all do best in full sun.

Several daisies are everlasting, thanks to showy bracts that resemble petals. Best known of the everlasting daisies is strawflower (*Helichrysum bracteatum*), which blooms in shades of yellow, orange, rose, salmon, red, pink and white. There are tall cultivars, about 3 feet (1 m), and dwarfs less than half that height. Acroclinium, or helipterum, is similar but is smaller and blooms only in shades of white, pink and rose. Xeranthemum is another, with lilac, pink or white flowers on 2-foot (60 cm) stems. Golden ageratum (*Lonas inodora*) has flattened clusters of yellow flowers on 1-foot-tall (30 cm) stems. None are especially attractive garden plants, so they are best confined to a cutting garden or a corner of a vegetable garden. They should be picked when just beginning to open, because they will open a little more after picking and look best partly open. Push a florist's wire up the center of the stem if you want the flower upright.

Among other popular everlastings:

• Baby's-breath (*Gypsophila* spp) should be cut when the flowers are fully open. For drying, perennial gypsophila is better than the annual.

• Globe amaranth (*Gomphrena globosa*), available in pink, purple, white, red, lilac and orange, will dry satisfactorily on the stem outdoors, though it should not be allowed to open fully before it is picked.

• Statice (*Limonium sinuatum*) will also dry on the stem in the garden. Sow it indoors about 2 months before the last spring frost date. There are blues, yellows and whites. Perennial statice, or sea lavender (*L. latifolium*), grows 20 to 30 inches (50-75 cm) tall, depending on the cultivar, and is lavender or white, lacking the bright colors of the annual.

Many seed pods are valued for dry arrangements, including those of poppy, clarkia, love-in-a-mist (*Nigella damascena*) and the somewhat weedy hardy perennials silver dollar (*Lunaria biennis*) and Chinese lantern (*Physalis franchetii*).

Flowering Cabbage; Kale
(Cruciferae, *Brassica oleracea*)
Flowering Kale
Although flowering cabbage and flowering kale are not, strictly speaking, flowers, their ornamental foliage helps them fulfill that role in the garden. They are northern favorites because they are admirably frost-hardy. Although they are annuals, they persist longer than almost anything else in the fall garden and are still colorful under the first light snows: green, white, pink or maroon, with leaves that may be smooth or lacy. Their roundish shapes, however, make them difficult to place artistically in the garden. They look best in groups at the foot of something taller—a house wall, fence or shrubs. The leaves are edible.
Culture: Plants are available in spring, but they are easy from seeds, grown like cabbage (see page 70). Plants grown from seeds are full-sized from late summer till winter, when their color is most appreciated. Plant 16 inches (40 cm) apart in fertile soil in sun or partial shade, and water once a week.
Pests & Diseases: Ornamental cabbage and kale are vulnerable to the same predators as other brassicas—flea beetles, green cabbageworms, deer and rodents. So prepare to spray with a blend of insecticidal soap and cayenne pepper.

Flowering Flax
(Linaceae, *Linum* spp)
There are two common hardy perennial forms of flax. They may not survive severe winters, but both will self-sow if happy, so new seedlings often appear to replace the old. *L. perenne* has sky-blue flowers from spring till fall on relaxed 14-inch (35 cm) stems with small gray-green leaves; there is also a white form. *L. flavum compactum*, the other

hardy perennial, has small golden flowers and dark evergreen foliage. An annual type, scarlet flax (*L. grandiflorum*), has red flowers; there are also pink and white versions. On all types of linum, flowers last just a day apiece, but the stems are dotted with buds that promise tomorrow morning's color.
Culture: Sow seeds directly in the garden in early spring, or buy plants and set them 6 inches (15 cm) apart in good, well-drained soil in sun.
Pests & Diseases: None of note.

Forget-Me-Not
(Boraginaceae, *Myosotis sylvatica*;
Cynoglossum amabile)
The usual forget-me-not, a lovely ground cover that blooms in spring, is *M. sylvatica*, with tiny sky-blue, pink or white stars on downy-leaved plants. It is tolerant of dry or poor soil in sun or partial shade, and though it is an annual, it spreads easily from self-sown seeds. Once you have forget-me-nots, you usually have them for keeps—hence the name, but they are easy to weed out. Sow seeds in early spring.

Chinese forget-me-not (*C. amabile*) is a taller version, up to 2 feet (60 cm), that also self-sows easily. The bright blue flowers and grayish leaves are lovely in summer. There are also pink and white forms.
Culture: It is often possible to buy forget-me-nots in spring or to obtain plants from horticultural-society sales. Otherwise, both types are easy from seeds sown directly in a partly sunny spot in the garden: forget-me-not in early spring, Chinese forget-me-not in late spring, around the last frost date. Grow both types in groups, thinning plants so that they just touch as they grow.
Pests & Diseases: None of note.

Four-O'Clock
(Nyctaginaceae, *Mirabilis jalapa*)
Marvel-of-Peru
This tender perennial, grown in the North as an annual, obtained its usual common name from flow-

ers that open in late afternoon. The 2-inch-long (5 cm) trumpets are white, yellow, pink, rose or red. In the warm, sheltered spot it prefers, mirabilis becomes a mounded shrub 2 to 3 feet (0.6-1 m) high and wide.

Culture: Seeds can be sown directly in the garden when nights are consistently warm, about a week after the average last spring frost date. Sow seeds on the surface; they germinate at a soil temperature of about 70 degrees F (21°C). Blooming begins in midsummer and continues till frost.

Pests & Diseases: None of note.

Foxglove

(Scrophulariaceae, *Digitalis purpurea*)

Most foxgloves are biennials, flowers that take 2 years to bloom. That leisurely schedule makes them most suitable in woodlands or relaxed cottage gardens along with other biennials such as Canterbury bells, hollyhocks and sweet William.

The tallest types of foxgloves, which may reach 8 feet (2.5 m), are likely to spend their first year as a ground-hugging rosette of downy leaves, blooming the second. But shorter foxgloves, such as 'Foxy,' may bloom the first year. If you obtain plants in spring that have flower stalks, you'll know they are on their way to blooming that year, producing spires of long bells in shades of purple, red, pink, yellow or cream.

Culture: Foxgloves appreciate moist, loamy soil in partial shade, but they will bloom almost anywhere, provided they have shelter from wind and high heat. Grow them about 1 to 2 feet (30-60 cm) apart at the back of a flower border, among trees or next to a wall, where their height will not block shorter plants. Often, they will self-sow and naturalize. Obtain plants in spring, or sow seeds in early spring on the soil surface directly where they will grow, thinning them as they sprout. Water steadily in dry weather.

Pests & Diseases: None of note.

Fritillaria

(Liliaceae, *Fritillaria* spp)

Checkered Lily; Crown Imperial

This is a genus of hardy bulbous plants that bloom at the same time as tulips but are less well known. The charming little snake's-head, or checkered lily (*F. meleagris*), grows about 1 foot (30 cm) tall, with nodding purple or white bell flowers that have a checkered pattern. They bloom in sun or shade and tolerate poor soil. The 3-foot-tall (1 m) crown imperial (*F. imperialis*) is a showstopper, with bright yellow, red or orange flowers under a top-knot of green leaves. It is malodorous if you bend down to sniff.

Culture: Obtain bulbs in fall. Crown imperial is temperamental, producing foliage but no flowers where conditions do not suit it, but it is easy in sunshine and well-drained limy soil. It is hardy to zone 5. The checkered lily is more dependable and somewhat hardier.

Pests & Diseases: None of note.

Fuchsia

(Onagraceae, *Fuchsia* spp)

A favorite hanging-basket plant and one that attracts hummingbirds, this tender perennial is available in many species and cultivars, all versions on the same theme: dangling flowers on graceful stems, usually in shades of white, pink, magenta and, of course, fuchsia. Fuchsia is grown as an annual by most Northerners, but its true nature is enjoyed by those gardeners who lovingly overwinter plants indoors. Where winters are mild, fuchsia grows into a shrub outdoors.

Culture: All fuchsias do best in shade, warmth and high humidity, in fertile, moist soil sheltered from wind. Water regularly all summer, and fertilize every 2 weeks. Take cuttings of tip growth in fall to propagate.

Pests & Diseases: Fuchsia grown as an annual seldom has problems except with heat, wind and drought. Indoors, fuchsia is commonly infested with whiteflies. Spray plants with insecticidal soap before bringing them indoors, and prepare to spray again if infestations occur.

Gaillardia

(Compositae, *Gaillardia* spp)
Indian Blanket; Blanket Flower
Annual gaillardia (*G. pulchella*), Indian blanket, is a bright, multicolored maroon, orange, red and yellow daisy that does well in sun. Plants grow as tall as 2 feet (60 cm), with fuzzy leaves. The hardy perennial blanket flower is *G.* x *grandiflora*. Flowers are 3 to 4 inches (7.5-10 cm) wide, orange, red, yellow or maroon, on stems about 18 inches (45 cm) long. A 1-foot-tall (30 cm) version is 'Goblin.'
Culture: Obtain plants in spring, or grow gaillardia from seeds sown indoors on the soil surface 6 weeks before the last spring frost date. Seeds sprout at a temperature of about 70 degrees F (21°C). Around the last frost date, set plants 6 to 12 inches (15-30 cm) apart, depending upon the eventual height of the plant. Gaillardia often self-sows and spreads gradually in dry, sunny, warm places, even in poor soil. Seedlings may act like biennials, blooming the second year.
Pests & Diseases: Gaillardia may be infected with aster yellows late in the season. See Aster.

Gazania

(Compositae, *Gazania rigens*)
Treasure Flower
This South African daisy is a tender perennial grown as an annual in the North. In warm soil and sun, it grows quickly. The big flowers, as wide as 5 inches (13 cm), bloom in bright colors—orange in the species, but also pink, red, gold and cream in the hybrids—all with grayish foliage. The centers are outlined with dots. The flowers close at night and in cloudy weather. Plants grow about 1 foot (30 cm) tall and wide. Give them well-drained soil in full sun. They are well suited to sunny window boxes and other containers.
Culture: Gazania is slow from seed, so it is easiest to obtain plants in spring. Otherwise, sow seeds

indoors 3 months before the last spring frost date. Seeds need a week of total darkness and a temperature of 60 degrees F (15°C) for germination. In the hot conditions they prefer, plants grow bushy, 6 to 12 inches (15-30 cm) tall and wide. Take cuttings in fall, and keep them in pots on a sunny windowsill for next summer's garden.
Pests & Diseases: None of note.

Geranium

(Geraniaceae, *Geranium* spp;
Pelargonium x *hortorum*)
Two distinct plants are called geraniums. The tender perennials most gardeners call geraniums are members of the genus *Pelargonium*. Popular garden and conservatory plants for more than a century, these South African natives bloom in a spectrum of warm shades, from bright pink through rose and salmon to white. Flower heads, modest or as big as 5 inches (13 cm) across, are borne on stiff stems held above the rounded foliage. Geraniums are well suited to containers, window boxes and patio tubs, and all can be brought indoors in fall, either entire plants or cuttings, for renewed life in sunny windows. For hanging baskets, use the trailing or ivy-leaved varieties (*P. peltatum*), such as the 'Tornado' hybrids and 'Summer Showers.'

The genus *Geranium* is a group of hardy North American perennials also known as cranesbills, because of their long, thin seed pods. These are the true geraniums, lovers of woodlands that will tolerate partial shade. Some tolerate drought; others put up with damp soil. Most flower in the color range of purple, magenta, pink and white. The foliage is glossy and attractive all season. They are easy, beautiful and worth including in any perennial border that is not too dry and hot. The bigroot geranium (*G. macrorrhizum*) will survive in dry shade, one of the garden's most difficult areas to beautify, and is hardy to zone 3. Some geraniums are invasive and should be kept in pots buried up to their rims in the garden bed.

Culture: Buy pelargoniums as bedding plants in spring or as houseplants any time of year. Plants can often be propagated from cuttings rooted in potting soil or water. Snap off the tip of a stem about 4 inches (10 cm) long. Pull off all but the top two leaves, and set the cutting deep enough to cover the bottom couple of leaf nodes. Keep cuttings warm and moist. Set plants outdoors after the last spring frost in full sun or partial shade. When pelargonium flowers fade, snap off the flower stems.

Plants of the genus *Geranium* are becoming increasingly available for purchase in spring, as more cultivars are developed and their popularity grows. Also, specialty seed houses carry a wide variety of species. In fall, sow the seeds, just covered, in pots in a sheltered place and leave outdoors over the winter.

Pests & Diseases: Geraniums are largely pest- and disease-free, but pelargoniums are subject to a number of disorders. Many of the new hybrids, bred for larger flowers on compact plants, are especially likely to suffer from black root rot and blackleg, which makes it difficult to root cuttings. Indoors, aphids and whiteflies may infest plants. Spray plants with insecticidal soap before bringing indoors and again if infestation occurs.

Gerbera

(Compositae, *Gerbera jamesonii*)

Popular among florists as a cut flower or pot plant, gerbera has tall, strong stems holding long-lasting daisies so large and so perfect, with bright petals and dark centers, that they scarcely look real. Colors range from bright shades of orange, pink, yellow and red to lavender and cream. Dwarf varieties such as 'Ebony Eyes' have stocky 8-inch (20 cm) stems; standard varieties are 18 inches (45 cm) tall, with 5-to-6-inch (13-15 cm) flowers. Blooming can continue for 2 months.

Culture: Gerbera is a South African tender perennial that is slow from seed. The easiest route is to obtain plants in spring. Potted plants can be tipped out and set in the garden after frost in rich, well-drained soil in sun. Seeds should be started about 6 months before the last spring frost date. After the

last frost, set plants in fertile, well-drained soil in sun or partial shade, being careful not to bury the crown, which causes rotting. Bring gerbera indoors to double as a houseplant. It is a good candidate for a cool greenhouse, as it prefers night temperatures around 60 degrees F (15°C).

Pests & Diseases: In the garden, gerbera is a favorite of snails and slugs. Indoors, spray with insecticidal soap if it becomes infested with aphids, whiteflies or spider mites.

Globe Thistle

(Compositae, *Echinops ritro*)

Not every gardener's cup of tea, globe thistle is, nevertheless, impressive, with spiny, metallic blue globes held on erect stems above thorny, grayish leaves in summer. It is a hardy perennial whose stems grow about 2 feet (60 cm) tall, best for mid-border. Globe thistle also makes a good everlasting if flowers are picked before they open.

Culture: Buy plants in spring or start seeds indoors 8 weeks before the last spring frost date, or in fall, sow seeds in pots left outdoors in a sheltered place over winter. Seeds need light to germinate, so do not cover with soil. Set plants 2 feet (60 cm) apart in well-drained soil in full sun. They will put up with poor soil and partial shade. Plants spread fairly quickly by underground rhizomes and can be divided after a couple of years. By the same token, they are difficult to eradicate; choose their position carefully from the outset.

Pests & Diseases: None of note.

Godetia

(Onagraceae, *Godetia grandiflora*)

Silky-looking flowers, resembling pink, rose and white poppies, are beautiful in the garden and the vase. Like its cousin clarkia, godetia, also an annual, does best in cool, moist soil in partial shade.

Culture: Sow seeds directly outdoors a couple of weeks before the last spring frost date, like clarkia.

Farmyard favorites, hollyhock spires draw the eye to the back of the border in early summer.

Thin to several inches apart. There are both single and double types, with stems 1 to 2 feet (30-60 cm) tall. Taller stems must be staked.

Pests & Diseases: See Clarkia.

Grape Hyacinth

(Liliaceae, *Muscari* spp)
Named for its resemblance to a bunch of tiny grapes on a 4-to-6-inch (10-15 cm) upright stem, muscari is charming along pathways, in containers, around trees and between larger bulbs. It forms clusters of stems and blooms in late spring. The usual purple-blue color complements not only green foliage but the colors of other flowers blooming nearby. There are also whites and pale blues.

Culture: Plant the corms 6 inches (15 cm) deep in sun or light shade, like narcissus. Unlike most other hardy bulbs, some species of muscari produce a grasslike clump of foliage in summer. Leave this to allow the plant to build its strength.

Pests & Diseases: None of note.

Heliotrope

(Boraginaceae, *Heliotropium peruvianum*)
This old-fashioned annual bears large clusters of white, lilac or purple flowers. Plants are shrublike, self-supporting and about 18 inches (45 cm) tall. Heliotrope makes a good cut flower. It is appreciated in part for its scent, but not all cultivars are fragrant; check the fine print.

Culture: Buy bedding plants, or start seeds about 10 weeks before the last spring frost date for flowers in July. Seeds should be lightly covered. They germinate at a temperature of 70 to 80 degrees F (21-27°C). Plant in the middle of the border or in their own bed 8 inches (20 cm) apart a week after the last spring frost. Heliotrope needs a place sheltered from wind and cold.

Pests & Diseases: None of note.

Hibiscus

(Malvaceae, *Hibiscus* spp)
The hibiscus that is best known is a tropical native, a woody shrub grown as a houseplant in the North, but there are also showy annuals and hardy perennials that can be grown in northern gardens. Annuals such as 'Southern Belle' and 'Dixie Belle' have dinner-plate-sized flowers on 5-foot-tall (1.5 m) and 2-foot-tall (60 cm) plants, respectively. Cut back in fall, these may survive a mild winter to reappear in spring. *H. trionum* is an annual that grows into a shrub about 2 feet (60 cm) tall. Each

cream-colored 2-inch (5 cm) flower lasts only a day, but the plant blooms for many weeks.

The perennial rose mallow (*H. moscheutos*), a native of eastern North America, is hardy to zone 4. Flowers may be as wide as 1 foot (30 cm), white or pink through rose, on a shrubby plant 6 feet (2 m) tall. Wild red mallow (*H. coccineus*) is about the same height but somewhat more winter-tender, hardy to zone 7, with smaller 6-inch (15 cm) red flowers. Like peonies, both perennials die back to the ground in winter.

Culture: Soak seeds overnight, then sow directly in the garden after the last spring frost, in sun or light shade. The soil must be warm, about 80 degrees F (27°C), for germination. Hibiscus resents transplanting. It grows best in full sun and moist soil but will tolerate dryness. Most varieties bloom from late July till frost.

Pests & Diseases: All mallows are favored by rodents and deer. Aphids may infest plants. Spray with insecticidal soap if the infestation is severe.

Hollyhock
(Malvaceae, *Althaea rosea*)

A farmyard and cottage-garden favorite, the hollyhock demands a place where it can grow tall without blowing over; standard plants can reach 6 feet (2 m), though 'Majorette,' an annual, is just half that height. All look best in front of a wall, fence or hedge, where their vertical habit is highlighted. Double varieties are now more common than the wilder-looking singles, especially among spring bedding plants, but the latter are more graceful. Flowers, which are edible, bloom in white and shades of pink through rose and purple. Depending on cultivar and climate, hollyhocks may be annuals, perennials or biennials that will form a rosette of foliage the first year and flowers the second year.

Culture: Hollyhocks are available as bedding plants in spring, but they are easy from seeds sown in peat pots indoors 6 to 8 weeks before the last spring frost date or, around the last spring frost, directly where they will grow. Thin to stand 1 foot (30 cm) apart.

Pests & Diseases: Hollyhocks are vulnerable to rust late in the season, which discolors and kills lower leaves and may spread over entire plants. Annuals are less susceptible. Grow hollyhocks behind shorter plants that will mask the lower leaves.

Hosta
(Liliaceae, *Hosta* spp)

North America's most popular perennial, hosta is known not so much for its flowers as for its plentiful, sometimes textured foliage, which grows in a clump directly from the ground. Leaves may be large or small, flat or pleated and colored green, bluish or yellowish or variegated with contrasting stripes or edgings. Depending on the cultivar, the lily flowers, white or lilac, that appear on stalks in summer may be an asset to the garden or a distraction to be pinched off. Hosta looks best in masses—under shade trees, in front of walls as foundation plantings or along paths.

Culture: Hosta is valued as a plant for shade. Grown as a ground cover or a low border plant, it can provide an easy-care answer for a difficult place, though it does appreciate decent soil and a good water supply. Where hosta is content, it will gradually expand to form a solid ground cover. It is easy to divide in fall by slicing established clumps into sections. Plants die back to the ground in winter and emerge in late spring. Generally purchased as plants, hosta can be grown from seed, though seedlings grow slowly and will probably not look like the parent. Planting seeds is, therefore, an adventure in genetics.

Bearded irises in subdued colors bloom in synchrony with the more intense Oriental poppies.

Pests & Diseases: Young plants are vulnerable to damage by slugs and snails.

Hyacinth

(Liliaceae, *Hyacinthus orientalis*)

This bulb, hardy to about zone 5, produces one of the most fragrant spring flowers; a few hyacinths can perfume a garden. Hyacinths are rather stiff and top-heavy, however, so they look best in masses, surrounded by softer foliage plants, such as lamb's ears or sedums. There are pink, blue, lilac, purple, yellow, orange and white versions.

Culture: Plant the bulbs in early fall about as deep as the length of your hand. Give them well-drained, decent soil in some sun, let their spot in the garden dry out in summer, and they should reappear for several years. In places with wet summers, lift the bulbs after blooming and store in dry peat until planting time in fall.

Pests & Diseases: None of note.

Hyacinth Bean

(Leguminosae, *Dolichos lablab*)

This annual climber, a lover of warmth, is grown as a food crop in some tropical countries. Young pods up to 2 inches (5 cm) long can be eaten whole. In northern gardens, however, hyacinth bean is more appreciated for rapid growth—to heights as great as 20 feet (6 m)—and a thick cover of glossy leaves on a trellis or wall. In summer or fall, there are fragrant white or lilac flowers followed by bright, shiny purple pods.

Culture: Soak seeds overnight before sowing a few inches apart and 1 foot (30 cm) out from a sunny wall or trellis around the date of the last spring frost. Thin seedlings to 1 foot (30 cm) apart. Water during dry weather.

Pests & Diseases: None of note.

Impatiens
(Balsaminaceae, *Impatiens* spp)

North America's favorite "annual" is actually a tender perennial (*I. wallerana*) that was scarcely known a generation ago except as a houseplant. Now, there are many hybrids in a range of pale to bright pinks, reds, mauves and oranges, as well as bicolors and white. Impatiens is valued because it is a nonstop bloomer, even in shade, and it sheds fading petals, so it never looks tired. The foliage is glossy and nicely rounded, and plants are just the right height for the front of a border or the edge of a container. They can also be massed as a ground cover under trees or grown in shady containers or window boxes. A grouped planting of a single color looks best. Flowers are edible and add a lovely touch to salads, especially the doubles, which resemble small roses. Balsam (*I. balsamina*) has similar flowers on upright stems about 18 inches (45 cm) tall; 'Tom Thumb' is half that height. New Guinea impatiens (*I. hawkeri; I. petersiana*) grows about 1 foot (30 cm) tall and is more sun-tolerant, with larger dark green, bronze or variegated leaves.

Culture: Impatiens can be grown from seed (though not by the impatient), but plants are available almost everywhere in spring. The seeds need light to germinate, so they must be scattered on moist soil mix 9 to 10 weeks before the last spring frost date. After the last frost, set plants about 8 inches (20 cm) apart, close enough so that they are almost touching. The bare soil between them will be covered as they grow. Keep the soil watered during dry weather for best appearance. In fall, lift plants or root cuttings of favorite cultivars, and keep them in pots indoors till next spring.

Pests & Diseases: None of note.

Iris
(Iridaceae, *Iris* spp)

The fleur-de-lis decorates the spring garden in many forms. First to bloom are the 6-inch-tall (15 cm) species irises, including yellow *I. danfordiae* and purple *I. reticulata*. These gems grow from bulbs that are best planted in fall, at least 4 inches (10 cm) deep, in a sunny, well-drained place.

The common bearded iris (*I. x germanica*) blooms in all colors. There are very tall cultivars, some with huge flowers that need staking. Old-fashioned varieties tend to have smaller flowers that can be left unstaked and often fit better in the garden design. Dwarfs never need staking and are fine in midborder.

Orris root (*I. pallida*) is similar, with lilac-colored flowers. Its rhizomes, dried and powdered, are used as a fragrance fixative in potpourri mixtures. There is a form with variegated foliage.

The Siberian iris (*I. sibirica*) is less well known, yet this hardier species, which overwinters without mulch in zone 3, has many additional virtues. Chief among them is attractive season-long foliage, 2 to 3 feet (0.6-1 m) tall, resembling a clump of wide-bladed, dark green grass. But the flowers are also beautiful: slender and elegant, in clear shades of blue to purple and burgundy.

Culture: The bearded iris grows from a rhizome that needs to be planted just at the soil surface, eyes pointing upward. In cold winter areas, zone 3 or 4, mulch with fallen leaves or grass clippings in autumn. When the clumps become crowded or too large, dig them up in late summer, pull the rhizomes into sections and replant the best ones.

Grow Siberian irises in sun or partial shade, preferably where the soil is not too dry. They are among the few plants that enjoy wet soil, and although they will survive drought, they will not grow as large. They are best by a pond or wherever the flowers are easy to see in late spring. When flowering is finished, the foliage will cover the stems of taller plants growing behind.

Pests & Diseases: The root borer is a troublesome pest of bearded iris that can be combated with beneficial nematodes sold under the brand name Biosafe. Destroy any infected rhizomes. Also, rhizomes growing in constantly wet ground may rot. Cut away damaged portions, and plant in a better-drained area if possible; otherwise, treat the rhizome and surrounding soil with copper dust. A bacterial disease can cause wet, brown lesions to appear on foliage, and viruses can produce streaking and mottling. Cut off affected foliage, or destroy plants that are badly diseased.

Kochia
(Chenopodiaceae, *Kochia scoparia trichophylla*)
Burning Bush
Small, slender leaves are produced so densely that kochia becomes a concentrated oval of green about 2 feet (60 cm) tall by early summer. The flowers are inconspicuous and tiny. In late summer, most kochia foliage turns pink, then dark red, though the cultivar 'Evergreen' stays green.

Culture: Seeds of this fast-growing annual can be sown directly in the ground any time in spring. When the weather warms, plants grow with determination—kochia is a noxious weed in some areas. The central stem is stiff, so the plant can look awkward if it settles into any position but perfectly upright. It looks best grown as a low hedge or behind the front plants in a border. Kochia will self-sow and reappear in most gardens but is easily weeded out.

Pests & Diseases: None of note.

Lavatera
(Malvaceae, *Lavatera trimestris*)
This showy annual is unusual enough to attract attention. Woody stems are self-supporting, foliage is dark green, and blooming can be spectacular.

Lavatera 'Silver Cup' is one of many mallows that grow swiftly from seeds sown in warm soil.

The silky flowers, 2 to 3 inches (5-7.5 cm) wide, are white, pale pink or rose. Most cultivars are about 2 feet (60 cm) tall, but 'Loveliness' can be twice as tall.

There are also species of lavatera that are short-lived perennials. Lavatera 'Barnsley' forms a shrub as tall as 6 feet (2 m) and bears pinkish white flowers from summer till fall. All lavatera species make good cut flowers.

Culture: Lavatera resents transplanting, so it is unlikely to show up as a bedding plant; it should be grown from seeds sown directly in a sunny, sheltered spot in the garden in early summer. In warm, moist soil, plants grow quickly. Thin to 1 foot (30 cm) apart. Blooming lasts for about 4 weeks.

Pests & Diseases: Like all mallows, lavatera may be eaten by rodents and deer.

Leopard's-Bane
(Compositae, *Doronicum columnae*; *D. caucasicum*; *D. cordatum*)
The surprise with leopard's-bane, named for its legendary ability to poison wild cats, is yellow daisies

in spring, when you least expect this dash of summer color. Leopard's-bane is also an easy plant, especially where summers are cool. It is hardy as far north as zone 4, is tolerant of poor soil and will grow anywhere from full sun to partial shade.

Plants grow 1 to 3 feet (0.3-1 m) tall, although the species *D. plantagineum* is somewhat taller. They become dormant in summer, evidenced by a blank spot of soil over their roots, so grow them behind low, leafy plants that will camouflage their quiet season.

Culture: Doronicum is widely available in spring, but you may have to resort to seeds to grow unusual cultivars or species. Seeds need light to germinate. Eight weeks before the last spring frost date, sow seeds on the surface of moist potting soil; they germinate at a temperature of about 70 degrees F (21°C). Leopard's-bane looks best in groups of at least three plants set 1 foot (30 cm) apart.

Pests & Diseases: Slugs and snails eat doronicum foliage. After every rain, sprinkle leaves with diatomaceous earth or spray with a soap solution.

Liatris
(Compositae, *Liatris spicata*)
Blazing Star; Gay-Feather

Liatris is a North American native naturally suited to northern gardens. The common name comes from spikes of feathery pink- or lilac-colored flowers that open from the tip downward in late summer, when many other flowers have faded. Cultivars range in height from 1½ to 3 feet (45-90 cm). Plants will grow in sun or light shade, but well-drained soil is essential, especially for winter survival. In fairly dry soil, liatris is hardy to zone 3. It is an excellent cut flower.

Culture: The most common varieties of liatris are widely available as bedding plants in spring. Additional species can be grown from seed. Liatris dies to the ground in fall and is late to appear in spring. Mark its position to avoid inadvertently

damaging the roots. Divide clumps in spring or fall.
Pests & Diseases: None of note.

Lily
(Liliaceae, *Lilium* spp)

Despite their exotic appearance, lilies are not difficult plants. Many of the showiest lilies are imported, but several species are native to North America and are worth seeking out if you have a wild garden or enjoy the grace of the Turk's-caps or tigers. The imports and the hybrids are easy too. All need well-drained soil and a spot that is not too windy, but they will put up with full sun to light shade. Many are hardy enough for zone 3.

Hybrid lilies are classified by the way their flowers point: upfacing, downfacing or outfacing. Within these three categories, there are flowers in all colors except blue, predominantly in the warm range of pink, yellow, orange, red and cream. Some lilies are fragrant, and most look best when growing in clumps, which they will form on their own, sometimes with surprising speed.

Many lilies grow very tall, 6 feet (2 m) or so, and look best at the back of the border. The foliage gradually fades to brown by the end of the season, when stems can be clipped off close to the ground.

Culture: Plants can be purchased for spring planting, or the bulbs, which may be bigger than your fist, can be planted any time in fall, even when the ground is frozen. The exception is the Madonna lily (*L. candidum*), which must be planted shallowly in early fall. Lily bulbs never become totally dormant, so they should be planted immediately. Plant them in groups of three toward the middle or back of a perennial bed, in large containers or in dappled sun in well-drained soil. Multiply lilies in fall by dividing clumps, by pulling small bulbs off bigger ones or by planting the bulblets that grow in the leaf axils.

Pests & Diseases: Slugs and snails enjoy the young shoots. Control aphids with soap spray. Lilies are vulnerable to virus diseases, which are

Lobelia, top right, is popular on its own or in combination with almost any other potted flowers.

passed on by vegetative reproduction. Growing from seeds eliminates this problem. Growth from seed is slow and is most easily done by sowing the seeds in pots, keeping the soil watered and leaving them outdoors all year.

Lily of the Valley
(Liliaceae, *Convallaria majalis*)
A Victorian favorite, lily of the valley has a sweet fragrance outdoors that lingers indoors when it is cut for small bouquets. Grasslike foliage appears in early spring, followed a month later by small bells, usually white but also pink. Lily of the valley makes a lovely ground cover about 4 inches (10

cm) high in sun or partial shade, but the downside, as with many ground covers, is invasiveness, especially in places where the soil is fertile and winters are cold. If you keep this aggressive little plant away from delicate things and let it spread where little else will grow, under deciduous trees and next to walls, it will reward you with an increasing choir of perfumed bells every spring.

Culture: Plant and divide lily of the valley any time of year.

Pests & Diseases: None of note. Leafcutter bees enjoy the foliage, which they will decorate with scallop-shaped cuts.

Lisianthus
(Gentianaceae, *Eustoma grandiflorum*)
This North American native began to appear in seed catalogs in the 1970s and immediately became popular. The large flowers—deep purple, lilac, white or pink—which look like a marriage of tulips and roses, are loved by flower arrangers. The foliage is

gray-blue. Lisianthus is slender-stemmed and can appear top-heavy in the garden, so it is best grown behind lower plants, such as dianthus or violas. It does best with warmth and light shade. When happy in rich soil, with consistent watering, the standard cultivars can become 2 to 3 feet (0.6-1 m) tall and shrublike. There are also dwarf varieties.

Culture: Lisianthus is available from many nurseries in spring, the best route if possible, because it is a biennial that is slow from seed. The tiny seeds must be started about 5 months before the last spring frost date if plants are to bloom by the end of summer. Seeds germinate at 70 degrees F (21°C). Set plants in the garden when frosty weather has passed.

Pests & Diseases: None of note.

Lobelia
(Lobeliaceae, *Lobelia* spp)

Lobelias, tall and short, are lovers of moisture and shade. The little trailing annual lobelia (*L. erinus*) is almost irreplaceable in window boxes, hanging baskets and containers, especially in the cool, damp, shady conditions it appreciates. Its flowers, in shades of pink, white and especially light or dark blue, are like small jewels on wiry stems 1 foot (30 cm) long. Too much sun, heat or wind, and lobelia fades and may die back until it is revived by cool weather. Frost kills it.

Cardinal flower (*L. cardinalis*) is a very hardy perennial (to about zone 2) for damp places, such as pool edges. The summer flowers are brilliant red, on 3-foot (1 m) spires. *L. siphilitica* grows about the same height, with small blue flowers that resemble monkshood. It is invasive.

Culture: Annual lobelia is widely available as a bedding plant in spring. For a greater cultivar selection, it is easy from seeds sown 8 weeks before the last spring frost date. Sprinkle seeds on moist soil mix, as they need light to germinate at about 70 degrees F (21°C). Set outdoors when the

weather is frost-free. Perennial lobelia seeds must be stratified in the refrigerator for 3 months to encourage germination.

Pests & Diseases: None of note.

Lupin
(Leguminosae, *Lupinus* spp)

Perennial lupins gone wild create a fabulous June show in the eastern provinces and on roadsides in the North, illustrating what can happen when a plant is content enough to self-sow. In gardens, too, *L. regalis* often spreads modestly so that a planting continues even if individuals die. The 3-to-5-foot (1-1.5 m) spires of white, pink, purple, rose, yellow, orange and bicolored flowers and the radiating leaves are equally attractive. There are also dwarf cultivars. Perennial lupin is a welcome sight in the late-spring garden. Less common in northern gardens are a couple of 1-foot-tall (30 cm) annual lupins whose lovely spires sometimes show up in wildflower mixtures: pale lilac *L. nanus* and blue Texas bluebonnet (*L. texensis*).

Culture: Perennial lupin is widely available as a bedding plant in spring. It can also be grown easily from seeds sown indoors or directly in the garden, in the manner of sweet peas (see page 152).

Pests & Diseases: Slugs, snails and green blister beetles enjoy the leaves. Combat mildew with a baking-soda spray (see page 192). Mottled leaves and brown stems are caused by cucumber mosaic virus. Infected plants should be destroyed.

Mallow
(Malvaceae, *Malva* spp)

Lavatera, hibiscus, hollyhock, sidalcea and mallow are all members of the same family, and sometimes it is difficult to tell where one genus leaves off and another begins. All have similar silky flowers, mostly in shades of white through pink, purple and burgundy.

There are several malvas for northern gardens: the 2-to-3-foot (0.6-1 m) musk mallow (*M. moschata*), a wild-looking plant that forms a loose mound; *M. sylvestris*, woody and twice the height; and the 3-foot (1 m) *M.* 'Zebrina,' with striped flowers. Hollyhock mallow (*M. alcea* 'Fastigiata') has 2-inch (5 cm) summer flowers on 3-foot (1 m) upright stems.

Culture: All mallows are short-lived perennials that can be grown as hardy annuals, and most will spread by seed. They are easy from seeds sown indoors a month before the last spring frost date or directly in the garden in late spring. Give them sun or partial shade in an area sheltered from strong winds, and water regularly. They also benefit from fertilizing every 2 weeks throughout spring and early summer.

Pests & Diseases: Mallows are entirely edible, so they are among the first choice of deer and rodents. If predation is a problem, spray with cayenne pepper after each rain.

Marigold

(Compositae, *Tagetes* spp)
Marigolds are sunny, generous bloomers that bring joy and innocence to the garden and demand very little work, especially if you buy bedding plants in the spring.

The African, or American, marigolds (*T. erecta*) are among the most dramatic. The 'Climax' series, for instance, are taller than 3 feet (1 m) but do not need staking. American marigolds bloom in colors from cream to yellow and orange, all semidouble or double.

Triploid marigolds offer larger flowers that bloom early and, because they are sterile, continue blooming throughout the season until frost.

The smaller species include the so-called French marigolds (*T. patula*), which are often bicolored and may be delightful singles, such as the orange-and-mahogany 'Granada.' Another group of single marigolds with innocent charm is the 'Gem' series of signet marigolds (*T. signata*), which are perfect for sunny pots and window boxes. Heights vary

from 8 to 12 inches (20-30 cm), and flowers are 1 to 2 inches (2.5-5 cm) wide. These marigolds produce plenty of seeds that can be gathered for next year. Irish lace (*T. tenuifolia*) forms a small globe of fragrant, ferny foliage and just a few small flowers.

Marigolds are effective along a driveway, in a sunny border or edging a vegetable garden, where they can help control nematodes. They make long-lasting but slightly malodorous vase flowers.

Culture: Bedding plants are widely available in spring, but for greater variety, start seeds indoors 2 months before the last spring frost date or sow smaller types directly in the garden in late spring. Seeds germinate at a soil temperature of 75 to 80 degrees F (24-27°C). Plant outdoors in well-drained soil in sun after the last spring frost.

Pests & Diseases: Red spider mites can be combated with an insecticidal soap spray. Near the end of the season, flowers may be infected with botrytis, a fungal disease that turns the base of the petals brown. The simplest way to control the disease is to remove spent flower heads.

Monarda

(Labiatae, *Monarda didyma*; *M. fistulosa*)
Bee Balm; Bergamot
This North American native perennial, about 3 feet (1 m) tall, is distinctive, with large flowers, usually scarlet or pink, and fragrant, lemony foliage that can be used to make herbal tea. There are several cultivars, including dwarfs, but the species are as beautiful as any. The tall varieties look best on their own or in a clump at the back of a perennial border.

Culture: Monarda is easily grown from seeds started indoors 8 weeks before the last spring frost date, but established plantings can be divided, so plants are often available in spring. Give plants good soil in full sun. Monarda is one of the few

Morning glory 'Heavenly Blue' quickly clambers to 10 feet (3 m) after an early-summer seeding.

perennials that does well in constant dampness.
Pests & Diseases: Mildew may infest entire plants or just the lower leaves, especially in dry places with poor air circulation. It may be necessary to move the entire clump to a better position.

Monkshood

(Ranunculaceae, *Aconitum napellus*)
One of the most poisonous plants in the garden is also one of the most beautiful, with a mound of finely divided foliage in spring, followed by tall spires of hooded flowers, usually blue, in late summer. There are species and varieties of monkshood from 1 to 6 feet (0.3-2 m) tall, including the 6-foot (2 m) *A. carmichaelii* and the yellow *A. vulparia*.

The so-called winter aconite, a hardy tuber with beautiful bright yellow flowers in early spring, is *Eranthis hyemalis*, not a true aconite at all, though it is a member of the same family, Ranunculaceae, and the foliage is similar.

Culture: Monkshood appreciates moist, rich soil in partial shade. Water during dry summers, and feed in spring with a topdressing of manure or compost. Tall stems require staking. Plants do not move or divide well, and growing from seeds is somewhat difficult. The easiest route is to obtain plants in spring or to sow seeds in fall in pots that are left outdoors all winter.
Pests & Diseases: None of note.

Moonflower

(Polemoniaceae, *Ipomoea alba*)
Moonflower is an annual vine much like its cousin, the morning glory, except its flowers are larger and creamy white in color, and they open in late afternoon. Each flower lasts just one night and will wilt by late morning of the next day. There are many buds, however, so flowers continue to appear all summer till frost.
Culture: Moonflower seeds can be sown indoors in spring, then set in the garden a month later, around the last frost date. Or the big seeds can be sown directly in the garden when the soil is warm and the nights frost-free. The vines grow about 4 feet (1.2 m) tall and require a trellis, shrub or vertical strings to twine around.
Pests & Diseases: None of note.

Morning Glory

(Polemoniaceae, *Ipomoea* spp)
The Northerner's most popular annual flowering vine is a frost-tender tropical native that grows so quickly and flowers so abundantly that the bit of work involved in sowing a few seeds in early summer is well worthwhile. Choose a place near a trellis, woody shrub or other support; otherwise, morning glories will climb up and ramble over neighboring plants. Vines grow about 10 feet (3 m) tall, though some species are smaller. Flowers bloom just a day apiece, but new buds form as long

as the weather is warm. *I. tricolor* 'Heavenly Blue' brings surprising sky-blue to the garden, but there are also lovely pinks, reds and creams.

Culture: Sow seeds indoors in peat pots 4 weeks early or directly outdoors as soon as the soil is warm in spring; they require a soil temperature of 70 to 80 degrees F (21-27°C) to germinate. Soak the seeds overnight before sowing to encourage germination. Thin plants to stand 1 foot (30 cm) apart. Plants are rapidly killed by frost. Morning glories sometimes self-sow.

Pests & Diseases: None of note.

Nasturtium

(Tropaeolaceae, *Tropaeolum majus*)

The lily-pad foliage and the distinctively shaped flowers are as pretty in a flower garden, window box or hanging basket as at bed ends in a vegetable garden, a traditional spot for this edible flower. Seed pods can be pickled as a substitute for capers, and both flowers and foliage have a peppery flavor reminiscent of a relative, watercress. Most varieties form a low bush that suits a border edge— *T. m. nanum* 'Alaska' has variegated foliage—but there are also vining types that will climb a trellis or vertical strings to about 6 feet (2 m). Most nasturtiums are sold in color mixtures, though single colors are available by mail order.

Culture: Nasturtiums are sold as bedding plants in spring, or you can grow them from seeds, a good idea if you want a quantity. The big seeds need darkness to germinate, so sow them about ½ inch (1 cm) deep. They can go directly in the garden after the last frost. Seeds sprout when the soil warms to 65 to 70 degrees F (18-21°C), begin to bloom a few weeks later and continue steadily until fall frost. Nasturtiums do best in a sunny place but should not be allowed to dry out. They often give their best show when summer's hottest days

have passed and autumn rains have begun to fall.

Pests & Diseases: None of note.

Nicotiana; Flowering Tobacco

(Solanaceae, *Nicotiana* spp)

Although the best-known types of nicotiana are only about 1 foot (30 cm) tall, with blooms in shades of pink, mauve, red, yellow and white, there are several taller white types that are more graceful and more fragrant. All nicotianas have tubular flowers. In general, the taller the plant, the longer the flower—to foot-long (30 cm) trumpets on the 8-foot (2.5 m) *N. sylvestris*. *N. affinis*, or *N. alata grandiflora*, grows 2 to 3 feet (0.6-1 m) tall, with long, slender white bells that are freshest in late afternoon and evening. This species and *N. sylvestris* are sweetly perfumed.

Culture: Nicotiana hybrids are widely available as bedding plants in spring, but you must grow more unusual species from seed. Nicotiana seed is very fine. Sprinkle it on the surface of moist potting soil 3 months before the last spring frost date or directly on damp garden soil in early spring. Thin seedlings later on so that plants just touch as they grow. The plants often self-sow in the garden, to bloom again the next year.

The usual types sold as spring bedding plants are *N. alata* hybrids, including the popular 'Nicki' series. Plant them 6 inches (15 cm) apart in good soil in sun. Deadhead plants regularly.

Pests & Diseases: Nicotiana occasionally attracts stray Colorado potato beetles. Hand-pick, or spray with rotenone.

Painted Tongue

(Solanaceae, *Salpiglossis sinuata*)

This annual looks much like its cousin, the petunia, but painted tongue is taller and more upright, with streaked petals. Plants grow 2 to 3 feet (0.6-1 m) tall but do not need staking. Painted tongue thrives in cooler conditions than those that suit petunias.

Culture: Plants are available from larger nurseries in spring. Alternatively, painted tongue seeds can be sown directly in the garden around the last spring frost date or, for early flowers, indoors 8 weeks ahead. Seeds need darkness and a temperature of 70 to 75 degrees F (21-24°C) to germinate. After frost, group plants 1 foot (30 cm) apart in a sunny or partly shaded, sheltered place.

Pests & Diseases: None of note.

Pansy

See Violet.

Penstemon

(Scrophulariaceae, *Penstemon* spp)
Beardtongue

Penstemons are a varied group of perennials that are becoming increasingly popular as more enter the nursery trade. Their tubular flowers resemble foxgloves and attract hummingbirds. Flowers may be white, pink, blue, purple, yellow, red or orange. Easiest to find is *P. digitalis*, a showy herbaceous plant that grows roughly 3 feet (1 m) high and half as wide. It has finger-sized white flowers. 'Husker Red' has bronze foliage and was chosen plant of the year for 1996 by the Perennial Plant Association.

Culture: Most penstemons are North American natives of rocky slopes and other well-drained soils, so they are somewhat drought-tolerant, dislike wet soil and require full sun. Plants are available from a few nurseries, but for a greater variety, grow them from seeds, available from specialist suppliers (see Sources). Seeds can be sown in pots in fall and left outdoors all winter.

Pests & Diseases: None of note.

Peony

(Paeoniaceae, *Paeonia* spp)

Considering their exotic appearance, peonies are surprisingly hardy, surviving even in abandoned gardens as far north as zone 4. The flowers may be single or double, white to pink, rose or purple and up to 6 inches (15 cm) wide. Yellow peonies are harder to find but worth the search, because they are fragrant. Japanese peonies have contrasting colors in outer and inner petals.

Peonies are shrubby plants that grow 2 to 3 feet (0.6-1 m) tall. Although flowering lasts only about 2 weeks in late spring, the attractive, dark green foliage persists till fall, when it turns brown. Grow peonies along a driveway, as specimen plants or in the middle of the perennial bed.

Culture: Obtain plants in spring, and set in a sunny place in fertile, well-drained soil. Peonies are long-lived perennials, so early soil preparation is important. Peony flowers, particularly doubles, are so heavy that their stems often bend to the ground, especially after a rain. To prop them up, surround the entire plants in spring with tomato cages or circles of stakes and strings that will be hidden in the foliage as the plants grow. Little additional care is required. Cut flower stems off at the base when flowers are spent. Cut the dead foliage and stems back to the ground in fall or spring. Partly open flowers can be hung to dry.

Pests & Diseases: In northern gardens, where summers are fairly dry and winters are cold, the peony is usually problem-free, but in wet weather, fungal diseases may attack the plant, producing a gray mold or purple or brown spots on leaves and sometimes preventing flowers from opening. Pick off moldy leaves and flowers, and spray with baking-soda solution (see page 192). Late-spring frost can also prevent flowers from opening fully.

Periwinkle

(Apocynaceae, *Vinca minor*)
Myrtle

Periwinkle is one of the few herbaceous ground covers that are evergreen in most northern gardens. Dig under the snow, and its leathery green leaves are revealed. It is also valued for long-season attractiveness in shade but will tolerate full sun if

The fleeting beauty of annual corn, or Shirley, poppies is a highlight of the northern flower garden.

it is not too hot and dry. In June, 1-inch (2.5 cm) flowers bloom, usually periwinkle-blue. Other species, cultivars and colors are less hardy. Stems grow outward, rooting wherever the nodes touch the soil. Eventually, periwinkle forms a fairly solid mat 1 foot (30 cm) deep that swamps small flowers, though tall perennials and hardy bulbs will bloom through it.

Culture: Periwinkle is widely available as a bedding plant in spring. After the second or third season, rooted stems can be snipped from the mother plant and planted elsewhere.

Pests & Diseases: None of note.

Petunia

(Solanaceae, *Petunia* x *hybrida*)

Petunias are justifiably popular for their provision of color from the time they begin blooming in late spring till after a few fall frosts. The grandifloras have big, floppy flowers as wide as 5 inches (13 cm); the multifloras produce smaller flowers, about 3 inches (7.5 cm) wide, and the millifloras, such as the 'Fantasy' series, have the smallest flower of all, only 1 inch (2.5 cm) wide. Multifloras and millifloras flower in greater profusion, are more dependable in rainy weather and are easier to balance in a garden design than are grandifloras. There are also low-growing spreading petunias, such as the surfinias, 'Purple Wave' and the 'Supercascade' series. White, blue and lilac cultivars are sweetly fragrant in late afternoon and evening, so they are ideal near a patio or path or in window boxes.

Culture: A wide and varied selection is sold as bedding plants, but nurseries favor the cultivars, mostly grandifloras, that bloom early enough to be sold already flowering. Surfinias cannot be grown from seed, but all the others can, including some that self-sow freely, such as 'Snowball,' from J.L. Hudson (see Sources). Sow seeds on the surface of moist soil mix 8 weeks before the last spring frost date at a temperature of 70 to 80 degrees F (21-27°C). Plant petunias 6 inches (15 cm) apart in sun or light shade. Pinch stems back to encourage bushiness.

Pests & Diseases: None of note. Stray Colorado potato beetles may show up occasionally. Handpick, or dust with rotenone.

Phlox

(Polemoniaceae, *Phlox* spp)

There are annual and perennial phlox for the northern garden. The annual *P. drummondii* blooms in all pastel shades from spring till fall, the dwarfs on 6-inch (15 cm) stems, the grandifloras twice as tall. Annual phlox tolerates dry soil.

Perennial phlox (*P. paniculata*) grows 2 to 4 feet (0.6-1.2 m) tall, with clusters of pink, white or rose flowers on stem tips in early summer. It does not require staking. Grow perennial phlox behind plants with long-lasting foliage, such as peonies or Siberian irises.

Moss phlox (*P. subulata*) is a very hardy ground cover for the border front. Its ½-inch (1 cm) flowers are rose, white, purple, red or pink in spring. The ground-hugging finely cut foliage is evergreen where winters are not too harsh. Cut it back after flowering, and divide in fall.

Culture: Annual phlox is easy from seeds sown directly outdoors in early May or indoors a month before the last spring frost date. Space plants 6 inches (15 cm) apart in groups or rows in full sun or a little shade. Seeds of perennial phlox must freeze before they will germinate; sow them in pots in fall and leave them outdoors. Germination begins in spring, when the soil temperature reaches about 70 degrees F (21°C). Set plants 1 foot (30 cm) apart in a sunny place with good, well-drained soil. Self-sown seedlings usually revert to magenta flowers, so they should be removed unless you want that wildflower color. Divide the clumps every few years.

Pests & Diseases: Hot, humid weather encourages powdery mildew, which causes the lower leaves to discolor and drop off. Leaf spot disfigures leaves with colored round or oval spots. Spray regularly with baking-soda solution (see page 192).

Poppy

(Papaveraceae, *Eschscholtzia californica*; *Papaver* spp)

There are many poppies for northern gardens, annual and perennial, tall and short. What they have in common is lovely, silky-petaled flowers in jewel tones. Generally, poppies are a resilient group, lovers of sun that are tolerant of heat, drought and poor soil, but they resent transplanting, and each flower lasts only a day. They look best grown in groups, either on their own or in the company of longer-lasting annuals, perennials and shrubs.

Among the annuals are California poppies (*Eschscholtzia californica*), with soft stems about 1 foot (30 cm) long and feathery, bluish foliage. The species is orange or gold, but pinks and crimsons have been developed. Shirley, Flanders or corn poppies (*Papaver rhoeas*) are twice as tall, with stiff, hairy stems supporting flowers in shades of red through pink, lavender, purple and white. Opium poppies (*P. somniferum*), sometimes called peony or carnation poppies in their double form, are taller still, up to 4 feet (1.2 m), with smooth stems and flowers that are correspondingly large, single or double, sometimes with a dark spot at the petal base. The big ornamental seed pods contain edible seeds used in pastries and cakes.

Among the perennials are Iceland poppies (*P. nudicaule*), which are hardy but often short-lived. They grow 1 to 2 feet (30-60 cm) tall, with early summer flowers in warm shades of yellow, orange, pink, red and white. Alpine poppies are smaller versions. Biggest of the perennials is the Oriental poppy (*P. orientale*), with stems as tall as 5 feet (1.5 m), bearing big white, pink, orange, salmon or scarlet flowers. These early-summer showstoppers can be invasive but are fairly easy to rout out. All poppies make good vase flowers that will last longer if you singe the cut stem ends with a match or hot water.

Culture: The annuals are easy to grow from seeds sprinkled on the ground any time in winter or spring. They will self-sow if some seed pods are left on the plants, or you can collect pods to save your own seeds. Plants of the perennial types can be obtained in spring, but they are also easy from seeds. Again, they are best sown outdoors, *in situ*, in early spring, because poppies suffer from transplanting. Scatter the seeds on the soil surface, and keep the area watered until germination occurs at a temperature of about 55 degrees F (13°C). Thin seedlings gradually so that plants are never closer than just touching.

Pests & Diseases: Leaf spot, caused by a number of diseases, may disfigure leaves with colored round or oval spots. Spray with baking-soda solution (see page 192).

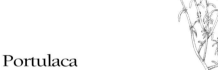

Portulaca
(Portulacaceae, *Portulaca grandiflora*)
Moss Rose

Portulaca is a self-reliant annual ground hugger that thrives in heat, even drought, and so is excellent anywhere you are not likely to water: beside a driveway, between the stones in a pathway, at the front of a sunny border, in a patio container. Above small, fleshy leaves, portulaca flashes some of the brightest colors in the garden, like little neon lights—pink, orange, red, yellow and white. It is one of the few flowers that look as good grown in a mixture of colors as a single tint.

Flowers open in the morning and bloom till afternoon. Older cultivars closed when the sun did not shine, but 'Cloudbeater' and other new cultivars stay open whatever the weather. Flowers are

2½ inches (6.3 cm) wide. Plants spread about 1 foot (30 cm) wide and grow into a mat 6 to 8 inches (15-20 cm) tall.

Culture: Buy portulacas as bedding plants in spring, or sprinkle seeds in the garden after the last spring frost. Flowers bloom about 8 weeks after sowing and may self-sow. Grow portulacas in masses, close enough so that they will overlap. Their only demand is well-drained soil. This is a desert plant that does poorly with too much rain or prolonged cold.

Pests & Diseases: None of note.

Primrose
(Primulaceae, *Primula* spp)

Lovers of shade and damp soil, the true primroses—as opposed to evening primroses and other flowers that borrow the name—bring an assortment of bright colors to the spring garden. Most common are the polyanthus primroses, which bear a bouquet of upward-facing flowers in all colors and combinations over a basal rosette of crinkly green leaves. Hardiness varies and depends in part on plant size; the 'Pacific Giant' hybrids are some of the hardiest. Most species are hardy to at least minus 31 degrees F (–35°C), especially under mulch. Primulas are best used as a ground cover under leafy trees or along the edge of a shady path.

There are many additional hardy perennials. Gardeners with moist, shady gardens should search specialist seed catalogs and nurseries for species such as 9-inch (23 cm) *P. auricula*, 2-to-3-foot (0.6-1 m) *P. bulleyana*, 2-foot (60 cm) fragrant white *P. chionantha,* the drumstick primrose (*P. denticulata*) and the common primrose of English hedgerows, *P. vulgaris.*

German primrose (*P. obconica*) is an annual with 1-inch-wide (2.5 cm) flowers and frilled leaves. Growing from seed is very slow, so the best route is purchased plants, which can be set in the ground as soon as the soil can be worked in early spring. Space plants 6 inches (15 cm) apart in shade. Mulch to keep the soil cool and damp. *P. obconica* causes dermatitis in some people. Wear gloves when tending the plants. *P. malacoides*, another annual that is available flowering in pots around Christmastime, can also move into the garden in spring and does not cause dermatitis.

Culture: Plants of some of the more common primulas are widely available in spring. To grow primulas from seed, sprinkle seeds on the surface of moist soil mix in pots 3 months before the last spring frost date. Place pots in plastic bags in the refrigerator for 2 days, then move to a greenhouse or windowsill. Seeds need cold before they will germinate, which occurs when the soil warms to about 55 to 60 degrees F (13-15°C). Keep soil constantly moist. Seedlings can be planted in the garden as soon as the soil can be worked. Give them soil rich in organic matter in a sheltered, partly shaded place. If frost threatens during blooming, cover the flowers till the danger is past. After a few years, plants can be divided in early summer as soon as they have finished blooming.

Pests & Diseases: Leaf spot, caused by a number of diseases, may disfigure foliage with colored round or oval spots. Spray with baking-soda solution (see page 192).

Purple Coneflower

(Compositae, *Echinacea purpurea*)
Beautiful and medicinal—the roots have antibiotic properties—purple coneflower is a native North American hardy perennial that is easy to grow. It has distinctive downward-slanting mauve petals and protruding orange-brown centers that have caused some confusion with the genus *Rudbeckia*. There are also white cultivars.

Stems may grow as tall as 4 feet (1.2 m) but are generally self-supporting. Smaller cultivars have been developed. Give purple coneflower full sun or partial shade, and grow it in front of a wall, in the company of other tall daisies or against a backdrop of evergreens that will complement its subtle colors.

Culture: Purple coneflower is now quite common as a bedding plant in spring. It is also easy

from seed, though blooming will likely take 2 years. Sow seeds indoors 8 weeks before the last spring frost date. Germination takes place at 70 to 75 degrees F (21-24°C). Set plants in the garden 1 foot (30 cm) apart around the last spring frost date. Purple coneflower does best with weekly waterings throughout summer, though it will survive a short drought and self-sows modestly where it is content.

Pests & Diseases: None of note.

Rose

(Rosaceae, *Rosa* spp)
A rose may be a *Rosa*, but roses vary enormously in color and size, from tiny to huge, hardy to tender. What all have in common is a need for fertile, absolutely well-drained soil in a place that has at least 6 hours of sun a day but is not too windy.

Hybrid tea roses, floribundas and grandifloras are generally fairly difficult to overwinter in all but the mildest places. Antique, heirloom and wild, or species, roses may be hardier, but their shortcoming is that they bloom just once, usually in June or July. They are best in a wild garden or at the back of a bed of lower perennials, where it won't matter that all they can offer most of the year is foliage. The flowers are usually fabulous.

Miniature roses are smaller versions of regular roses, no bigger than 2 feet (60 cm) tall. They are perfect along formal pathways, at border fronts and in containers, indoors or out, but they can look out of place amid wildflowers or large perennials. Their winter hardiness varies, so when overwintering them outdoors anywhere from zone 6 north, play it safe and cover them heavily with mulch in fall.

Climbing roses do not cling to supports the way many vines do. They need some training and tying as they grow. Their hooked thorns help them hang on, thanks to the weight of the stems. In places where climbing roses are marginally hardy, grow them near a south- or east-facing wall. Prune them back in late fall to about 1 foot (30 cm) from the ground, or pull them down and cover with mulch.

British gardener David Austin produced a 20th-century series of English roses that resemble old-fashioned roses in appearance and fragrance but bloom longer and are more disease-resistant. Some are also quite winter-hardy. There are scores in all colors and sizes, but one of the most popular is the golden yellow 'Graham Thomas.' The plant is bushy and upright and grows to 6 feet (2 m) tall, with glossy, dark green foliage. 'Graham Thomas' is hardy to zone 5.

Breeding programs in the American Midwest and Canada have produced dozens of extremely hardy, disease-resistant cultivars that are beautiful and recurrent in flowering and can survive northern winters without mulch. Some of the best are the Explorer series, developed in Ontario and Quebec, and the Parkland series, from Manitoba. Alberta offers another winner, 'Therese Bugnet,' with pale pink double flowers on a 6-foot (2 m) shrub.

This is one of many tough though brief-blooming hybrids of *R. rugosa*, which can survive prairie winters without protection. Among the best are the fragrant, double white 'Blanc Double de Coubert,' 4 to 6 feet (1.2-2 m) tall, and, for single pink flowers, 'Frau Dagmar Hastrup,' which also produces red hips in abundance.

Culture: Buy roses in spring from local nurseries or from mail-order sources that specialize in them. Plant in rich, deeply dug, well-drained soil in full sun, and leave a 1-foot-wide (30 cm) area mulched around the stem so that no other plants compete. Water regularly, and fertilize with manure tea or fish fertilizer every 2 weeks from April until July. In cold-winter areas, be sure the graft—the bulge on the stem where the named variety was grafted onto the roots—is at least 2 inches (5 cm) below the soil surface. (Some roses are not grafted.) In late fall, if your roses are marginally hardy for your area, prune the plants back and cover with soil, straw or pine boughs to help them survive the winter.

Pests & Diseases: Roses are among the most disease-susceptible of garden flowers. Black spot is a disfiguring fungal ailment that turns stem tips black. Rust is another common disease that may discolor leaf edges. Use a sulfur spray in spring,

and apply a baking-soda solution weekly (see page 192). If you are watering late in the day, do not wet the foliage. Newer varieties are often selected for disease resistance. Read the catalog descriptions.

Rose Campion

(Caryophyllaceae, *Lychnis* spp)
Campion; Jerusalem Cross; Maltese Cross
The foliage of rose campion (*L. coronaria*) is fuzzy and gray, so plants resemble lamb's ears (*Stachys lanata*) in spring, but the surprise in early summer is bright magenta flowers on 18-inch (45 cm) stems. Rose campion will self-sow in most gardens and is easily routed out where it is not wanted.

There are several additional perennial *Lychnis* species for Northerners. What they have in common is jewel-toned pink or red flowers. Other than that, they vary widely. The best-known, Jerusalem cross (*L. chalcedonica*), is 3 feet (1 m) tall, with summer clusters of flowers that are usually bright red but may be pink, white or violet. It tolerates wet ground.

Culture: Lychnis does best in full sun. Seeds need chilling, so they should be sown directly in the garden or in pots in fall. Sprinkle seeds on the ground. They need light and a temperature of 70 degrees F (21°C) to germinate. In spring, set plants 8 inches (20 cm) apart.

Pests & Diseases: None of note.

Rudbeckia

(Compositae, *Rudbeckia* spp)
Black-Eyed Susan; Coneflower; Gloriosa Daisy; Golden-Glow
Rudbeckia resembles a small sunflower, with hairy leaves, golden rays and slightly conical centers that are usually dark. The perennial is *R. fulgida* 'Goldsturm.' The annual is *R. hirta*, which may act like a biennial, forming a fuzzy rosette of foliage the first year and blooming the second. Plants grow

Single rudbeckia often self-sows to grace next summer's garden with sunny drifts of long-lasting color.

into clumps about 3 feet (1 m) high and wide. Flowers may be wider than 5 inches (13 cm). The All-America Selection 'Indian Summer' produces 9-inch (23 cm) flowers on 3-foot (1 m) stems that do not need staking. There are also dwarf and double cultivars. *R. hirta* often self-sows, creating drifts of long-lasting sunny color in midsummer. Both are excellent cut flowers that last for weeks.

Culture: Plants are often available in spring, and either type can be grown from seeds sown indoors about 6 weeks before the last spring frost date. Set plants outdoors in well-drained soil in full sun.

A favorite farmyard perennial is golden-glow (*R. laciniata*). It does not produce seeds and must be grown from divisions, but where happy, it is a permanent resident, producing impressive, often self-supporting 6-to-8-foot (2-2.5 m) stalks topped with golden double daisies in summer. It can be invasive. **Pests & Diseases:** None of note.

Russian Sage

(Labiatae, *Perovskia atriplicifolia*)

A recent arrival on the horticultural scene, Russian sage was voted Perennial of the Year for 1995 by the Perennial Plant Association, because it is adaptable to almost all conditions, will grow as far north as zone 3 and is ornamental for a long season. It is very heat- and drought-resistant and appreciates full sun; plants tend to be leggy and sprawling in shade. Russian sage has an airy, shrubby form to about 4 feet (1.2 m) tall. The foliage is grayish, a little like a tall perennial dusty miller. The blue flower spikes, which are pretty but not showy, appear in late summer and early fall and often continue blooming till late fall. Plants look best in groups or grown toward the back of a border in sun.

Culture: The usual way to start with Russian sage is to obtain plants in spring. Dipped in rooting hormone, tip cuttings of new growth root easily in peat pots under glass in a shady place in summer. Seeds are available from a few specialists, such as Thompson & Morgan (see Sources).

Pests & Diseases: None of note.

Salvia

(Labiatae, *Salvia* spp)

There are both annual and perennial salvias in a range of colors. Most have vertical flower spires and are good plants for hot, relatively dry gardens, although they also tolerate partial shade and considerable moisture.

Annual salvia, or scarlet sage (*S. splendens*), can fill the middle of a garden bed or define the edges of a pathway with brilliant color. This easy annual blooms soon after planting and continues till the first fall frost. The flowers are borne on vertical spikes. Eventual height depends on the cultivar: dwarfs are 8 inches (20 cm) tall, while the later bloomers may be as tall as 2 feet (60 cm). Brilliant orange-red or blood-red are the usual colors, but there are also lavender, salmon, purple, rose, cream and bicolors. Salvia is most attractive when massed together, especially just one color. Set plants 8 inches (20 cm) apart.

The best hardy perennial sage is *S. x superba*, available in blue or white. The plant grows 2 feet (60 cm) tall and about half as wide and is self-supporting, with thin, densely flowered spikes in early summer. Cut the spikes back after flowering. The foliage is grayish and has an aroma reminiscent of cooking sage. Give it full sun or partial shade. Another hardy perennial, *S. horminum*, has 18-inch (45 cm) spikes of florets that resemble insect wings. Perennial salvias can be massed in the middle of a flower border or grown as specimens on their own.

Culture: If you are growing annual salvia from seed, sow the seeds on the soil surface; they need light to germinate and a temperature of 68 to 80 degrees F (20-27°C). Perennial salvias are variable from seed and best grown from divisions or cuttings. The perennial species *S. farinacea*, which is less hardy, cannot be grown from seed at all, because the plant is sterile.

Pests & Diseases: None of note.

Sanvitalia

(Compositae, *Sanvitalia procumbens*)
Creeping Zinnia

Sanvitalia is an excellent annual ground cover for the front of a dry, sunny border. Plants grow about 6 inches (15 cm) high and 1 foot (30 cm) wide, with trailing stems and yellow or orange daisies 1 inch (2.5 cm) wide.

Culture: Sow seeds directly in the garden in a sunny place in well-drained soil after the last spring frost, or start seeds indoors 2 months earlier by sprinkling on the soil surface. They need light to germinate and a temperature of about 70 degrees F (21°C). Transplant with as large a rootball as possible, since sanvitalia roots are easily damaged.

Pests & Diseases: None of note.

Scabiosa

(Dipsacaceae, *Scabiosa* spp)
Pincushion Flower

Scabiosa is not well known, yet some of these flowers, in shades of lilac and blue and also white, are very hardy and interesting, resembling a cross between a daisy and a poppy. The stamens stick up like pins in a cushion, inspiring its common name, pincushion flower. There are annual and perennial types, all unusual enough to attract attention. *S. caucasica* is a hardy perennial that grows 2 to 3 feet (0.6-1 m) tall, depending on the cultivar. Slender stalks bearing 2-inch-wide (5 cm) flowers grow

Drought-tolerant and requiring almost no care, sedum 'Autumn Joy' brings weeks of late-summer color.

from a clump of grayish foliage. The annual version is *S. atropurpurea*.

Culture: The easiest way to grow scabiosa from seed is to sow seeds outdoors in pots or directly in the garden after the last spring frost. Space plants 1 foot (30 cm) apart. Annuals bloom the same year; perennials bloom the summer of the following year. Scabiosa does best in slightly alkaline soil with good drainage and with watering during dry weather.

Pests & Diseases: None of note.

Scilla
(Liliaceae, *Scilla* spp)
Squill
This hardy bulb can form a blanket of sky-blue in spring. Individual flowers are small and delicate,

but where it is happy and undisturbed, scilla will multiply. It grows less than 8 inches (20 cm) tall, with several stems from each bulb, and looks best at the front of a border, under deciduous shrubs or in pots. *S. sibirica* is hardy to zone 3. There are taller, less hardy species, and flowers may be pink or white.

Culture: Plant scilla in fall in groups, with bulbs a few inches apart and 3 to 4 inches (7.5-10 cm) deep. Plant some in pots to bring indoors in January.

Pests & Diseases: None of note.

Sedum
(Crassulaceae, *Sedum* spp)
Stonecrop
Many types of sedum are ideal ground covers for sunny, dry gardens. Drought-tolerant, hardy and colorful, with yellow, red, pink or purple flowers, and easy to rout out if they spread too far, sedums are popular for border fronts and rock gardens. Among the ground-hugging types are: *S. acre*, a determined 2-inch-high (5 cm) spreader with bright

yellow flowers, sometimes allowed to spread in lawns; *S. kamtschaticum*, larger and less invasive, also with yellow flowers; *S. spurium* 'Dragon's Blood,' with purple foliage and magenta flowers; and *S.* 'Ruby Glow,' 1 foot (30 cm) tall with green foliage and red flowers.

A taller upright type, *S. spectabile,* is available in several cultivars, including the green-and-gold variegated 'Brilliant' and the hybrid 'Autumn Joy.' Long-lasting clumps of dark to light pink flowers bloom in late summer on stems 2 to 3 feet (0.6-1 m) tall. Flowers cut just before they open will last for weeks in a vase indoors and may take root to yield more garden plants next spring.

Culture: Several species and varieties are commonly available as spring bedding plants. Sedums are easy to divide in spring or fall. Several can also be grown from seed, a method that is easy but slow. Check the larger flower catalogs for seed, which is often available in mixtures. Seeds can be sown on the soil surface directly outdoors in early spring. Germination occurs at about 50 degrees F (10°C).

Pests & Diseases: None of note.

Shasta Daisy

See Chrysanthemum.

Snakeroot

(Ranunculaceae, *Cimicifuga* spp)

Black Snakeroot; Bugbane

Six-foot (2 m) spires of white flowers grow from snakeroot (*C. racemosa*), a North American native that is one of the few tall perennials that love shade. It has purplish foliage and looks best in groups rather than grown as single specimens. Set plants 2 feet (60 cm) apart near a shady wall or at the back of a partly shaded perennial border. *C. americana* grows about half as tall. Snakeroot blooms in summer in warmer zones, later in the cooler parts of its range, continuing for about a month.

Culture: Plants are available in spring from specialty nurseries. Seeds can be purchased from large seed houses, such as Thompson & Morgan (see Sources), but seeds are slow to germinate. The best method is to sow seeds in moist soil in pots and leave the pots outdoors in a sheltered place over the winter. Given moist soil, snakeroot, once established,

is impressive and requires virtually no attention.

Pests & Diseases: Fungal diseases can cause brown leaf spots. Spray with baking-soda solution (see page 192).

Snapdragon

(Scrophulariaceae, *Antirrhinum majus*)

This native of the Mediterranean and southern Europe has been grown for centuries for its edible oil. It is better appreciated now for a wide spectrum of long-lasting colors in the summer garden. Best-looking are the single flowers—the Latin name means "like a snout"; the Chinese name means "goldfish flower," because when you squeeze the flower at the sides, its "muzzle" opens. There are both standard and dwarf types. The latter are bushy and may be only 6 inches (15 cm) tall, while standards can reach 4 feet (1.2 m), perfect for cutting. In the garden, they need staking to keep them upright in wind and rain.

Culture: Snapdragons are widely available as bedding plants in spring, are easy from seed and often reappear where they grew last year. Indoors, 8 weeks before the last spring frost date, sow seeds on the soil surface; they need light and a temperature of 65 to 75 degrees F (18-24°C) to germinate. They go outdoors at about 3 inches (7.5 cm) tall and can withstand light frost. Give snapdragons sun or light shade and moderately rich, well-drained soil. They fare best in cool weather and may stop blooming in summer's heat.

Pests & Diseases: Downy mildew may be a problem in damp weather. Remove affected plants, or spray with baking-soda solution (see page 192).

Snowdrop

(Amaryllidaceae, *Galanthus nivalis*)

The first sign of spring in many northern gardens is slender stalks sporting fragrant white bells emerging through the snow, usually in April or May. Spring snow and frost do not harm snowdrops.

All stocks, including the so-called 10-week stocks, are easy from seeds sown in the spring garden.

Most are small and single, but 'Flore Pleno' bears double flowers and can reach 1 foot (30 cm) tall.

Culture: In fall, plant clusters of snowdrop bulbs about 3 inches (7.5 cm) deep along pathways, under shrubs or deciduous trees and in pots. Bulbs gradually spread to form clumps, and flowers also spread by seed. Snowdrop division must be done immediately after flowering, while there are still green leaves on the bulbs.

Pests & Diseases: None of note.

Snow-in-Summer

(Caryophyllaceae, *Cerastium tomentosum*)
A beautiful perennial ground cover for a sunny, well-drained area, snow-in-summer is named for its carpet of white flowers in late spring and a fairly solid mat of grayish foliage, about 1 foot (30 cm) high, through the summer. It is very invasive, a positive characteristic if you want to cover a lot of ground in a hurry, a negative one in a flowerbed.

Surround snow-in-summer with lawn, grow it in a pot, or use it as a lawn substitute in places of light foot traffic.

Culture: Buy bedding plants in spring, and set 1 foot (30 cm) apart, or sow seeds outdoors in late spring, around the date of the last frost. Seeds just covered with soil germinate quickly when the soil warms to 70 to 75 degrees F (21-24°C). Snow-in-summer needs well-drained soil, so it suits rockeries and other fairly dry places.

Pests & Diseases: None of note.

Stocks

(Cruciferae, *Malcolmia maritima*; *Matthiola* spp)
There are several related garden annuals called stocks. Most common is the so-called 10-week stocks (*Matthiola incana*), with spires of white and pink through rose to purple flowers for sun or light shade. Evening scented stocks (*M. longipetala*; *M. bicornis*) is a small, modest lilac flower on a reclining 1-to-2-foot (30-60 cm) stem, but the fragrance, in afternoon and evening, is sweet and powerful. It blooms all summer and is a good flower to mix among showier things.

Virginia stocks (*Malcolmia maritima*) is better known in England than in North America, where it can be hard to find. Its virtue is its ability to bloom quickly from seeds sprinkled on the garden soil in spring and to self-sow in years to come, beginning to bloom by the end of June. At the front of a sunny or partly shaded border, it provides small, fragrant pink, lilac and white stars throughout summer, as long as it receives occasional watering. Reclining stems are about 1 foot (30 cm) long.

Culture: All stocks are easy from seed, which is the best route, because they also look best in masses. Sow the seeds early indoors, or about a month before the last spring frost date, sprinkle them directly where the flowers will grow, gradually thinning the seedlings so that the plants just touch as they grow.

Pests & Diseases: All members of the family Cruciferae are vulnerable to leaf perforation by flea beetles early in the season. Dust with rotenone if the infestation is severe.

Stokesia

(Compositae, *Stokesia laevis*; *S. cyanea*)
Stokes' Aster

Stokesia (whose name has nothing to do with the Canadian company Stokes Seeds) is a perennial, with relaxed 2-foot (60 cm) stems topped for weeks in summer by 3-inch (7.5 cm) daisies of, most popularly, lavender-blue. There are also pale blue, white, pink and pale yellow versions.

Culture: Buy plants, or sow seeds 8 weeks early indoors. Plant 18 inches (45 cm) apart in sun or partial shade. Stokesia tolerates heat but requires occasional watering. It is hardy only in the milder regions of Canada, to about zone 5. In marginal places, mulch it for the winter. Clumps can be divided in spring.

Pests & Diseases: None of note.

Summer Bulbs

An assortment of flowering bulbs, corms and rhizomes too tender to spend winters in the frozen ground can be treated much like bedding annuals: planted in spring around the last frost date and either replaced every year or overwintered indoors. In summer, all do best with regular watering in fertile soil.

• Gladiolus are the best-known. Glads have tall, stiff stems, and their flowers of white to yellow through pink, strawberry-red and bicolors last a long time in a vase. In the garden, however, they are difficult to situate; unless staked, the stems end up pointing at odd angles. Consider a row in a vegetable garden, where they are easy to reach for cutting. Corms are vulnerable to rotting in storage or in wet soil in the garden. To combat fungi, dust

corms with sulfur before storing in fall. Any infected corms should be discarded. Thrips are tiny black insects that may cause silvery flecking of flowers and foliage. Spray insecticidal soap on foliage, not flowers.

• Acidanthera, butterfly flower, is a 3-foot-tall (1 m) gladiolus relative with creamy white flowers that have the added bonus of an intoxicating fragrance. Give it sun or partial shade near the back of a flower border. Treat corms like gladiolus.

• Agapanthus, called African lily or lily-of-the-Nile, is common in southerly gardens, where it overwinters and forms spreading clumps. In the North, it is best grown in containers that can be moved indoors in winter and kept fairly dry by a cool, bright window. Tall stems bear long-lasting tubular blue, pink or white flowers. Do not divide rhizomes until they become crowded.

• Caladium is a tuber often grown as a houseplant. In summer, the big, colorful heart-shaped leaves can also decorate shady corners of the garden or containers.

• Canna grows from a tuber. The lilylike flowers, in yellow, pink or red, grow several feet tall on standard plants; miniatures or dwarfs are less than 2 feet (60 cm) high. Canna blooms best in a warm, sunny place with moist soil. If happy, it can quickly dominate a bed, but it can be restricted in a large pot filled with rich soil. Remove withered flower spikes to encourage more flowering.

• Tigridia, also called tiger flower or Mexican shell-flower, is a corm that produces an 18-inch (45 cm) stem topped by 4-inch (10 cm) white, yellow, pink or red flowers in late summer. The inner part of the flower is spotted. Tigridia blooms for weeks, but like day lilies, the individual flowers last just a day apiece.

• Zantedeschia, formerly called calla lily, produces a sheathlike flower in midsummer, like that of its relative, jack-in-the-pulpit. There are several species, ranging in height from 2 to 3 feet (0.6-1 m). Flower color varies from white or yellow to pink or rosy purple. Give zantedeschia a sunny, sheltered spot and plenty of water. It can be overwintered indoors in a pot.

Overwinter zantedeschia, caladium and agapanthus in pots. With the others, cut the stems back to the ground soon after the first fall frost. Dig up

Acidanthera is a gladiolus relative whose graceful white flowers have an intoxicating perfume.

the corms, roots or rhizomes, dry them outdoors in the sun for a day, dust them off, then pack in dry peat or vermiculite in paper bags and store in a cool, dry place. For an early start, plant indoors in pots 2 months ahead. Plants already growing should not be put outdoors until nights are warm. For outdoor planting, do so about a week before the last spring frost date.

Sunflower

(Compositae, *Helianthus annuus; Heliopsis* spp)
The most famous cultivar of sunflower is 'Giant Mammoth,' also called 'Russian Giant,' although, like all sunflowers, it is native to North America. Truly giant, its 10-foot-or-taller (3 m) stems may bear flowers 1 foot (30 cm) wide. The oily seeds are sweet and delicious, if you can beat the squirrels and birds to them. This monster is best confined to the northern boundary of a vegetable garden or to a few chosen spots where it can be impressive. There are many other cultivars, some as short as

marigolds, which are prettier for home gardens and which make excellent, long-lasting cut flowers. Almost all have dark brown centers. Some have a branching habit. Flowers are borne from midsummer till frost, with later flowers somewhat smaller than the first ones. Mixtures include all warm colors, from the standard yellow petals to peach, bronze, orange, pink and bicolors. Seed mixtures do not include white, but the cultivars 'Italian White' and 'Vanilla Ice' are lovely. False sunflower (*Heliopsis* spp) has smaller flowers and is a hardy perennial.

Culture: Sunflowers are easy from seeds sown in a sunny place as soon as the soil can be worked in spring. When the soil warms to 70 to 75 degrees F (21-24°C), seedlings sprout and grow quickly. Thin them to stand about 2 feet (60 cm) apart. Thinned seedlings transplant easily. As the flowers grow, staking may be necessary in windy places, but otherwise, their strong stems are self-supporting. Sunflowers put up with heat and drought and will self-sow if you allow some of the flowers to dry on the stems. All sunflowers, even the small ones, are somewhat domineering, so keep them away from delicate plants.

Pests & Diseases: Sunflowers may suffer from stem rot, which causes plants to wilt and topple. Remove affected plants.

Sweet Pea

(Leguminosae, *Lathyrus odoratus*)

Sweet peas are one of a rare group of annuals that thrive in cool weather and damp soil. They are sown about the same time as garden peas and produce vines short or long, depending on the cultivar, then a crop of pea flowers in white, pastel colors or dark red, purple or blue. Some are sweetly perfumed. All make good cut flowers, especially those bred for long stems.

Culture: Soak the big seeds overnight in cool water, then as soon as the ground can be worked in spring, sow ½ inch (1 cm) deep and 1 inch (2.5 cm) apart close to a trellis, vertical strings or fence. All except the dwarf varieties need support. Thin to 4 inches (10 cm) apart. For an even earlier start, keen sweet-pea growers sow seeds indoors a month ahead. Use peat pots; otherwise, transplanting can set the plants back. Seeds germinate at a temperature of 55 to 65 degrees F (13-18°C).

Pests & Diseases: Where summers are hot and dry, sweet peas are susceptible to mildew and burn out quickly.

Tithonia

(Compositae, *Tithonia rotundifolia*)

Mexican Sunflower

Tithonia is a tall, shrubby annual daisy, up to 6 feet (2 m) high and half as wide, for the back of a border or a focal point in the sun. The flowers of 'Goldfinger' are brilliant orange with raised yellow centers. There is also a yellow cultivar.

Culture: Sow seeds directly in the garden after

the last frost, thinning plants to 2 feet (60 cm) apart, or start seeds indoors a month early. Sow seeds on the surface of moist soil mix; they need light and a temperature of about 70 degrees F (21°C) to germinate. Plant outdoors after the last frost. Tithonia sometimes self-sows. It fares best in hot, dry weather. Stake the stems if you plant in a windy place or if the ground is moist and rich.

Pests & Diseases: None of note.

Tradescantia

(Commelinaceae, *Tradescantia* x *andersoniana*)

Spiderwort; Trinity Flower

Bearing a distinctive, showy three-petaled bloom, tradescantia is a dependable perennial. Too dependable, in fact, for very fertile or manicured places: the plant is invasive in all but the worst growing conditions. Slender leaves 1 to 2 feet (30-60 cm) tall are reminiscent of day lilies, topped in late spring and in fall by flowers that are typically blue, although there are also pink, magenta, white and bicolor versions. Some are semidouble.

Culture: Tradescantia spreads so easily that plants are usually available from horticultural-society sales in spring and also from bedding-plant growers. Seeds can be purchased from some specialist sources. Just covered, seeds sprout in about a month at 70 degrees F (21°C). Give tradescantia sun or shade in any soil, and keep an eye on its wandering habits.

Pests & Diseases: None of note.

Tulip

(Liliaceae, *Tulipa* spp)

All tulips are generally problem-free. First to bloom in spring are species such as *T. tarda* and *T. foster-*

ana. Later come the larger cultivated types, such as the Darwin and Cottage tulips. There are early, midseason and late varieties, so it is possible to have tulips in bloom for as long as 2 months. Some cultivars die out after a year, but tulips can be long-lasting perennials, requiring no care other than weeding. Among the cultivars likely to last many years without replacement are 'Holland's Glorie,' 'Oxford' and any cultivar that includes the word 'Apeldoorn.' There are both single and double cultivars of hybrid tulips. The doubles, which resemble roses, last longer in bloom than the singles.

Culture: Plant tulip bulbs in fall 6 inches (15 cm) deep in a sunny place in fertile soil before the first frost. They must have well-drained soil, not constant moisture. Tulips look best in groups of the same color, planted about 6 inches (15 cm) apart. Mixing them up produces a speckled effect. After tulips finish blooming, cut the flower stems but leave the foliage in place to manufacture food for next year's flowers. Hide the fading foliage behind other leafy plants. If tulips are content, they will gradually form a cluster of bulbs that can be separated after the foliage dies back.

Pests & Diseases: The worst pests are squirrels, so in susceptible gardens, mostly in cities, the planted area should be covered with chicken wire just under the soil surface. Covering the soil with cayenne pepper flakes also helps. So-called broken tulips, whose petals are streaked and mottled, are infected with a virus disease that can create beautiful flowers but also makes plants short-lived.

Verbena
(Verbenaceae, *Verbena* x *hybrida*)

There are perennial types of verbena for gardens with mild winters, but the most common verbena for Northerners is an annual. It grows 6 to 12 inches (15-30 cm) tall, with small, pointed leaves and starry clusters of flowers in white or bright pink, red, blue or purple, often with a contrasting eye. Individually, verbena plants look stiff, but they can be attractive when grown in a mass. There is also a new trailing type, 'Imagination,' with soft 2-foot (60 cm) stems, lacy foliage and blue flowers, ideal for hanging baskets or window boxes in sun.

Culture: Plants are generally available in spring, but growing from seed increases your choice of cultivars. Start verbena seeds indoors 6 weeks early. Seeds germinate at a temperature of 70 to 75 degrees F (21-24°C). Keep seedlings slightly on the dry side. After the last frost, set outdoors in pots or in the garden 6 inches (15 cm) apart in sun or a little shade. In fall, take tip cuttings of trailing verbena and root indoors for next year's plants.

Pests & Diseases: Verbena is one of the favorite foods of rabbits and other rodents. Spraying with cayenne pepper acts as a deterrent.

Veronica
(Scrophulariaceae, *Veronica* spp)
Speedwell

Along with salvia, monkshood and delphinium, veronica provides spikes of blue flowers in the hardy perennial bed in spring or early summer. There are several species and many cultivars. Veronica varieties may be as short as 18 inches (45 cm) or as tall as 30 inches (75 cm). One of the best of the blues is *V. latifolia* (*V. teucrium*) 'Crater Lake Blue.' There are also whites and pinks. Woolly speedwell (*V. incana*), another hardy perennial, is a fuzzy ground cover about 1 foot (30 cm) tall, with pale blue flowers in summer.

Culture: A limited number of cultivars are widely available as bedding plants in spring. Some types can be sown from seed directly in the garden around the last spring frost date and will bloom the following summer. Veronica does best in sun or with some shade in ordinary well-drained soil. In dry weather, it needs deep watering. Clumps can be divided in spring as soon as the new growth appears. Shear it back after the flowers fade.

Pests & Diseases: None of note.

Violet
(Violaceae, *Viola* spp)
Pansy; Viola

Pansies and violets belong to the genus *Viola* and are distinguished from one another largely by flower size. Both are lovely in bloom but are especially valuable in the North for their tolerance of frost, shade and damp ground. The foliage, roundish and glossy green, is also pretty. Many have biennial tendencies: they form a leafy clump the first year from seed and bloom the second, sometimes setting seed that germinates for next year's flowers.

At the front of a shady border, violets are eye-catchers when their blue, yellow, white or purple flowers begin to bloom in late spring. Often first to bloom are Johnny-jump-ups and cultivars of *V. cornuta*. Flowering can continue for weeks if the weather stays coolish and the ground is not too dry. Another small species, the purple violet (*V. cucullata*), is the provincial emblem of New Brunswick. There are many additional wild violets that will appear in your garden if you are fortunate. They seed generously and can be weeded out if you prefer.

Violets are about 1 inch (2.5 cm) wide, but the flowers of their big brothers, the hybrid pansies, may be 4 inches (10 cm). Some are plain, but more charming are the pansies with "faces," suggested by blotches of a different color. Many of these act like annuals, while others bloom a second year.

Pansy and violet flowers are edible. The smallest violets are especially lovely as garnishes on desserts or cheese spreads.

Culture: Many types of hybrid pansy and a few violets are available as bedding plants in spring. If you want to grow violets or pansies from seed, start them early, around January or February, because the seeds are tiny and slow. They can be sown in pots in fall and left outdoors over the winter, as they require chilling. Indoors, cover pots with newspaper, because germination requires darkness at a soil temperature of 65 to 70 degrees F (18-21°C). Uncover pots as soon as the seeds sprout. When heavy frosts are past, group plants 4 inches (10 cm) apart any place where their small size—about 6 inches (15 cm) tall—will be an asset.

Pests & Diseases: None of note, though the foliage may be grazed by rodents and deer.

Wallflower
(Cruciferae, *Cheiranthus cheiri*; *Erysimum* spp)

The wallflower is a fragrant biennial. Seeds sown in spring develop rosettes of leaves. Next year, there are 1-foot-tall (30 cm) flower stems and brilliant flowers: orange, yellow, red, pink, purple or rose, often fragrant. 'Tom Thumb' grows about half as tall. There are also several species of Siberian wallflower (*Erysimum* spp) that are similar, although some are perennial where winters are mild and summers fairly cool.

Culture: Sow wallflower seeds directly in a sunny spot in the garden in midspring, a couple of weeks before the last frost date.

Pests & Diseases: None of note.

Yarrow
(Compositae, *Achillea* spp)
Milfoil

Drought-tolerant and very hardy even in poor soil and full sun, yarrow is attractive spring through fall and may be in bloom for as long as 15 weeks, from June to October. If yarrow seems too good to be true, its virtues are balanced by a common fault of tough plants, invasiveness. Keep an eye on it, dividing it every year if necessary, and yarrow can be just the thing for a spot that is seldom watered but needs a plant as tall as 3 feet (1 m). Woolly yarrow (*A. tomentosa*) and *A. filipendulina* have bright yellow flowers. The foliage is fernlike. Cultivars of *A. millefolium* have pink, rose or purple flowers; 'Lilac Beauty' and 'Sawa Sawa' were rated best overall in trials at the Chicago Botanic Garden. *A. ptarmica* 'The Pearl' was the best of the whites in the trial. This species is different from the others, with dark green foliage, relaxed stems and button flowers. It can be invasive but puts up with wet ground and blooms for 6 weeks in July and August. *A.* 'Moonshine,' another popular choice, lost points in the trials because of occasional flopping.

Culture: Yarrow plants can be purchased in spring. Yarrow is also easy from seeds sown 8 weeks before the last spring frost date. Press seeds into the surface of moist growing mix, as they need light to germinate at about 68 degrees F (20°C). Set outdoors 1 foot (30 cm) apart around the last frost date. Plants usually bloom a year later. Divide plants in spring or fall.

Pests & Diseases: None of note.

Zinnia

(Compositae, *Zinnia* spp)

Zinnias are easy, bright daisies for the summer garden. Some are singles, which suggest their daisy heritage better than many of the exotic doubles. *Z. angustifolia* is a ground cover much like sanvitalia: 2-inch (5 cm) daisies grow on 1-foot-tall (30 cm) plants that look best at the front of the border.

Zinnias are heat-resistant, and provided you remember to snap off spent flowers and water them occasionally, zinnias will bloom constantly through summer's hottest weather, creating a beautiful show of warm colors.

Culture: The cheapest way to grow zinnias in quantity is to sow the large seeds in late spring

Yarrow color varies with species and cultivar. A. filipendulina, *foreground, is sunny yellow.*

directly where you want them in the garden. Cover lightly with soil and keep watered till the seedlings sprout when the soil temperature reaches 70 to 80 degrees F (21-27°C). Seedlings grow quickly in warm, wet soil, and may catch up to purchased transplants. Flowers bloom in about 6 weeks, and if you cut off fading flowers, blooming will continue till frost. Easiest from seeds are the smaller types, such as 'Rose Pinwheel' or 'Dreamland.' You can also grow zinnias from bedding plants, but transplanting usually hampers their growth. Transplants may produce huge, top-heavy flowers that require staking. On the other hand, if you are prepared to coddle them, the big zinnias can be showstoppers in the garden and wonderful in a vase.

Pests & Diseases: Botrytis, or gray mold, is a fluffy gray covering that may occur on stems in wet weather. Remove affected plants, or spray weekly with a baking-soda solution (see page 192).

Chapter Six

A Northern Bouquet Garni

"There were others that are known to the Natives and make a part of their food, especially fern roots, a root of licorice taste and some others unknown to me . . ."

—The Journals of Captain James Cook, 1778

In describing the diet of the inhabitants of coastal British Columbia, Captain James Cook listed plants the local people knew intimately. The plants may have been ones we would consider vegetables, or perhaps we would call them herbs. It makes little difference. All plants have an effect, good or ill, on the body. Some are tastier and more palatable than others, and plants run the gamut from wholesome to toxic—but there is no clear dividing line between food and medicine.

Nevertheless, today we divide edible plants into just those two fairly distinct groups, food and medicine, calling the first group vegetables or fruits and the second group herbs. Herbs are a loosely associated fraternity of edible plants whose strong flavor suits many of them to another role as seasonings or teas.

Our use of herbs as seasonings, supposedly without medicinal side effects, is so recent that our refrigerators and spice cabinets are filled with little pharmacopoeias of forgotten knowledge. Plant names offer hints. The species name of many herbs, *officinalis*, describes a plant used officially, in medicine. Another common species name, *sativa*, suggests edibility. Many genus names also tell a story. For instance, the genus name of sage, *Salvia*, comes from the same root word as "salvation," suggesting that the plant has life-saving qualities. Salvia has been recommended at various times for everything from mending broken bones to curing nervous disorders, but now it is more likely to show up in stuffed turkey than in a tonic or salve.

All the herbs in this chapter have some reputed effect on human health, but that is not why they have been included. They are here because they are the easiest, most dependable culinary herbs for Northerners to grow. Whether or not they are therapeutic, they will certainly help to enliven casseroles and bland salads.

Herb Gardens

The essential oils that give these plants their characteristic flavor and fragrance—and their medicinal properties—are part of the plants' own insect- and herbivore-repelling strategies. Obviously, the ploy has done little to repel people, but it does mean that

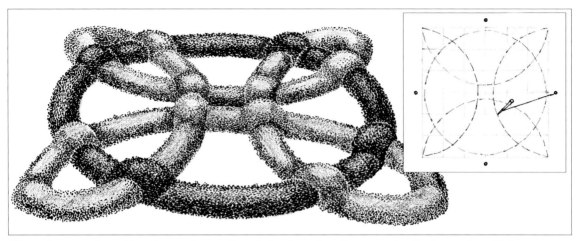

Plan a knot garden with string and a marker, right, then plant low-growing herbs, and mulch between.

in the garden, herbs tend to have few pests and diseases. Still in possession of their wild survival tactics, many herbs are also capable of thriving in infertile soils where vegetables often languish.

All herbs, however, must be sheltered from harsh winds, and all except parsley, chervil, mint, lovage and bergamot do best in well-drained, even dry soil. In wet places, some of the drought-tolerant perennials will not survive winter. For a herb garden, plan to use humusy or sandy soil, perhaps in raised beds to help drainage. Gardeners in the driest areas of the country can get away with heavy soil that may even require a summer mulch, but in most areas, a mixture of 1 part sand, 2 parts topsoil and 1 part compost will produce an adequate herb-garden soil.

Because herbs are generally quite resilient and attractive and because most gardeners need only a few plants of any particular variety, herbs are very versatile plants: grow them in containers, in flower gardens, in their own bed or in a border along a path. Raised beds surrounded by stones, bricks, concrete blocks, railroad ties or boards create an attractive display.

At one time, intricate herb gardens were popular. The knot gardens of Tudor and Stewart England featured low-growing herbs whose prunings made their way into soups, stews and medicines. These gardens were meant to be viewed from above, from a high window, where, as William Coles wrote in 1656, there would be no better way

to refresh one's vision "than to view the pleasant greennesse of Herbes."

To be suitable for a knot garden, herbs should be perennial and lend themselves to pruning and shaping. Chives, sage, thyme, winter savory, salad burnet and hyssop are northern possibilities, as well as some perennial medicinal herbs such as horehound and wormwood. Where lavender is hardy, its graygreen fragrant foliage is a beautiful addition, as is santolina, hardy to zone 6 or 7. Low-growing annual flowers or foliage plants, such as dusty miller, coleus, dwarf marigolds and alyssum, can be planted every spring to fill in areas of the design, as can the perfectly globe-shaped basil 'Spicy Globe.' Alpine strawberries were sometimes included in traditional gardens. All plants must be set close together to fill in as a continuous mat and must be kept trimmed, suckers and volunteer plants removed and any dead plants replaced. In short, knot gardens are projects for devoted gardeners.

Ornamental herbs can be included in the flower garden. Most herbs are decorative, chiefly for foliage rather than flowers, and all you need to do is position them like any other ornamental: tall at the back, low at the front. You can also give perennial herbs a bed of their own. Knot gardens took formality to the extreme, but a simpler design, perhaps a circle or square divided into quadrants or triangles, can be very effective. A sundial, birdbath or raised pond makes an eye-catching center.

Annual herbs—basil, borage, summer savory,

chervil, anise, nasturtiums, chile peppers and dill—can be raised in the vegetable garden. A biennial such as parsley is also well suited to the vegetable garden, but if you want a bonus of spring greens and summer seeds next year, remember not to till or spade the roots in fall or in spring before they resprout. If you grow perennial herbs in the vegetable garden, give them a corner of their own and plan their positions carefully. Some of them, like mint and horseradish, tend to spread; some, like lovage, grow very tall; others, like thyme, are small and easily crowded out.

Overwintering

Whether or not a perennial herb will survive the winter depends on many things: the herb's own capacity to withstand cold, its need for dormancy, the temperature, the snow cover and the moisture level in the ground during any particular winter. Very hardy herbs may perish in waterlogged frozen soil, while half-hardy ones might survive a winter with a deep snow cover yet die during a winter that is warmer but has less snow.

Check with other gardeners, with nurseries and with local horticultural societies to determine which herbs are likely to be hardy in your area. If there is any doubt, mulch heavily with leaves or straw before fall's first heavy frost. For added insurance, root cuttings and keep them indoors over the winter.

This process is not without its own hazards, either, because indoor growing is not optimal for herbs, most of which require cool air and plenty of sunlight. Protect tender herbs from frost, and bring them indoors before the days are cold. Hardy herbs, on the other hand, must have some winter cold in order to continue to grow well; do not bring them indoors until just before the soil freezes. Water indoor herbs whenever the soil is dry ½ inch (1 cm) below the surface, and if you are harvesting leaves throughout the winter, fertilize the plant every month.

The Harvest

Herb leaves and stems can be pinched off anytime, provided you don't pinch off so much that the plant is seriously set back in its growth. The youngest (top) leaves are usually the tenderest and most desirable. Harvest them in the morning as soon as the dew has dried, and wash only if necessary. In fall or just before the plant goes to seed, whichever is appropriate for each herb, pick a single large harvest for winter storage.

Herbs taste best when they are fresh, but fresh leaves are not always available year-round. If preservation is necessary, drying is usually most convenient—the process is very inexpensive, and the finished product takes up little space. In recipes, substitute 1 part dried herbs for 2 parts fresh—that is, ½ teaspoon (2 mL) crushed dried herbs instead of 1 teaspoon (5 mL) chopped fresh herbs.

Herb drying is most successful if it takes place fairly quickly in relative darkness and in temperatures of 70 to 95 degrees F (21-35°C). Excessive heat and light cause additional flavor losses. The heat from the pilot light of a gas oven is ideal. Leaves spread in a single layer on a cookie sheet should be dry in 2 to 14 days, depending on the thickness and wetness of the leaves.

Microwave drying can also work well, though you must watch the plants closely, since there may be only a few seconds between dry and burned. Place a layer of sprigs on a paper towel, and microwave for about 1 minute. Let the herbs cool. If they are not completely dry, microwave for another 30 seconds or as required.

Alternatively, plants may be spread on screens or cookie sheets in a dry room, in the open-doored oven of a warm wood stove or in an electric oven set at its lowest setting—no higher than 100 degrees F (38°C) if the door is closed, 150 degrees (66°C) with the door ajar. If you are drying herbs outdoors, leave them on screening in a shady place and be sure to bring them in overnight and whenever the weather is wet—any dampness during the drying process will cause a darkening of the leaves, loss of flavor and perhaps rotting.

Store crackling-dry herbs in labeled glass jars, not in paper or cardboard, which will absorb essential oils. Place the containers in a cool, dark cupboard. If, after the first week or two, moisture can be seen condensing on the inside of the container or if the herbs do not crush easily, they must be removed for further drying. Leafy herbs can also

Annual herbs such as dill can grow in the vegetable garden or add an ornamental touch to flowers.

be hung upside down in bunches to dry and to store. Bunches of thyme, sage, savory or oregano tied with ribbon can be quite decorative in a kitchen or pantry, although they do become dusty. Do not crush dried herbs until just before using.

Herbs can also be frozen, a storage method that works especially well with chervil, tarragon, parsley and basil. The herbs are simply washed, packed in small plastic bags, labeled and placed in the freezer.

While not primarily a means of herb storage, herb vinegars do accomplish that end, as do herb jellies or herbs stored in vegetable oils. Pesto, a mixture of basil, garlic, pine nuts, cheese and olive oil, is the most common herb-and-oil mixture. It can be stored frozen in meal-sized portions.

To make herb vinegar, add 4 parts vinegar to 1 part fresh herbs in a glass jar. In 2 weeks, strain liquid, add 1 part fresh leaves again, and let stand for another 2 weeks. Strain and store, with one herb sprig added to the bottle for decoration and identification. Especially good herb vinegars are made with mint, basil, dill, garlic and tarragon.

Because herbs are so easy to grow and store, at least one or two should be included in any Northerner's garden plan. Herbs could not possibly be called an essential part of the diet, but they are the bouquet garni of the garden, providing pleasure for the eyes, nose and taste buds.

Herbal Chemistry

The flavor, fragrance and medicinal value of plants come from unusual chemical components. A few of these components are:

• terpenoids, which are substances that can often be detected by scent. The characteristic aroma of basil, mint, oregano and sage comes in part from terpenoids (as does the smell of turpentine);

• steroids, substances produced by both plants and animals. The foxglove (*Digitalis* spp) is a rich source of steroids. Plants considered toxic because of their steroid content include lily of the valley (*Convallaria majalis*). The bitter component of cucurbits, cucurbitacin, is also a steroid;

• alkaloids, found in many drug plants and some plants with a bitter flavor. Piperine of black pepper is an example. So is caffeine, which is present in many plants in small quantities. Additional alkaloids are morphine, cocaine, atropine and quinine.

Angelica

(Umbelliferae, *Angelica archangelica*)

This herb's heavenly name suggests its healing mercies and its legendary ability to ward off evils. Angelica was once believed to cure colds, bronchitis, pleurisy, colic, rheumatism and indigestion. Many liqueurs, such as Benedictine, include it. One of several related herbs with anise-flavored leaves, angelica grows into what resembles a shrubby celery plant as tall as 5 feet (1.5 m), in the manner of lovage.

Culture: The seeds, which must be fresh, need exposure to light for germination. Press them into the surface of moist seeding mix outdoors in fall, or plant them in early spring in fertile soil directly where they will grow, in sun or a little shade. Transplanting must be done when seedlings are small, as root disturbance sets plants back and can lead to decline. Angelica is a biennial or short-lived perennial, but it is hardy and may last as long as 3 years if the seed stalks are picked off as soon as they appear. On the other hand, plants allowed to go to seed may self-sow, and the seed heads are attractive in floral arrangements.

Harvest: All parts of the plant are most commonly used in desserts and candies, although leaves and tender stem tips can be added to salads, used as a garnish or boiled or roasted in the manner of Florence fennel.

Pests & Diseases: None of note. Parsleyworms can be hand-picked.

Anise
(Umbelliferae, *Pimpinella anisum*)
The licorice flavor of anise is now almost unknown beyond the candy store and such liqueurs as anisette, ouzo and Pernod, although aniseed cakes are popular in German cuisine. At one time, however, the herb was highly esteemed. The early Romans considered anise a cure for many ailments. Pliny the Elder claimed that stuffed in a pillow, anise would help a sleeper avoid nightmares. Sixteenth-century herbalist John Gerard noted that the plant was "good against belchings and upbraidings of the stomacke....Bechewed it maketh the breath sweet," which was why anise liqueur was supposed to be good after a meal. Maude Grieve added in *A Modern Herbal* in 1931: "The taste is sweet and spicey, and the odour aromatic and agreeable." The plant grows 1 to 2 feet (30-60 cm) tall and resembles celery, producing its small grayish seed, the most favored part of the plant, in late summer.

Culture: An annual, anise is easy to grow, but it does require about 4 months of warm, frost-free weather to produce seed, although the leaves of non-seed-producing plants can be used for teas and garnishes. Northerners who want seed have the best chance if they start plants indoors in March or April, about 4 weeks before the last spring frost. Since the seedling forms a taproot and thus is difficult to transplant, seeds should be sown on peat pellets or in peat pots filled with potting mix. Seeds will germinate in about a week at 68 degrees F

(20°C). Set outdoors 4 inches (10 cm) apart after the last spring frost date, choosing a sunny spot where the soil is well drained and free of weeds.

Harvest: A few leaves may be picked from each plant throughout the growing season and sprinkled on cooked vegetables or fruit salads or used as a soothing tea for colds. In August, each plant should produce up to half a dozen seed stalks bearing a small umbel of white flowers. As soon as a few seeds have ripened, cut the seed stalks and place them in a paper bag so that the seeds will not be lost as they fall. The seeds are usually crushed before they are used in confectionery or baked goods. Some seeds may be saved for planting next spring.

Pests & Diseases: None of note.

Anise-Hyssop
(Labiatae, *Agastache foeniculum*; *A. anethiodora*)
Fragrant Giant Hyssop; Fennel Giant Hyssop
Used by North American native people to make a medicinal tea, anise-hyssop is a fairly recent arrival in the herb gardens of Europeans. It grows 3 to 4 feet (1 m) tall and has broad, mintlike leaves, which are downy white underneath, and lavender flowers that attract bees. It is a hardy perennial well suited to being positioned at the back of a herb garden, even against a wall, because it grows straight and tall and is not invasive. It often self-sows.

Culture: Obtain plants in spring, or sow seeds directly in the garden in fall or early spring. Thin plants to 1 foot (30 cm) apart. Anise-hyssop tolerates full sun or partial shade and grows best in decent soil watered once a week.

Harvest: Pinch off leaves as needed to brew a delicious fragrant tea, or use the leaves dried or fresh, in the manner of sage.

Pests & Diseases: None of note.

Balm
(Labiatae, *Melissa officinalis*)
Lemon Balm; Melissa
The gray-green leaves of this tender perennial make a delicious citrus-flavored tea and can con-

Balm contributes lemon flavor to teas and foods.

tribute lemon flavor to many dishes, especially those including chicken and mushrooms. "The bees do delight in ye herb," wrote Dioscorides, and perhaps for the same reason, balm is well suited to fragrant potpourris. Herbalist John Gerard wrote in 1597 that balm "maketh the hart merrie and joiful and strengtheneth the vitall spirits." It grows 3 to 4 feet (1 m) tall.

Culture: It is often possible, and indeed advisable, to buy plants from a nursery. Otherwise, in early spring, soak the seeds in warm water for 24 hours before sprinkling them on the surface of a container of seeding mix. Keep it damp by covering the container with plastic or placing it in a shallow pan of warm water. Seeds germinate in about a month. When the seedlings are 2 inches (5 cm) tall, transplant into a sunny or partly shaded patch of well-drained soil at 1-foot (30 cm) intervals. In later years, the plants can be propagated by dividing the clumps. The plant may self-sow in the garden. Cut it back in late fall and mulch, or bring

plants indoors wherever winters are severe. At the Devonian Botanic Garden, near Edmonton, Alberta, the balm plants are overwintered in a greenhouse.

Harvest: Do not harvest the first year after seeding. Thereafter, pinch off leaves and plant tips as needed. Cut off stems in fall and dry.

Pests & Diseases: None of note.

Basil

(Labiatae, *Ocimum* spp)

Basileus means "king" in Greek, an indication of this herb's standing in the ancient culinary arts. Now favored as a seasoning for tomatoes, basil has a pleasant, slightly sweet, clovelike flavor that suits it to all kinds of meat and vegetable dishes. Because this fast-growing annual can be harvested as soon as 6 weeks after sowing in early summer, it suits all northern gardens, however short the growing season, provided it is covered in case of untimely frost, to which it is very sensitive. There are several versions of the common sweet basil. *O. basilicum,* the one carried by most seed houses, has large green leaves and grows about 18 inches (45 cm) tall. Opal basil has decorative purple foliage, while lettuce-leaf basil has larger foliage than normal, sometimes as long as 8 inches (20 cm) and half as wide. Bush basil, including the cultivar 'Spicy Globe,' is a low-growing, small-leaved version ideal for containers. In addition, other unusual types of basil can be purchased from seed houses specializing in herbs:

• Camphor basil (*O. kilimandscharicum*) is strong in flavor and odor and is grown commercially for camphor. It grows about 5 feet (1.5 m) tall.

• East Indian basil (*O. gratissimum*) has a stronger, more clovelike flavor and scent than common basil and grows about 5 feet (1.5 m) tall.

• Sacred basil (*O. sanctum*), also more clovelike than common basil, grows to about 20 inches (50 cm).

• Lemon basil (*O. americanum*) has a strong lemon fragrance that makes it useful in teas, potpourris and fish dishes. It is about 6 inches (15 cm) tall and goes to flower earlier than most other types.

Culture: Although basil is perennial in southern Asia, where it is native, it is grown as an annual in the North. Seeds may be sown indoors 6 weeks before the last spring frost date or directly in the garden from the last frost date until midsummer. Choose a sunny, sheltered spot where the soil is well drained, preferably sandy. Seeds germinate in 7 days at the preferred soil temperature of about 65 degrees F (18°C). Thin plants gradually to stand 6 inches (15 cm) apart. Thinnings may be used in salads or as seasoning, or they may be transplanted into other garden areas. Basil must be kept warm throughout its short season; cover with a plastic tunnel or half of a plastic pop bottle if the weather is cool. Mulching and regular watering and fertilizing will help produce tender leaves. Basil can also be sown in a pot indoors, but it needs plenty of light, or it will become leggy.

Harvest: Leaves may be pinched off individually as needed until the plant flowers. To extend the harvest, pinch off flowers as they form. The harvest must be completed before the first frost and the entire plants cut and dried or the leaves frozen or preserved in pesto or vinegar.

Pests & Diseases: None of note.

Bay Laurel

(Lauraceae, *Laurus nobilis*)
Bay Leaf; Sweet Bay
Literally noble laurel, bay has a long and honorable history. Greek and Roman poets and heroes wore garlands of it. "It resisteth witchcraft very potently," pronounced Nicholas Culpeper in 1652. "Neither witch nor devil, thunder nor lightning, will hurt a man where a bay tree is." Bay reputedly healed wounds, detoxified poisons, helped during childbirth, killed intestinal worms, cured coughs and flatulence and cleaned off marks on the skin. There was nothing it didn't do. Bay laurel is a tender evergreen perennial, and as such, it cannot winter outdoors in the North, but it is an easy houseplant that can spend summers outdoors.

Culture: Obtain bay as a plant. Seeds take as long as 3 months to germinate, and few companies carry them. Plant bay in potting soil. Keep it on the dry side during winter, and fertilize once a month from late winter till midsummer. Keep it in a win-

Bay is a perennial that needs protection from frost.

dow or greenhouse that is bright but not too hot. After the last frost, gradually move it outdoors to a shady, protected place for the summer. Slowly accustom it to the indoors again around the date of the first fall frost. Transplant it into a larger pot every couple of years if you wish; otherwise, prune it back to size or whenever it becomes leggy. It has the potential to become as tall as 6 feet (2 m) in a tub—40 feet (12 m) outdoors in its native Mediterranean climate—but can be kept much smaller. To propagate, air layer by splitting the stem, applying rooting hormone to the wound, then tying on moist peat moss held in a plastic bag. When roots become visible, remove the rooted part of the stem. Rooting tip cuttings is more difficult.

Harvest: Take bay leaves as needed, but never strip the plant.

Pests & Diseases: Indoors, bay can become infested with mealybug or scale insect. Apply alcohol with a cotton swab or spray with insecticidal soap.

Bergamot

(Labiatae, *Monarda* spp)
Bee Balm; Oswego Tea; Wild Bergamot
Bergamot, which is also described in Chapter Five under Monarda, is one of the less familiar herbs, mainly because it is a North American native and

was therefore not known at the time of the older European herbals. But it is hardy and prolific. Its showy bright red or pink flowers and green, mint-like leaves are attractive at the back of the herb garden, where its 20-to-36-inch (50-90 cm) height will not shade other plants. Oswego tea, made from bergamot, had been used by the indigenous people of eastern North America for generations before the Boston Tea Party made it popular among immigrants. Chopped leaves may be used in potpourris or sparingly in salads, while the flowers are an edible garnish. The perennial plant attracts bees and hummingbirds.

Culture: See Monarda.

Harvest: Both leaves and flowers are used. Cut flowers when newly opened. Cut leaves for drying when the flowers begin to form.

Pests & Diseases: Powdery mildew can disfigure plants in places that are too dry. Move plants, or apply a baking-soda spray (see page 192).

Borage

(Boraginaceae, *Borago officinalis*)
Beebread

The saying "borage for courage" reflects an old belief that this plant can induce euphoria—perhaps enough to inspire a folly that might pass for bravery. "The leaves, flowers and seed, all or any of them, are good to expel pensiveness and melancholy," wrote Nicholas Culpeper in the 17th century. The foliage of borage has a cucumber flavor that suits salads, eggs, pickles and cold summer drinks. The young leaves can even be cooked like spinach; the older leaves are unpleasantly fuzzy. The dried flowers, which are bright blue, add color to potpourris and salads. An annual, borage grows 2 to 3 feet (0.6-1 m) tall and has gray-green velvety leaves. The plant attracts bees so dependably that it is nicknamed beebread.

Culture: Because borage is difficult to transplant, the seeds should be sown outdoors where they will grow. About 2 weeks before the last frost date, sow seeds in a fairly dry location in sun or light shade.

Chamomile flowers left unpicked will self-sow.

Thin seedlings to 1 foot (30 cm) apart. They mature in about 80 days but can be sown every 3 weeks until midsummer to prolong the harvest of young, tender leaves. If allowed to bloom, borage will often self-sow.

Harvest: Pinch off young leaves as needed, and extend the harvest by pinching off flowers. Borage is only good when fresh.

Pests & Diseases: None of note.

Catnip

(Labiatae, *Nepeta cataria*)

The species name *cataria* literally means "of cats," and if catnip is growing on your property, cats will find it, rolling in it and chewing it as soon as it emerges from the soil in spring. Catnip is not entirely for cats, however. A medicinal herb of long-standing reputation, it is also used to ease coughs, flatulence and headaches, and catnip tea is a calming beverage. Catnip is a hardy perennial about 2 feet (60 cm) tall with ragged-looking foliage that resembles nettles. Purple flower heads appear in summer. It often self-sows so generously that this native of Europe and Asia has become a weedy nuisance in some North American farmyards.

Culture: Buy plants in spring, or grow from seeds. Seeds need darkness to germinate. Sow them, just covered, either directly where they will grow in the garden or indoors about 6 weeks before the last frost. Thin to 6 inches (15 cm) apart. Catnip does best in full sun and will tolerate poor, dry soil.

Harvest: Use fresh for tea, or dry for later. To make cat toys, dry the leaves but do not crush them. Sew a strong fabric mouse, and stuff with leaves.

Pests & Diseases: None of note.

Chamomile
(Compositae, *Matricaria recutita*;
Chamaemelum nobile; Anthemis nobilis)
German Chamomile; Sweet False Chamomile
Chamomile, which is such an honored medicine that it is still included in the pharmacopoeia of more than 20 countries, is one of many herbs most appreciated now simply because of its appealing taste. Its medicinal benefits are anti-inflammatory, antiseptic, carminative, healing and sedative. The leaves are bitter and the flowers too chewy for salads, but steeped in boiling water, they yield one of the most popular herbal teas. There are several types, but the one most easily grown in the North for tea is German, or sweet false, chamomile, an annual whose fragrant white-petaled, yellow-centered daisies bloom in summer on relaxed 1-foot (30 cm) stems. Chamomile self-sows freely, so unless you pick every blossom, you will likely have chamomile again next year.

Culture: Grow German chamomile from seeds sown directly in the garden any time in spring. They will germinate and grow as the soil warms. Thin to 4 inches (10 cm) apart. The plant does best in a sunny location in well-drained soil and will tolerate poor, dry soil once established.

Harvest: Pick the flowers at any stage, and dry thoroughly before storing in jars for use in teas and baths. Constant picking will prolong the harvest.

Chervil
(Umbelliferae, *Anthriscus cerefolium*)
French Parsley
Chervil is an annual with delicate, fernlike leaves that have a licorice-parsley flavor especially esteemed in France. They can be used in Béarnaise sauce, in salads, with chicken, veal and omelets or as a garnish. The plant, which grows about 2 feet (60 cm) tall, will tolerate light frost.

Culture: Because chervil is difficult to transplant, the seeds are best sown outdoors in early spring on a shady patch of moist soil. Sprinkle the seeds on the soil, then press down lightly, keeping the patch watered with a fine spray until the seeds sprout in about 2 weeks. When they are 2 inches (5 cm) tall, thin seedlings to stand 6 inches (15 cm) apart. If allowed to flower, chervil may self-sow in the garden.

Harvest: At first, cut only the outside leaves so that the center will continue growing. Later, the entire plant can be cut once or twice. Chervil leaves are far better fresh or frozen than dried, when they lose most of their flavor. Seeds may be sown in a windowsill pot for a winter supply of fresh leaves.

Pests & Diseases: None of note.

Chile Pepper
(Solanaceae, *Capsicum frutescens*)
All peppers, including the sweet peppers described on page 92, are sometimes called chiles to distinguish them from white or black pepper, the common seasonings that are natives of Asia. All chiles are South American perennials that are usually grown as annuals in the North. They vary in the size of the plant and in the size and appearance of the fruit and its degree of hotness. Some of the more common chiles include:

• Cayenne: very thin, about 6 inches (15 cm) long, fiery hot, turning from dark green to red with maturity.

• Tabasco: thin, about 1 inch (2.5 cm) long, hot, turning from light green to red with maturity.

• Jalapeño: about 2 inches (5 cm) wide and 4 inches (10 cm) long, medium hot, turning from dark green to red with maturity.

• Ancho: similar in size and shape to a bell pepper, mild to hot, turning from dark green to red to brown with maturity.

• Hungarian Wax, or Yellow Banana: a little longer than a jalapeño, medium to hot, turning from yellow to red with maturity.

• Ornamental peppers, whose seed is often listed in the flower section of seed catalogs, produce very hot, tiny peppers on small plants that are ideally suited to window ledges or flower gardens. Allow a 6-inch (15 cm) pot of rich soil for each plant.

Culture: See Pepper.

Harvest: These peppers can be left on the plant until they have reached their mature color and dried; if the weather is inclement, they can be harvested earlier. Pull entire plants, and hang them upside down; the fruit will continue to ripen. The plants must be protected from frost or harvested. Be careful when handling chiles, and wash your hands thoroughly afterward. The hottest part is the membrane inside the skin. Some chiles are so hot that the juice will cause painful, though not visible, burns, especially if you rub your eyes or nose. Fruits may be pickled, frozen or dried whole or sliced. When thoroughly dry, peppers should be stored whole or ground for use as cayenne or chile pepper. Because few of these peppers are hybrid, their seeds can usually be saved for planting next year. See the instructions for saving pepper seeds on page 202.

Pests & Diseases: See Pepper.

Chives
(Amaryllidaceae, *Allium* spp)
Hardy, spreading and very versatile in the kitchen, chives are an attractive addition to most northern herb gardens, where they will do well as long as they are adequately watered. A mild substitute for onions, chives are used fresh in salads, cooked in stir-fry dishes and added to various meats and vegetables. The common garden chive (*A. schoenoprasum*) grows into rounded clumps about 1 foot (30 cm) tall and bears rosy lavender flowers in early summer. The garlic chive (*A. tuberosum*) produces white flowers and flatter, paler green leaves with a mild garlic flavor. Garlic chives are somewhat

Common chives produce beautiful purple flowers that can complement an ornamental garden.

taller and a little less winter-hardy than common chives but will overwinter in most places if mulched.

Culture: Chives are sufficiently popular and prolific that most gardeners should be able to obtain a few bulbs from a friend or a nursery. The plant can also be grown fairly easily from seeds sown indoors or outdoors in the same way as onions. In early spring—but after heavy frosts are over—set plants in groups of two or three at 1-foot (30 cm) intervals in a sunny or partially shaded location and fairly well-drained soil. Chives can also be grown in pots: A clump can be dug in fall and planted in potting mix to provide fresh chives indoors all winter, as long as the plant has adequate light and water. In the garden, chives spread gradually and may self-sow. Clumps are easy to divide in spring or fall.

Harvest: Because chives can be picked all year and do not dry or freeze very successfully, they are usually used fresh. Snip them off just above the base.

Pests & Diseases: None of note.

Coriander

(Umbelliferae, *Coriandrum sativum*)

Chinese Parsley; Cilantro

A herb of ancient reputation, coriander is used in cooking almost worldwide, although in very different ways. Some cultures know it best as a seed, others as a green leaf. East Indian cooks often use the seeds in their curries, and Europeans sometimes use them in cakes, breads, liqueurs and sausages. Spanish and South American cooks make frequent use of the leaves, which they call cilantro. Another name, Chinese parsley, attests to the popularity of the leaves in Oriental dishes. The ripe seeds have a flavor reminiscent of lemon and camphor. The flavor of cilantro leaves is similar to parsley but more distinctive, and the smell is considered unpleasant by some people, thus the genus name that comes from the Greek *koris,* meaning "bedbug." The flowers attract bees.

Culture: Coriander is an annual that resembles Italian parsley. Since it does not transplant easily, it should be sown directly in the garden in full sun. In warm soil, the seeds germinate quickly and, thereafter, can tolerate drought. Thin to 8 to 10 inches (20-25 cm) apart. As soon as the seeds are ripe, they must be harvested, or they will scatter. Seeds can be kept in jars and used for seasoning or for next year's plants.

Harvest: Pinch off leaves and shoots as needed in Oriental or Mexican dishes. Leaves must be used fresh, not dried. When the flower stalks appear in summer, leaf production stops.

Pests & Diseases: Coriander is sometimes infested by carrot rust fly. See Carrot.

Dill

(Umbelliferae, *Anethum graveolens*)

The umbrellalike seed heads of this blue-green herb are better known than are those of its biennial relatives, carrot, parsley and parsnip. Dill is an annual that is usually planted in the vegetable garden. The fragrant greens in spring are a delicious garnish for salads and fish dishes. The summer seed heads are prized for pickles, potato salads, eastern European dishes, breads and dressings. The seed stalks can grow 2 to 3 feet (0.6-1 m) tall but are too wispy to present a serious shading problem for neighboring vegetables. The ornamental cultivar 'Fernleaf' is about half as tall. Dill was said by John Parkinson in 1629 to have a therapeutic effect on the gastrointestinal system, "it being stronger than Fenel is of the more force to expel wind in the body. Some use to eat the seed to stay Hicock." Nicholas Culpeper agreed a few years later that dill "stayeth the hiccough, being boiled in wine and but smelled unto."

Culture: Dill does not transplant well, so seeds should be sown directly in the garden. If transplants are used, try not to disturb the roots. A couple of weeks before the last frost date or early enough to allow the plants about 70 days to mature before frost, sow seeds in a sunny or partially shaded spot. Thin plants to 4 inches (10 cm) apart. Dill often self-sows if the plant is allowed to drop some seeds in the garden. Sown indoors in pots, dill is used for leaves but may not go to seed.

Harvest: Dill leaves can be used as soon as they appear, or the heads can be cut as they open but before the seeds fall. They taste best when still green. Leaves and seed heads may be dried, frozen or used in herb vinegar. After the seeds mature and turn brown, they can be stripped from the heads for use as seasoning or next year's seed.

Pests & Diseases: Dill is sometimes infested with carrot rust fly. See Carrot.

Fennel

(Umbelliferae, *Foeniculum vulgare*)

Florence Fennel; Finochio; Anise

There are many types of fennel grown for seeds, roots and foliage, but Florence fennel (*F. vulgare azoricum*), a native perennial of southern Europe and the Mediterranean area, is grown as an annual primarily for its enlarged bulb—actually a thickened base of the leaves, which resemble those of

Able to grow almost anywhere, horseradish can take over the garden if its pungent roots are tilled.

celery. Increasingly available in specialty markets and often sold as anise, because it has a similar licorice flavor, fennel is also easy to grow in the garden, and every bit of it is edible.

Culture: There are varieties for spring, summer and fall/winter production. Florence fennel can be grown from seeds or transplants, but it is a long-season crop so is best started early indoors. Set plants 8 to 10 inches (20-25 cm) apart. Since they can grow as tall as 4 to 5 feet (1.2-1.5 m), they should be situated where they will not shade sun-loving plants. Fennel does best in cool weather with frequent watering and has a tendency to bolt to seed as the temperature rises.

Harvest: Fennel leaves and stems can be used in salads and as garnishes. The root can be grated into salads. Harvest entire plants after the bulb fattens but before flowering begins. Trim off the top of the foliage and the roots, wash the bulb, and store it in the refrigerator. Fennel can be used raw, steamed, sautéed or roasted.

Pests & Diseases: Fennel is sometimes infested with carrot rust fly. See Carrot.

Horseradish

(Cruciferae, *Armoracia rusticana*)
One of the most persistent of perennials, horseradish has a tendency to take over and is difficult to clear out of a spot once established. It is usually best relegated to a northern corner of the vegetable garden, where its 2-foot-tall (60 cm) broad-leaved foliage will not shade or crowd other plants. Do not till the horseradish bed, because cut pieces of roots will grow into new plants.

Culture: Horseradish cannot be grown from seeds. Obtain plants, or plant pieces of root, about 3 inches (7.5 cm) long, just below the soil surface and 18 inches (45 cm) apart. Horseradish can be planted in early spring or in fall, before the soil freezes. As with other root crops, the straightest, fattest horseradish roots grow in soil that has been deeply worked and is rich in organic matter, but horseradish is a hardy plant that will survive almost any soil condition except standing water or a prolonged drought.

Harvest: For the hottest roots, dig horseradish just before the ground freezes in fall or immediately after it thaws in spring. Warmer soil means milder roots, but horseradish can be dug anytime. Wash the roots, and grate them right away for sauces and dressings, or store the roots in perforated plastic bags in the refrigerator until needed. Horseradish, like onion, releases volatile compounds as it is grated or chopped, so be prepared for tears.

Pests & Diseases: None of note.

Hyssop

(Labiatae, *Hyssopus officinalis*)

A hardy perennial native of southern Europe, hyssop is an attractive plant that will overwinter in most northern gardens, especially under a mulch, but it is not likely to be used in many kitchens, because it is bitter. Nicholas Culpeper, who wrote in the 17th century that "the plant is of a pretty strong aromatic smell," recommended that hyssop be applied externally for cuts and bruises. During this century, Maude Grieve recommended hyssop tea sweetened with honey as a cure for rheumatism. But whether or not it is used, the plant—a shrub about 18 inches (45 cm) high, with small evergreen leaves and blue, rose or white flowers—is beautiful and easy and lends itself to formal designs such as knot gardens. When in bloom, it is a favorite of bees.

Culture: Hyssop grows easily from seeds sown outdoors 4 weeks before the last spring frost date or sown indoors a month before that. The seeds germinate in about 10 days. Transplant or thin seedlings 12 to 18 inches (30-45 cm) apart in any weed-free, well-drained spot. Hyssop tolerates sun or shade. The plant may later be propagated by dividing clumps. Also, hyssop self-sows in most gardens, and new seedlings that appear in spring can be transplanted readily.

Harvest: Before the plant flowers, pick leaves and branch tips to use in cooking.

Pests & Diseases: None of note.

Lavender

(Labiatae, *Lavandula angustifolia*; *L. officinalis*)

Lavender is something of a luxury in a northern garden, but it is perennial, even if short-lived. While most Northerners will never grow the knee-high shrubs that overwinter in mild gardens, some varieties, such as 'Munstead' and 'Lady' are hardy enough to survive winter temperatures of minus 4 degrees F (–20°C) to minus 22 degrees (–30°C) when mulched. Plants die to the ground in winter and reappear in spring, growing 1 foot (30 cm) tall by fall. Lavender has whitish foliage, sprays of lavender-colored flowers in summer and a distinctive, sweet fragrance when touched.

Culture: The cultivar 'Lady,' an All-America Selection in 1994, can be grown easily from seed, will flower the first year and is hardy to zone 5. Start seeds indoors 6 to 12 weeks before the last spring frost date. Seeds require light for germination, so press them against the surface of potting mix. Germination is slow. Otherwise, root cuttings or obtain plants and set 1 foot (30 cm) apart. Lavender does best in full sun or a little shade in well-drained soil that is not too rich. This is a good plant for a 1-foot-wide (30 cm) pot. In late fall, set the entire pot in the ground up to its rim, then cover both pot and plant with about a foot (30 cm) of hay or fallen leaves. Do not remove the mulch in spring until heavy frosts have passed. Lavender can be propagated from cuttings, by layering, by division or, in the case of 'Lady,' by seed.

Harvest: Harvest top shoots to dry for potpourris and sachets and to use sparingly to flavor desserts, jellies, dressings and wines. Picking should be done only until midsummer. Harvesting later can weaken the plant and cause the growth of fragile stems that are vulnerable to winterkill.

Pests & Diseases: None of note.

Lemon Verbena

(Verbenaceae, *Aloysia triphylla*; *Lippia citriodora*)
The strongest lemon flavor in the herb garden comes from this tender perennial that, like bay laurel, suits itself to the northern garden by spending winters indoors. Unlike bay, however, lemon verbena is deciduous. It spends the winter in a leafless or semi-leafless condition, then grows a new crop of slender, lemon-scented leaves as the days lengthen in spring. In summer, it produces a crop of small white flowers. Outdoors in the South, lemon verbena grows into a shrub 10 feet (3 m) tall, but in pots, it stays small.

Culture: Obtain lemon verbena plants; this herb cannot be grown from seeds. To propagate, root tip cuttings. Water whenever the top ½ inch (1 cm) of soil is dry. Apply fish fertilizer or manure tea every 2 weeks in spring and early summer. Accustom the plant gradually to the outdoors by putting it first in a shady place, though it should spend the summer in a sheltered spot that is mostly sunny. Bring it indoors before heavy fall frosts. Cut stems back if the plant becomes leggy.

Harvest: Pick foliage as needed in spring and summer. Lemon verbena foliage dries well, retaining its lemon flavor for winter teas and its fragrance for potpourris when the plant is bare.

Pests & Diseases: Indoors, lemon verbena may become infested with aphids, spider mites or whiteflies. Keep it away from other houseplants. Spray the plant with insecticidal soap before bringing it indoors and again if infestation occurs.

Lovage

(Umbelliferae, *Levisticum officinale*)
During the 17th century, Nicholas Culpeper wrote that lovage tea "takes away the redness and dimness of the eyes if dropped into them; it removes spots and freckles from the face." More to the point today, lovage has a pleasant flavor which blends that of two of its relatives, parsley and celery. Easy to grow in most areas, it is a hardy perennial that thrives in damp soil and partial shade. It looks like overgrown, leafy celery that has shot up to 6 feet (2 m) tall.

Culture: One plant will supply a typical family with all the lovage it needs, so a single transplant is sufficient. Plants can also be started from seeds sown outdoors in moist soil in spring. Thin them gradually to stand 2 feet (60 cm) apart. Regular watering and occasional fertilizing in spring and early summer will ensure a constant supply of large, tender leaves. Clumps gradually enlarge. The plant may be propagated by dividing the clumps as soon as shoots appear in spring.

Harvest: Harvest branches and leaves as needed for fresh use. The fresh leaves are used sparingly in salads or sandwiches. Use fresh sprigs to decorate and flavor tomato beverages. Use the leaves, fresh or dried, in soups, stews, breads and stuffings. Seeds can be stripped from mature seed heads for use as seasoning. Leaves can be dried or frozen, and young stems can be blanched as a cooked-celery substitute. The root is also edible in soups and stews.

Pests & Diseases: None of note.

Marjoram

(Labiatae, *Origanum majorana*)
Sweet Marjoram; Knotted Marjoram
Sweet marjoram is a tender perennial grown as an annual in the North. Bushy, with small, gray-green, rounded, velvety leaves, the plant grows about 10 inches (25 cm) tall, tolerates light frost and occasionally overwinters in milder areas. According to William Turner in 1551, marjoram leaves should be "layd unto the styngyng of a scorpyone with salt and vinegre." In 1629, John Parkinson added that the plant could be used in "sweete powders, sweete bags and sweete washing water." Now, marjoram is used in soups and stews and with lamb, carrots, mushrooms, veal and poultry. It is more delicately flavored and more highly esteemed for culinary use than its hardier cousin, oregano.

Culture: Buy transplants, and plant sweet marjoram outdoors a week after the last spring frost date. Or sow the fine seeds as described for balm. Germination may be poor and can take more than 3 weeks. Seeds should be kept in the shade until they sprout, after which they must be moved into sunlight. Transplant outdoors at 1-foot (30 cm) intervals in a sunny spot with well-drained sandy soil. Sweet marjoram may be potted in fall and brought indoors to a sunny windowsill for winter use, then replanted in the garden after the last spring frost.

Harvest: Pinch off stems or leaves as needed, and cut stalks as they begin to flower. The best flavor is in the green, knotlike buds that have given sweet marjoram the name knotted marjoram. Leaves can be dried or frozen.

Pests & Diseases: None of note.

Mint

(Labiatae, *Mentha* spp)

Most mints are hardy perennials that spread by runners and tend to take over the garden if they are not pruned back every year. Native field mint (*M. arvenis*) grows 8 to 30 inches (20-75 cm) tall and looks much like its relative, the stinging nettle, with hairy, toothed, pointed leaves and flowers growing in the leaf axils. It has less flavor than and is not as sweet as the cultivated mints but was consumed as a tea and used as a condiment and medicine by North American native people.

There are many varieties of mint. Among the most common:

• Spearmint, or garden mint (*M. spicata* or *M. viridis*), has a distinctive sweet flavor that makes it and its relatives the most valued of mints in cooking. One variety, curly mint, has broad, crumpled leaves. Spearmint grows 2 to 3 feet (0.6-1 m) tall and spreads quickly, especially in damp ground. A hybrid of spearmint and water mint (*M. aquatica*) is *M.* x *piperita*, peppermint or candymint. There are many forms, some variegated.

• Apple mint (*M. suaveolens*) has soft, gray-green leaves with an apple fragrance. One variation, pineapple mint, is a sprawling plant with attractive variegated green-and-white leaves and a pineapple fragrance. It grows about 1 foot (30 cm) tall and may be invasive where winters are mild, although it is unlikely to survive harsh winters.

• Orange, or bergamot, mint (*M. citrata*) grows about 2 feet (60 cm) tall. Its leaves have purplish margins and a slight orange fragrance and flavor.

• Corsican mint (*M. requienii*), which is not hardy in most of the North, is a creeper that forms a lovely fragrant temporary ground cover for a herb garden. Sow the seeds directly in the garden where they will grow.

• Pennyroyal (*M. pulegium*) was a pioneer favorite that grows into a prostrate shrub about 1 foot (30 cm) tall and wide. It was traditionally planted near the front door to help repel flies, ants and fleas. It is not invasive and will not survive harsh winters.

Culture: The best way to start is to obtain plants, preferably by smelling and tasting the foliage before buying, because mints are so variable. Seeds are sometimes untrustworthy in their purity and variety and tend to germinate poorly. Gardeners who do obtain seeds should follow the directions for balm. When seedlings are 2 inches (5 cm) tall, set them outdoors 6 inches (15 cm) apart. Unlike most herbs, mint will tolerate shade, crowding and a great deal of moisture. Because the hardy perennial types spread quickly, only two to five plants are needed at the beginning. Control the plants by digging up runners every spring—these can be used for propagation if desired—or by growing plants in large pots or drainage tiles submerged in the soil, the rim extending just above the soil surface. On most mints, the flower spikes are not particularly attractive and can be sheared off.

Harvest: Harvest mint leaves and stem tips as desired throughout the season to use fresh, or preserve by drying or freezing. Mints are a fragrant addition to herbal baths. They suit fruit salads and summer drinks and, of course, partner lamb dishes in the form of jelly or sauce. Mint is the source of menthol, still used in cold remedies and as a flavoring agent.

Pests & Diseases: Rust may appear on plants growing in overly rich soil. Dig up infected plants,

The leaves and flowers of nasturtium are edible, as are the seed pods left after the petals fall.

burn or discard them, and replant mint in a new location the following year.

Nasturtium

(Tropaeolaceae, *Tropaeolum* spp)
Indian Cress

The common garden nasturtiums (*T. majus* and *T. nanum*) are Peruvian perennials whose ornamental virtues are described on page 138. But the same plants were once respected for medicine and food, when they were known as Indian cresses, plants "rare and faire." Medicinally, they were used to treat urinary and respiratory infections. Their use as food is suggested by the common name "nasturtium," which is the same as the genus of watercress (*Nasturtium officinale*), whose leaves also have a peppery

flavor. There are both climbing and bush varieties.

Harvest: The young green fruits, or seed pods, left behind after the petals fall can be pickled to use as a substitute for capers. Collect the pods, and cover with a brine made of 8 parts water and 1 part pickling salt. Continue to collect seeds until you have enough, replacing the brine every 3 days. Pour off the brine. Pack the seed pods into small, sterilized jars, cover with boiling vinegar, and seal. The flowers and leaves are edible in sandwiches and salads and can be used as beautiful garnishes for any summer foods.

Pests & Diseases: None of note.

Oregano

(Labiatae, *Origanum vulgare*)
Wild Marjoram

This staple of Italian cuisine is closely related to marjoram and has a similar but stronger flavor. It is a sprawling perennial that grows about 2 feet (60 cm) tall. A crop of small pink or white flowers appears in early summer. Oregano is good with pasta and pizza as well as lamb, guacamole and green beans. It was once esteemed as a gargle for sore throats, and herbalist John Gerard claimed in 1597 that it also "healeth scabs, itchings and scurviness, being used in bathes." During the next century, Nicholas Culpeper wrote that "it strengthens the stomach and head much; there is scarcely a better herb growing for relieving a sour stomach, loss of appetite, cough, congestion of the lungs."

Culture: Greek, or true, oregano (*O. vulgare*; *O. heracleoticum*) is a half-hardy perennial treated as an annual or moved indoors in most of the North. There are several additional tender perennial species of oregano that can be cultivated the same way. Pot a plant before heavy frost in fall, and set it beside a sunny window for winter use, replanting it outdoors after the last heavy frost in spring. Wild oregano, or common or pot marjoram (*O. vulgare*), is a hardy perennial, but its flavor is not as fine as that of true oregano. It produces a clump 2 feet (60 cm) tall and has broad, oval leaves with blunted tips. The subspecies 'Aureum,' golden creeping oregano, forms a beautiful yellow ground cover in a herb garden, though the leaves have little flavor. The flowers, ranging from pale pink to purple, attract bees. Oregano is best grown from transplants. The outcome of growing from seeds is unreliable. Set plants at 1-foot (30 cm) intervals in light, well-drained soil in a sunny place. Growth is slow, so the bed must be kept weeded to prevent crowding. Replace plants every 3 or 4 years, starting new ones by layering stems (see page 199).

Harvest: Pinch off fresh leaves as needed, and complete the harvest when plants start to flower. Pinching off the flowers as they develop will prolong the harvest.

Pests & Diseases: None of note.

Parsley

(Umbelliferae, *Petroselinum crispum*)

Curled, or moss-curled, parsley is the type that is best known as a garnish. The small celerylike leaves of the plain-leaved varieties, called French, Italian or Greek, have a more subtle flavor and are more winter-hardy. Hamburg, or turnip-rooted, parsley (*Carum petroselinum*) produces a slender parsnip-like root that can be used in soups and stews and stored in a root cellar like beets or carrots. Parsley leaves can be used in almost every meal, in soups, stews, sandwich fillings, sauces and stuffings and, of course, as a garnish. Thomas Hyll wrote in 1568 that "chawinge of the fresh and grene Parceleye doth cause a swete smelling breath." The Greeks used the plant as a garden border.

Culture: Parsley is slow from seed and dislikes being transplanted. Sow seeds indoors 8 weeks before the last spring frost date or outdoors as soon as the soil can be worked in spring. Soaking the seeds in warm water for 24 hours before sowing will speed germination, which may take as long as 3 weeks. Thin plants gradually to stand 6 inches

(15 cm) apart, using the thinnings as salad greens or seasoning. Plants will grow in full sun or, more slowly, in partial shade. They do best when watered regularly and fertilized with manure tea once a week. Mulching encourages good growth. Parsley is a hardy biennial, so any plant that has not been harvested too heavily may overwinter and go to seed the following summer. Or a plant may be carefully dug in fall and replanted in a deep 12-inch-diameter (30 cm) pot of rich soil for fresh greens indoors for the early part of the winter.

Harvest: Pinch off leaves and sprigs as needed. In late fall, pick most foliage for drying or freezing or, alternatively, replant in pots as described above and bring indoors to a sunny window.

Pests & Diseases: Hand-pick parsleyworms. Parsley is sometimes infested with carrot rust fly. See Carrot.

Rosemary

(Labiatae, *Rosmarinus officinalis*)

This attractive plant, with its grayish evergreen leaves and woody stems, has traditionally been associated with fidelity: "Rosemary for remembrance." Peter Treveris's *Grete Herball* of 1526 recommended that those suffering from "weyknesse of ye brayne" inhale the smoke of rosemary that had been soaked in wine. Perhaps the patient, his or her "brayne" strengthened, would regain lost memories, thus fortifying the plant's reputation. Rosemary is perennial in its native southern Europe, where it may grow 6 feet (2 m) or taller, but in most of the North, it must be wintered indoors. Many Northerners keep rosemary in pots year-round so that the plants can be easily moved indoors and outdoors.

Culture: Rosemary seeds germinate slowly and poorly, and the plant itself grows so slowly that none can be harvested for a couple of years. Instead, obtain potted plants or root cuttings. Rosemary can also be easily tip-layered (see page 199).

The many faces of salvia include common sage, left, and the less hardy 'Aurea,' 'Tricolor' and 'Purpurea.'

If the plant is in a pot, root the tip in another pot placed next to it. Once the tip has rooted, it can be cut from the parent plant. After the last spring frost, plants can be set outdoors in pots or in sandy, well-drained soil. Rosemary will tolerate full sun or partial shade but must not be allowed to dry out for any length of time, a particular hazard for potted plants outdoors. Before bringing plants indoors, prune them lightly. Indoors, the plant does best in a bright, cool place where the air is moist, difficult to find in most homes, though it will survive greater warmth and dryness. Mist the plant occasionally. Harden it off (see page 53) before setting it outdoors again in spring.

Harvest: Rosemary is best when it is used fresh. Pinch off leaves sparingly as needed for cooking with lamb and chicken and in fruit salads, breads and medicinal teas. Leaves may also be dried for later use.
Pests & Diseases: None of note.

Sage
(Labiatae, *Salvia* spp)
A Latin proverb of the Middle Ages posed the question, "Why should a man die while sage is in his garden?" The plant was reputed to cure everything from toothaches and coughs to wounds, failing memory and gray hair, which the juice was said to darken. "If it were possible," wrote one herbalist of Tudor times, "it would make man immortal."

Sage has a strong, distinctive flavor that complements poultry, sausages, peas, rabbit and fish and is good in herb breads or mixed with cream cheese. Common garden sage (*S. officinalis*) is also such an attractive plant, with its gray-green foliage and spires of blue flowers, that it suits the flower garden. It is a hardy perennial that grows about 18 inches (45 cm) tall and dies back to the soil every winter in most northern gardens. Survival is best in well-drained, dryish soil. At the Devonian Botanic Garden, near Edmonton, Alberta, however, sage is not hardy and so is grown as an annual. The varieties 'Icterina' and 'Tricolor,' both with variegated foliage, cannot tolerate severe winters and must be overwintered indoors in most of the North. Do not confuse the variety 'Tricolor' with tricolor sage (*S. viridis*), an ornamental annual. Pineapple sage (*S. elegans*), whose leaves are delightfully scented and flavored like pineapple, is one of several fruit-scented types that are beautiful but frost-tender. Root tip cuttings in water to pot up indoors for the winter, and set plants back outdoors after the last spring frost.

Culture: Sage can be grown easily from seeds sown in the manner of salvia (see page 146). Tip cuttings are also easy to root. Set plants about 1 foot (30 cm) apart in sandy soil in a sunny place. Perennials tend to be short-lived, so expect to replace plants every 3 or 4 years.

Harvest: Pinch off leaves and plant tips as needed, completing the harvest when the plant begins to flower. The leaves are fairly thick, so drying time is longer than for most herbs. Sage can also be preserved in vinegar.

Pests & Diseases: None of note.

Salad Burnet

(Rosaceae, *Poterium sanguisorba*; *Sanguisorba minor*) A short-lived perennial that is evergreen in most northern gardens, salad burnet is little known but was, at one time, according to herbalist John Gerard, "thought to make the hart merry and glad." That recalls the reputation of borage, another herb that tastes of cucumber, a flavor that must have cheered the medieval palate. In William Turner's herbal of 1551, he poetically described the plant as having "two little leaves like onto the wings of birds, standing out as the bird setteth her wings out as she intendeth to flye." Salad burnet grows 1 to 2 feet (30-60 cm) tall and is attractive enough to border a herb garden. A bonus is a crop of small crimson flowers in summer.

Culture: Sow the seeds outdoors ½ inch (1 cm) deep, in fall or early spring. Salad burnet will grow in any well-drained soil and does best in full sun, although it will tolerate shade. Transplants may be set outdoors at 12-inch (30 cm) intervals in early spring. Later, the plant can be propagated by dividing the entire clump, although it is just as easily left to self-sow in the garden.

Harvest: Pinch off the top leaves throughout the season, using only these young leaves in salads, cold drinks and casseroles. Removal of the flower stalks will prolong the harvest, which should be discontinued once the flowers have bloomed. Allow the plant to go to seed if you intend it to self-sow. Leaves may be dried for later use, although some flavor will be lost. Salad burnet leaves also make a good herb vinegar.

Pests & Diseases: None of note.

Savory

(Labiatae, *Satureja* spp)
Winter savory (*S. montana*) is a low-growing 8-inch (20 cm) hardy perennial with small, stiff leaves that are evergreen in warmer places. Its flavor is stronger and not as highly esteemed as that of summer savory, but it is used in much the same way. Summer savory (*S. hortensis*) is an erect, branching annual that grows about 12 to 18 inches (30-45 cm) tall. With pink flowers and small, gray-green leaves, it is attractive enough for perennial borders and annual flower gardens. The mild-flavored leaves are used in soups and sauces and in egg, poultry and bean dishes. Because its flavor complements beans, peas and lentils, savory is some-

times called the bean herb—its German name, *Bohnenkraut*, means just that.

Culture: Winter savory may be grown from seed (follow the instructions for balm), although transplants short-cut the growing process. Set plants outdoors after the last spring frost date, 1 foot (30 cm) apart, in well-drained soil and full sun. A clump of winter savory can be dug up and potted for indoor use during the winter. Summer savory does not transplant well and is much easier to grow from seed, which can be sown outdoors, just covered, around the last spring frost date. Sow seeds close together, and thin plants to several inches apart.

Harvest: Strip off leaves as needed until flowers start to open in midsummer, then cut stalks for drying or freezing.

Pests & Diseases: None of note.

Sorrel

(Polygonaceae, *Rumex* spp)

Sourgrass

Sorrel, which is related to buckwheat and the weed dock, has a flavor that some find reminiscent of citrus fruits and others describe as just plain sour; the name comes from the Old French *surele*, meaning "sour." A leafy, bushy plant that grows from 10 inches (25 cm) to 3 feet (1 m) tall and is perennial in its native southern Europe, sorrel is grown as a hardy annual throughout most of the North. French sorrel (*R. scutatus*) has broad leaves and the mildest flavor, while garden sorrel (*R. acetosa*) has narrow leaves. Although the herb lends a distinct *haute cuisine* flavor to some dishes, especially salads, casseroles and sorrel soup, sorrel should not be eaten in large quantity—the flavor is partly due to a high level of oxalates, which have been responsible for the poisoning of animals and people.

Culture: Sow seeds outdoors about 4 weeks before the last spring frost date in fertile, moist soil in a sunny or shady spot. The plant tolerates light frost and does best in cool weather. When the seedlings are about 1 inch (2.5 cm) tall, thin them to stand 8 inches (20 cm) apart, using the thinnings in the kitchen.

Harvest: The young leaves have the mildest flavor and are best for salads and sandwiches, while the older, stronger-tasting leaves are a better complement to soups and casseroles. The leaves may be harvested anytime, as long as the plant is not weakened by overpicking. Leaves may be dried for storage, but some of the distinctive flavor will be lost. Plants may self-sow if allowed to go to seed in summer.

Pests & Diseases: None of note.

Sweet Cicely

(Umbelliferae, *Myrrhis odorata*)

Declared "exceeding good, wholesome and pleasant among other sallad herbs" by John Gerard in his 16th-century herbal, sweet cicely is a hardy perennial that, along with anise, fennel, anise-hyssop and angelica, provides licorice-flavored leaves and seeds. This plant's common name suggests that it is sweeter than the others, however. It is also one of the most attractive, with lovely fernlike fronds several feet long, decorated in summer by spiring seed stalks bearing a froth of tiny white flowers sought out by honeybees.

Culture: Sow as angelica. Thin to 2 feet (60 cm) apart. This perennial tends to self-sow, so be ready for it to spread or be diligent about removing seedlings. It is very attractive at the back of a herb garden in sun or partial shade.

Harvest: Use the leaves, immature seeds and tender young stems in salads and herb teas and as garnishes. Cooked, they can also be added to soups, casseroles and desserts. Gerard writes: "The roots are likewise most excellent in a sallad, if they be boiled and afterwards dressed as the cunning Cooke knoweth how better than my selfe; notwithstanding I use to eat them with oile and vinegar, being first boiled; which is very good for old people that are dull and without courage; it rejoiceth and comforteth the heart, and increaseth their lust and strength."

Tarragon

(Compositae, *Artemisia dracunculus sativa*)

Estragon; French Tarragon

The ancient Romans believed tarragon was so repellent to snakes that anyone who carried a sprig of it would be safe from snakebites. No doubt it earned this reputation from the appearance of its snakelike roots, which also inspired its Latin species name *dracunculus*, meaning "little dragon." True, or French, tarragon is a hardy perennial with a strong anise flavor. French tarragon grows about 2 feet (60 cm) tall and has long, thin, green leaves quite different from other artemisias but much esteemed in cordon bleu cuisine, especially in vinegar, Béarnaise sauce, tartar sauce and blends of fines herbes, with fish, shellfish and spinach.

Culture: French tarragon can be grown only from transplants or root divisions. The seed sold as tarragon is that of Russian tarragon (*A. dracunculus; A. redowskii*), which lacks the characteristic flavor and so is scarcely worth growing as a culinary herb. French tarragon will tolerate either sun or partial shade but requires well-drained soil—dampness will lead to winterkill. Cut stems back before the soil freezes, and mulch plants heavily, removing the mulch in spring. Divide plants every third spring.

Harvest: Leaves may be stripped from stems as needed but are best before the plant blooms in midsummer. Afterward, leave the plant to gain strength for winter. Leaves are best fresh but can be frozen to preserve. Tarragon makes a very good herb vinegar.

Pests & Diseases: None of note.

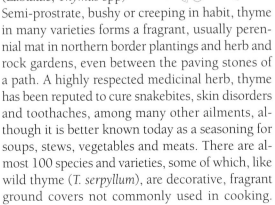

Thyme

(Labiatae, *Thymus* spp)

Semi-prostrate, bushy or creeping in habit, thyme in many varieties forms a fragrant, usually perennial mat in northern border plantings and herb and rock gardens, even between the paving stones of a path. A highly respected medicinal herb, thyme has been reputed to cure snakebites, skin disorders and toothaches, among many other ailments, although it is better known today as a seasoning for soups, stews, vegetables and meats. There are almost 100 species and varieties, some of which, like wild thyme (*T. serpyllum*), are decorative, fragrant ground covers not commonly used in cooking.

Unusual varieties can be purchased from seed companies specializing in herbs. Among the most popular types:

• Common, or garden, thyme (*T. vulgaris*) is very variable, creeping or shrubby, with small, dark green leaves. Taste plants, if possible, before you buy. This is one of the hardier species, although mulching in zone 5 or colder gardens will provide added insurance of winter survival.

• Caraway thyme (*T. herba-barona*) has a distinctive caraway flavor and aroma. It forms a low mat of small, dark green leaves and deep pink flowers. The name comes from the use of this herb as a seasoning for baron of beef in the Middle Ages. Mulch it over the winter from zone 5 north.

• Lemon thyme (*T. x citriodorus*) has a distinctive lemony fragrance and flavor. It grows into a small woody shrub about 1 foot (30 cm) tall. It is less hardy than *T. vulgaris* and should be cut back and mulched heavily to overwinter in zone 5 or colder gardens. Cultivars 'Argenteus,' 'Aureus' and 'Silver Queen' have silver or golden leaves.

• Creeping lemon, or Pennsylvania Dutch tea, thyme (*T. pulegioides*) is a hardy creeper with a strong lemon fragrance. The tea is used to treat sore throats and coughs. The cultivar 'Doone Valley,' with gold variegated leaves, needs winter protection in most gardens.

Culture: Thyme is easily grown from transplants or from established plants propagated by tip-layering. Gardeners who wish to grow thyme from seed should follow the directions given for balm, but as is true of many herbs, seed-grown plants are unpredictable. Around the last spring frost date, set plants outdoors 6 inches (15 cm) apart in a sunny spot in well-drained soil with little competition from other plants. In cold areas, mulch plants, and if there is a possibility of winterkill, overwinter some of the plants indoors.

Harvest: Pinch off branches and strip leaves from plant as needed. Flowers may also be harvested for use. All may be dried or frozen. In some places, thyme can be picked all winter, remaining evergreen under the snow. Always leave enough foliage on the plant in fall and winter to ensure that it is not weakened.

Pests & Diseases: None of note.

Chapter Seven

The Blooming of Summer

"I have contemplated a well-hoed ridge of potatoes
on that bush farm with as much delight as in years long past
I had experienced in examining a fine painting."

—Susanna Moodie

Roughing It in the Bush, 1852

Throughout the North, sometime between the end of one winter and the beginning of the next, a rapid and momentous transformation takes place. One day, vegetation struggles along, an invisible insect manages an early bite of a winter-whitened forearm, and birds arrive sporadically, like early guests at a party. And the next day, the celebration begins. The lawn has to be mowed, sunrise brings heat, and the garden bursts with life: insects, worms, birds, squirrels, flowers to pick, weeds growing like, well, weeds and, praise be, the first vegetables ready for harvest.

Coping with summer is generally the least of the northern gardener's concerns. Better to concentrate your energy on those tricky borderline times: spring and fall. If the gardener is spared untimely frosts, the summer may be spent in the garden doing little more than weeding, harvesting and enjoying. But in many areas, summer means less rain and more petal-withering heat and wind than most plants can tolerate. It also means generations of vegetation-eating larvae determined to munch their way to adulthood before the cool weather comes again. Watering, mulching and pest control are vital parts of the summer routine.

Watering

Most garden plants need a thorough soaking once a week with about 1 inch (2.5 cm) of water. A particular garden's need for water varies, however, with many things: the weather (hot, windy weather speeds evaporation from plants and soil); the layout of the garden; and the soil. Soil high in organic matter can retain water far better than soil that is chiefly silt, clay or sand. A very important part of a gardener's drought-proofing program comes from soil improvements (see Chapter Two).

Whatever the soil type, it is the plant roots in it that make the best use of water. Watering foliage wastes water and encourages the growth and spread of fungus diseases, especially in calm, hot, damp weather. So a watering system that applies the water directly to the soil surface around the plants will conserve water while helping to maintain a healthy garden. Sprinkling, on the other hand, not only pours water on foliage but requires

Sprinklers drench the foliage, wasting water and creating an environment for fungal diseases.

Although labor-intensive, hand-watering has the advantage of placing water exactly where it is most needed. Spot-watering makes very efficient use of a small amount of water. The best system of all links hand-watering with rainwater. Rainwater is better than tap water for the garden. Soft, slightly acidic and free of water-treatment additives, rainwater is also at ambient temperature, which helps plants grow; cold tap water can slow plant growth. Set up a clean oil drum or other large barrel under the downspout of eavestroughs to collect rainwater. If there is not enough, fill the barrels from a hose and let the water warm to the ambient temperature before using.

Schedule watering for a certain time each day or every second day. Take care of a portion of the garden each time, and pay most attention to seedlings, newly planted perennials, hanging baskets and other containers. Established annuals and perennials are lower on the list. Many thrive when kept on the dry side. In perennial beds or the vegetable garden, water if plants are wilted in the morning or begin to wilt before noon. On the other hand, wilting in the afternoon or evening on a hot, windy day can happen even when soil moisture levels are adequate.

Mulching

Mulches help retain moisture in the soil, especially if applied thickly after a drenching rain. Plastic mulches also assist in warming the soil. Organic mulches, such as grass clippings, hay, bark chips and fallen leaves, do not warm the soil, but their insulating properties help retain its warmth on summer nights and in fall. A deep organic mulch may make watering unnecessary, even during long, dry spells. The constantly mulched Connecticut garden of Ruth Stout, the "mother of mulch" during the 1960s, was never watered and seldom weeded or fertilized. Connecticut is, however, a relatively warm area, and such a year-round mulch system can slow soil warming and therefore retard spring growth in shorter-season gardens.

There are, in fact, a couple of cases in which organic mulches should be used sparingly, if at all. Where the season is very short or cool, do not use them except on dirt pathways. In very wet gardens, mulches can worsen slug and disease problems;

high water pressure and can waste about half the sprayed water to evaporation, even more to pathways, patios and other structures in the water's path. If you must use a sprinkler, try to direct the spray, and do so on calm evenings when evaporation is minimal. Do not work with the plants until the foliage has dried, because you may spread fungal spores.

A better watering system is a perforated, or weeping, hose that can be laid on the soil next to the plants. Trickle-irrigation equipment can be purchased at garden shops and from some mail-order suppliers. These systems can be connected directly to an outdoor tap. Household "gray" water, from washing and bathing, can be used for about half the irrigation if it has been filtered and does not contain borax, fabric softeners, bleaches or detergents (although some soap is fine). Check local bylaws, however, as gray water cannot be recycled legally in some places.

A straw mulch keeps the soil moist, weed-free and cool around the roots of a clump of garlic chives.

confine the mulches to dirt pathways and the driest areas of the garden.

The most suitable organic mulching materials for a particular garden depend on availability, cost and appearance. In the vegetable garden, choose something that is inexpensive and plentiful. Rural gardeners can usually obtain straw or spoiled hay, while city gardeners may be able to find large supplies of fallen leaves and grass clippings, especially if they can count on the contributions of neighbors, and pile or bag them in fall. Do not use grass clippings from a lawn recently sprayed with herbicides, and do not use the leaves of walnut or butternut trees, because they contain juglone, a fungicide that is harmful to some vegetables. Evergreen needles can be used, but they tend to make the soil more acidic, so do not place them around plants that prefer alkaline conditions.

For those who have access to it, seaweed is an excellent mulching material. It does not need to be rinsed to remove salt before use. Freshwater weeds are a substitute for the landlocked. Compost is another good mulch, but it is usually in too short supply to be used as anything other than a soil conditioner and mild fertilizer.

Organic mulches have a further advantage: as they decay, they contribute organic matter and nutrients to the soil. Straw, for instance, contains about 0.5 percent nitrogen, 0.2 percent phosphorus and 1 percent potassium as well as many other nutrients. Sawdust contains a little less nitrogen and potassium but slightly more phosphorus. Seaweed contains even less nitrogen and phosphorus but may have an astonishing 4.6 percent potassium content, valuable in most garden soils.

The mulch material's contribution of nutrients and fiber to the soil depends not only on its fertility but also on its carbon-to-nitrogen (C:N) ratio. In general, drier, older materials contain a higher proportion of carbon than do fresher, moister substances, the preferred mulches. Materials high in carbon will eventually add fiber and fertility to the soil, but they do so initially at the expense of soil nitrogen. For that reason, wood chips, sawdust and paper should be used sparingly or confined to pathways. Wood or bark chips make an attractive mulch for a flowerbed, but mulched plants should be fortified with a feeding of fish fertilizer or manure tea once a week. Despite its high carbon content, newspaper is so plentiful and can be so helpful in weed control that it is especially valuable where weeds are persistent. Spread several layers on the watered soil around plants, then cover with a more attractive mulch that will also prevent the paper from blowing in the wind.

While plastic mulches may be laid early in the vegetable garden so that soil warming precedes sowing or transplanting, the application of organic mulch should be delayed, because it has the opposite effect. Mulch applied too early slows the warming of the soil and can retard plant growth. Mid-June is about the right time for mulching with hay, leaves, straw or grass clippings in most northern gardens. By then, the soil is warm and the plants are growing rapidly.

First, weed the garden; then, after a rain, lay down newspaper in rows and between plants—

wherever practical—weighing down its edges with soil. Cover it with a further 4 to 6 inches (10-15 cm) of another mulch, which may reach right up under the plants and around their stems. In the small spaces between plants, where newspaper is impractical, pile straw, grass clippings, compost or leaf mold. If mulching materials are in short supply, concentrate first on the cool-loving crops in the vegetable garden, such as potatoes and leafy vegetables. Next, mulch around those plants whose fruit would otherwise rest on the ground (sprawling tomatoes, cucumbers and melons).

Weeding

Because mulches conserve water *and* control weeds, they are very popular with gardeners, few of whom really enjoy the otherwise endless task of weeding. Weeds grow faster than virtually all cultivated plants, and left on their own, these sturdy native or, more commonly, naturalized plants will take the lion's share of the light, moisture and soil nutrients, leaving the flowers and vegetables waning in their shadows.

Not only do weeds take care of their immediate needs with gusto, they also ensure that their progeny will inhabit future gardens. One hedge mustard plant can produce half a million seeds in a season; redroot pigweed and purslane produce about 200,000. The seeds of some weeds such as lamb's-quarters, purslane, pigweed and wild mustard can spring to life 40 years after being buried in the soil. No wonder successive diggings bring new flushes of weeds.

Some of the hardy biennial or perennial weeds, such as dandelions and burdock, have long taproots that must be dug almost entirely if the plant is not to rebound. Quack, or twitch, grass, which infests fields and gardens across the country, is a perennial that spreads by underground stemlike rhizomes with a number of buds or growing points, any of which can develop new shoots when the plant is broken up. It also spreads by seed and so is an exceedingly persistent plant that requires diligent digging.

Newly cleared garden plots produce the greatest crop of weeds, especially until midsummer. Keep up with any that sprout from seeds or roots, and you will gradually notice a difference.

No one ever decisively wins the battle with weeds, but then weeds are not so much enemies as competitors. They do have their good points, bringing up nutrients from deep in the soil and, after they are pulled, contributing organic matter to the garden or the compost pile. And many are as edible as the vegetables they surround. Dandelion, lamb's-quarters, wild mustard, purslane, redroot pigweed and stinging nettle are nutritious and tasty, especially when very young and tender. Wear gloves, of course, when picking and preparing stinging nettle shoot tips, which should be cooked in soups or stews, not eaten fresh. Their stinging quality is lost in cooking.

Despite the use of mulches, some weeding will have to be done in any garden. Weeds can be easily removed when young by scraping over the soil with a hoe or the edge of a trowel to decapitate them; the tops can be left where they are. If this is repeated about once a week, weeding need never be a backbreaking chore. If weeds do become more mature, they must be dug or pulled. This is most easily done after a rain, when the soil is soft. Weeds may reroot if whole plants are tossed onto the soil, so remove them to their own pile or leave them, roots up, on the mulch. Quack grass should not be composted; bag it with the garbage, throw it on dry mulch or confine it to its own pile, where you can watch it for signs of resprouting.

In perennial flower gardens, perennial grasses are the worst weeds. The ground must be free of grasses and their rhizomes before any planting is done, and thereafter, any trace of grass should be pulled and dug out as soon as you see it. A season of neglect can mean an infested perennial border that needs to be dug up so that grass roots can be painstakingly untangled from the flowers, which must then be replanted.

Insects: Friendly & Unfriendly

Second in importance to weed control is pest control. Most pests arrive in droves—a dramatic increase in plant damage can be clearly related to a sudden rise in the population of pests, often because the temperature has risen high enough to permit egg-hatching. In fact, many pests overwinter in the garden, and many more are there as

Damaged plants—and the invaders themselves—are sure signs of the inevitable onslaught of insect pests.

mating adults or eggs long before any damage appears. Removing plant debris from the garden in fall is a simple way to help control the pest population. Rotating vegetable crops (see chart on page 38) and keeping related plants apart also helps, as does regular watering, planting in warm soil and anything else that encourages the steady growth of sturdy, healthy plants. Insects and diseases are more likely to attack plants weakened by drought, early planting, overfertilization or poor soil.

Physical barriers are also effective means of pest control in some cases. To fend off cutworms, place cardboard collars or tin cans, both ends removed, over vegetable seedlings (see page 188). Use collars of window screening to keep slugs from climbing plant stems, and use blankets of cheesecloth, screening or spunbonded polyester fabric, such as

Reemay, to cover rows of vegetables vulnerable to damage by the larvae of moths or flies.

If pests do infest the plants, the best way to control them—best in terms of controls that are least harmful to the gardener or to garden allies—is by hand-picking the pests, their eggs or, sometimes, the leaves bearing egg clusters. If hand-picking seems distasteful, use a stick to knock the offenders into a jar half full of water that has a little dish-washing detergent added. A hard jet of water applied to foliage will wash off some pests. The use of baits, such as beer for slugs or a molasses solution for grasshoppers, helps the hand-picking process, and some birds will quite happily do the work for the gardener. If they find suitable nesting sites around the garden, swallows, purple martins, kingbirds and other insect-eating birds will spend virtually all their time in pursuit of their prey. A birdbath filled daily and set by a tree that provides perches will help attract beneficial birds.

Companion Planting

Another benign method of pest and disease control is companion planting, which involves arranging garden plants according to their beneficial effects on one another. Making sure that tall plants do not shade short, sun-loving plants is one of the simplest forms of companion planting, as is planting tall, wind-resistant plants where they can shelter more delicate things.

One way to confound pests is to separate plants that are members of the same botanical family. In a small garden, plants from different families will almost inevitably find themselves growing next to one another, and usually, this is just as well. Pole beans and corn, for instance, are traditional companions: beans contribute nitrogen to the soil, while corn is a heavy feeder. If the corn is given a couple of weeks' head start, the beans can use the cornstalks for support.

Explorer Samuel de Champlain noted just this system in use by indigenous peoples when he traveled up the St. Lawrence in 1604. The aboriginals planted the corn in hills of three or four kernels, each hill 3 feet (1 m) from the next. Then, wrote Champlain, "with this corn, they put in each hill three or four Brazilian beans [kidney beans], which are of different colors. When they grow up, they interlace with the corn, which reaches to the height of from 5 to 6 feet [1.5-2 m], and they keep the ground very free from weeds."

But companion planting involves more than sensible interplantings or crop rotations to make the best use of light, space and soil nutrients. Its most publicized aspect is the theory that some garden plants have an immediate, positive effect on others, often on pest control, and that furthermore, the wrong companions may have a detrimental effect. The evidence for this has been in small part scientifically documented, in large part a matter of subjective observation and, as such, liable to change with the climate, the cultivar and the pest populations and weather during any particular season. For instance, some gardeners have found that

Companion-planting nasturtiums with brassicas may fend off pest problems while adding beauty.

nasturtiums help produce healthy, pest-free brassicas, while in his experiments at Cornell University, Richard Root demonstrated that nasturtiums increased the population of flea beetles on collards. Tests at Prince Edward Island's Ark Project produced similar results, and research in 1981 in Alberta showed that neither flea-beetle nor cabbage-worm damage to cabbage was lessened by the use of any of nine species of recommended companion plants. Several of the companions, moreover, competed with the vegetables for water and nutrients, stunting cabbage growth. And, in addition to feeding on the cabbage, flea beetles also ate tansy flowers and nibbled the nasturtiums.

Nevertheless, one thing is clear: Nasturtiums are colorful and edible and, whether companionable or not, certainly provide the gardener with a more pleasant place in which to work. Companion-planting success seems to depend on the conditions in one's own garden, so experimentation is certainly worthwhile. Thoroughly companion-planted gardens are among the most attractive you can find anywhere—a pleasing mix of herbs, flowers and vegetables.

Some companions have proved beneficial everywhere. The French marigold (*Tagetes patula*) has a repellent effect that can help protect tomato and potato roots from nematode infestation if the flowers encircle the vegetables. The tall Mexican marigold (*T. minuta*) has a repellent effect on wireworms. Garlic oil has been found to be a potent larvicide and is used in sprays. Garlic, then, is a suitable companion for everything except other onions, provided the garlic is not so badly overshadowed that its own maturity is endangered. All onions have some repellent effect and so may be grown throughout the garden.

Pesticides

When hand-picking and washing is not enough to keep up with pest damage, you may want to try a spray. Before you buy insecticides from your local garden store, read the warning on the label. Most are highly toxic substances that can be harmful to you, your pets and children and the plants you spray, especially food plants. These substances may be valued by commercial growers who need perfect crops, but home gardeners should be prepared to accept a few blemishes in the cause of nurturing a safe environment. Certain pesticides, however, are considered acceptable in an organic garden.

***Bacillus thuringiensis* (Bt):** Bacterial spores sold in concentrated form are diluted with water before being sprayed on plants. Bt is an effective and very selective control of the larvae of butterflies and moths (Lepidoptera), such as cabbage loopers, tomato hornworms, gypsy moth caterpillars, tent caterpillars and parsleyworms, all of which die about 3 days after ingesting sprayed plant material. The use of Bt in aerial spray programs has been controversial, because it kills all lepidopterous insects, but when targeted directly on pests in a garden situation, it can be effective as well as safe. There is also a strain that kills the larvae of Colorado potato beetles. Apparently, neither strain has a harmful effect on humans, animals, birds, fish or earthworms.

A pump-type sprayer helps the gardener apply a pest-repellent solution of garlic, soap and cayenne.

Mineral Oil: Oil sprays are available commercially for killing overwintering pests on fruit trees and other woody perennials in early spring before the buds open. Also, ¼ teaspoon (1 mL) of light mineral oil placed on the tips of corn silks just after they have wilted helps control corn earworms.

Insecticidal Soap: Soap is a surprisingly wide-ranging pesticide that kills most insects on contact, but it is also somewhat harmful to plants, especially if it contains certain additives. Special insecticidal soaps can be purchased, or you can make your own from additive-free dishwashing liquid (*not* dishwasher detergent). Use 1 teaspoon (5 mL) dishwashing liquid to 1 cup (250 mL) water in a spray bottle. Soaps are especially effective against aphids, whiteflies, mealybugs, earwigs and spider mites. Insecticidal soap is not otherwise toxic and readily biodegrades. It must be reapplied after a rain.

Diatomaceous Earth: This is the pulverized remains of diatoms, tiny hard-shelled sea creatures.

Its particles are so sharp-edged that they can pierce the soft skin of slugs and snails and the hard shells of beetles. Diatomaceous earth is usually sold in combination with rotenone or pyrethrum, so its effectiveness by itself is difficult to measure, but it is most effective on plants and soil that are dry. Reapplication is necessary after a rain.

Alcohol: A half-and-half solution of water and rubbing alcohol (70 percent isopropyl alcohol, available at drugstores) or grain alcohol (available at liquor stores), with or without a small amount of insecticidal soap, kills a number of indoor plant pests, including scale insects, aphids, spider mites, thrips, whiteflies and mealybugs. Either spray the plants, which causes leaf-burning of some species, or use a cotton swab to contact the pests directly.

Citrus Oil: The oil in the outer skin of citrus fruit, including oranges, lemons, limes and grapefruit, is toxic to a wide range of insects. Shake the grated zest of any citrus fruit with a small amount of water, strain through a sieve, and apply to infested plants.

Pheromone Lures: The natural attractant substances produced by certain insects have been produced or synthesized in the laboratory. When these substances are used to bait a trap, pests can be gathered and destroyed. In most cases, the traps are intended to monitor pest populations rather than eradicate them. Traps can catch large numbers of gypsy moths, Japanese beetles and yellow jackets, however. Other traps, for aphids, whiteflies and thrips, are most effective in a greenhouse (see Sources).

Other Remedies: Using the cedar tree's own pest-repelling properties, a tea of cedar bark and water has been shown to kill squash bugs and Mexican bean beetles. By the same token, a tea made from fresh tomato leaves discourages diamondback moths from laying eggs on brassicas. Garlic is a proven pesticide that is often crushed and used alone—it kills snails and slugs, for instance—or is included in homemade sprays along with herbs such as tansy, catnip and cayenne pepper. To any such spray, add a few drops of mild soap or dishwashing liquid (*not* dishwasher detergent) to facilitate mixing and adherence to plants and to increase its effectiveness. Hot pepper seeds or flakes sprinkled on the soil and plants also fend off small animals.

Beneficial Imports: Beneficial insects, such as lady beetles, soldier bugs, parasitic wasps (see page 189) and praying mantids, can be purchased for release into the garden. This is not recommended anywhere but in a greenhouse, however, because, of course, once outdoors, the new arrivals cannot be persuaded to stay where they are wanted. Every garden naturally attracts its own population of native beneficial insects in numbers the garden can support. Take care of these, rather than buying new ones. To encourage a population of beneficial insects, avoid wide-spectrum insecticides, grow a variety of plants that bloom at different times and aim any insecticidal sprays carefully. Another strategy is to let a few plants that are members of the carrot family, Umbelliferae, produce flowers. These feed parasitic wasps.

The following botanical pesticides, though considered organic because their manufacture is relatively benign and they biodegrade quickly, are as powerful as some of the synthetics. They may kill toads, lady beetles and honeybees on contact. Most can be dangerous to people and pets, so you should not come in contact with them, breathe them or eat anything treated with them before washing it thoroughly. Use these pesticides if you must, but use them carefully. Do not wear contact lenses during spraying, and if any gets into your eyes, flush them immediately with plenty of water. Spray on a calm day, and keep children and pets out of the garden for at least a day after spraying. Wash your hands and clothing after spraying.

Rotenone: A botanical pesticide produced in the roots of several tropical legumes, rotenone is so powerful that it is usually sold in concentrations of only about 1 percent. It is an effective and fast-acting killer of many beetles, aphids, caterpillars, larvae and bugs, but it is also highly toxic to cold-blooded creatures, such as fish, frogs and toads. It is harmful to humans on contact, although its toxicity disappears soon after the powder is applied or when it ages. Buy rotenone fresh every year. Apply it with care, and do not use it during the week before harvesting vegetables.

Pyrethrum: A botanical pesticide, pyrethrum is made from pyrethrin, which is obtained from the small white blossoms of *Chrysanthemum ciner-*

ariifolium, the pyrethrum daisy. (The blossoms of the red, white, pink or purple *C. coccineum*, often called pyrethrum, contain only a minute quantity of pyrethrin.) The pyrethrin in the flowers is released when they are crushed. Pyrethrum provides fast knockdown upon contact with a range of caterpillars, aphids, beetles and thrips, then biodegrades quickly into harmless by-products. Like rotenone, pyrethrum is toxic to cold-blooded animals, such as fish, toads and snakes, and is also harmful to humans when fresh. Do not apply pyrethrum during the week before harvesting vegetables. Pyrethroids, synthetic elements of pyrethrin, are stronger and longer-lasting and should be considered in the same league as other synthetic pesticides. Some insects have developed a resistance to pyrethroids.

Neem: Extracts of seeds of the neem tree, a tropical relative of mahogany, have been proved to have insecticidal and fungicidal properties. Neem products are licensed for sale in the United States but not in Canada at the time of publication.

Know These Bugs

Aphid: This tiny, soft-bodied sap-sucking insect thrives in colonies on all sorts of plants, especially on young leaves and tender branch tips. Aphids, which may be white, green, purple or black, can be a problem both indoors and out. They can kill young plants, weaken older plants and sometimes spread disease. If you find them on an indoor plant, check all other plants for infestations and treat immediately. Aphids breed very rapidly, both sexually and asexually, and they have a winged stage during which they migrate to other plants. Small numbers can be squashed on the leaves or knocked onto the ground. Insecticidal soaps provide good control. Earwigs and lady beetles eat aphids.

Cabbage Looper & Cabbageworm: Several similar larvae infest brassicas, chewing holes in foliage and inflorescences. They are the imported cabbageworm, the diamondback moth larva and the cabbage looper. All are green and up to 1 inch (2.5 cm) or so in length. Their round or oval whitish eggs can be scraped off leaves in spring, soon after cabbage butterflies are seen in the garden. Later, the green caterpillars can be

Where potatoes grow, Colorado potato beetles follow.

hand-picked or sprayed with a homemade insecticidal mixture, with *Bacillus thuringiensis* or, in severe cases, with rotenone or pyrethrum.

Colorado Potato Beetle: This orange-and-black North American beetle has followed the spread of Solanaceae, especially potatoes, around the world. Because adults can overwinter in the garden, clean out all potato foliage in fall and rotate the potato patch from one season to the next. In early spring, destroy the masses of orange eggs found on the undersides of potato leaves. The orange or brown larvae that hatch in early summer chew the foliage of potato plants and occasionally infest other Solanaceae, including eggplants and nicotiana. Hand-pick into a jar of soapy water, use a spray of tansy leaves, or for severe infestations, apply pyrethrum, rotenone or M-Trak, a strain of *Bacillus thuringiensis*.

Cucumber Beetle: Whether striped or spotted, the cucumber beetle is found mostly in the Northeast, where it is a common pest of Cucurbitaceae —cucumbers, melons and squashes—eating the foliage and sometimes spreading disease. The spotted cucumber beetle is yellow-green with 12 black spots, while the striped cucumber beetle has three lengthwise black stripes on a yellow background. They are attracted to cucurbitacins, bitter substances in cucurbits, so infestation is less severe on

The parsleyworm can be forgiven its foraging, for it will soon become a swallowtail butterfly.

some of the sweeter types of cucumber. Cucumber beetles occasionally spread to corn, beans, peas and blossoms. For severe infestations, use pyrethrum or rotenone.

Cutworm: There are hundreds of species of cutworm throughout the continent. All are plump, hairless caterpillars, gray to brown or black, about 1 inch (2.5 cm) long, that live underground, chewing plant stems at the soil line at night or crawling up the stems to strip the foliage. All are most easily disposed of in spring, when tilling or spading exposes them. Later, they are most troublesome around tender vegetable seedlings. Protect transplants using cardboard collars that extend 1½ inches (3.8 cm) above and below the soil line or collars made from tin cans with both ends removed. If few or no seedlings emerge from warm soil (or if a seedling is lopped off), dig around the area to find and destroy the cutworms.

Earwig: This quick-moving bug with its lobster-like pincers infests more gardens every year, eating a wide variety of seedlings and even mature plants. On the positive side, earwigs have a voracious appetite for aphids, slug eggs and insect larvae. To limit the earwig population, keep the garden clean; earwigs hide in the damp shadows in debris and will eat food scraps. Earwigs can be trapped in canned-fish tins full of soapy water that are buried almost to their rims in the garden or in rolled lengths of corrugated cardboard. The earwigs will crawl into the small spaces and can be dumped in the garbage or burned. Especially vulnerable plants should be grown in plastic or glazed pots, where the earwigs cannot reach them.

Flea Beetle: A tiny beetle that jumps when disturbed, the flea beetle perforates foliage and can destroy seedlings when they are first planted out, especially eggplants. All other members of the tomato family, Solanaceae, as well as the mustard family, Cruciferae, both vegetables and flowers, can also be severely damaged. As the beetle is fast-moving, you are more likely to spot its damage—peppery holes in young leaves—than you are to catch sight of the perpetrator itself. There are eight common garden types of flea beetle, most glossy black and most attracted to certain plant genera. Flea beetles seldom destroy entire plantings, so succession planting and heavy sowing of seeds can make up for losses. Regular fertilizing and watering, planting in warm soil and anything else that helps plants grow quickly and steadily allow them to outpace the damage. Flea beetles locate their preferred crop by smell, so sprays of strong-smelling unrelated plants, such as tansy, clover, citrus or garlic, can repel them. A floating cover such as Reemay excludes them.

Lady Beetle: One of the gardener's best friends, the lady beetle is a carnivore that eats sap-sucking pests such as aphids and scale insects. Its orange eggs are laid in clusters on the undersides of leaves; they are smaller and more cylindrical than the eggs of the Colorado potato beetle. The larvae are flat and grayish. Lady beetles can have red, orange or white wing casings that may or may not be spotted.

Onion Maggot: This is the larva of a small fly, *Hylemya antiqua,* that lays its eggs on the soil near onions. The larva then tunnels into onion bulbs. Where infestations are common, place a fine-meshed cover, such as nylon netting or Reemay, over the crop. Control of the 1/3-inch-long (8 mm) larva is also possible by crop rotation and applications of diatomaceous earth to the soil around onions in affected gardens.

Parasitic Wasp: Hardly visible, the parasitic wasp is tiny but powerful. It injects its eggs into various insect eggs or larvae, which die as the wasps hatch and mature. Some species of parasitic wasp can be purchased to control greenhouse pests, including scale insects, whiteflies and more than 200 species of moth. In the garden, existing parasitic-wasp populations can be encouraged. If you use any broad-spectrum pesticides, including organic or homemade ones, aim them carefully. Allow some plants of the family Umbelliferae to flower in the garden—the tiny flowers of plants such as Queen Anne's lace, sweet cicely and angelica are favored nectar sources for parasitic wasps.

Parsleyworm: The distinctly green-and-black-striped larva of the black swallowtail butterfly eats the foliage of Umbelliferae—parsley, parsnips, carrots, dill and other herbs. Hand-pick, or leave them in peace to turn into butterflies.

Praying Mantid: Various species of this 2 1/2-inch-long (6.3 cm) insect, also known as a praying mantis, prey on insects, flies and bugs in many North American gardens. Although praying mantids do not discern between friend and foe, their predation is welcomed by most gardeners. Praying mantids can be purchased from some pest-control companies. Their eggs are laid in a hard, foamy mass on stems and twigs.

Slug & Snail: Mollusks that can vary in length from 1/3 inch (8 mm) to 10 inches (25 cm), slugs and snails will eat most vegetables and certain flowers like delphiniums, particularly in the damp, shady conditions they need. Garlic sprays are toxic to slugs and snails. Traps can be made by placing saucers or jar lids filled with beer or, better, a solution of table sugar and water in the soil around affected plants. An old remedy is a solution of 2 ounces (57 g) of alum in 1 gallon (4 L) of water, soaked into the ground around the plants. Or lay boards or cabbage leaves on the ground near the plants; slugs and snails, which are nocturnal in habit, will congregate under them at night and can be removed in the morning. Collars of window screening around stems will prevent mollusks from climbing the stems.

Squash Bug: These ugly, flat, gray, black or dark brown bugs sometimes congregate near the base of cucurbits, especially squashes and pumpkins, sucking juice from the leaves, stems and vines. The eggs, which are laid on the undersides of squash leaves in early summer, are first yellow but soon turn brown. Control the bugs with cedar-bark tea or by placing boards or shingles around the bases of plants. Like slugs, squash bugs will gather under the boards at night and can be removed in the morning.

Tomato Hornworm: Capable of ballooning up to 4 inches (10 cm) in length in a couple of weeks, this larva is so large that its damage to leaves and fruit is dramatic; its size also makes it easy to hand-pick. Control may be maintained with *Bacillus thuringiensis.* The yellow-green eggs are laid on host plants, which occasionally include other members of the family Solanaceae.

White Grub: The large, pale C-shaped larvae of June beetles are most likely to infest newly cleared ground following their 3-year cycle of growth. Damage, therefore, is most severe every 3 years, with lawns and root crops, especially potatoes, being the worst-hit. Brown patches of lawn grass may signal the destruction of roots by white grubs. When spading or tilling a garden, check for larvae and adults—large rust-brown beetles. Rotate potato plantings. Buried chunks of potato may be used as bait among other crops. Dig up the bait, and replace it throughout the season. Biosafe, Scanmask or Ecomask are brand names for a type of nematode that attacks many species of underground larvae. Apply it to lawns or gardens that are infested with grubs or leatherjackets.

Wireworm: This fast-moving, tough-skinned cylindrical worm, usually reddish brown, is the larva of a click beetle. It consumes seeds, roots and tubers. Remove wireworms that are exposed while tilling or spading. As well, pieces of potato can be buried as bait. Dig up and destroy the pieces, then replace throughout the season.

Plant Diseases & Disorders

Plants, like people, are subject to myriad diseases and disorders. And, like people, the best-fed, best-tended plants seem to suffer the fewest ailments. In a typical well-managed garden, diseases seldom result in plant death, though they may produce discolored, spotted, specked and dropped leaves, flowers and fruit. Good soil maintenance, proper crop rotations and the use of suitable varieties and growing methods will help to alleviate all serious problems, whether they are caused by soil-nutrient deficiencies, pests, the weather or diseases.

Diseases and deficiencies are often difficult to diagnose for several reasons: many have similar symptoms; a plant may suffer from more than one ailment at a time; and symptoms that resemble those of a disease may instead signal a nutrient problem or a physical disorder. For instance, a long cold spell can cause heat-loving plants to fade and die even if frost does not occur. Their leaves become pale and sometimes purplish. Air pollution and too much or too little water can all result in unhealthy plants. Many plants die as soon as their propagation requirements have been fulfilled. Early-seeding annuals, such as peas and poppies, turn yellow and die in midsummer, while only the foliage dies on plants with underground storage organs, such as potatoes, onions and spring bulbs.

Diseases result in wilting, disfiguration and sometimes death when plants should be green and growing. Disease symptoms appear most frequently in mid- or late season when the weather is hot, foliage is dense and disease-spreading insects are moving from plant to plant. Bacteria, fungi and viruses are all causes of disease.

Bacterial Diseases: These are most prevalent during hot, humid weather, when bacteria in the soil multiply freely and attack vulnerable plants. Rotate crops, and if you have problems, buy fresh seed of a new variety next year. Destroy affected plants.

• Bacterial blight causes pea stems to turn purplish or black at ground level and small, water-soaked spots to appear on leaves and pods.

• Bacterial ring rot affects potatoes, causing leaf margins to turn inward and become leathery and tubers to develop a dark ring just beneath the skin.

• Bacterial soft rot affects lettuce, cabbage and taproots such as carrots, turning them into a soft, pulpy mass. Outer leaves of cabbage and lettuce rot first.

Viral Diseases: Highly infectious, these diseases are often spread by aphids and beetles. Covering plants with cheesecloth, which prevents contact with disease-carrying insects, may help. Viruses are also spread by vegetative reproduction organs, such as bulbs and rhizomes. Growing from seed promises a fresh, virus-free beginning.

• Mosaic is a common disease that can infect almost all garden plants, especially tomatoes, potatoes, cucumbers and summer squashes, producing mottled, mosaiclike designs on fruit and leaves. Mosaics can be spread to plants in the Solanaceae family from tobacco; smokers should wash their hands before gardening.

Fungal Diseases: Responsible for most disease problems in the northern garden, fungi may produce molds, galls and watery or rotten spots on leaves or fruit. Most, with the notable exceptions of smut and scab, are worse in hot, humid weather. Thin plants to encourage air circulation, choose resistant varieties, and rotate crops. Remove any diseased plants, and dispose of them away from the garden. Clean all dead and dying plants from the garden at the end of the season. Do not tend wet plants.

• Anthracnose affects many garden plants. Mature tomato or pepper fruits have small black bumps or wrinkled, uneven areas of decay. Bean seed coats bear dark brown indented spots, and lower leaves may have dark red or purplish veins. Also affected are rhubarb and all cucurbits.

• Blackleg affects most Solanaceae and Cruciferae (see page 38 for a list of plant families). They exhibit a black lesion at the base of the stem that causes the plant to wilt, topple over and die. Pelargonium and other cuttings may become infected and die before they root, especially when temperatures are low or the soil mix is not sterile. The same fungus can cause crown rot of campanulas.

• Black spot is a common disease of roses. Susceptible varieties are covered with a sooty black coating in summer.

• Botrytis, also descriptively called gray mold, produces a fluffy gray covering on leaves and stems. Among susceptible food plants are globe artichoke, cucurbit, lettuce, berries and fruit. Flowers include chrysanthemum, clarkia, dahlia, godetia, lily, peony, petunia and zinnia. Some resistant cultivars are available. Botrytis rot of onions is often not evident until after the harvest. Because this form usually appears at the top of the bulb, it is also known as neck rot.

• Clubroot affects all Cruciferae, especially in wet, acidic soil. Leaves become yellow, and plants may wilt even when watered. When pulled up, the roots appear large and misshapen, eventually becoming mushy or moldy. Some resistant varieties are available. Raising the pH of the soil helps.

• Damping-off is caused by water molds that need water to spread. It attacks young seedlings before or after emergence (see page 53). Marigolds are especially susceptible.

• Downy mildew produces cottony white patches on the pods or leaves of lettuce, lima beans, onions and peas. Stake the peas and beans, thin the onions and lettuce, and in wet areas, grow them in well-drained soil, perhaps in raised beds.

• Early blight, or alternaria, is "early" because it attacks plants while they are still blossoming. This disease affects all plants in the Solanaceae family.

On tomato, eggplant and pepper fruit, the rot begins in cracks or in areas where there has been pest damage and gradually spreads into flattened black patches. Leaves bear concentric circular spots, which has led to another name for the disease: target spot. Determinate tomatoes, particularly, are likely to contract this disease late in the season.

• Late blight, which caused Ireland's potato famine, attacks solanaceous plants after they blossom and is most serious in areas where the weather is cool and damp late in the season. New, more virulent strains of late blight are especially dangerous to tomatoes and potatoes. Dark watery spots suddenly appear on branches, fruit and leaves, spreading rapidly. A whitish mold may grow under the leaves. When severe, the disease produces a foul smell. Plants usually die. Resistant potato varieties include 'Cherokee,' 'Chieftain,' 'Epicure,' 'Kennebec,' 'Nooksak' and 'Sebago.'

• Powdery mildew produces a white, powdery coating on the leaves, fruit and stems of azaleas, berry bushes, chrysanthemums, cucumbers, fruit trees, lilacs, melons, monarda, oaks, peas, phlox, roses, squashes, verbena, zinnias and many other plants. Plants can become infected if warm days are followed by cool nights and sunlight and air movement are restricted. There are resistant cultivars. See also the list of fungicides on page 192.

• Rust is the descriptive term for a raised orange fungus that may coat chrysanthemums, dianthus, hollyhocks, pelargoniums, snapdragons and others. Remove and destroy affected leaves. There are resistant forms of asparagus.

• Scab produces corky brown marks on potatoes, turnips, beets, radishes and cucurbits. Although unsightly, scab does not affect the edibility of the vegetables. It is most severe in warm, dry, alkaline soils. Lowering the pH should eradicate it. Do not save scabby potatoes for use as seed.

• Smut is among the most destructive of corn diseases, producing galls (swellings) that may be tiny or several inches across. Destroy all affected plants before the galls burst, releasing black spores. Dry weather, late planting, poor soil or an overabundance of nitrogen all encourage smut.

• Verticillium wilt affects members of the Solanaceae family around blossoming time. Leaves wilt and die progressively from the base of the plant upward. Yields may be lowered, or plants may die. Do not rotate solanaceous plants with others in the same family or with strawberries, raspberries or Brussels sprouts. Resistant tomato cultivars bear the initial "V" after their names.

Disease Resistance

Certain plants are susceptible to certain diseases, and plant breeders have attempted to produce cultivars resistant to the most troublesome. Seed-catalog descriptions usually indicate which cultivars are resistant. Buying these can make a dramatic difference. There are roses resistant to black spot, apples resistant to scab, asters resistant to aster yellows, tomatoes resistant to verticillium wilt, and so forth.

There are also a couple of organically approved sprays that help control disease outbreaks and reduce damage:

Baking Soda: Ordinary household baking soda (sodium bicarbonate), at the rate of about ¼ ounce (7 g) to 1 gallon (4 L) water, or 1 teaspoon (5 mL) to 1 quart (1 L) water, has proved an excellent spray to prevent fungal diseases. It has been used to pre-vent black spot of roses and powdery mildew on euonymus, cucumbers, eggplants, strawberries and squashes. The same solution may include 1 part mineral oil to 2 parts baking soda. If there are already affected leaves on the plant, remove them before spraying to prevent the spread of disease. Higher concentrations of baking soda can burn foliage.

Sulfur: Sulfur has been used in agriculture for thousands of years to kill a number of pests, such as mites, scale insects and aphids and to counter a wide range of fungal diseases. Sold alone or in combination with copper and other substances, sulfur is used to treat dormant fruit trees in early spring. On the negative side, sulfur can kill beneficial insects and harm certain plants, especially within 2 months of an oil-spray application.

Other Fungicides: A solution of 1 part crushed garlic to 20 parts water has been shown to help protect cucumber plants from powdery mildew and to lessen black-spot infection of roses—the leaf tops and undersides were sprayed. Cinnamon has proved effective against crown rot of orchids and mildew of begonias. It may also work against some bacterial diseases.

The Bedside Companion: Vegetable Pollination

The 1930s saw the publication of a book entitled *Just Like the Flowers, Dear: A Botany for Parents*. A gardener's companion manual might well be called *Not Very Much Like People, Dear: A Sex Manual for Gardeners*.

Plants lead a passive love life, depending on various active agents—wind, insects, water, birds and animals—to be their matchmakers. The way plants, especially vegetables, make use of these go-betweens is of concern to the gardener for several reasons: It influences plant spacing, the segregation of varieties and seed-saving. As far as the harvest is concerned, plant pollination is most critical when the edible part is a fruit, such as a tomato, pepper, cucumber, squash, melon or ear of corn.

Fruiting plants that are entirely insect-pollinated will not produce a crop if there are no suitable insects in the garden at the right time, something which might happen if the garden is either downtown or near an area recently sprayed with insecticides, if the weather is inclement or if the plants are growing in a greenhouse. Pollination must be done by the gardener.

Insect-pollinated vegetables include squashes and melons as well as most garden cucumbers. All these plants are termed monoecious: male and female reproductive organs are segregated in separate flowers. The female flower, which often appears a little later than the male, is easily distinguished by a small, immature fruit —cucumber, squash or melon—at its base. If there are bees in the area, pollination will likely take place as soon as the flower opens and the weather is calm, warm and dry; otherwise, the gardener must transfer pollen from a male flower to the stigma—the center of the female flower—using a small paintbrush or a swab. With tiny flowers such as cucumbers, the entire stamen—the pollen-headed fila-

For fruit to form, a lemon cucumber blossom needs to be pollinated, by either insect or gardener.

ment in the male flower—can be removed and touched against the stigma. After pollination occurs, the petals drop, and the fruit begins to swell and mature. Greenhouse cucumbers and the seedless garden types are parthenocarpic: fruit develops without fertilization, and the quality is lower if pollination occurs.

Most other fruit-producing crops—beans, peppers, tomatoes, peas, eggplants, and such—are primarily self-pollinated. These plants are termed hermaphroditic: each flower contains both male and female organs, and pollination is achieved when the plant is moved in the wind, bumped by a passing gardener or perhaps visited by an insect.

Hand pollination of these plants is needed only when they are grown under cover—they or their blossoms can be simply bumped or touched—or when their cross-breeding is controlled for seed production, as described in the following chapter.

Like the melon family, corn is monoecious, but pollination is assisted by the wind, which transfers pollen from the spokelike tassels, high on the plant, to the silks on each ear. Every strand of silk must be pollinated for the kernels to fill the entire cob. Because this is very much a hit-and-miss affair, each corn cultivar should be grown in a close grouping rather than just in a single row, and different cultivars that mature at the

same time should be segregated from one another.

Of course, lack of fruit formation need not always be caused by the lack of a suitable pollinating agent. Fruit will form irregularly, if at all, when the plant is under stress. In northern gardens, this typically happens when temperatures are too low; but it also occurs when temperatures are too high, when plants are diseased or malnourished, when drought or rainy conditions persist or when the soil is too rich in nitrogen. All in all, the successful production of fruit is usually the sign of a good working relationship between the gardener, the garden and that most fickle of gardening partners, the weather.

Chapter Eight

As You Reap, So Shall You Sow

"A few large carrots should be laid by to plant out
early in spring for seed. Onions the same, also beets, parsnips
and some of your best cabbages."

—Catharine Parr Traill

The Canadian Settler's Guide, 1855

At the time when Catharine Parr Traill was advising Upper Canadian settlers to save their own garden seeds, high-quality seeds of good varieties were hard to come by. Seeds for a favorite old-world vegetable or flower might not be available at all—unless the settlers had had the foresight to include some with their baggage and the seeds were types that would remain viable for months. So people were willing to do what we might consider to be too much trouble: save biennials over the winter so that they would set seed the next year.

Today, the situation has changed completely. Rather than too few seed choices, gardeners are faced with too many. And all of those choices are likely to be fresh, clean seeds that are true to the variety name and the color picture on the packet. And if you don't want to start plants from seeds, you can find suitable bedding plants on the market in spring.

Yet there are still very good reasons for gardeners to save seeds from their own plants. One reason is obvious: if plants produce their own seeds, why not use them? They are free for the taking, the

garden's investment in its own future, so saving seeds saves money. Ironically, the most expensive seeds—bulky ones like beans, peas, morning glories and sunflowers—are often the easiest to save at home. Just one plant may provide all of next year's seeds.

Another reason to save your own seeds is more subtle and was as true in Traill's day as it is in our own. There is a certain satisfaction that comes from seeing the gardening process through from beginning to end to beginning again. Your knowledge of botany and of the peculiarities of your own garden will also grow. After several years of carefully saving seeds from your best plants, you will end up with custom-designed cultivars that suit your own garden better than anything on the market. Unsuitable plants simply die out, leaving the stronger, better-adapted ones to produce seeds.

Saving your own seeds has broader consequences as well. A seed retailer can carry only a limited selection of cultivars; every year, as new selections are introduced, older ones must be dropped, sometimes never to reappear. The home

Big seeds like those of sunflowers are the easiest to save. One flower provides plenty for next year.

gardener who has been saving a personal seed supply can still grow the discontinued cultivars and perhaps produce enough seeds to share with other gardeners. In both Canada and the United States, seed exchanges have been established for the barter and sale of hard-to-find or heirloom vegetables and flowers. These older varieties are among the easiest and safest to save, because they are not hybrids.

Hybrid vs. Standard

Seeds on the market are either hybrid or non-hybrid (also called standard, or open-pollinated). Most hybrids sold are F1, which stands for filial-one, the first-generation offspring of two inbred parents. What makes F1 hybrids popular are qualities of improved vigor and greater uniformity. Corn is one plant that has changed dramatically through hybridization, which has meant larger cobs and bigger, sweeter kernels. Hybrid seedless cucumbers are also noticeably different from their open-pollinated seedy counterparts. Some hybrid

melons are remarkably early. Hybrid flowers are generally larger and bloom longer. Tetraploids, which have three sets of chromosomes rather than the usual two, are a group of hybrids that may have huge flowers, as with some day lilies, or huge fruits, such as certain apples.

If hybrids are popular with some growers, they are even more so with many seed companies. Hybrid seeds are relatively expensive, and more important, growers must return to the seed company every year for a new supply, ensuring guaranteed sales. Some hybrids produce no seeds at all. Fully double flowers are examples. Other hybrids do produce viable seeds, but if you plant them, the offspring may hark back to a tough-skinned, drab-colored, disease-susceptible or small-fruited forebear. Or the offspring may be even better than its parent. This kind of experimentation is too risky for commercial growers, but in your own garden, planting the seeds produced by a hybrid plant is horticultural pioneering. F2 hybrids (filial-two) are the offspring of F1 parents. Often, F2 plants are very much like their parents. A few F2 hybrid flowers, such as calendula 'Neon' and petunia 'Rainbow,' are even sold in catalogs.

Standard, or open-pollinated, plants, on the other hand, produce seeds that grow into plants very much like the parents, provided cross-pollination among different cultivars has not taken place. Open-pollinated seeds or plants you buy will have been grown this way. If you wish to save your own seed, open-pollinated varieties will give you the most predictable results. In seed catalogs and on packets, hybrids are usually identified as such. If you do not see a plant identified as a hybrid, it is probably open-pollinated. Most flowers are open-pollinated, as are most vegetables, with the exception of most sweet corn and some varieties of carrot, cucumber, melon, onion, radish and squash, as well as members of the cabbage and tomato families.

In any case, experiment. There is a mystique surrounding seed production and collection that is seldom justified. Certainly there are plants which present seed-collection problems, often because the northern season is too short or too wet for success or because the isolation of plants that normally cross-pollinate is difficult to ensure in crowded urban or suburban areas. Some seeds are a challenge to germinate. But many plants practically hold their seeds out for you and are very easy to grow from seeds you have collected. A little collecting in late summer and fall can mean a garden full of homegrown plants next year.

Plant Selection

Some experimentation will be required before you know which seeds you can easily collect. Because properly stored seeds of most plant families (except, notably, Amaryllidaceae and Umbelliferae) last longer than one year, it is not necessary to save the seeds of every crop every year. In fact, with a little cooperation among several gardeners, seed-saving could be reduced to just one or two plants a year for each gardener.

Isolation of varieties and consequent seed purity is very important to commercial seed producers with reputations to maintain and government regulations to meet. It is far less important in home

The seeds of nonhybrid flowers can be saved to produce offspring much like the parent plants.

flower gardens, where accidental crossings, if they occur at all, may have happy conclusions. In the vegetable garden, however, frequent crossings will almost inevitably lead to a decline in quality. This is especially true with corn, cucumbers, squashes and tomatoes. If you intend to save seeds, grow just one cultivar or keep cultivars as far apart as possible.

For vegetable seeds, always choose the healthiest, most productive and, in most places, earliest-bearing plant. This requires a considerable amount of willpower: The plant bearing the earliest beans, for example, must be marked and those beans allowed to mature and dry on the branches while you are anxiously awaiting your first harvest. Remember to take the whole plant into consideration. A tomato as big as your fist may look tempting, but if it is the only fruit the plant has produced, you might prefer to save the seeds from a plant with more than one tomato, even if they are smaller. Plants in more sun or in a patch of fertile soil

An overwintered parsnip obligingly offers its seed heads the summer after its year of planting.

might look better than less favored ones, but their superiority will not be carried with the seeds.

Seed Storage

Whether seed is grown commercially or domestically, it must be mature in order to keep over the winter and, later, to germinate successfully. Fruits, then—peppers, squashes, tomatoes and such— must be fully mature but not yet rotting when they are cut open for seed collection. If they cannot be left to ripen on the vine, they can spend the final week or two indoors. Dried fruits or pods, such as those of beans, cabbage, peas, radishes, hollyhocks, lupins, petunias and poppies should be papery dry and the seeds inside hard. Again, maturation is most successful if it occurs on the plant, but pods that are almost dry can, if necessary, be brought indoors for final ripening. Seeds borne on umbels—members of the family Umbelliferae, such as carrots, dill, parsley, parsnips, angelica and lovage—are ready for harvest when they are brown and papery. Seeds of onions and other alliums will begin to fall from the seed heads when they are shiny, black and mature. Seeds of daisies must be gathered before they blow or drop from the plant in summer.

All seeds must be thoroughly dry to keep well. Even if they look dry when you gather them, allow the seeds to sit a further week in a warm place where air circulation is good. They should be exposed to temperatures no higher than 100 degrees F (38°C), and they should not be allowed to become wet during drying. If they dry outdoors, bring them indoors every night and during damp weather.

Home-stored seeds often contain bits of dried stem, leaf or pod. Some of this can be removed by hand or by winnowing (allowing the seed to drop from one container to another while an electric fan or a stiff breeze carries the chaff away). Don't be too concerned about clean seed, however. Bits of dry plant material will not affect seed germination.

Even if you do not wish to save your own garden seeds, you should save commercial seeds left over from spring planting. Many will keep for several years if stored in a dry, cool place. Write the date of purchase on seed packets. Home-collected seeds can be placed in labeled envelopes, paper bags, jars or cans. Put envelopes or bags, marked with the cultivar name, in rodent-proof airtight jars or cookie tins with some moisture-absorbing material, such as silica gel, cotton wool or a couple of spoonfuls of skim-milk powder wrapped in a few layers of facial tissue. Place the containers in a cool, dark cupboard or in the freezer. Freezing works well as a storage method for all but a few tropical species.

Dampness is the worst enemy of stored seeds, causing germination or rotting. The general rule is that the best storage conditions occur when the sum of the percentage of relative humidity and the temperature in Fahrenheit degrees totals less than 100. Avoid storage temperatures over 70 degrees F (21°C) if possible.

To check the viability of old seeds, place 10 seeds in warm, moist paper toweling about a month before the seeding date in spring. If, after 3 weeks, five seeds have not germinated, consider discarding the seeds and buying a fresh supply. If a few have germinated, the seeds can be sown thickly to compensate for germination failure.

Vegetative Reproduction

Seed-saving is easiest, generally, with annuals in the vegetable garden and both annuals and biennials in the flowerbed. But when it comes to established perennials, the easiest way to propagate most of them is vegetatively, which means that you make a clone, a genetic copy of the parent plant— "literally a chip off the old block," writes one gardener. There are several methods of vegetative, or asexual, propagation for home gardeners. The usual ones are division, layering and cuttings.

Division

Most perennials that spread outward are easy to propagate by division. This is best done in early spring, when the plant first appears, or in fall, after leaf drop. Perennials with fleshy roots, including irises, peonies and Oriental poppies, are best divided in fall—September in most of the North. In spring or fall, divide plants soon after a rain or

Multiply perennial clumps easily by division.

deep watering, when soil will cling to the roots and the plant will be able to root quickly in its new location. Depending on the size of the plant, you can use a hand trowel or spade to dig into it and cut away sections to plant elsewhere. Discard any parts that seem weak or old, usually in the center. Plant the divisions immediately, and water. If the weather is hot and dry, mulch the divisions and provide a bit of shade. Fall-planted divisions should be mulched for their first winter.

Among the plants that are easy to divide are the vegetables asparagus and rhubarb; the herbs chives, lemon balm, lovage, mint, monarda, oregano and thyme; and the flowers artemisia, aster, astilbe, campanula, centaurea, coreopsis, day lily, echinacea, echinopsis, hosta, iris, lamb's ears, liatris, lily, phlox, primula, rudbeckia, scabiosa, sedum, Solomon's-seal, sweet woodruff, tradescantia, veronica and yarrow. A few that do not like to be disturbed but may survive careful division are aconitum, anemone, baby's-breath, balloon flower, bleeding heart, delphinium, hibiscus and peony.

Layering

This is an easy propagation technique that some plants do naturally: periwinkle, strawberries, sweet woodruff, thyme and other creeping plants root where the leaf nodes touch the ground. Perennials that are otherwise difficult to propagate, such as azalea and rhododendron, can sometimes be coaxed to do the same thing. Rosemary is easier. Take an outside branch of a soft-stemmed perennial, strip off all the lower foliage, push the branch to the ground, and bend it gently where it contacts the soil. Press the bend firmly into the soil, and hold it in place with a hairpin or a heavy wire bent into a U-shape. Cover the buried stem with more soil, and keep it moist. If the mother plant is in a container, secure the stem in the soil in a smaller pot placed on top of or beside the first container. When the layered stem has rooted and sends up new growth, cut the stem joining the new plant to the mother plant.

Cuttings

Once a gardener has tasted success, propagating by cuttings is a fascinating procedure that can be habit-forming. This is a good way to multiply plants that are either too small to divide or resent division. One unusual candidate is the tomato. Remove suckers that grow from the leaf nodes, and plant them half-buried in the garden or in pots, keeping them moist until they take root. Many perennials can be propagated in this way.

There are books about working with cuttings, but the fundamental rules are few. First, you should purchase rooting hormone, which is available from all good garden stores. Second, take new growth at the tip of the plant; a piece of stem 3 to 5 inches (7.5-13 cm) usually works best. It must include leaf nodes, as this is where roots grow. Strip off all the lower leaves. Third, take more cuttings than you need. It is unlikely that they will all root. Fourth, avoid stress on the cuttings by keeping them moist and shaded until new growth appears, when they can be planted normally. One system that works well is to press each cutting into its own peat pot full of moist soil mix. Push several such peat pots into moist soil mix in a bucket. Cover the bucket with clear plastic held tightly in place, and put the bucket in a warm, shady spot. Fifth, don't give up too soon. As long as the cutting is alive, not withered or brown, be patient. New growth means rooting has occurred.

Some flowers root so easily that you should not need rooting hormone. Rooting is easiest, however, when soil temperatures are fairly high and plants are actively growing. Wax begonia, coleus, impatiens, pelargonium and sedum may even root in jars of water, as will branches of willow. Flowers more likely to need rooting hormone include artemisia, centaurea, chrysanthemum, dahlia, dianthus, fuchsia, gazania and Russian sage.

Among the herbs that are fairly easy from cuttings are scented geranium, horehound, lemon verbena, sweet marjoram, rosemary, sage, winter savory and thyme.

The Best Vegetables for Seed-Saving

Beans & Peas: These are among the easiest seeds to save, which is one reason why seed exchanges carry an impressive variety of dry beans. Bean and pea flowers generally self-pollinate, though enough crossing occurs that the gardener should keep different varieties as far apart as possible. Leave the pods on the plants until they have become dry and papery, or harvest almost dry pods to finish drying indoors. Harvesting can be left until after the first light fall frost, which will not harm pods that are nearly dry. Shell them, then continue to dry indoors until they cannot be easily dented with your fingernail. Store in glass jars or tins.

Corn: Open-pollinated sweet-corn seed is fairly easy to save but is seldom grown. You may want to keep popcorn or ornamental corn, however. For seed-saving and for eating, corn should be kept isolated from other cultivars that mature at the same time. As corn will cross-pollinate at distances of up to 1,000 feet (305 m), the home gardener should plant one cultivar only or several that mature at different times or should stagger plantings at 2-week intervals. To ensure that cross-pollination does not occur among different cultivars—if, for instance, a neighbor nearby is growing a different cultivar—cover the earliest-developing ears with paper bags as soon as the silks have formed. When pollen is produced on the tassels of more plants of the same cultivar, remove the bag, break off part of a tassel from another plant and sprinkle pollen on the silks. Repeat for 3 or 4 days in succession. Between pollinations, replace the bag

Sage and rosemary are among the herbs best vegetatively propagated from tip cuttings.

and leave it on the ear until the silks turn brown.

Leave the ears on the plants until the kernels are dry, even if this means leaving them past the first few light frosts. Then pick the ears, shuck them, and hang them indoors to dry until the kernels are brittle. The kernels can be left on the cobs all winter or rubbed off and stored in jars or cans.

Cress: When the plant begins to go to seed, pull it up and hang it under cover with a paper bag tied over the head to catch seeds as they fall. When it has completely dried, shake any seeds remaining on the plant into the bag.

Lettuce: The tendency of lettuce to go to seed in hot weather is somewhat frustrating to gardeners lusting after summer salads. To grow the longest-standing lettuce in future years, collect the seeds of the last plants to bolt—as long as those plants have other desirable characteristics as well. Very slow-bolting cultivars may have to be started sooner indoors so that they will bolt early enough for seed collection. The seed of looseleaf types is easier to collect than that of heading lettuce. Because lettuce usually self-pollinates, different cultivars can be placed quite close together, although seed purity will be more certain if different cultivars are set apart in the garden—or if all cultivars but one are harvested before bolting. About a month after bolting, the flowers will begin to feather, just as dandelions do when going to seed. When this happens, shake the seed heads into a bag. Because the seeds mature over several days, this procedure can be repeated from time to time. In mild areas, seeds may be sown in fall for seed collection the following summer.

Parsnips: Parsnip seed is the easiest to save of all biennial vegetables. It often overwinters in the garden without mulching, later presenting the gardener with large, papery seeds that are easy to strip from the seed stalks. The only problem with parsnips is that like carrots and parsley, varietal crossing can take place over long distances. As few varieties exist, however, this is seldom a problem, even in city gardens. Where winters are severe, dig roots in fall to store in a cool root cellar, and replant in spring.

Peppers: Northerners who grow sweet peppers usually grow hybrids, and these are chancy to save for seed, but open-pollinated chile peppers are good candidates. Peppers must be fully ripe for the seed to be mature. Some peppers are not ripe until they have turned red. In other cases, leave fruit to ripen about a month past its first indication of ripeness. Mark the fruit so that it is not picked early. It can, if necessary, be further ripened indoors at room temperature. Peppers usually self-pollinate, but to ensure purity, gardeners who wish to save seed should keep different cultivars about 25 feet (7.5 m) apart. You can store chiles whole and dry, or when the fruit is fully ripe, you can scrape out the seeds and dry them in a warm, dry place.

Potatoes: As long as the potato crop is not diseased, sound tubers may be saved indoors for planting the following spring. Potatoes store best at 45 to 50 degrees F (7-10°C) and must be kept in the dark. In spring, cut into eyes and plant as usual. If the tubers have already developed long sprouts in storage, do not break them off; simply cut them back, leaving just a leaf or two. Never plant tubers that show any signs of fungus infection.

The fruit borne by some potato plants contains seeds that may be dried and saved, but for genetic reasons, the quality of tubers that result from planting such seeds is unpredictable.

Squashes & Pumpkins: Summer squashes, winter squashes and pumpkins often sprout next year in the garden, a sure sign of a plant whose seeds are easy to save. The catch is that they cross-pollinate readily with any members of the same species growing within 100 feet (30 m), possibly farther. Therefore, gardeners who wish to save seed should either ensure that hand pollination occurs with the fruits which are to be saved for seed or grow no more than one selection from any of the following species of *Cucurbita*:

• *C. maxima*—buttercup; hubbard; delicious; banana
• *C. moschata*—butternut; sweet potato squash
• *C. pepo*—all common summer squashes; acorn; pumpkin; spaghetti squash

The seeds of all squashes are ready to harvest when the fruits are mature, so summer squashes must be left on the vine past their normal harvesting date. The skin will become as hard as that of winter squashes and may change color. All squash for seed may be left on the vine past the first fall frost. Then scoop out the seeds, wash them, and spread on cookie sheets or screens to dry indoors for about a week in a warm, dry place.

Sunflowers: Like squashes, sunflowers often sprout in next year's garden. Mature, dried sunflower seeds from a large-seeded cultivar such as 'Russian Giant' will store for several years, provided they are left unshelled. Discard seeds that are undersized or damaged. Harvest and store in the same manner as seeds used for eating. Ornamental-sunflower seeds are too small to be practical for food but can be saved for birdseed or the flower garden.

Tomatoes: Open-pollinated, or nonhybrid, tomato seeds are easily collected and stored. Tomatoes generally self-pollinate, but separating different cultivars is nevertheless wise if seed is to be collected. On the best-producing plant, allow one fruit to become overripe but not rotten—mark the tomato with a string so that it is not harvested early by mistake. Then pick the tomato, crush it in a jar, and let the mixture ferment in a warm place for 1 to 3 days, or until the pulp is soft and separates readily from the seeds and skin. Fill the jar with water, stir vigorously, then let the seeds settle for a minute. Pour off some of the mixture, refill the jar, stir and pour off again, repeating the refilling and emptying several times. Pour the seeds into a sieve, remove any remaining bits of tomato by hand, and shake off excess water. Spread the wet seeds out to dry in a warm, dry place.

Seed-Sharing

As a historical footnote to the subject of seed-saving, keep in mind a little advice from Catharine Parr Traill: "If you have more than a sufficiency for yourself, do not begrudge a friend a share of your superfluous garden seeds. In a new country like Canada, a kind and liberal spirit should be encouraged; in out-of-the-way country places, people are dependent upon each other for many acts of friendship."

Pollination of Vegetable Crops

Family	Vegetable	Self	Pollination Cross	Method*	Seed-bearing habit
Amaryllidaceae	Chives	—	100%	insects	perennial
	Garlic	—	100%	insects, bees	biennial
	Leeks	—	100%	insects, bees	biennial
	Onion	—	100%	insects, bees	biennial
	Shallot	—	100%	insects, bees	biennial
Chenopodiaceae	Beet	—	100%	wind	biennial
	Spinach	—	100%	wind	annual
	Swiss chard	—	100%	wind	biennial
Umbelliferae	Carrot	—	100%	insects	biennial
	Celeriac, Celery	—	100%	insects	biennial
	Parsley	—	100%	insects	biennial
	Parsnip	—	100%	insects	biennial
Compositae	Artichoke, globe	95%	5%	wind, insects	annual
	Artichoke, Jerusalem	—	100%	insects	perennial
	Endive	95%	5%	wind, insects	annual
	Lettuce	95%	5%	wind, insects	annual
	Salsify	—	100%	insects	biennial
Cruciferae	Broccoli	—	100%	bees, insects	annual
	Brussels sprouts	—	100%	insects	biennial
	Cabbage	—	100%	insects, bees	biennial
	Cauliflower	—	100%	insects, bees	biennial
	Cress	—	100%	insects, bees	annual
	Horseradish	—	100%	insects, bees	perennial
	Kale, Kohlrabi	—	100%	insects, bees	biennial
	Radish	—	100%	insects, bees	annual or biennial
	Rutabaga, Turnip	—	100%	bees, insects	biennial
	Watercress	—	100%	insects, bees	perennial
Solanaceae	Eggplant	55%	45%	wind, insects	annual
	Pepper	70%	30%	wind, insects	perennial
	Potato	100%	—	wind	annual
	Tomato	95%	5%	wind, insects	annual
Cucurbitaceae	Cucumber	25%	75%	bees, insects	annual
	Melon	25%	75%	bees, insects	annual
	Squash, Pumpkin	25%	75%	bees, insects	annual
Leguminosae	Bean	90%	10%	tripped by bees	annual
	Pea	97%	3%	tripped by bees	annual
	Peanut	—	100%	insects	annual
Gramineae	Sweet Corn	5%	95%	wind	annual

*the most common is mentioned first

Chapter Nine

Of Balconies, Bins & Boxes

"Young, middle-aged and elderly people were so enthusiastic, in fact, that extra courses had to be given and a waiting list made for those wanting garden boxes."
—Susan Alward, Ron Alward & Witold Rybczynski
Rooftop Wastelands, 1976

One of the most exciting frontiers for northern gardeners is the portable garden: the garden planted in containers. Where the climate is not always accommodating, plants can be moved from one place to another to follow the sun or to go under cover when necessary. Potted plants can be outdoors in summer, indoors in winter. Even where there is little or no soil—on a patio, a deck, a balcony or a wall—there can be a garden.

Containers offer aesthetic advantages too. Their different heights, textures and colors are appealing in the garden. Containers can be suspended or attached to a wall or under a window. On the ground, they often look best arranged in groups and can easily be moved whenever you want a design change. The pots themselves can be ordinary or exotic, purchased, recycled or homemade. In McGill University's landmark roof-gardening project, quoted above, a downtown Montreal roof became the site of a vast container garden of wooden boxes full of edible plants. The roof garden was complete with compost bins and a solar greenhouse.

Anything that can be grown in the ground can be grown in a container, but container growing can be hard on plants and on gardeners. Plants growing aboveground in a restricted amount of soil are more vulnerable to thirst, starvation and extremes of temperature and are more dependent upon the care of their keepers. Perennials considered fully hardy for your area may not survive the winter in their containers, because plant roots are far less hardy than plant shoots, and in containers, roots are poorly insulated from the weather. The same principle may cause roots to bake in summer, especially those in dark-colored pots in full sun. Soil temperatures higher than 95 degrees F (35°C) will slow growth.

Container growing separates devoted gardeners from part-timers and self-reliant plants from those which demand daily care. A container may be just the place for a plant too invasive to be trusted in the garden. Lily of the valley, snow-in-summer, goutweed, mint, yarrow and many other aggressive perennials are tough enough to overwinter outdoors in a container, attractive when kept in their place and safe within the container's bounds.

Anything that can hold soil can become a plant container, and any plant is a candidate.

On the other hand, gardeners tend to favor, for containers, plants that are more productive or floriferous. In containers, such plants may need water every day. Check by feeling the soil: if it is dry 1 inch (2.5 cm) beneath the surface for a large pot, half that depth for a small one, it is time to water.

If you have an extensive container garden and don't enjoy daily watering, consider a drip or pop-up watering system. For a few pots, double potting or mulching can afford some short-term watering relief, especially if you have to leave the garden during hot, dry weather. Before you go away, move all the pots to a sheltered, shady place. To double-pot, put a planted container inside a larger water-tight one with several inches of sand or vermiculite at the bottom. Pour in water to the depth of this layer, and place the planted pot inside. Similarly,

several smaller pots can be placed inside a large tray. A mulch of grass clippings—provided they have not been treated with weedkiller—will insulate the pots and slow evaporation from the soil surface. Plastic pots with attached water reservoirs are available on the market.

Soil-drying winds present problems to plants in containers. Tender leaves wilt even before the soil has dried out, and small containers sometimes topple over. Wind may be almost constant on a balcony or roof, where a cloth or wooden partition can be used as a barrier on the windward side. A trellis will do double duty by providing a place for sturdy vines.

If you have bare outdoor walls but are in a rental place where you cannot build, consider using a staple gun on wood, or masonry nails on brick or concrete, and hang plastic netting or install strings to support annual twining vines, including cup-and-saucer vine, hyacinth bean, moonflower and morning glory. Sow the vine seeds directly in pots of soil at the wall's base, and water frequently.

Choosing Containers

Whatever the situation, suitable plant containers must meet two conditions: They must be big enough for the plant in question, and they must hold soil securely for at least one season. Expect to lavish more care on smaller pots, because they dry out faster. Within these criteria, the range of possibilities is almost endless. Besides a variety of terra-cotta, plastic and ceramic pots sold especially for plants, there are all kinds of containers meant for other jobs: packing crates, ice-cream pails, garbage bags or pails, half-barrels and wastepaper baskets.

There is one more qualification you may or may not require. In many cases, especially in a rainy or shady garden, you will need a pot that drains from the bottom. This ensures that the plant will not develop root rot from standing in water. If your garden is dry and windy, however, you may do better with pots that do not drain, especially if the pots are small and densely planted. In such a situation, line terra-cotta pots or wicker baskets with plastic before filling them with soil. Cut the plastic back even with the soil surface so that it does not show.

In their Montreal rooftop experiment, the McGill researchers used wooden packing crates that measured about 2 by 3 by 2 feet (0.6 x 1 x 0.6 m). One box, they found, would comfortably hold either one summer squash or broccoli plant or two tomato plants or eggplants or three miniature cabbages or three rows of peas or two rows of beans. Or they could broadcast lettuce or carrot seeds on the soil surface of a single box, later thinning plants to leave 2 to 6 inches (5-15 cm) between them. Although heading members of the cabbage family —broccoli, Brussels sprouts, cabbage and cauliflower—can be grown in containers, the return per unit of space is so low that precious soil is better spent on cut-and-come-again leafy greens, herbs or fruiting plants, such as beans, peas, peppers, scallions, summer squashes and tomatoes. Among the best herbs are basil, bay laurel, chives, dill,

The best flowers for containers look good all season, like petunias and pelargoniums.

lavender, lemon verbena, mint, parsley, rosemary, sage, summer savory and thyme.

Ornamentals, both annual and perennial, suit containers, but they look best if they are attractive throughout the season, even if there is only foliage. The most popular choices are the annuals or tender perennials that bloom or provide leafy color almost nonstop from spring till fall—ageratum, wax and tuberous begonias, browallia, coleus, dusty miller, impatiens, nasturtium, pelargonium, petunia and vinca (catharanthus). But widening your horizons provides some exciting possibilities: alyssum, canna, kochia, marigold, ornamental grass, portulaca and zinnia. Plant closely; the best containers look like miniature jungles.

Among the perennials recommended for all winter on a city rooftop garden are *Aquilegia canadensis*, aster, coreopsis, day lily, gaillardia, *Geranium maculatum, Gypsophila paniculata*, Siberian iris, liatris, phlox, rudbeckia, veronica and yarrow. In

Stairways, balconies, patios and rooftops are ideal places for container-grown flowers and vegetables.

zone 5 or colder, however, even these hardy plants should have their containers surrounded by mulch.

Soil Mixes & Fertility

A fertile, well-drained medium is best for all container growing. Straight compost works well for most plants. If you are gardening on a rooftop or balcony, weight is an important consideration. Soil is heavy, especially when wet, so include about 50 percent of a lightweight ingredient: perlite or vermiculite. The McGill researchers reported success with a heavier mix of seven-eighths good topsoil and one-eighth vermiculite, perlite and peat moss. They placed a 1-inch (2.5 cm) layer of half-and-half peat moss and vermiculite on the bottom of their large containers to aid drainage and to prevent soil leakage. An alternative is polystyrene peanuts or broken pieces of packing polystyrene.

Where light weight is important and pots are too deep, consider covering the bottom with an over-turned plastic pot or with one or more of the nursery 6-packs used to sell transplants. Ask the building superintendent for advice before you start planting large containers aboveground. On rooftops, situate containers near the edge or directly over structural supports. On balconies, keep the largest containers next to the building walls. Consider drainage as well. You may need to place all pots inside watertight trays or tubs so that they do not drip onto other balconies.

Potted plants must be fertilized more frequently than garden plants. For annuals, including vegetables, use a balanced liquid fertilizer every 2 weeks. Fertilize herbs and flowering perennials once a month from March until August.

On their rooftop, the Montreal researchers installed a compost bin into which leaves, plant material and household garbage were piled. They noted that the compost was "the ideal fertilizer" and used it whenever possible. Few container gardeners can fit a compost bin into their plans, but bagged compost can be purchased.

The same soil can be used for several seasons, although before spring planting, about one-quarter of the old soil should be removed from the container and replaced with compost or with half-and-half topsoil and composted manure, again with a lightweight filler if necessary. After the potted soil has dried over the winter, you may need to work water into it before it is ready for use again.

Seasonal Routines

Usually, you will start your garden with plants, rather than seeds, especially any plants that are slow or difficult from seeds. While this will limit your variety options, it is often the most practical choice. Container gardeners generally want only a few plants, perhaps just one, and if you live in an apartment, you probably won't have the time or facilities to produce the best home-grown transplants.

As soon as the transplants are brought home, the hardening-off process can begin (see page 53). While the plants are still in their temporary flats or pots, begin leaving them in their outdoor growing spot for increasing lengths of time each day (provided the weather is amenable), starting with just an

Container gardens are most easily started not from seeds but from transplants set close together.

hour the first day. In about a week, the plants can be left out all day and all night—but, of course, do not leave frost-tender plants outdoors on frosty nights.

When the weather is suitable for the plants to take up permanent residence outdoors, fill the larger containers with soil mix, and in the position each transplant will occupy, dig a depression as deep as the transplant rootball or, in the case of tomatoes, as deep as the first true leaves. Water both the transplant and the soil in the pot thoroughly. Then carefully tap out single plants by holding them upside down, two fingers straddling the plant stem and held against the soil surface to support the plant when it comes out of its pot. If there are several plants in one flat, cut between them with a knife to the bottom of the flat, and pry out each one. In every case, keep as much of the rootball intact as possible. Set each transplant into the depression in the soil of the container, fill around it with soil, press down firmly on the surface around the plant stem, and water again. To

ease the shock of transplanting, the plant should be kept watered and protected from severe winds and daylong sun for the first few days.

Some plants are best grown directly from seeds. When sown in pots, seeds must be kept moist until they sprout. Covering containers with glass or plastic will help retain soil moisture in shade, but in sunny places, transparent covers can raise soil temperatures too much. In all but the coldest areas, remove the covering as soon as the sprouts begin to appear through the soil.

Planting dates for container vegetables are similar to those of their less restricted relatives, but the microclimate of a balcony or rooftop is likely to be so singular that some experimentation will be necessary. As a rule, the growing season is longer off the ground, and the frost-free season is longer in a city than in the surrounding countryside. Richmond W. Longley wrote about Edmonton, Alberta, in the *Canadian Journal of Plant Science*: "Heat from large cities tends to keep temperatures in the vicinity a few degrees higher than over the surrounding area, particularly on cool nights. This effect has caused late-spring and early-fall frosts to be less common at the airport than in the country." The Montreal researchers found that their rooftop tended to be about 9 Fahrenheit degrees (5C°) hotter than surrounding land, a boon in spring and fall but perhaps too much of a good thing in summer, when temperatures are elevated by the heat reflected off pavement and car roofs.

Direct sun, too, is likely to be either restricted or excessive in a city garden. Keep black pots in partly shaded places or, where summers are cool, use in full sun for warmth-loving plants. While a north-facing balcony will not mature fruiting plants, one that faces south may require a screen on one side to provide the plants with a little shade. Roofs and patios offer gardeners more options.

Overwintering

Perennials that would be perfectly hardy in the garden may die after a winter in a container, where the soil temperature fluctuates more. So perennials that will spend the winters outdoors need their roots protected. Containers meant for perennials can be lined with polystyrene-foam insulation, then with plastic. Unlined containers can be hilled with soil or surrounded with fallen leaves, bales of hay or straw or sheets of bubble wrap. Cover the soil with hay or a sheet of polystyrene foam, weighted down. You can also bury pots in soil up to their rims for the winter. Do not remove the pot or outer insulation until heavy frosts are past in spring.

In general, gardeners who use containers work with some of the most challenging limitations. But, as the Montreal team discovered, there are more rewards from cultivating plants in outdoor containers than from growing houseplants. The researchers found that rooftop plantings could actually enhance the quality of urban living. Their container garden of vegetables and herbs was an aesthetic as well as a practical improvement of the environment that gave city dwellers welcome control over something directly affecting their lives.

Suspended Animation

Hanging planters bring a new spatial dimension to the art of container gardening. Flowers, houseplants, herbs, even certain vegetables can be grown in their own little patches of soil suspended above the ground.

The plants best suited to hanging baskets or to sconces—half-containers that fit flat against a wall—are either compact or trailing. Compact plants, preferably less than 10 inches (25 cm) tall, fill the upper part of the container, while trailers add grace and movement. Among flowers, some favorites for hanging planters are alyssum, browallia, calceolaria, fuchsia, ivy, lobelia, nasturtium, upright and trailing pelargoniums, periwinkle, schizanthus,

viscaria and, of course, flowering vines such as balloon vine, canary creeper and thunbergia. All three of these vines and several more can be grown from seeds sown directly in the pots. Stay away from more rambunctious vines like morning glory and cup-and-saucer vine; they need about a half-barrel of soil apiece and lots of room to spread.

The best vegetables and fruits for hanging planters are chile peppers, vining cucumbers, leaf lettuce, strawberries and indeterminate cherry tomatoes such as 'Sweet 100.' Among herbs, consider chamomile, marjoram, mint, rosemary, thyme and, for upright interest in midpot, basil, chives, 'Fernleaf' dill (a small cultivar),

lavender, marjoram, parsley, sage, savory and sorrel.

You may want to grow just one type of plant or a combination of several. Grow cucumbers, strawberries and tomatoes on their own, because they need all the water and nutrients they can obtain. With herbs and flowers, set the plants closer together than you would in the garden. For a container 1 foot (30 cm) wide, you will need five or six plants. For herbs and vegetables, line wire baskets or other porous baskets with plastic so that the soil is slower to dry out.

There are several types of hanging container available. Most common are plastic pots, usually white and usually sold already planted with petunias or geraniums. They are plain-looking, so you may want to fill them with trailing plants that will disguise them. These pots come with their own wires for hanging, as do fiber baskets and hanging baskets made of wire. Wire baskets are meant to be lined with sphagnum moss or with purchased coconut-fiber liners. If you use sphagnum, you can plant through the sides as well as on the top. These baskets are so porous that they dry out quickly, so they are best used where the climate is rainy and cloudy or else in a sheltered, partly shaded place. Line at least the lower part of the sphagnum with plastic, and prepare to water them once or twice a day.

Any regular plant pot with a single drainage hole can also be converted into a hanging pot. There are special wires on the market for this conversion, or you can make your own. Drill a narrow hole through a small block of wood about 1 inch (2.5 cm) square. Pass a piece of heavy wire down through the pot's drainage hole, then through the hole in the piece of wood. Press the wire into a coil under the wood to hold it in place when the pot hangs. The wire will now stay more or less upright in the pot. Hook the top of the wire, then fill the pot with soil.

If you are using terra-cotta, wood or other porous materials for hanging planters, consider lining them with plastic. The chief maintenance problem with hanging planters is watering, and a plastic lining will give you a bit of relief. Some garden suppliers sell plastic hanging planters and window

Hanging baskets display trailing plants gracefully.

boxes that have an attached dish underneath, which acts as a reservoir. Water is fed to the roots by capillary action from the reservoir for several days between refills.

The larger and heavier the pot, the sturdier its suspending wires and supports must be. Make sure you have a strong place to hang the pots before you set them up. A sconce is held against the wall, and there are wall brackets available to hold a hanging pot away from the wall. Consider also an archway, pergola, porch or tree branch for hanging baskets. For a window box, you will need a window that will allow you to reach the plants easily, from either indoors or outdoors.

The best places for all containers are those which are protected from the wind and receive shade for part of the day. If you grow houseplants and other shade lovers, you can make do with no direct sun at all. All leafy and vining houseplants are suitable, but even in shade, they will likely

have more light than they had indoors, so harden them off by leaving them outdoors for short periods of time at first. For a window box, you can simply leave houseplants in their indoor pots, set inside the box and packed into wet peat moss that acts as insulation and humidifier. For containers of flowers in full sun, consider geranium, lantana, small marigolds, nasturtium, petunia, portulaca, verbena, vinca (catharanthus) and the small vines mentioned above.

To plant the basket, fill it almost to the top with compost, a purchased light soil mixture or a mixture of peat moss, compost and vermiculite or perlite. Water thoroughly. Nestle transplants or seeds in the top, with trailers toward the edge. Set plants just 3 to 4 inches (7.5-10 cm) apart. Water again, using a liquid fertilizer. Hang the pots. Water whenever the top $\frac{1}{2}$ inch (1 cm) of soil is dry. This may be a couple of times a day in hot or windy weather. Check first thing in the morning and again in the late afternoon. Fertilize every 2 weeks with a liquid fertilizer or manure tea. If plants fade during summer, cut back to just a couple of inches long. Some will not last the summer and can be replaced, but others will sprout anew.

In fall, clean out the baskets and store them for next spring. All can be used again, although plastic pots eventually lose their flexibility and become fragile due to photodegradation. Fiber baskets and wire baskets lined with sphagnum can be used at least once more; be sure you store them in a place where mice will not be tempted to use them for nesting material.

Chapter Ten

Harvest Days, Frosty Nights

"That harvest was the happiest we have ever spent in the bush.
We had enough of the common necessaries of life."

—Susanna Moodie

Roughing It in the Bush, 1852

Fall is the time of reckoning, the time to tally your successes and shortcomings, the practices and plants you want to keep or change, the quirks of climate on your own unique little patch of land. But it is also a busy time, especially for vegetable gardeners. Almost everything must be harvested, and much of that must be preserved. In the flower garden, too, there are things to do before the weather becomes colder and the days shorter. Hardy bulbs have to be planted, tender plants protected from frost and the garden cleaned up, ready for a new season under snow and ice.

For Northerners, what marks the onset of fall and the beginning of the end of the growing season is the date of the first frost. Frosty nights may have occurred earlier in the summer—an untimely cold spell that the gardener may or may not have anticipated—but by late summer, the approach of killing frost is as inevitable as the fall of leaves from the trees. Some plants will die abruptly, while others will continue growing, but at a slower rate. A light frost, which occurs when temperatures drop into the range between 32 and 29 degrees F (0 to –1.7°C),

can kill exposed tender plants, but other plants are not harmed. A moderate frost, 28 to 25 degrees (–2 to –4°C), damages fruit blossoms, flowers and most other vegetation. Most damaging is a severe frost, defined as 24 degrees (–4.4°C) or colder.

Frost Hardiness

Other chapters described how different plants vary in their capacity to withstand cold weather. Some seeds are sown outdoors as soon as the soil thaws or even sooner on the snow, while others are sown indoors in a warm, sunny window, where the seedlings are coddled until all danger of frost has passed. Once out in the garden, these frost-tender plants grow better if they are protected under plastic or glass for the first couple of weeks. Similarly, different plants stop growing and die at different times as the temperature drops in autumn. Now that plants are bigger, the plastic or glass that protected them in spring might not be spacious enough, so you may have to be inventive. At this end of the season, too, a little protection can mean weeks of extra growth and productivity.

Tender plants can be killed by frost alone, but hardy ones can endure weeks under ice and snow.

After a few years, northern gardeners become skilled at predicting frost. The weather report might provide a warning, but if you have an outdoor thermometer, remember that a late-afternoon temperature above 41 degrees F (5°C) probably means no frost, while a late-afternoon temperature below 36 degrees (2°C) usually promises frost, especially if the sky is clear. Clouds and wind keep frost away. The early-morning light following the first frost reveals a garden glazed with white.

As soon as the warming sun hits the garden, that first fall frost demonstrates quickly and graphically which plants are hardy and which are not. Exposed tender plants show the first and worst damage. These include the vegetables cucumber, eggplant, lima bean, melon, okra, pepper, snap bean, soy bean, squash and tomato and the herbs basil and summer savory and the flowers begonia, coleus, cosmos, dahlia and pelargonium. There are many more. The first frost may not kill these lovers of warmth, but all the foliage that was frozen will be limp and lifeless as soon as the temperature rises above freezing in the morning. Tender fruit touched by frost will be discolored and will soon rot, outdoors or in storage. Flowers droop and turn brown. The second frost usually completes the job, killing the plants.

Even prolonged temperatures just *above* freezing will kill most tender plants. Just 48 hours at an air temperature of 35 degrees F (1.7°C) can damage half the leaves of begonia and peperomia. Corn and beans stop growing as soon as the soil temperature drops below 50 degrees (10°C), tomatoes and squashes at 55 degrees (13°C).

But there are many other garden plants that continue to be green, upright and very much alive. Some are weeds, the toughest plants in the garden. Many more are the trees, shrubs and herbaceous perennials upon which Northerners depend. While young asparagus shoots will be harmed by frost, the plant itself is a hardy perennial that can survive most northern winters. There are also some precious annuals that can take frost. The last vegetables and herbs to remain conspicuously alive are a tenacious band of roots and greens—Brussels sprouts, cabbage, carrots, collards, corn salad, kale, leeks, lovage, onions, parsley, parsnips, rutabagas, salsify, spinach, Swiss chard, turnips—whose greens are very hardy, although the bulbs will not keep well if touched by frost. Conversely, potato foliage will die at 30 degrees F (–1°C), but the underground tubers will remain unharmed, unharvested ones sometimes overwintering to sprout next spring. Pea and broad-bean plants can survive lower temperatures than their pods, which freeze when the temperature dips to 30 degrees (–1°C).

This does not mean that these hardy plants continue to grow at their summer pace during frosty weather. Although lettuce and spinach can survive light frost, lettuce stops growing at 40 degrees F (4.5°C), spinach at 36 degrees (2°C). The planting dates of even the hardiest crops, such as Brussels sprouts and kale, are calculated so that the plants will mature by the first frost date, even though they may survive weeks longer. The entire garden stops growing with the first severe frost, but hardy plants do promise a prolonged harvest of fresh vegetables and herbs, and hardy flowers fill garden beds with interesting foliage and the last colors of chrysanthemums, pansies and the heads of ornamental grasses.

Hardy perennials stop growing and begin the process of acclimatization as the temperature falls and the days shorten. These plants lose their leaves and prepare to enter a period of dormancy, or rest, which enables them to survive much colder weather in winter than they could in summer. Do not fertilize perennials after midsummer, because this encourages the growth of tender new shoots that are less frost-hardy. Before the acclimatization process is complete, a hard frost can be deadly. After 15 years of robust growth in gardens near Edmonton, Alberta, *Sedum spectabile* 'Autumn Joy' died to the ground following a sudden drop in temperature to about minus 4 degrees F (–20°C) in mid-October 1984.

After acclimatization, some hardy perennials can survive extreme cold unscathed, but others do better when protected with a layer of mulch. Chrysanthemums, irises, lythrum and roses are a

Average Date of the Last Fall Frost

This list provides the average date of the first light frost, 32 degrees F (0°C) in fall. There is a 50 percent chance of a frost occurrence before these dates. This information comes from Environment Canada.

Alberta	Calgary	September 12
Alberta	Edmonton	September 17
British Columbia	Kamloops	October 1
British Columbia	Vancouver	October 30
British Columbia	Victoria	November 2
Manitoba	Winnipeg	September 21
New Brunswick	Fredericton	September 26
Newfoundland	St. John's	September 19
Northwest Territories	Yellowknife	September 16
Nova Scotia	Halifax	October 15
Ontario	Ottawa	September 28
Ontario	Thunder Bay	September 10
Ontario	Toronto	October 30
Prince Edward Island	Charlottetown	October 16
Quebec	Gaspé	September 26
Quebec	Montreal	October 7
Quebec	Sherbrooke	September 27
Saskatchewan	Saskatoon	September 15
Yukon Territory	Whitehorse	September 1

few perennials best mulched in marginal places. If you have any doubts about the hardiness of a new plant, mulch it, especially the year of planting. Perennials are most vulnerable during their first winter.

If the day has been cool, the sky is clear and the weather station warns of frost "in low-lying areas," the gardener has a number of options. Flowers can be picked for indoors, and cuttings can be taken from begonias, impatiens and pelargoniums. Many tender vegetables can be picked right away: tiny summer squashes for delectable dining, small cucumbers for pickling. Tomatoes that have begun to turn color, appearing white or pinkish, will probably ripen if brought indoors and spread out, not touching, on paper and left at a temperature of 55 to 70 degrees F (13-21°C). Wrapping each fruit in paper encourages ripening by reducing air circulation around the tomatoes. Light is neither essential nor harmful in the ripening process. Muskmelons that are full-sized but not yet ripe will ripen the same way. Immature peppers can be eaten, as can young peas and beans.

Dig up a few pepper plants, and keeping the rootball as intact as possible, put each one in a 12-inch (30 cm) pot. Fill around the rootball with compost, drench the plant and soil with diluted insecticidal soap to help control aphids and whiteflies, and place the plants indoors in a sunny window. Kept watered throughout the winter, the plants will probably not set fruit but will provide very early peppers when planted outdoors the next spring after all danger of frost has passed. Several herbs, too, can be potted in fall for indoor use in winter (see Chapter Six).

The next strategy—covering the plants—is particularly recommended if the weather is expected to improve soon, providing a few warm weeks of Indian summer. Covering the plants prevents damage caused by dew settling on leaves or fruit, then freezing. While a cover will not protect tender plants from really low temperatures, almost anything—blankets, bedsheets, garbage bags, sheets of plastic or newspaper—laid over plants in the early evening and secured so that it won't blow off will keep the plants alive through light or even moderate frosts. Some gardeners make special

Covering plants in spring and fall extends the season by holding in the soil's warmth.

large, plastic-covered wooden frames for just this purpose. Low-growing plants can be lightly covered with mulch. If the plants are already growing under cover, they are out of danger from light frost, but adding another layer of covering will help protect them from lower temperatures. Covers that exclude light should be removed as soon as the temperature rises above freezing in the morning.

What if frost catches you and your garden unprepared? Before the sun strikes the garden, sprinkle frosted plants with water from a hose or a watering can, which prevents damage from a light frost. This method works because water releases heat as it freezes. It can prevent damage from even colder weather if the plants are sprinkled all night, but increasing amounts of water are needed as the temperature falls. In experiments in the Yukon Territory during the 1960s, Agriculture Canada scientist Gerard H. Gubbels found that "potato foliage and peas were not injured seriously when maintained above minus 1.1 degrees C [30°F]. To maintain plant temperatures above minus 1.1 degrees required 0.9 mm per hour of water when the air was down to minus 2.8 degrees [27°F], 1.2 mm per hour down to minus 3.3 degrees [26°F], 1.6 mm per hour down to minus 4.4 degrees [24°F], 2.2 mm per hour down to minus 5.5 degrees [22°F] and 2.9 mm per hour down to minus 7.2 degrees [19°F]."

Space heaters or smoky bonfires situated throughout the garden also help keep temperatures above freezing on frosty nights but are so labor-intensive, fuel-hungry and polluting that they are out of the question unless your winter food supply depends on your garden.

Vegetable-Garden Cleanup

As fall approaches, the most tender plants must be harvested first. The fruit of summer and winter squashes and pumpkins, for the most part hidden under huge leaves, is protected from the first frost. But once the foliage is dead, the fruit must be picked before the next frost if you hope to store it for any length of time.

Roots or tubers can generally be left until just before the soil freezes, even though the plant foliage may be dead. By the time you dig the potatoes, there may be only a dead stem marking the position of each hill of tubers. Onions are the opposite, with frost-hardy tops growing above bulbs that should be harvested before the first frost. Harvesting, curing and storage instructions for each vegetable are described in Chapter Four.

As each crop is harvested, any remaining plant refuse should be carted out of the garden and added to the compost heap. This is a matter of not only neatness but also future crop health. Many pests and diseases overwinter in the garden on crop refuse. For example, bean rust and bacterial wilt remain on infested debris; corn earworms and European corn borers spend the winter inside cornstalks; Colorado potato beetles and striped cucumber beetles overwinter in the debris of their respective hosts. Burn any diseased plants, or send them off with the garbage collector, and avoid growing a related plant in that spot next spring. Thick stems such as those of broccoli and corn will

not break down quickly enough for the compost pile. Put them through a compost shredder or power lawn mower, or pile them separately where their gradual decomposition will not slow the compost pile's work.

After each row or bed has been completely cleared, the soil can be tilled or spaded or a cover crop such as ryegrass can be sown for green manuring in spring (see pages 36 and 37). Spare the beds that hold newly planted garlic and overwintering root crops. Some root vegetables can be overwintered in the ground under a heavy layer of mulch such as bales of hay or straw. Jerusalem artichokes, beets, carrots, parsnips and salsify may be kept this way. Jerusalem artichokes and parsnips will survive most winters without mulching, although unlike mulched roots, they cannot be harvested until the soil thaws in spring.

Flower-Garden Cleanup

Cleaning up the flowerbeds is mostly a matter of aesthetics. No gardener wants to spend the winter looking out at a garden full of dead flowers and rotting vegetation. Collect seeds, and divide plants according to the directions in Chapter Eight. Remove the least attractive of the dead annuals and the aboveground remains of the perennials, but leave some vegetation behind. A number of annual and perennial stems are attractive even when dried and brown and should be left for winter interest and to help collect drifting snow, which acts as mulch and as a water reservoir. Mulch perennial beds with about 4 inches (10 cm) of hay, fallen leaves or grass clippings that have not been treated with herbicides.

There are a few more end-of-season tasks:
• Fall is a good time to have a soil test done (see the list of addresses on page 43). Organic materials and lime or sulfur, in amounts recommended by the report, may be tilled or spaded in before winter.
• In your garden notebook, write down all the harvest dates and your comments on the success of each plant, along with frost dates. Make a note of anything you might want to try next year.
• Rake up fallen leaves, and use them as mulch or pile them to compost.
• Some vegetable and flower seeds can be sown in

Vegetables must be harvested according to their hardiness, or frosty weather will spoil them.

fall, a risky process but one that can bring very early flowers and vegetables if the winter weather is cooperative. In the 1982 edition of *The Prairie Garden*, Joe Tsukamoto wrote that in Brandon, Manitoba, he was successful with beets, carrots, lettuce, onions, parsley, radishes and spinach, all sown "as close to the time of freeze-up as possible." These fall-sown seeds emerged earlier and matured faster than their spring-sown counterparts. Flower possibilities include alyssum, baby-blue-eyes (*Nemophila menziesii*), annual baby's-breath, California poppy, candytuft, clarkia, cleome, corn-flower, cosmos, cynoglossum, gloriosa daisy, larkspur, love-in-a-mist (*Nigella damascena*), pot marigold, Shirley poppy and snapdragon. Sprinkle the seeds on the ground any time after the soil freezes until early spring, even on snow. The seeds will soak into the ground as the snow melts and will germinate as the soil warms. Many hardy

perennials can also be sown outdoors in fall. It is best to sow them in pots or in a cold frame so that you can easily find the little sprouts in spring. Suit-able flowers include delphinium, Oriental poppy, painted daisy, pansy, stokesia and viola.

• This is the time to plant hardy spring-flowering bulbs, including some that will go into pots for winter forcing in a cool shed or greenhouse or in a refrigerator in the house.

• This is also an alternative time for planting Jerusalem artichokes, asparagus and rhubarb.

• If you wish to enlarge the garden or start a new one, begin preparing the site as soon as possible (see Chapter Two).

• Clean tools, sharpen them if necessary, wipe metal blades with an oily rag, and store tools un-der cover for the winter. Collect plant stakes, trel-lises and any other garden hardware, and store un-der cover. Power mowers, shredders and tillers should be prepared for winter according to the manufacturer's directions.

Vegetable Storage

Most crops are stored indoors over the winter. Methods of storage include pickling, canning, freezing, drying, cool storage and the preparation of jellies and jams. In every case, vegetable maturation and spoilage is slowed or stopped, sometimes with the help of the plant's own ability to remain dormant, sometimes by artificial means that exclude decay organisms. Each method has its own advantages and disadvantages and suits a few crops best.

Home Canning

Home canning might better be called home jarring, because foods are preserved in sturdy glass jars capable of holding an airtight seal, thanks to specially designed tight-fitting lids. When food is processed in these jars at high temperatures for a specified time, harmful microorganisms are destroyed. If the canning has been done properly, the airtight seal prevents further microorganisms from entering the jar, and the food will store safely at room temperature for years.

The most dangerous contaminant of canned food is the spore-forming bacterium *Clostridium botulinum*, which is naturally present in soil and on most produce. In the oxygen-free environment of a sealed container, this botulism bacterium can multiply, producing a deadly toxin. High-acid foods prevent the multiplication of *C. botulinum* and thus are the only ones that can be safely canned at a temperature as low as the boiling point of water. Low-acid foods, including all vegetables, should be processed at 240 degrees F (115°C), a temperature that can be reached safely only in a pressure canner.

Tomatoes have a high enough acid content to allow processing in hot water, but they are considered borderline in acidity by Agriculture Canada, which recommends the addition of 1/4 teaspoon (1 mL) citric acid or 1 tablespoon (15 mL) reconstituted lemon juice to each pint (500 mL) of stewed tomatoes. Add twice that amount to quart jars. Citric acid is a natural constituent of tomatoes, so its addition will have little effect on the flavor of the canned produce. Fresh lemon juice is not recom-

mended, because its acid content is too variable.

For canning high-acid food, you need a canning kettle, also called a hot-water bath, which can be purchased in most hardware stores and country general stores in summer and fall. The size of the pot you buy will depend on whether you are going to use pint or quart jars. The pot should be deep enough so that water will cover the jars by 1 to 2 inches (2.5-5 cm). Do not use a steam canner—this piece of equipment has not yet been proved capable of sustaining the high temperatures required for safe canning.

You can buy canning jars in half-pint (250 mL), pint (500 mL) and quart (1 L) sizes. Some places sell quart jars with a wide mouth, best suited to whole-cucumber pickles or whole tomatoes. All canning jars have securely fitting metal lids and screw bands that can be replaced every year. Older canning jars featured a rubber ring that was squeezed against the jar rim by a glass lid held in turn by a metal screw band. These, too, are reliable if used properly.

Rather than buying jars, many cooks use recycled jam jars, pickle jars and the like. They often come with sealer lids or will fit standard commercial lids. Food experts at Agriculture Canada, however, recommend that recycled jars *not* be used for processing. Use them, instead, for storing dried foods.

With a hot-water bath and a supply of strong, washed jars and lids, anyone wishing to preserve fruits, tomatoes, pickles, relishes and jams needs little else except perhaps a ladle, a pair of pot holders and standard kitchen equipment. Wash the food, and if necessary, hull, trim or peel it. Whole tomatoes peel easily after they have been boiled for about a minute, then dipped into ice water. In some cases, the fruits or tomatoes are cooked before they are processed (to make jam or ketchup, for instance), but this is a matter of personal preference only and not a matter of safety. There are many good books on canning and on making specific types of home-canned foods, such as jellies, jams, salsas and pickles.

Fill only as many jars as can be processed in one batch—usually seven. Pack the whole or sliced fruits into the jars to within 1 inch (2.5 cm) of the rim (that empty top inch is called "headspace"), then fill the jars with boiling water, juice or sugar syrup, leaving ½ inch (1 cm) of headspace in quart jars, ¼ inch (6 mm) in pint jars. Sugar syrup may contain from ¾ to 3 cups (175-750 mL) water to every 1 cup (250 mL) sugar, honey or corn syrup, depending on your preference. The amount and type of sweetener will affect the flavor of the food, but sweeteners are not necessary for safe preservation.

Once the jars are filled, insert a rubber spatula down the inside edge of each jar to release air bubbles, adding more liquid if needed. When canning juices, sauces and syrups, just pour in the liquid until the appropriate headspace remains.

Wipe the rim of each jar with a clean, wet cloth, wet the lids or rubber rings, place one lid or ring on each jar, then screw the retaining band on tightly. With the rubber-ring system *only*, the band is then slightly loosened—turn it back no more than 1 inch (2.5 cm)—before processing.

Fill the water bath about halfway with hot water, and place the jars on the rack that fits inside. Lower the rack to rest on the bottom of the bath, and add enough water to cover the jars. Put the lid on the kettle, set it on high heat, and as soon as the water reaches a rolling boil, begin timing. The processing times given on this page are for altitudes less than 2,000 feet (610 m) above sea level. At altitudes from 2,000 to 3,000 feet (610-915 m), add one-fifth to the time listed; from 3,000 to 4,000 feet (915-1,220 m), add two-fifths; and so on, adding one additional fifth for each successive rise of 1,000 feet (305 m) above sea level.
• Process whole berries, except cherries, for 15 minutes in pints or 20 minutes in quarts.
• Berry and rhubarb juices and syrups, 10 minutes in pints and quarts.*
• Whole or sliced cherries, 20 minutes in pints or 25 minutes in quarts.
• Tomatoes, 55 minutes in pints or 60 minutes in quarts.
• Tomato juice, sauce and ketchup, 40 minutes in pints and quarts.
*When the processing time is less than 15 minutes, the jars and their lids should first be sterilized. Immerse them in boiling water for 15 minutes just before they are filled.

Maintain a full boil throughout the timing.

When the time is up, turn off the heat, remove the kettle lid, lift the basket—it should have handles that will hook over the edges of the canning kettle—and carefully remove each jar, using pot holders or a jar lifter. Place the jars, not touching, on a dish towel on a counter, where they can sit undisturbed until cool.

Any hissing during cooling indicates an unsealed jar. A loud "ping" during cooling, on the other hand, indicates a good seal on a snap lid, a type of metal lid designed to give that reassuring signal. When the jars are cool, check each seal. The metal lids should be indented and, as with glass lids, will not leak when the jar is turned upside down. The screw bands may be *gently* removed for further seal checking and for jar storage—but be careful, as tightening or loosening the band vigorously may break the seal. You should not be able to remove either the glass or the metal lids with your thumb. Any jars that are not properly sealed can be given a new sterilized lid or rubber ring and reprocessed for 15 minutes, or they can be refrigerated and the food used as soon as possible.

Store full jars upright in a cool, dark cupboard. Light can cause food to fade. Properly canned food will store for several years, but most cooks try to estimate their yearly needs so that fresh produce is canned as soon as the previous year's supply runs out. If food looks at all suspect when you open the jars, discard it where it will not be tasted by people or animals. The jars must then be washed and sterilized in boiling water for 15 minutes. *Never* taste canned food that looks spoiled in any way.

Jams, Jellies & Pickles

Jams and jellies make use of the naturally acidic properties of fruit for preservation. Pectin, gelatin and other thickeners are usually added, along with honey or sugar for flavor, thickening and preservation. Pickles and relishes use the acidity of vinegar and the preserving power of salt so that low-acid foods such as cucumbers and corn can be stored safely at room temperature without pressure canning. Sauerkraut is a fermented cabbage product that includes salt. Dill pickles can be prepared by a similar process.

When you make pickles or relishes, follow the

Drying and pickling are preservation methods well suited to a few choice vegetables and herbs.

recipe exactly—measurements have been calculated so that the food will be safe for water-bath canning. When making jams and jellies, some cooks choose to top the jars with a double layer of paraffin (let one layer cool before adding the second) rather than using a sealer lid. Make sure that the fruit goes above the shoulder of the jar, or the paraffin will be very difficult to remove.

Before being filled with jams, jellies or pickles, the jars should be sterilized. Do this by immersing washed jars in boiling water for 15 minutes, then filling the hot jars with boiling produce. Unless processing is recommended in the recipe, it is not necessary for pickles and relishes. Tests by Agriculture Canada have indicated that processing these foods makes the product less crisp and does not improve its keeping quality.

Vegetables on Ice

The preparation of food for freezing requires less energy and less equipment, but freezing itself is expensive, requiring the maintenance of a closed environment of 0 degrees F (–18°C) or colder. Frozen food is, however, safe to eat, and the quality can remain high for months. Certain vegetables, properly prepared and frozen, are almost identical in flavor and texture to fresh ones that have been cooked. There is gradual deterioration, so after a year, discard frozen vegetables and fruits.

Most vegetables should be blanched before freezing. The only items not blanched are those which would become mushy if they were: herbs, tomatoes, peppers, mushrooms and onions. Spread these in a single layer on cookie sheets, and freeze them, then pour the food into plastic bags, jars or recycled containers.

Fruits can be packed with or without sugar. If sugar is to be added, it may be dry or in a cold syrup. Pour the syrup, which may contain from ¾ to 2 parts water to every 1 part sugar or honey, into containers packed with berries, chopped rhubarb or melon. Leave at least 1 inch (2.5 cm) of head-

An attractive way to dry quantities of everlasting flowers is to hang them upside down indoors.

space between the surface of the fruit and the rim of any rigid container, because the liquid will expand as it freezes.

All other foods can be blanched to destroy enzymes that otherwise cause the texture and flavor to deteriorate more quickly in storage. If you plan to use the food within about 4 months, though, you may want to freeze it raw. Unblanched food is safe to eat, and studies have indicated a greater loss of vitamin C in blanched green beans, broccoli, spinach and squash than in the unblanched food after 3 months' storage. Other research has shown that carotene (vitamin A) levels remain higher in blanched vegetables. To blanch vegetables, bring a large pot half filled with water to a boil, add the vegetables, put on a lid, leave the pot on high heat and time the blanching until the vegetables are hot right through.

As soon as the time is up, pour off the water. Retain and reuse the water if you are doing several batches of the same vegetable. Pour the hot veg-etables into a sink of ice water. As soon as they are cool, lift them into a colander to drain for a few minutes, then pack in containers, and place in the freezer right away.

Flexible containers should be as full as possible, because any air enclosed with the vegetables will lower the food quality. With a drinking straw, suck the air out of filled freezer bags, then pinch the top shut, and secure it with a twist tie. If possible, freeze no more than 3 pounds (1.4 kg) of food for every 1 cubic foot (0.03 m³) of freezer capacity at one time, and place the new bags of vegetables so that they do not touch and can freeze as quickly as possible. Once frozen, the bags can be stored together in one area.

Home-frozen vegetables usually retain enough blanching water that none need be added when they are heated to serve. Without adding water, heat the frozen vegetables gently in a lidded pot, turning them occasionally, and serve as soon as they are hot. Frozen cobs of corn can be buttered, wrapped in foil and baked for 20 minutes at 400 degrees F (200°C).

Dried Produce

Home-dried food is noticeably different in flavor and texture from fresh, even after reconstitution, but its preparation is easy and inexpensive, and storage requires very little space. Some foods adapt particularly well to drying—herbs, spinach and other leafy greens, for instance, as well as thinly sliced mushrooms, onions, carrots and parsnips. As is the case with frozen foods, items that will otherwise become mushy, such as herbs, peppers, tomatoes, onions and mushrooms, need not be blanched before drying. Other foods should be blanched until they are warmed slightly, or the flavor and nutrient content of the food will gradually deteriorate in storage.

Vegetables to be dried should be sliced $\frac{1}{8}$ to $\frac{1}{4}$ inch (3-6 mm) thick, if appropriate, before blanching. Leafy vegetables and herbs can be left whole (see Chapter Six for information on drying herbs). Blanched vegetables that are to be dried need not be cooled. Just drain, blot dry, then place the vegetables, still hot, in a single layer on cookie sheets or on cheesecloth or screening (not galvanized) stretched on a frame. Set in a warm, dry spot with good air circulation. The ideal temperature range for drying is 100 to 140 degrees F (38-60°C), hot enough for quick drying but not hot enough to cook the food. There are commercial food dryers, but ready-made possibilities include the sill of an open screened window, the oven of a gas stove, a shady spot outdoors in dry weather and an electric oven at its lowest setting, with the door left ajar.

Food should not become damp once drying has begun. Bring anything drying outdoors back in overnight or whenever the weather is damp. In the best conditions, leafy vegetables and herbs should dry in a day, other vegetables in less than a week. Fast drying means best quality. Drying may take much longer if conditions are not optimal.

Snap beans, berries, mushrooms, pumpkins, root vegetables and squashes will feel tough and leathery when ready to store. Broccoli, cabbage, celery, cucumbers, herbs, onions, potatoes and leafy vegetables should be paper-dry and crumbly

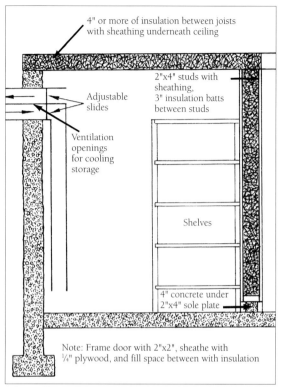

This 5-by-8-foot (1.5 x 2.5 m) root cellar will hold about 30 bushels (1,000 L) of food.

or brittle. Beans, corn and shelled peas should be too hard to dent with a fingernail. If in doubt, let the food dry longer, perhaps in paper bags. Insufficiently dried foods will spoil.

As soon as the food is dry and cool, pour it into clean, labeled glass jars with lids. Store in a cool, dry, dark cupboard. The food will gradually deteriorate while in storage and so should be used within a year. Dried vegetables and fruits are especially suited for backpacking and for use in dishes that have enough liquid to reconstitute them: soups, stews, puddings or pies. Remember that dried foods may be less than half as bulky as their fresh counterparts, so add correspondingly less to the recipe and be prepared to use extra liquid. Dried fruits are also ideal snack foods.

Root Storage

Some foods designed by nature to be dormant through the winter can be stored without any special equipment at all if you can give them the right

Store onions and garlic on their own so that their strong odors do not contaminate other foods.

environment. A few things will keep in the garden, provided the winter is not too harsh: carrots, parsnips and potatoes. If they are under heavy mulch, you can dig up a few as needed.

If you have lots of space and plenty of food to store, you may want to build a root cellar, which can be constructed either outdoors or indoors. The advantage of the outdoor cellar, which is built underground or bermed with earth, is that temperatures can be naturally maintained around freezing all winter. The optimum relative humidity in a root cellar is 80 to 95 percent. Most hardware stores stock a combination thermometer/hygrometer, which measures temperature and humidity.

Indoor root cellars allow easy accessibility. While an unheated basement is the perfect environment for such a storage room, a heated basement can be suitable if the root cellar is well insulated and is provided with a window that will allow cold air to enter. During winter, the window will need to be opened only infrequently to keep the temperature

within the correct storage range. A storage room 5 by 8 feet (1.5 x 2.5 m) will hold about 30 bushel hampers. Alternatively, a refrigerator set at its highest temperature will keep a small quantity of bagged produce crisp and moist.

Not all foods should be stored together. Apples, apricots, muskmelons, peaches, pears, plums and tomatoes produce ethylene gas, which speeds up the aging process of vegetables, shortening their storage life. Cabbage, celery and onions have strong odors that may be picked up by other vegetables. Most of these foods would not be stored together in any case, but where they are together, consider packing one item in polyethylene or keeping them as far removed from each other as possible. Avoid the following combinations:
• celery with onions or carrots
• apples, pears or tomatoes with celery, cabbage, lettuce, carrots, rutabagas, potatoes or onions
• root crops with fruit or leafy vegetables
Store only sound, whole produce; bruises, cuts

and insect damage allow the growth of molds. Beets, carrots, horseradish, parsnips, winter radishes, salsify and scorzonera can be packed in perforated polyethylene bags and stored at 32 degrees F (0°C), or they can be left unbagged, layered with peat, sand or straw and stored in boxes in a dark, cool root cellar at a temperature at or just above freezing. Potatoes should also be kept in darkness, although their environment should be drier and warmer, preferably about 45 to 50 degrees (7-10°C). There might be a relatively cool spot in the basement or a relatively warm spot on the porch for a carton, basket or bag of potatoes. Cabbages will keep a few weeks in a cool place. Either wrap them in newspaper and store on a shelf in the root cellar, or pack them in polyethylene bags in the refrigerator. Winter squashes and pumpkins store best in a dry place at about 50 to 60 degrees (10-15°C), in or out of light. In the same environment, watermelons will keep for about a month. Onions and garlic need the driest surroundings of all, and although they keep best at temperatures just above freezing, the hardest varieties of storage onions will keep well even at a somewhat cool room temperature. They may be stored loose in bags, boxes, baskets or nylon stockings hung from hooks; or the dried tops can be braided with a string and the completed braids hung in a cool, dry room.

To store well, these vegetables should first be cured for a day. This dries the skin of the produce so that it helps contain the moisture within. Squashes, pumpkins, roots and tubers should be harvested on a dry morning and spread out in a single layer on newspaper or a sunny porch. After a few hours, turn each vegetable over, exposing the damp underside, and rub off any clinging lumps of soil. Onions should be cured for several days, until the skins are papery and the tops are dry. Cover or bring indoors during damp weather or overnight. Alternatively, onions can be cured in a warm, dry room with good air circulation.

Flower-Bulb Storage

Tender perennials such as acidanthera, dahlias and gladiolus can be stored in much the same manner as onions. They need to be kept from freezing, from drying out and from becoming moldy. Glads and other flowers with a papery corm are easy to store in paper bags in a cool, dry place. Dahlia roots are vulnerable to drying out, but if they are piled under glad corms, the corms will help protect them. Alternatively, dahlias can be stored in boxes of peat moss or vermiculite. (See page 150 for more information about summer bulbs.)

In the North, this quiet time of storage and dormancy takes the gardener through until sowing and planting time comes again.

Bulb Hardiness

According to horticulturists at the University of Minnesota, the bulbs listed here can be severely injured by the soil (not air) temperatures indicated. You may not know your soil temperature, but what this table indicates is relative hardiness. If you know one species will survive for you, others that are similarly hardy probably will as well. Bulbs that are less hardy should be mulched or brought indoors for the winter.

Temperature	Species
5°F (–15°C)	*Camassia quamash*
8°F (–13°C)	*Tulipa fosterana* 'Red Emperor'; *Tulipa gesnerana* 'Apeldoorn'
12°F (–11°C)	*Eranthis hyemalis*; *Puschkinia scilloides*; *Scilla siberica*
16°F (–9°C)	*Anemone blanda*; *Crocus speciosus*; *Endymion hispanicus*; *Galanthus nivalis*; *Hyacinthus orientalis* 'King of the Blues'; *Lycoris radiata*; *Muscari armeniacum* 'Blue Spike'; *Scilla tubergeniana*; *Tulipa kaufmanniana*
21°F (–6°C)	*Allium moly*; *Leucojum aestivum*; *Sternbergia lutea*
28°F (–2°C)	*Ixia* spp; *Ranunculus* spp; *Sparaxis tricolor*

This simplified version of the U.S. Department of Agriculture's latest climatic-zone map indicates general temperature trends throughout Canada and the United States. The temperature ranges indicate average minimum winter temperatures. Colder zones have lower numbers. Nursery catalogs usually indicate the coldest zone in which a plant will thrive. Plants that are successful in your zone and in zones with numbers lower than yours should survive winters in your garden. Plants that prefer zones with higher numbers than yours may not be winter-hardy for you.

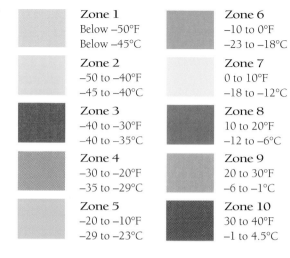

Zone 1
Below −50°F
Below −45°C

Zone 2
−50 to −40°F
−45 to −40°C

Zone 3
−40 to −30°F
−40 to −35°C

Zone 4
−30 to −20°F
−35 to −29°C

Zone 5
−20 to −10°F
−29 to −23°C

Zone 6
−10 to 0°F
−23 to −18°C

Zone 7
0 to 10°F
−18 to −12°C

Zone 8
10 to 20°F
−12 to −6°C

Zone 9
20 to 30°F
−6 to −1°C

Zone 10
30 to 40°F
−1 to 4.5°C

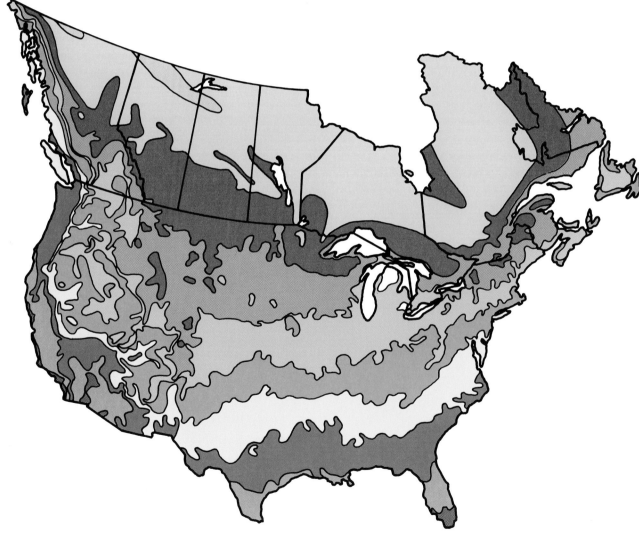

Glossary

Acidic: refers to soil with a pH below 7, which is neutral. For the best growth of most plants, an ideal garden soil is slightly acidic, with a pH of about 6.5. Sulfur compounds tend to make soil more acidic, or "sour." Acidic soils are usually found in areas of high rainfall.

Alkaline: the opposite of acidic; refers to soil with a pH above 7. Liming compounds such as calcium carbonate or magnesium carbonate make soil more alkaline. Alkaline soils are usually found in areas of low rainfall or where the bedrock consists of alkaline materials.

Annual: a plant that completes its entire life cycle within one year. Many tropical perennial plants are treated as annuals in the North—planted or sown outdoors in spring and allowed to die in fall.

Axil: the crotch between a large stem and a smaller stem or a leaf.

Bedding Plant: a young plant purchased in a container, ready to go into the garden. The term has traditionally been used for flowering annuals.

Biennial: a plant that must survive one winter or a certain period of low temperatures before it will produce seed.

Blanch: in the garden, the process of shading a vegetable so that its color is lightened and its flavor becomes milder. Strong-tasting vegetables such as dandelions, chicory and endive are best after being blanched for a week or two. Cauliflower is blanched by tying leaves over the developing head, which then stays white; unblanched heads turn green or purple and have a stronger flavor. Blanched vegetables are somewhat lower in nutrients than their unblanched counterparts. In the kitchen, blanching denotes the processing of vegetables prior to freezing or drying.

Bolt: the process in which some plants produce seed stalks quickly. Lettuce and spinach are said to bolt to seed in hot weather. When crops bolt, the edible parts deteriorate in flavor and texture.

Brassica: a member of the *Brassica* genus of plants, including broccoli, Brussels sprouts, cabbage, cauliflower, collards, kale and kohlrabi. All brassicas suffer from similar diseases and pests.

Bulb: a plant storage organ, usually underground, whose fleshy scales are modified leaves. Tulips, narcissus, alliums and onions have bulbs.

Clone: an exact genetic replica of the parent, propagated from part of the parent rather than from seed. Cuttings, potato eyes, rhizomes and runners all produce plants that are clones of the parent. The word may also be used as a verb that denotes such propagation.

Compost: organic matter in a state of partial and continuing decay. Compost is usually a mixture of leaves, animal manure, hay and other biodegradable ingredients that is kept wet and aerated as it decays, releasing heat and killing harmful microorganisms. As soon as it is crumbly, which may take from 2 weeks to several years, depending on the amount and type of materials in the pile, the size of the pile and the ambient temperatures, compost can be used as a fertilizer, mulch or potting mixture. The word is also used as a verb that denotes the process of composting.

Corm: a plant storage organ formed as a thickened base of the stem. Crocuses and gladiolus have corms. Newly developing corms are called cormels or cormlets.

Cotyledon: the first leaf produced by a plant; also called a seedling leaf. The cotyledon looks different from later-developing true leaves. Cotyledons are usually very simple in structure and appearance, lacking indentations and other characteristics of all later-developing leaves. Monocotyledons (or monocots), such as lily, grass and corn, produce only one cotyledon, while dicotyledons (or dicots), such as tomato and rose, produce two.

Cross-Pollination: occurs when pollen is passed from the male part of one flower to the female part of another. Also called crossing or crossbreeding.

Cultivar: a human-created plant variety, short for *cultiv*ated *variety*. For example, while *Brassica oleracea capitata* designates cabbage (*capitata* being the variety name), 'Stonehead' is a cultivar.

Cutting: a shoot or twig of a plant that can be used for propagation. Placed in water or a wet growing medium to root, it produces a clone of the parent.

Daisy: a member of the Compositae family, the largest plant family on Earth and one with many representatives in flower gardens, including marigolds, dahlias and asters. Single daisies have composite flowers composed of rays, or ray flowers, the so-called petals, and a center of disk flowers. Doubles may be composed of ray flowers only.

Damping-Off: a fungus disease that spreads in unsterilized soil, especially when it is cool and wet and when plants are overcrowded. The disease kills seedlings either before they emerge through the soil or soon after, when the base of the stem becomes pinched and the seedling finally topples and dies.

Deadhead: to remove dead flowers. Frequent deadheading helps certain ornamentals look neat and encourages continued flowering.

Determinate: a type of plant that reaches a certain size and stops growing because each stem terminates in a flower bud. The opposite is indeterminate. The adjectives are usually used to describe tomatoes, sometimes cucumbers or summer squashes. Seed catalogs or packets often refer to determinate cultivars as bush types.

Double: a flower with more than the number of petals usual for the wild species. Double flowers may have an extra ring of petals, sometimes called semidouble, or they may be a mass of petals forming a round pompon. Fully double flowers are generally sterile.

Drip Line: the ground under the outermost extent of the foliage of a plant. Rain that is shed off the plant will first fall most heavily along this line, hence the name.

F1, F2: designations for hybrid plants. F1 means filial-one. It is the first generation of offspring from a cross between two related species or cultivars. F2 is the offspring of an F1 hybrid.

Flat: container about 3 inches (7.5 cm) deep and up to 18 inches (45 cm) long and wide that is filled with growing medium and used for germinating seeds and for holding seedlings before they are transplanted into deeper soil.

Fungicide: a substance that kills fungi (plural of fungus). The word usually applies to any of a number of synthetic substances used mostly by commercial growers.

Fungus: a plant that does not manufacture its own chlorophyll and so must live off other plants or organic materials. Mushrooms are fungi, as are many diseases that infect garden plants. Most fungi thrive in wet conditions.

Genus: a grouping of closely related plants within a large family. The usual botanical name of a plant includes a genus and species. The genus name goes first and is capitalized and written in italics. The species name follows, in lowercase italics. For instance, both the potato and the garden huckleberry belong to the genus *Solanum*; the first is known as *Solanum tuberosum*, the latter as *Solanum nigrum*. The plural is genera.

Germination: the sprouting of a seed.

Gray Water: household wastewater from washing or bathing. As long as it does not contain detergents, borax, bleaches or other chemicals (although some soap is all right), it may be used sparingly in the garden. However, the use of gray water is illegal in many urban areas.

Green Manure: a crop that is grown for the purpose of being plowed under while still immature, thus adding nutrients and organic matter to the soil. Common green-manure crops include buckwheat, ryegrass and field peas.

Harden Off: to acclimatize a plant to a change in its environment, usually a change from indoors to outdoors. Plants that are not slowly acclimatized, or hardened off, before making such a move may die. In hardening off plants, then, the gardener gradually exposes them to increasingly long periods of time in the conditions of their new environment, a process that usually takes several days. Less frequent watering helps plants harden off.

Herbaceous: an adjective used to describe perennial plants that die to the ground in winter. All common garden flowering perennials are herbaceous. The opposite term is woody. Shrubs and trees are woody perennials.

Herbicide: a substance that kills certain plants. The word usually applies to a number of synthetic substances used mostly by commercial growers.

Hybrid: a plant that does not have the same genetic makeup as either of its parents, which may be members of different species, varieties or cultivars. Hybrid plants possess "hybrid vigor," some of the best characteristics of both parents, and so may be superior in some ways to nonhybrid, open-pollinated or standard plants. On the other hand, hybrids may not be markedly superior but are often more expensive, more profitable and thus more heavily promoted. The seed of a hybrid seldom produces offspring just like the parent.

Indeterminate: a type of plant that continues to grow and blossom throughout the season. The opposite type is determinate. The term is usually used to describe tomatoes, occasionally cucumbers and summer squashes, but in reality, many perennial plants are indeterminate. Seed catalogs often refer to indeterminate tomatoes as staking tomatoes, because they are likely to grow tall during the season. Semi-determinate tomatoes possess characteristics of both determinates and indeterminates.

Inflorescence: a flower. The term usually denotes a tight cluster of flowers, whether opened or closed, such as the head of broccoli or of cauliflower.

Inoculation: the process of inoculating legume seeds with the proper type of *Rhizobium* bacteria to ensure nitrogen fixation in the soil, enhancing soil fertility. Inoculant can be purchased from many seed houses. Seeds are coated with the inoculant powder before they are planted.

Insecticide: a substance that kills insects, bugs, larvae and such. The word usually applies to any of a number of synthetic substances used mostly by commercial growers. Insecticides, herbicides and fungicides are all covered by the blanket term pesticide, which is preferred now over the word insecticide.

Larva: the stage between egg and adult of a moth, butterfly, beetle or fly. Larvae are often called caterpillars, loopers, grubs or maggots.

Leggy: describes a plant, especially a seedling, that has become tall and weak, usually as a result of too little light, often in combination with too much fertilizer, water and warmth.

Legume: a member of the pea family, Leguminosae. These plants, which include beans, lentils, peanuts and vetch, have the ability to obtain, or "fix," nitrogen from the air with the help of certain bacteria.

Manure Tea: the liquid produced after a quantity of livestock manure has been allowed to steep for about a day in 5 to 10 times as much water. The tea is then used as a mild fertilizer.

Mulch: a covering on the soil that is meant to slow or stop the growth of some plants, usually weeds, and to encourage the growth of vegetables, herbs, flowers, shrubs and trees. Mulches may consist of inorganic materials, such as plastic, boards, stones or carpeting, or they may be organic matter, such as leaves, seaweed, grass clippings, straw or sawdust. Plastic mulches help warm the soil; organic mulches may cool the soil in summer but also provide it with additional organic matter and nutrients as they decay.

Nitrogen Fixation: the process of changing the nitrogen in the atmosphere into a form that can be used by plants, thus enhancing soil fertility. Certain bacteria of the *Rhizobium* genus, which inhabit small nodes or nodules on legume roots, actually "fix" the nitrogen.

Perennial: a plant that, under normal circumstances, will live for more than 2 years. It may set seed every year or less frequently.

Pesticide: an insecticide, a herbicide or a fungicide; a substance, usually synthetic, that kills a living thing labeled a pest by agriculturists.

pH: a scale that ranges from 0 to 14 and denotes acidity or alkalinity. The higher the number, the more alkaline; the lower the number, the more acidic. The number 7 represents neutral. Thus numbers lower than 7 indicate increasingly acidic conditions, and numbers higher than 7 indicate increasingly alkaline conditions. The scale is logarithmic, so each number denotes a value 10 times greater than its predecessor. The symbol pH stands for potential hydrogen.

Pollination: the process by which pollen is transferred to the female part of a flower from the male part. Pollination is usually accomplished by wind, insects, water or animals.

Potpourri: French for "rotten pot," a mixture of dried or preserved herbs and/or flowers that is kept for its appearance and fragrance. Preservatives such as pickling salt or orris root are often added to make the scent last longer.

Rhizome: the fleshy underground stem used by some plants for food storage and for spreading over a larger area. Quack grass and bearded irises have rhizomes. Rhizomes have nodes, roots and buds or leaves and so can be distinguished from roots.

Seedling: a young plant, usually with only its cotyledons, or first true leaves.

Self-Sterile: a flower in which fertilization will not occur if its own pollen is used on its own stigma. Such plants must cross-pollinate if fertilization and eventual seed production are to take place.

Set: a small bulb, especially of an onion or shallot. It is planted in spring to develop into a full-sized bulb by fall. Fruit is said to have set when pollination and fertilization have occurred and the fruit has begun to swell.

Side-Dressing: a method of midseason fertilization by which nutrients are spread on the soil beside plants, usually under the drip line of their foliage. In this way, fertilizer is gradually utilized by the roots.

Single: when used to describe a flower, indicates that the flower has the usual number of petals for the wild species. A wild rose, for instance, has five petals, as does a single rose. A semidouble or double rose has many more.

Solanaceous: describes a member of the plant family Solanaceae, which includes tomatoes, potatoes, peppers, ground cherries, browallia, petunias and nicotiana.

Species: a subdivision of a genus; members of the same species appear similar and are capable of interbreeding. Swiss chard and beets belong to the same species, as do celery and celeriac.

Stamen: the male part of a flower, consisting of a threadlike stem—the filament—that supports an anther upon which pollen is produced. There are usually several stamens surrounding a central stigma, although some flowers produce only stamens.

Stigma: the part of a flower that receives pollen. The stigma is the top of the female part of a flower, the pistil, at the base of which is an immature ovary, an undeveloped fruit.

Sucker: a fast-growing shoot that may develop at the expense of the rest of the plant. It often grows where shoots are not desirable for reasons of plant health, longevity, neatness or size of harvest.

Taproot: a swollen root where the plant stores food that is usually used when the plant resumes growth in spring. Carrots, parsnips and dandelions all have taproots.

Tendril: a slender shoot that twines itself around anything it touches, thereby supporting the plant from which it grows. Peas and sweet peas have tendrils.

Transplant: as a verb, denotes the transfer of a live plant from one growing medium to another; as a noun, refers to the plant that will be moved, is being moved or has recently been moved.

True Leaf: any leaf produced by a plant subsequent to the development of its cotyledons, or seedling leaves.

Tuber: a swelling on an underground stem that the plant uses for the storage of food. The edible part of the potato plant is a tuber.

Umbel: a seed head in which the flowers have stalks that originate at a common point on the stem. The umbel may be globe- or umbrella-shaped. Members of the plant family Umbelliferae, such as dill, carrot and parsley, derive their family name from their umbels. Onions and dandelions also produce umbels.

Variety: the narrowest botanical classification by which a plant is identified; subdivision of a species. The word is also used to mean cultivar.

Sources

The following list is up to date as this book is published, but because addresses and catalog prices inevitably change, please inquire before ordering. Seeds can travel freely within Canada and fairly freely across international boundaries. There are restrictions, however, including sweet corn and seeds of trees and shrubs, which cannot be imported without a permit. A permit is required, too, for all plant materials, from flower bulbs to potted plants. The foreign company must be willing to supply the paperwork, and the buyer in Canada must pay a fee and apply to:
The Food Production and Inspection Branch
Plant Protection Division
Agriculture Canada
59 Camelot Drive, Second Floor, West Wing
Nepean, Ontario K1A 0Y9
   To import plant materials from Canada into the United States, write for information from:
The U.S. Department of Agriculture, APHIS
Plant Protection and Quarantine
Permit Unit
4700 River Road, Unit 136
Riverdale, Maryland 20737-1236

Mail-Order Seeds & Plants: Canada

Aimers
81 Temperance Street
Aurora, Ontario L4G 2R1
Seeds and bulbs for domestic flowers and wildflowers, exotica, rare seeds.

Alberta Nurseries & Seeds Ltd.
Box 20
Bowden, Alberta T0M 0K0
Flower and vegetable seeds, bulbs, shrubs, trees.

Ward Barkley Select Perennials
RR 1
Morrisburg, Ontario K0C 1X0
Hostas, day lily plants.

Beachwood Lilies
Box 60240, Fraser Postal Outlet
Vancouver, British Columbia V5W 4B5
Day lilies.

Becker's Seed Potatoes
RR 1
Trout Creek, Ontario P0H 2L0
Seed potatoes, common and rare.

Bluestem Grasses
1949 Fife Road
Christina Lake, British Columbia V0H 1E3
Ornamental grasses.

Boughen Nurseries Valley River, Ltd.
Box 12
Valley River, Manitoba R0L 2B0
Berries, fruit trees, ornamental shrubs and trees.

Brackenstone Herbs
Box 752
Nelson, British Columbia V1L 5R7
Herb plants and seeds, scented geraniums.

Bradner Bulb Gardens
6735 Bradner Road, RR 1
Mt. Lehman, British Columbia V4X 2C6
Hardy spring-flowering bulbs.

Bramley Gardens
RR 4
Waterford, Ontario N0E 1V0
Day lilies.

The Butchart Gardens, Ltd.
Box 4010
Victoria, British Columbia V8M 1J8
Victorian favorite flower seeds.

Leonard W. Butt
Huttonville, Ontario L0J 1B0
Gladiolus, lilies.

Chuck Chapman Iris
11 Harts Lane
Guelph, Ontario N1L 1B1
Irises of all types.

The Conservancy
51563 Range Road, 212A
Sherwood Park, Alberta T8G 1B1
Seeds of native Alberta and arctic plants.

Corn Hill Nurseries, Inc.
RR 5
Petitcodiac, New Brunswick E0A 2H0
Fruit trees, berry bushes, roses, perennials.

Cruickshank's Inc.
1015 Mount Pleasant Road
Toronto, Ontario M4P 2M1
Flower bulbs and seeds, garden tools and accessories.

Dacha Barinka
46232 Strathcona Road
Chilliwack, British Columbia V2P 3T2
Seeds for unusual vegetables, garlic, everlasting flowers.

Dahlias Galore
RR 1, Legion Site C-22
Sechelt, British Columbia V0N 3A0
Dahlias.

William Dam Seeds, Ltd.
Box 8400
Dundas, Ontario L9H 6M1
Vegetable, flower, herb seeds, many European specialties.

Dominion Seed House
Box 2500
Georgetown, Ontario L7G 5L6
Flower, herb and vegetable seeds, bulbs, garden tools and accessories.

Early's Flower & Garden Centre, Inc.
2615 Lorne Avenue
Saskatoon, Saskatchewan S7J 0S5
Flower, herb and vegetable seeds, bulbs, garden tools and accessories.

Erikson's Daylily Gardens
24642 - 51st Avenue
Langley, British Columbia V2Z 1H9
Day lilies.

Ferncliff Gardens
8394 McTaggart Street, S.S.1
Mission, British Columbia V2V 6S6
Flower seeds and plants.

Fox Lily Ranch
RR 2
Millet, Alberta T0C 1Z0
Lilies.

Fraser's Thimble Farms
175 Arbutus Road
Salt Spring Island, British Columbia V8K 1A3
Native plants, ferns, unusual perennials, shrubs, trees.

Gardenimport, Inc.
Box 760
Thornhill, Ontario L3T 4A5
Perennial plants, bulbs, flower and vegetable seeds, garden tools and supplies.

Gardens North
5984 Third Line Road N., RR 3
North Gower, Ontario K0A 2T0
Seeds for hardy perennials, ornamental grasses.

Gleneden Gardens
51405-C, Nevin Road
Rosedale, British Columbia V0X 1X0
Day lilies, hostas, irises.

Halifax Seed Co., Inc.
Box 8026
5860 Kane Street
Halifax, Nova Scotia B3K 5L8
Flower, herb and vegetable seeds, garden tools and accessories.

Hardy Roses for the North
Box 2048C
Grand Forks, British Columbia V0H 1H0
Roses.

The Herb Farm
RR 4
Norton, New Brunswick E0G 2N0
Herb seeds and plants.

Heritage Seed Program
RR 3
Uxbridge, Ontario L9P 1R3
Exchange of heritage and other nonhybrid vegetable, herb and flower seeds; magazine.

Honeywood Lilies
Box 68
Parkside, Saskatchewan S0J 2A0
Lilies, peonies, perennials.

Hortico, Inc.
723 Robson Road, RR 1
Waterdown, Ontario L0R 2H1
Perennials, ornamental grasses, herbs, native plants.

Iris Plus
1269 Rte. 139, Box 903
Sutton, Quebec J0E 2K0
Irises.

Les Jardins Osiris
CP 336
Repentigny, Quebec J0S 1M0
Day lilies, hostas, irises, peonies.

The Lily Nook
Box 846A
Neepawa, Manitoba R0J 1H0
Prairie-hardy lilies.

Lindel Lilies
5510 - 239th Street
Langley, British Columbia V3A 7N6
Lilies.

Lindenberg Seeds Ltd.
803 Princess Avenue
Brandon, Manitoba R7A 0P5
Flower, herb and vegetable seeds, bulbs, garden
tools and accessories.

Living Prairie Museum
2795 Ness Avenue
Winnipeg, Manitoba R3J 3S4
Seeds of native flowers and grasses.

McConnell Nursery
Port Burwell, Ontario N0J 1T0
Perennials, roses, shrubs, trees, bulbs.

McFayden Seed Co.
30 - 9th Street, Suite 200
Brandon, Manitoba R7A 6N4
Flower, herb and vegetable seeds, bulbs, plants,
garden tools and accessories.

McMath's Daffodils
6340 Francis Road
Richmond, British Columbia V7C 1K5
Daffodils, narcissus.

McMillen's Iris Garden
RR 1
Norwich, Ontario N0J 1P0
Irises.

Mapple Farm
RR 1
Hillsborough, New Brunswick E0A 1X0
Sweet potatoes for the North; shallots, Jerusalem
artichokes, plastic mulch.

Mason Hogue Gardens
3520 Durham Road 1
RR 4
Uxbridge, Ontario L9P 1R4
Perennials, ornamental grasses, clematis.

Millar Mountain Nursery
5086 McLay Road, RR 3
Duncan, British Columbia V9L 2X1
Irises.

Monashee Perennials
RR 7, Site 6, Box 9
Vernon, British Columbia V1T 7Z3
Hardy perennial plants.

Mosswood Perennials
451 Creed Road, RR 6
Victoria, British Columbia V9E 1C9
Unusual perennials, mail-order seeds.

Naylor's Desert Plants
9091 Eighth Line Road, RR 2
Georgetown, Ontario L7G 4S5
Hardy cactus and succulents.

Ontario Seed Co. Ltd.
Box 7, 330 Phillip Street
Waterloo, Ontario N2J 3Z9
Flower, herb and vegetable seeds.

Pacific Northwest Seed Co.
Box 460
Vernon, British Columbia V1T 6M4
Flower, herb and vegetable seeds.

Carl Pallek & Son Nurseries
Box 137
Virgil, Ontario L0S 1T0
Roses.

Parkland Perennials
Box 3683
Spruce Grove, Alberta T7X 3A9
Lilies, day lilies.

Pickering Nurseries, Inc.
670 Kingston Road
Pickering, Ontario L1V 1A6

Prairie Grown Garden Seeds
Box 118
Cochin, Saskatchewan S0M 0L0
Organically grown vegetable seeds.

Prairie Habitats
Box 1
Argyle, Manitoba R0C 0B0
Seeds for native plants.

Prism Perennials
C-45, S-25, RR 1
Castlegar, British Columbia V1N 3H7
Perennials, irises, day lilies, ornamental grasses.

Rainforest Gardens
13139 - 224th Street, RR 2
Maple Ridge, British Columbia V2X 7E7
Organically grown perennials.

Rawlinson Garden Seeds
269 College Road
Truro, Nova Scotia B2N 2P6
Flower, herb and vegetable seeds.

Richters
357 Highway 47
Goodwood, Ontario L0C 1A0
Herb seeds and plants.

River View Herbs
Box 92
Maitland, Nova Scotia B0N 1T0
Herb plants, seeds, scented geraniums.

Salt Spring Island Nursery
355A Blackburn Road
Salt Spring Island, British Columbia V8K 2B8
Perennial and herb plants.

Salt Spring Seeds
Box 33
Ganges, British Columbia V0S 1E0
Beans and grains.

Select Perennials
Box 124, RR 1
Morrisburg, Ontario K0C 1X0
Hosta and day lily plants.

South Cove Nursery, Ltd.
Box 615
Yarmouth, Nova Scotia B5A 4B6
Perennial, herb plants.

Stirling Perennials
RR 1
Morpeth, Ontario N0P 1X0
Perennial plants.

Stokes Seeds Ltd.
39 James Street, Box 10
St. Catharines, Ontario L2R 6R6
Flower, herb and vegetable seeds, bulbs, garden tools and accessories.

Suttell's Dahlias
5543 Blezard Drive
Beamsville, Ontario L0R 1B3
Dahlias.

T&T Seeds Ltd.
Box 1710
Winnipeg, Manitoba R3C 3P6
Flower, herb and vegetable seeds, bulbs, perennial plants, garden tools and accessories.

Territorial Seeds (Canada) Ltd.
206 - 8745 Ontario Street
Vancouver, British Columbia V5X 3E8
Flower, herb and vegetable seeds, bulbs, garden tools and accessories.

Vesey's Seeds Ltd.
Box 9000
Charlottetown, Prince Edward Island C1A 8K6
Vegetable seeds, accessories.

Vivaces Nordiques
2400 Ch. Principale
St-Mathieu du Parc, Quebec G0X 1N0
Day lilies.

We're in the Hayfield Now
4704 Pollard Road, RR 1
Orono, Ontario L0B 1M0
Day lilies.

Whitehouse Perennials
RR 2
Almonte, Ontario K0A 1A0
Day lilies, hostas, Siberian iris, peonies.

Stanley Zubrowski
Box 26
Prairie River, Saskatchewan S0E 1J0
Clematis plants, tomato seeds.

Mail-Order Seeds & Plants: International
The following companies will ship to Canada. When inquiring about catalog prices, enclose an International Postal Reply Coupon, available at any post office.

Robert Bolton
Birdhook, Halstead
Essex CO9 4BQ
England
Sweet peas.

Chiltern Seeds
Bortree Stile, Ulverston
Cumbria LA12 7PB
England
Unusual annual and perennial seeds, vegetable seeds.

Mail-Order Seeds & Plants: United States
The following companies will ship to Canada. When inquiring about catalog prices, enclose an International Postal Reply Coupon, available at any post office.

Abundant Life Seed Foundation
Box 772
Port Townsend, Washington 98368
Organically grown seeds for native plants, vegetables, herbs.

American Daylily & Perennials
Box 7008
The Woodlands, Texas 77387
Perennial plants.

Companion Plants
7247 N. Coolville Ridge
Athens, Ohio 45701
Organically grown herb and native plants.

The Cook's Garden
Box 535
Londonderry, Vermont 05148
Seeds for salad vegetables, edible flowers, ornamental vegetables.

Evergreen Y.H. Enterprises
Box 17538
Anaheim, California 92817
Seeds for Oriental vegetables.

Far North Gardens
Box 126
New Hudson, Michigan 48165-0126
Seeds of rare and common flowers; primulas.

Gleckler's Seedmen
Metamora, Ohio 43540
Seeds for unusual vegetables.

Heirloom Old Garden Roses
24062 NE Riverside Drive
St. Paul, Oregon 97137
Roses. Catalog $5 (U.S.).

Heronswood Nursery
7530 - 288th Street NE
Kingston, Washington 98346
Perennials. Catalog $4 (U.S.).

J.L. Hudson, Seedsman
Box 1058
Redwood City, California 94064
Nonhybrid vegetables and flowers, many rare species.

Johnny's Select Seeds
310 Foss Hill Road
Albion, Maine 04910-9731
Seeds for vegetables and herbs.

Lowe's Own Root Roses
6 Sheffield Road
Nashua, New Hampshire 03062
Roses, not grafted. Catalog $2 (U.S.).

Moon Mountain Wildflowers
Box 725
Carpinteria, California 93014-1725
Wildflower seeds.

Native Seeds/Search
2509 N. Campbell Avenue #325
Tucson, Arizona 85719
Seeds for vegetables grown by indigenous people.

Park Seeds
Cokesbury Road
Greenwood, South Carolina 29647-0001
Flower, herb and vegetable seeds, bulbs, garden tools and accessories.

The Pepper Gal
Box 23006
Ft. Lauderdale, Florida 33307
Seeds for chile and sweet peppers.

The Redwood City Seed Co.
Box 361
Redwood City, California 94064
Organically grown vegetable and herb seeds.

Russell Graham Purveyor of Plants
4030 Eagle Crest Road NW
Salem, Oregon 97304
Perennials. Catalog $2 (U.S.).

Seeds of Change
Box 15700
Santa Fe, New Mexico 87506-5700
Seeds for open-pollinated vegetables. Catalog free.

Select Seeds
180 Stickney Hill Road
Union, Connecticut 06076
Seeds for old-fashioned flowers.

Shepherd's Garden Seeds
30 Irene Street
Torrington, Connecticut 06790
Flower, herb and vegetable seeds.

Stokes Seeds, Inc.
Box 548
Buffalo, New York 14240-0548
Seeds for flowers, vegetables and herbs; garden tools and accessories.

Thompson & Morgan, Inc.
Box 1308
Jackson, New Jersey 08527
Parent company is British. Seeds for unusual flowers, vegetables.

White Flower Farm
Litchfield, Connecticut 06759-0050
Perennial and shrub plants.

Mail-Order Tools & Supplies: Canada

Many seed houses also sell garden tools and supplies.

Better Yield Insects
RR 3
Belle River, Ontario N0R 1A0
Insects, pheromone traps.

House of Tools
100 Mayfield Common NW
Edmonton, Alberta T5P 4K9

International Irrigation Systems
Box 1133
St. Catharines, Ontario L2R 7A3
Drip-irrigation supplies and consultation.

Lee Valley Tools Ltd.
1080 Morrison Drive
Ottawa, Ontario K2H 8K7
Garden tools and structures.

Natural Insect Control

Box 171
Niagara Falls, Ontario L2E 6T3
Insects, pheromone traps, biological pesticides.

Mail-Order Tools & Supplies:
United States

Necessary Organics, Inc.

One Nature's Way
New Castle, Virginia 24127-0305
Organic-gardening supplies and information.

Walt Nicke Co.

36 McLeod Lane
Box 433
Topsfield, Massachusetts 01983
Garden tools and structures.

Index

Abelmoschus esculentus, 88. See also Okra
Acclimatization. See Hardening off
Achillea, 154-155. See also Yarrow
    filipendulina, 155; photo, 155
    millefolium, 23, 155
    ptarmica 'The Pearl,' 155
    tomentosa, 155
Acidanthera, 150, 225; photo, 151
Acidic soil, 33-36, 227
Aconite, winter, 137. See also *Eranthis*
    hyemalis
Aconitum
    carmichaelii, 137
    napellus, 137
    vulparia, 137
Acorn squash, 98-99. See also Squash,
    winter
Acroclinium, 123; photo, 122
Agapanthus, 150
Agaricus bisporus, 85-86. See also
    Mushrooms
Agastache
    anethiodora, 161
    foeniculum, 161
Ageratum, 39, 106, 207
    houstonianum, 106
Ageratum, golden (*Lonas*), 123; photo,
    122
Alcohol as pesticide, 186
Alfalfa as green manure, 37

Alkaline soil, 33-36, 227
Alkaloids in herbs, 160
Allium, 38, 166-167. See also Chives;
   Garlic; Leeks; Onions
    aflatunense, 106
    caeruleum, 106
    cepa, 88-89
    fistulosum, 88
    giganteum, 106
    moly, 106, 225
    ornamental, 38, 106
    porrum, 82
    sativum, 80
    schoenoprasum, 166
    tuberosum, 166
Aloysia triphylla, 170. See also Verbena,
   lemon
Alternaria, 117, 191. See also Blight,
   early
Althaea rosea, 129
Alyssum, 106-107; photo, 107
    and crop rotation, 39
    annual, 106-107
    container growing, 207, 210
    in knot gardens, 158
    perennial, 107
    sowing, 26, 218
Amaranth, 107
    globe, 23, 123
    green, 101

    vegetable, 100-101
Amaranthus, 107
    caudatus, 107
    retroflexus, 101
    tricolor, 100-101, 107
Amaryllis family and crop rotation, 38
Amethyst flower, 111-112. See also
    Browallia
Ancho pepper, 165
Anemone, 107-108
    blanda, 107, 108, 225
    coronaria, 107
    grapeleaf, 107
    Japanese, 107
    patens, 107, 118
    poppy-flowered, 107
    pulsatilla, 107
    tomentosa, 107
    x *hybrida*, 107
Anethum graveolens, 167. See also Dill
    'Fernleaf'
Angelica archangelica, 160-161; photo, 24
Angel's-trumpet, 120
Anise (*Foeniculum*), 167-168
Anise (*Pimpinella*), 39, 159, 161
Anise-hyssop, 161
Annuals
    characteristics, 105
    container growing, 207
    definition, 227

for cutting gardens, 23
for direct sowing, 26
Anthemis nobilis, 165. See also
  Chamomile
Anthracnose, 191
Anthriscus cerefolium, 165. See also
  Chervil
Antirrhinum majus, 50, 148. See also
  Snapdragons
Aphids, 65, 78, 91, 93, 97, 114, 185,
  186, 187, 192
Apium graveolens
    dulce, 73-74. See also Celery
    rapaceum, 73. See also Celeriac
Apple, thorn, 120
Apples, root-cellar storage, 224
Apricots, root-cellar storage, 224
Aquilegia, 116-117
    canadensis, 116, 207
Arabis, 108-109. See also *Aubrieta*
Arachis hypogaea, 91-92. See also
  Peanuts
Armoracia rusticana, 168-169. See also
  Horseradish
Armyworms, beet, 69, 93
Artemisia. See also Tarragon
    dracunculus sativa, 176-177
    redowskii, 177
Artichoke plume moth, 62
Artichokes
    French, 62
    globe, 39, 46, 47, 62, 203; photo, 63
    Jerusalem, 39, 62-63
    Jerusalem, fall planting, 218
    Jerusalem, location in garden, 17
    Jerusalem, overwintering in the
      ground, 217
    Jerusalem, pollination, 203
    Jerusalem, yield, 27
Arugula, 63
Ashes, wood
    as fertilizer, composition, 34
    as remedy for acidic soil, 35, 36
Asparagus beetle, 64
Asparagus officinalis, 63-65; photo, 64
    fall planting, 218
    frost hardiness, 214
    in single-row gardens, 20
    location in garden, 17
    planting time, 46
Aspermy virus and chrysanthemums,
  115
Aster, 39, 50, 108, 207
    novae-angliae, 108. See also Daisies,
      Michaelmas
    x *frikartii* 'Monch,' 23
Aster yellows, 108
Asters. See also *Aster*
    China, 108. See also *Callistephus
      chinensis*

Stokes', 150. See also *Stokesia*
Astilbe, 108; photo, 109
    x *arendsii*, 108
Atropine in plants, 160
Aubrieta, 39, 50, 108-109
    deltoidea, 108-109
Aurinia saxatilis, 106-107
Austin, David, rose series, 144
Axil, definition, 227
Azalea, 16, 200
Baby-blue-eyes, fall sowing, 218
Baby's-breath, 109, 123, 218. See also
  Gypsophila
Bachelor's-button, 117-118
Bacillus thuringiensis, 185
Bacterial diseases, 190
Bacterial wilt, 78, 217
Baits for insect control, 183
Baking soda for fungal diseases, 192
Balloon flower, 109. See also *Platycodon
  grandiflorus*
Balloon vine, 52, 210
Balm, 161-162; photo, 162
    bee, 136-137, 163-164
    lemon, 161-162
Balsam impatiens, 131
Banana pepper, 166
Bark chips as mulch, 181
Barley as green manure, 37
Base temperature, 19
Basella
    alba, 85
    rubra, 85
Basil, 162-163
    camphor, 162
    container growing, 207, 210
    East Indian, 162
    frost tenderness, 214
    in vegetable gardens, 158-159
    lemon, 162
    opal, 162
    planting time, 46
    sacred, 162
    'Spicy Globe,' 158, 162
    terpenoids in, 160
Basket flower, 117
Basket-of-gold, 106-107
Baskets, hanging, 210-211
Bay laurel, 163, 207; photo, 163
Bay leaf, 163
Bean beetles, Mexican, 67, 186
Bean herb, 176. See also Savory
Bean leaf beetle and soy beans, 68
Bean rust, overwintering, 217
Beans
    adzuki, 68
    and crop rotation, 39
    as green manure, 37
    asparagus, 68
    base temperature, 19

black turtle, 67
broad, 46, 65, 215
bush, 18, 67
container growing, 207
drying, 223
fava, 65. See also Beans, broad
filet, 66
garbanzo, 68
green, blanching for freezing, 222
horse, 65. See also Beans, broad
horticultural, 67
hyacinth, 39, 130-131, 207
kidney, 65-66
lima, 47, 66, 214
'Limelight,' 66
mung, 68
navy, 67
pinto, 67
planting time, 47
pole, 18, 67, 184
pollination, 193, 203
pre-germination, 52
'Princess of Artois,' 66
romano, 66
scarlet runner, 66; photo, 66
seed-saving, 200
snap, 66-67, 214, 223
soy, 47, 67-68, 214
space efficiency, 17
string, 66-67. See also Beans, snap
tick, 65. See also Beans, broad
Windsor, 65. See also Beans, broad
winged, 68
yield, 27
Beardtongue, 139
Bedding plants
    definition, 227
    transplanting into containers, 209
Beds
    digging, 30-31
    preparing, 29-32
    raised, 19, 22-23; photo, 18
    trenching, 30-31
Bee balm, 136-137, 163-164
Beebread, 164
Beet armyworm, 69, 93
Beet family and crop rotation, 39
Beet greens, 27, 68
Beet leafhopper, 69
Beetles
    asparagus, 64
    bean leaf, 68
    blister, 81, 101, 135
    carrot, 72
    Colorado potato, 37, 79, 80, 81, 94,
      185, 187, 217; photo, 187
    control, 186, 187
    cucumber, 78, 91, 99, 187-188, 217
    flea, 62, 70, 78-79, 80, 81, 96, 97,
      124, 184, 188-189

Japanese, 186
June, 94-95
lady, as beneficial, 186, 189
Mexican bean, 67, 186
Beetroot, 68-69. See also Beets
Beets, 68-69
    fall sowing, 218
    overwintering in the ground, 217
    planting time, 46
    pollination, 203
    root-cellar storage, 225
    sowing and transplanting, 49
    space efficiency, 17
    sugar, 68
    yield, 27
Begonia, 109-110; photo, 16
    container growing, 207
    fibrous, 110
    frost tenderness, 214
    planting time, 46
    tuberous, 109
    wax, 110
    x *semperflorens-cultorum*, 110
    x *tuberhybrida*, 109
Bellflowers
    Carpathian, 112
    peach-leaved, 112
Bellis perennis, 50
Bells of Ireland, 50, 110
Bergamot, 136-137, 163-164
Bergamot mint, 171
Bergenia, 18, 110-111
    cordifolia, 110-111
    heartleaf, 110-111
Berkeley compost method, 42
Berries
    drying, 223
    juices and syrups, processing time, 220
    processing time, 220
Beta vulgaris, 68-69. See also Beets
    cicla, 100. See also Swiss chard
Bibb lettuce, 83
Biennial, definition, 227
Bigroot geranium, 126
Biosafe, 190
Birds in insect control, 183-184
Black-eyed Susan, 144-145. See also
    Rudbeckia
Black-eyed-Susan vine, 111. See also
    Thunbergia alata
Black root rot, 110, 127
Black rot, 96, 121
Black spot, 144, 191, 192
Blackheart and celery, 74
Blackleg, 96, 127, 191
Blanching, 222, 227
Blanket flower, 126. See also *Gaillardia*
Blazing star, 133. See also *Liatris*
Bleeding heart, 111; photo, 13. See also

Dicentra spectabilis
Blight
    bacterial, 190
    early, 95, 102, 191. See also
        Alternaria
    late, 95, 191
Blister beetles, 81, 101, 135
Blood, dry, as fertilizer, composition, 34
Blossom-end rot, 98, 102
Bluebell, 112
Bluebonnet, Texas, 135
Bok choy, 87
Bolting, definition, 227-228
Bonemeal as fertilizer, composition, 34
Bonfires for frost protection, 217
Borage, 158-159, 164
Borago officinalis, 164
Borecole, 81. See also Kale
Borers
    corn, 76, 217
    root, 132
    squash vine, 78, 99
Botanical nomenclature, 38
Botrytis, 136, 191. See also Gray mold
Brachycome iberidifolia, 111
Brassica, 228
    and clubroot, 37
    chinensis, 87
    juncea, 87. See also Mustard greens
    napus, 96. See also Rutabagas
    oleracea (ornamental), 124
    oleracea acephala, 50, 81. See also
        Kale
    oleracea botrytis, 72-73. See also
        Cauliflower
    oleracea capitata, 70-71. See also
        Cabbage
    oleracea caulorapa, 81-82. See also
        Kohlrabi
    oleracea gemmifera, 70. See also
        Brussels sprouts
    oleracea italica, 69-70. See also
        Broccoli
    pekinensis, 75. See also Cabbage,
        Chinese
    planting time, 46
    rapa, 96, 102-103. See also Turnips
Broccoli, 69-70
    and crop rotation, 39
    blanching for freezing, 222
    Chinese, 69, 81
    container growing, 207
    drying, 223
    location in garden, 18
    planting time, 46
    pollination, 203
    'Premium Crop,' photo, 69
    raab, 69
    sowing and transplanting, 49
    space efficiency, 17

yield, 27
Bromegrass, smooth, as green manure, 37
Browallia, 18, 39, 111-112, 207, 210;
    photo, 110
    speciosa, 111-112
Brussels sprouts, 70
    and crop rotation, 39
    container growing, 207
    frost hardiness, 215
    planting time, 46
    pollination, 203
    sowing and transplanting, 49
    space efficiency, 17
    yield, 27
Bt, 185
Buckets, 26
Buckwheat as green manure, 37
Bugbane, 148
Bulbs
    definition, 228
    fall planting, 218
    hardiness, chart, 225
    storage, 225
    summer, 150-151
Bunching onions, 88, 89
Burdock as weed, 182
Burning bush, 132. See also *Kochia*
Buttercup squash, 98-99. See also
    Squash, winter
Butterflies
    black swallowtail, 72, 74, 189
    control, 185
Butterfly flower, 150. See also
    Acidanthera
Butterhead lettuce, 83; photo, 83
Butternut squash, 98-99. See also
    Squash, winter
Butternut trees as harmful to plants, 102, 181
Cabbage, 70-71
    and clubroot, 37
    and crop rotation, 39
    celery, 75. See also Cabbage, Chinese
    Chinese, 75
    Chinese, and crop rotation, 39
    Chinese, looseleaf, 87
    Chinese, shade tolerance, 17
    container growing, 207
    drying, 223
    flowering, 124
    frost hardiness, 215
    mustard, 87
    ornamental, 50, 124; photo, 71
    planting time, 46
    pollination, 203
    root-cellar storage, 224, 225
    sowing and transplanting, 49
    space efficiency, 17
    yield, 27

Cabbage looper, 185, 187
Cabbage moth, 70
Cabbageworm, 124, 184, 187
Caffeine in plants, 160
Caladium, 150
Calceolaria, 50, 210
Calcitic lime as remedy for acidic soil, 35
Calendula, 26, 39, 50, 112; photo, 22
  See also Marigolds, pot
    officinalis, 112
Calla lily, 150
Calliopsis, 26, 117
Callistephus chinensis, 26, 108
Camassia quamash, hardiness, 225
Campanula, 112
    carpatica, 112
    medium, 112
    persicifolia, 112
    rapunculoides, 112
Campion, rose, 144
Canary creeper, 112, 210
Candymint, 171
Candytuft, 39, 112-113, 218
    annual, 26, 46, 112-113
    perennial, 113
Canna, 150, 207
Canning instructions, 219-220
Cantaloupe, 25, 86
Canterbury bells, 112
Cape marigold, 122-123
Capsicum. See also Peppers
    annuum, 92-93
    frutescens, 165-166. See also Chile
      peppers
Caragana for wind protection, 18
Caraway and crop rotation, 39
Carbon-rich compost materials, 42
Cardinal flower, 135
Cardoon and crop rotation, 39
Carnation, 121-122. See also *Dianthus*
Carrot beetle, 72
Carrot rust fly, 72, 74, 173
Carrots, 71-72
    and crop rotation, 39
    container growing, 207
    drying, 223
    fall sowing, 218
    frost hardiness, 215
    overwintering in the ground, 217,
      224
    planting time, 46
    pollination, 203
    root-cellar storage, 224, 225
    space efficiency, 17
    yield, 27
Cartier, Jacques, 66, 70
Carts, garden, 26
Carum petroselinum, 173
Catharanthus, 113, 207, 211

Cathedral bells, 119. See also Cup-and-
  saucer vine
Catmint, 113. See also *Nepeta* x *faassenii*
Catnip, 113, 164-165
    in insecticidal sprays, 186
Cauliflower, 72-73; photo, 72
    and crop rotation, 39
    container growing, 207
    planting time, 46, 47
    pollination, 203
    sowing and transplanting, 49
    space efficiency, 17
    yield, 27
Cayenne pepper, 165
    in insecticidal sprays, 186
Cedar-bark tea as insecticide, 186
Celeriac, 39, 73, 203
Celery, 73-74
    and crop rotation, 39
    drying, 223
    planting time, 46, 47
    pollination, 203
    root-cellar storage, 224
    sowing and transplanting, 49
    space efficiency, 17
    turnip-rooted, 73. See also Celeriac
    yield, 27
Celosia, 113-114
    cristata, 113
    plumosa, 113
    spicata, 113
    wheat, 113
Centaurea, 117-118. See also Cornflower
    americana, 117
    montana, 117
Cerastium tomentosum, 149. See also
    Snow-in-summer
Chamaemelum nobile, 165. See also
    Chamomile
Chamomile, 39, 165, 210; photo, 164
    German, 165
    sweet false, 165
Champlain, Samuel de, 62, 184
Chard, Swiss, 100; photo, 100
    and crop rotation, 39
    frost hardiness, 215
    pollination, 203
    sowing and transplanting, 49
    space efficiency, 17
Charlie, creeping, 113
Cheiranthus cheiri, 154. See also
    Wallflowers
Chemical fertilizers, 32-33
Chenopodiaceae and crop rotation, 39
Chenopodium album, 97. See also Lamb's-
    quarters
Cherries
    ground, 39, 80-81; photo, 80
    processing time, 220
Chervil, 39, 159, 165

Chick peas. See Beans, garbanzo
Chicken manure as fertilizer,
  composition, 35
Chicory, 39, 74-75; photo, 74
    asparagus, 74
    leaf, 74
    Magdeburg, 74
    wild, 75
    witloof, 74
Chile peppers, 165-166
    in hanging baskets, 210
    in vegetable gardens, 159
    seed-saving, 202
Chinese lantern, 39, 124
Chives, 38, 106, 166-167
    common, 166; photo, 166
    container growing, 207, 210
    garden, 166
    garlic, 106, 166
    in knot gardens, 158
    pollination, 203
Chrysanthemum, 114-115
    and crop rotation, 39
    carinatum 'Court Jesters,' 114
    cinerariifolium, 186-187
    coccineum, 114, 187
    coronarium, 114
    mulching in fall, 215
    multicaule, 114
    tricolor, 114
    x *superbum*, 114
    zawadskii 'Clara Curtis,' 23
Cicely, sweet, 176
Cicer arietinum, 68
Cichorium
    endivia, 74, 79. See also Endive
    intybus, 74-75. See also Chicory
Cilantro, 167. See also Coriander
Cimicifuga, 148
    americana, 148
    racemosa, 148
Cineraria x *hybridus* in cool environment,
    50
Cinnamon to control crown rot and
    mildew, 192
Citrullus lanatus, 103. See also
    Watermelons
Citrus oil as pesticide, 186
City microclimates, 209-210
Clarkia, 115, 123, 218
    elegans, 115
    pulchella, 115
Clay soil, 32
Clearing land for a garden, 29
Clematis, 115
    florida, 115
    paniculata, 115
    tangutica, 115
    viltalba 'Traveler's Joy,' 115
    x *jackmanii*, 115

Clematis wilt, 115
Cleome, 26, 115-116, 218; photo, 114
    hasslerana, 115-116
Climatic zones, 19-20; map, 226
Climbing plants, 25
Clinging plants, 25
Cloches, 58
Clone, definition, 228
Clostridium botulinum, 219
Clover as green manure, 37
Clubroot, 37, 70, 96, 191
Cobaea scandens, 119. See also Cup-and-
    saucer vine
Cocaine in plants, 160
Cockscomb, 113
Coffee grounds in compost, 42
Colchicum, 118-119
Cold frames, 56-57; illustrations, 56, 57
    construction, 56
    installation, 57
Cold treatment for seedlings, 53
Coles, William, 158
Coleus, 116, 158, 207, 214
    x *hybridus*, 116
Collards, 17, 46, 184, 215
Colloidal phosphate as fertilizer,
    composition, 34
Colorado potato beetle, 37, 79, 80, 81,
    94, 185, 187, 217; photo, 187
Columbine, 116-117; photo, 116. See
    also *Aquilegia canadensis*
Companion planting, 184-185
Compositae and crop rotation, 39
Compost, 40-43
    as fertilizer, composition, 34
    as mulch, 181
    Berkeley method, 42
    containers, 40-41; illustration, 41
    definition, 228
    in container gardens, 208
    in seed-starting mixes, 51
    ingredients, 40
    process, 41-42
    speed, 42
    starters, 42-43
    sterilizing, 51
    turning, 42
Coneflower, 144-145
    purple, 39, 143
Consolida ambigua, 121. See also
    Larkspur
Container gardens, 205-211
    and compost, 208
    and wind, 206
    fertilization, 208
    hanging baskets, 210-211
    microclimates, 209-210
    mulching, 206
    overwintering, 210
    seasonal routines, 208-210

shade, 211
soil mixes, 208
sowing seeds directly, 209
suitable plants for, 207
sunny locations, 211
transplanting bedding plants, 209
vining plants in, 206
watering, 206
weight considerations, 208
window boxes, 211
Containers
    conversion to hanging pots, 211
    for compost, 40-41; illustration, 41
    for starting seeds, 48-50; photo, 49
    hanging, 210-211
    selecting, 207
Convallaria majalis, 134, 160. See also
    Lily of the valley
Cook, Captain James, 157
Cool indoor environment, flowers for, 50
Copper naphthenate, as nontoxic
    preservative, 22
Coral bells, 117
Coreopsis, 39, 117, 207. See also
    Calliopsis
    lanceolata, 117
    tinctoria, 117
    verticillata, 23, 117
Coriander, 39, 167
Coriandrum sativum, 167
Corm, definition, 228
Corn, 75-76. See also Popcorn
    as companion for pole beans, 184
    base temperature, 19
    drying, 223
    in single-row gardens, 20
    Indian, 76
    location in garden, 17
    ornamental, 76
    planting time, 46
    pollination, 193, 203
    seed-saving, 200-201
    space efficiency, 17
    squaw, 76
    yield, 27
Corn borer, 76, 217
Corn earworm, 76, 93, 185, 217
Corn family and crop rotation, 39
Corn salad, 77, 215
Corn smut, 76
Cornflower, 26, 39, 46, 117-118, 218
Corydalis, 118
    lutea, 23, 118
Cos lettuce, 83
Cosmos, 118; photo, 22
    and crop rotation, 39
    bipinnatus, 118
    bipinnatus 'Sensation Mixed,' 118;
        photo, 119
    direct sowing, 26

fall sowing, 218
frost tenderness, 214
sulphureus, 118
Cottonseed meal as fertilizer,
    composition, 34
Cotyledon, 50, 228
Covering plants for frost protection in
    fall, 216
Cow manure as fertilizer, composition,
    35
Cranberries, highbush, for wind
    protection, 18
Cranesbill, 126-127. See also *Geranium*
Creeping Charlie, 113
Cress, 39, 77, 201, 203
    Indian, 172
    rock, 50, 108-109. See also *Aubrieta*
Crickets, 102
Crocus, 118-119
    ancyrensis, 118
    chrysanthus, 118
    speciosus, hardiness, 225
Crocus, prairie (*Anemone*), 107, 118
Crookneck squash, 97-98. See also
    Squash, summer
Crop rotation and plant families, 37-39;
    chart, 38-39
Cross-pollination, definition, 228
Crown imperial, 125
Crown rot and cinnamon, 192
Cruciferae and crop rotation, 39
Cucumber beetle, 78, 91, 99, 187-188,
    217
Cucumber mosaic and lupins, 135
Cucumbers, 77-78
    and crop rotation, 39
    drying, 223
    frost tenderness, 214
    harvesting when frost threatens, 216
    in hanging baskets, 210
    in vertical gardens, 25
    lemon, photo, 188
    location in garden, 18
    planting time, 46, 47
    pollination, 192, 203
    pre-germination, 52
    sowing and transplanting, 49-50
    space efficiency, 17
    yield, 27
Cucumis
    melo, 86-87. See also Muskmelons
    sativus, 77-78. See also Cucumbers
Cucurbita. See also Squash
    maxima, 98-99
    moschata, 98-99
    pepo, 97-99
    seed-saving, 202
Cucurbitaceae and crop rotation, 39
Cucurbitacin in cucurbits, 160
Culpeper, Nicholas, 163, 164, 167, 169,

170, 172
Cultivar, definition, 228
Cup-and-saucer vine, 119, 207, 210
Curing vegetables before storage, 225
Currants for wind protection, 18
Cut-and-come-again greens, 85, 207
Cutting-garden annuals, 23
Cuttings, 200, 228
Cutworms, 70, 79, 93, 183, 188
Cynara scolymus, 62. See also Artichokes, globe
Cynoglossum amabile, 124, 218
Daffodils, 119-120
Dahlia, 39, 120, 214, 225
Daikon, 95. See also Radishes
Daisies
   and crop rotation, 39
     crown, 114
     definition, 228
     English, in cool environment, 50
     gloriosa, 144-145, 218. See also
       Rudbeckia
     Michaelmas, 50, 108
     painted, 114, 218
     Shasta, 114
     Swan River, 111
Damping-off, 46, 53, 191, 228
Dandelions, 39, 78-79, 182
Datura, 39, 120
   meteloides, 120
   sanguinea, 120
   stramonium, 120
   suaveolens, 120
Daucus carota, 71-72. See also Carrots
Day lilies, 120-121, 207. See also
   Hemerocallis
Deadheading, definition, 228
Deep digging, 31
Delphinium, 50, 121, 218
   ajacis, 121. See also Larkspur
   chinensis 'Dwarf Blue Butterfly,' 121
Determinates, 101, 228
Diamondback moth, control, 186, 187
Dianthus, 26, 50, 121-122
   barbatus x *chinensis*, 122
   deltoides 'Microchip,' 121
Diatomaceous earth, 185-186
Dicentra spectabilis, 23, 111. See also
   Bleeding heart
Digging
   deep, 31
   garden beds, 30-31
Digitalis
   purpurea, 125
   steroids in, 160
Dill, 167; photo, 160
   and crop rotation, 39
   container growing, 207
   'Fernleaf,' 167, 210
   in vegetable gardens, 159

Dill family, sowing and transplanting, 49-50
Dimorphotheca, 122-123
Dioecious, 63
Dioscorides, 162
Disease control, 192
Diseases of plants, 190-192. See also
   names of specific diseases
     bacterial, 190
     fungal, 190-192
     viral, 190
Dishwashing liquid as pesticide, 185
Division, 199; photo, 199
Dolichos lablab, 130-131. See also
   Hyacinth bean
Dolomitic lime as remedy for acidic soil, 35
Doronicum. See also Leopard's-bane
   caucasicum, 132-133
   columnae, 132-133
   cordatum, 132-133
   plantagineum, 133
Double flower, definition, 228
Double-potting, 206
Doucette, 77. See also Corn salad
Downy mildew, 191
Drip line, definition, 229
Drying
   everlasting flowers, photo, 222
   produce, 223
Dusty miller, 158, 207
Earthworms, 38-40
Earwigs, 76, 114, 185, 188
Earworm, corn, 76, 93, 185, 217
Echinacea purpurea, 143. See also
   Coneflower, purple
Echinops ritro, 127. See also Thistle, globe
Ecomask, 190
Edible flowers, 123
Egg trees, 79. See also Eggplant
Eggplant, 79
   and crop rotation, 39
   container growing, 207
   frost tenderness, 214
   length of growing season, 19
   planting time, 46
   pollination, 193, 203
   pre-germination, 52
   sowing and transplanting, 49
   space efficiency, 17
Eggshells in compost, 42
Egyptian onions, 88; photo, 88
Endive, 39, 79, 203
   Batavian, 79
   Belgian, 74. See also Chicory
   French, 74. See also Chicory
Endymion hispanicus, hardiness, 225
Eranthis hyemalis, 137, 225
Eruca sativa, 63
Erysimum, 154

Escarole, 39, 79. See also Endive
Eschscholtzia californica, 141. See also
   Poppies, California
Estragon, 176-177
Eustoma, 46
   grandiflorum, 134-135
Evening primrose, 123
Evergreen needles as mulch, 181
Everlasting flowers, 123-124; photos, 122, 222
F1 hybrids, 196, 229
F2 hybrids, 196-197, 229
Fall
   activities, 213-225
   cleanup, 217-219
   frost dates, first, 213; chart, 215
   plant protection, 216-217
   planting, 217-218
Families of plants and crop rotation, 37-39; chart, 38-39
Feldsalat, 77. See also Corn salad
Fencing, 25
Fennel, 39, 167-168
   Florence, 167, 168
   giant hyssop, 161
Ferns, shade tolerance, 18
Fertilizers, 32-40
   and perennials in fall, 215
   chemical, 32-33
   in containers, 208, 211
   organic, 35, 36-40; chart, 34
Fescue, creeping red, as green manure, 37
Filial-one hybrids, 196, 229
Filial-two hybrids, 196-197, 229
Finochio, 167-168. See also Fennel
First fall frost dates, 213; chart, 215
Fish emulsion as fertilizer, composition, 34
Flats, 229
   construction, 49
Flax, flowering, 124
Flea beetles, 62, 70, 78-79, 80, 81, 96, 97, 124, 184, 188-189
Fleming, Bob, 31
Flies
   carrot rust, 72, 74, 173
   narcissus bulb, 120
   white-, 185, 186
Flossflower, 106. See also *Ageratum*
Flower bulbs
   fall planting, 218
   hardiness, chart, 225
   storage, 225
   summer, 150-151
Flower gardens, 105-155
   and herbs, 158
   and light, 18
   designing, 23-24
   fall cleanup, 217

Flowers. See also Annuals; Perennials;
  names of specific plants
    difficult to divide, 199
    double, definition, 228
    easy to divide, 199
    easy to start by cuttings, 200
    edible, 123
    everlasting, 123-124; photos, 122,
      222
    fall sowing, 218
    for containers, 207, 210-211
    for cool greenhouses, chart, 50
    needing rooting hormone to start by
      cuttings, 200
    single, definition, 231
    species descriptions, 105-155
Foeniculum vulgare, 167-168. See also
  Fennel
    azoricum, 167
Forget-me-nots, 26, 124
    Chinese, 124. See also *Cynoglossum
      amabile*
Four-o'clocks, 124-125
Foxgloves, 125, 160
Freesia in cool environment, 50
Freezing vegetables and fruit, 221-223
Fritillaria, 125
    imperialis, 125
    meleagris, 125
Frost
    dates, first in fall, 213; chart, 215
    dates, last in spring, 46; chart, 47
    degrees of, 213
    hardiness, 213-215
    pocket, 19
    predicting, 214
    protection in fall, 216-217
    warnings, what to do about, 216
Frost-hardy plants, 214-215
Frost-tender plants, 214
Fruit
    freezing, 221-223
    in hanging baskets, 210
Fuchsia, 18, 125-126, 210
Fumitory, 118. See also *Corydalis lutea*
Fungal diseases, 190-192
Fungicide, definition, 229
Fungus, definition, 229
Fusarium wilt, 64, 102
Gaillardia, 39, 126, 207; photo, 22
    'Goblin,' 126
    pulchella, 126
    x *grandiflora*, 23, 126
Galanthus nivalis, 148-149, 225
Garden carts, 26
Gardens. See also Container gardens;
  Flower gardens; Herb gardens; Knot
  gardens; Vegetable gardens
    orientation, 16-17
    site evaluation, 16-19

size, 15-16
types, 20-24
Garlic, 38, 80; photo, 224
    as companion plant, 185
    as control for powdery mildew, 192
    as insecticide, 185, 186
    pollination, 203
    root-cellar storage, 225
Garlic chives, 106, 166
Gay-feather, 133. See also *Liatris*
Gazania, 39, 126
    rigens, 126
Genus, definition, 229
Geranium, 126-127. See also *Pelargonium*
    bigroot, 126
    in containers, 211
    macrorrhizum, 126
    maculatum, container growing, 207
    sanguineum 'Striatum,' 23
Gerard, John, 161, 162, 172, 175, 176
Gerbera, 39, 50, 127
    jamesonii, 127
Germination, 52-53, 229
    pre-germination, 52-53
Gladiolus, 16, 23, 150, 225
Glechoma hederacea, 113
Gloriosa daisy, 144-145, 218. See also
    Rudbeckia
Glossary, 227-231
Glycine max, 67-68. See also Beans, soy
Godetia grandiflora, 127-128
Golden-glow, 145. See also *Rudbeckia
    laciniata*
Gomphrena globosa, 123. See also
    Amaranth, globe
Gooseberries for wind protection, 18
Gourd family and crop rotation, 39
Gourds, 25, 46, 49-50
Goutweed, container growing, 205
Gramineae and crop rotation, 39
Granite meal as fertilizer, composition,
    34
Grape hyacinth, 128. See also *Muscari*
Grapeleaf anemone, 107
Grass clippings
    as mulch, 181
    in compost, 40, 42
Grasses
    ornamental, 39, 207
    perennial, weeds, 182
    quack, 30, 182
    twitch, 30, 182
Grasshoppers, control, 183
Gray mold, 114, 115, 191. See also
    Botrytis
Gray water, 180, 229
Green amaranth, 101
Green manures, 36-37, 217, 229
Greenhouses
    flowers for cool greenhouses, chart, 50

    freestanding, 56; photo, 59
    passive-solar, 55
    window, 55-56; photo, 55
Greensand as fertilizer, composition, 34
Grieve, Maude, 161, 169
Ground cherries, 39, 80-81; photo, 80
Growing season, length of, 19
Grubs, white, 190
Gubbels, Gerard H., 59, 216
Gumbo, 88. See also Okra
Guy Ion, 69, 81
Gypsophila, 109, 123. See also Baby's-
    breath
    elegans, 109
    paniculata, 109, 207
    repens, 109
Hand-picking insects, 183
Hand-watering, 180
Hanging baskets, 210-211
    conversion from regular containers,
      211
    fertilizing, 211
    planting, 211
    types, 210-211
Hardening off, 53-54, 208-209, 229
Harebell, 112
Harvesting vegetables in fall, 217
Hay
    as mulch, 181
    in compost, 40, 42
Heaters for frost protection, 217
Helianthus, 62-63, 151-152
    annuus, 151-152. See also Sunflowers
    tuberosus, 62-63. See also Artichokes,
      Jerusalem
Helichrysum bracteatum, 123. See also
    Strawflower
Heliopsis, 151-152; photo, 12
Heliotrope, 128
Heliotropium peruvianum, 128
Helipterum, 123
Hemerocallis, 23, 120-121. See also
    Day lilies
Herb gardens, 157-159
    and light, 16-18
    knot gardens, 158
Herb vinegars, how to make, 160
Herbaceous, definition, 229
Herbicides, definition, 229
Herbs, 157-177
    annual, 158-159
    characteristics, 157
    chemical components, 160
    container growing, 207, 210
    cultivation, 158
    dried and fresh equivalents, 160
    drying, 159-160, 223
    easy to divide, 199
    easy to start by cuttings, 200
    freezing, 160

harvesting, 159
in the flower garden, 158
in the vegetable garden, 158-159
overwintering, 159
perennial, 159
preservation and storage, 159-160
species descriptions, 160-177
Hermaphroditic, 193
Heuchera, 117
micrantha 'Palace Purple,' 117
Hibiscus, 128-129
coccineus, 129
moscheutos, 129
Hoes, 26
Holdfasts, 25
Hollow-heart, 95
Hollyhocks, 129; photo, 128
Honeydew melons, 86
Honeysuckle, photo, 24
Horehound in knot gardens, 158
Hormone, rooting, 200
Hornworm, tomato, 81, 102, 185, 189
Horse manure as fertilizer, composition, 35
Horseradish, 168-169; photo, 168
and crop rotation, 39
in vegetable gardens, 159
pollination, 203
root-cellar storage, 225
Hosta, 18, 129-130
Hot beds, 54, 56-58
construction, 56
heating methods, 57-58
Howard, Albert, 40, 41, 42
Huckleberries
garden, 39, 79-80
wild, 79
Hungarian wax pepper, 166
Hyacinth, 130. See also *Hyacinthus orientalis*
grape, 128. See also *Muscari*
Hyacinth bean, 39, 130-131, 207
Hyacinthus orientalis, 130
'King of the Blues,' hardiness, 225
Hybrids, 196-197, 229
Hylemya antiqua, 189
Hyll, Thomas, 173
Hyssop, 169
fennel giant, 161
fragrant giant, 161
in knot gardens, 158
Hyssopus officinalis, 169. See also Hyssop
Iberis, 112-113. See also Candytuft
sempervirens, 113
umbellata, 112-113
Impatiens, 18, 46, 131, 207
balsam, 131
hawkeri, 131
New Guinea, 131
petersiana, 131

wallerana, 131
Indeterminates, 101, 229
Indian blanket, 126
Indoor seed-sowing, 46, 51-52
schedule, 46
soil mixes, 50-51
Inflorescence, definition, 230
Inoculation of nitrogen-fixing plants, 37, 230
Insect control, 182-190
baits, 183
encouraging birds, 183-184
hand-picking, 183
physical barriers, 183
Insecticidal soaps, 185
Insecticides, definition, 230. See also Insect control
Insects. See also names of specific insects
beneficial, 186
to watch for, 187-190
Ipomoea, 137-138. See also Morning glories
alba, 137. See also Moonflower
batatas, 99-100. See also Sweet potatoes
tricolor 'Heavenly Blue,' 138; photo, 137
Iris, 131-132, 215
bearded, 131; photo, 130
danfordiae, 131
pallida, 131
reticulata, 131
Siberian, 131, 207
sibirica, 131
x *germanica*, 131
Irish lace, 136
Irrigation. See Watering
Ivy in hanging baskets, 210
Ixia, hardiness, 225
Jalapeño pepper, 165
Jams, 220-221
Jellies, 220-221
Jerusalem artichoke. See Artichokes, Jerusalem
Jerusalem cross, 144
Johnny-jump-up, 154
Joseph's-coat, 107
Juglone, 102, 181
June beetle, 94-95
Kale, 81
and crop rotation, 39
Chinese, 69, 81
flowering, 124
frost hardiness, 215
ornamental, 81, 124
planting time, 46
pollination, 203
Scotch, 81
Siberian, 81
space efficiency, 17

yield, 27
Kingbirds in insect control, 183
Kitchen waste in compost, 40, 42
Knot gardens, 158; illustration, 158
Kochia, 39, 132, 207
scoparia trichophylla, 132
Kohlrabi, 81-82
and crop rotation, 39
pollination, 203
space efficiency, 17
yield, 27
Lactuca sativa, 82-84. See also Lettuce
Lady beetle as beneficial insect, 186, 189
Lamb's lettuce, 77. See also Corn salad
Lamb's-quarters, 97, 182
Lantana in containers, 211
Larkspur, 26, 50, 121, 218
Larvae, 186, 230
Last spring frost dates, 46; chart, 47
Lathyrus odoratus, 152. See also Sweet pea
Laurus nobilis, 163. See also Bay laurel
Lavandula. See also Lavender
angustifolia, 169-170
officinalis, 169-170
Lavatera, 47, 132
'Silver Cup,' photo, 132
trimestris, 132
Lavender, 158, 169-170, 207, 210
sea, 123
Layering, 199-200
Leaf spot and poppies, 142
Leafhopper, beet, 69
Leaves
as mulch, 181
in compost, 40
seedling, 50
true, 50, 231
Leeks, 82
and crop rotation, 38
frost hardiness, 215
planting time, 46
pollination, 203
space efficiency, 17
yield, 27
Legginess, 48, 230
Legumes
and crop rotation, 39
as nitrogen-fixing plants, 37
definition, 230
Lens culinaris, 82. See also Lentils
Lentils, 39, 82
Leopard's-bane, 39, 132-133
Lepidium sativum, 77. See also Cress
Lettuce
and crop rotation, 39
Bibb, 83
butterhead, 83; photo, 83
cessation of growth in fall, 215
container growing, 207

cos, 83
fall sowing, 218
head, 82-84
lamb's, 77. See also Corn salad
leaf, 17, 84, 210
'Pirat,' photo, 83
planting time, 46
pollination, 203
romaine, 83
root-cellar storage, 224
seed-saving, 201
shade tolerance, 17
sowing and transplanting, 49
yield, 27
Leucojum aestivum, hardiness, 225
Levisticum officinale, 170. See also Lovage
Liatris, 39, 133, 207
spicata, 133
Light, 16-18
and container gardens, 211
for indoor seedlings, 47-48
Lilies, 133-134
African, 150
calla, 150
checkered, 125
day, 120-121, 207
Madonna, 133
Lilium, 133-134
candidum, 133
Lily-of-the-Nile, 150
Lily of the valley, 134, 160, 205
Limestone, calcitic and dolomitic, as soil
amendment, 35, 36
Limonium. See also Statice
latifolium, 123
sinuatum, 123
Linum, 124
flavum compactum, 124
grandiflorum, 124
perenne, 124
Lippia citriodora, 170. See also Verbena,
lemon
Lisianthus, 134-135. See also *Eustoma*
Livestock manures
as fertilizer, 34, 38; chart, 35
in compost, 40, 42
Loam soil, 32
Lobelia, 135; photo, 134
cardinalis, 135
erinus, 135
in cool environment, 50
in hanging baskets, 210
shade tolerance, 18
siphilitica, 135
trailing annual, 135
Lobularia maritima, 106-107. See also
Alyssum
Lonas inodora, 123. See also Ageratum,
golden
Longley, Richmond W., 209

Lovage, 39, 159, 170, 215
Love-in-a-mist, 123-124, 218
Love-lies-bleeding, 107
Luffa cylindrica, 84-85
Lunaria biennis, 124
Lupin, 39, 135
Lupinus, 135
Lures for insects, 186
Lychnis
chalcedonica, 144
coronaria, 144
Lycopersicon esculentum, 101-102. See
also Tomatoes
Lycoris radiata, hardiness, 225
Lythrum, mulching in fall, 215
Macdonald, Sir John A., 86
Mache, 77. See also Corn salad
Macoun, W.T., 93
Madagascar periwinkle, 113
Magdeburg chicory, 74
Maggots
onion, 89, 189
pepper, 93
root, 70
Mail-order sources, 232-239
Malcolmia maritima, 149-150. See also
Stocks, Virginia
Mallows, 135-136
hollyhock, 136
musk, 136
rose, 129
wild red, 129
Maltese cross, 144
Malva, 135-136
alcea 'Fastigiata,' 23, 136
moschata, 136
sylvestris, 136
Mangel, 68
Mantid, praying, as beneficial insect,
186, 189
Manure tea, 38, 230
Manures
as fertilizer, 34, 38; chart, 35
chicken, composition, 35
cow, composition, 35
green, 36-37, 217, 229
horse, composition, 35
in compost, 40, 42
pig, composition, 35
sheep, composition, 35
Mao du, 67-68. See also Beans, soy
Map, climatic zones, 226
Marigolds, 136
and crop rotation, 39
African, 136
American, 136
as cutting flowers, 23
as part of vegetable garden, 16
Cape, 122-123
container growing, 207, 211

dwarf, in knot gardens, 158
ease of starting from seed, 16
French, 102, 136, 185
in cool environment, 50
Mexican, as companion plant, 185
planting time, 47
pot, 50, 112, 218. See also *Calendula*
signet, 136
Marjoram, 170-171
in hanging baskets, 210
pot, 172
sweet, 170
wild, 172-173
Marrow, vegetable, 97-98. See also
Squash, summer
Martins, purple, in insect control, 183
Marvel-of-Peru, 124-125
Matricaria recutita, 165. See also
Chamomile
Matthiola, 50, 149-150
bicornis, 149
incana, 149
longipetala, 149
McCulloch, Thomas, *The Stepsure Letters*,
25
McGrath, Thomas, 77
Mealybugs, control, 185, 186
Melissa officinalis, 161-162
Melons. See also Muskmelons;
Watermelons
and crop rotation, 39
frost tenderness, 214
honeydew, 86
in vertical gardens, 25
planting time, 46
pollination, 192, 203
pre-germination, 52
sowing and transplanting, 49-50
space efficiency, 17
Mentha, 171-172. See also Mint
aquatica, 171
arvensis, 171
citrata, 171
pulegium, 171
requienii, 171
spicata, 171
suaveolens, 171
viridis, 171
x *piperita*, 171
Mesclun, 85. See also Cut-and-come-
again greens
Mexican bean beetle, 67, 186
Michihli, 75. See also Cabbage, Chinese
Microclimates in cities, 209-210
Mildew, 114, 135, 137, 192
downy, 191
powdery, 91, 99, 108, 121, 191, 192
Milfoil, 154-155. See also Yarrow
Mineral oil as pesticide, 185
Mint, 171-172

apple, 171
bergamot, 171
candymint, 171
container growing, 205, 207, 210
Corsican, 171
curly, 171
field, 171
garden, 171
in vegetable gardens, 159
orange, 171
pennyroyal, 171
peppermint, 171
pineapple, 171
spearmint, 171
terpenoids in, 160
water, 171
Mirabilis jalapa, 124-125
Mites, 192
spider, 136, 185, 186
Mold, gray, 114, 115, 191. See also Botrytis
Moluccella laevis, 50, 110
Monarda, 136-137, 163-164
didyma, 136-137
fistulosa, 136-137
Monkshood, 137
Monoecious, 192
Moodie, Susanna, *Roughing It in the Bush*, 78
Moonflower, 137, 207
Morning glories, 52, 137-138
container growing, 207, 210
'Heavenly Blue,' 138; photo, 137
Morphine in plants, 160
Mosaic, 78, 84, 115, 190
cucumber, 135
tobacco, 102
turnip, 96
Moss phlox, 141
Moss rose, 142. See also *Portulaca*
Moths
artichoke plume, 62
cabbage, 70
control, 185
diamondback, 186, 187
gypsy, 185, 186
Mulches, 180-182
definition, 230
on container plants, 206
on perennials in fall, 215-216, 217
organic, 180-181
plastic, 59, 181
timing, 181-182
Muscari, 128
armeniacum 'Blue Spike,' 225
Mushrooms
drying, 223
field, 85-86
freezing, 221
Muskmelons, 17, 27, 47, 86-87, 224

Mustard
hedge, as weed, 182
wild, as weed, 182
Mustard cabbage, 87
Mustard family and crop rotation, 39
Mustard greens, 17, 39, 87
Myosotis sylvatica, 124
Myrrhis odorata, 176
Myrtle, 139-140
Names of plants, botanical, 38
Narcissus, 119-120
Narcissus bulb fly, 120
Nasturtium (*Tropaeolum*), 138, 172; photos, 172, 184
as companion plant, experiments, 184
as part of vegetable garden, 16
container growing, 207, 210, 211
in vegetable gardens, 159
Nasturtium officinale, 103, 172. See also Watercress
Neck rot, 191. See also Botrytis
Neem, 187
Nematodes, 102, 185
beneficial, 190
Nemophila menziesii, fall sowing, 218
Nepeta
cataria, 113, 164-165. See also Catnip
hederacea, 113
mussinii, 113
x *faassenii*, 23, 113
Nettle, stinging, as weed, 182
Newspaper as mulch, 181
Nicotiana, 26, 39, 46, 138
affinis, 138
alata grandiflora, 138
alata 'Nicki,' 138; photo, 114
sylvestris, 138
Nigella damascena, 124, 218
Nightshade, Malabar, 85
Nightshade family and crop rotation, 39
Nitrogen fixation, 37, 230
Nitrogen-rich compost materials, 42
Ocimum, 162-163. See also Basil
americanum, 162
basilicum, 162
gratissimum, 162
kilimandscharicum, 162
sanctum, 162
'Spicy Globe,' 158, 162
Oenothera
fruticosa, 123
missourensis, 123
speciosa, 123
tetragona, 123
Oil, mineral, as pesticide, 185
Okra, 19, 52, 88, 214
Chinese, 84
Onion maggots, 89, 189

Onions, 38, 88-89; photo, 224
as companion plants, 185
bulb, 17, 27
bunching, 17, 88, 89
curing, 225
drying, 223
Egyptian, 88; photo, 88
fall sowing, 218
freezing, 221
frost hardiness, 215
globe, 88, 89
ornamental, 106
pearl, 88
pickling, 88
planting time, 46
pollination, 203
root-cellar storage, 224, 225
sowing and transplanting, 49
Spanish, 88
spring, 88
top, 88
tree, 88
Open-pollinated seeds, 196, 197
Orange mint, 171
Oregano, 172-173
common, 172
golden creeping, 173
Greek, 172
terpenoids in, 160
true, 172
wild, 172
Organic fertilizers, 35, 36-40; chart, 34
Organic material, 31-32
Orientation of garden and garden rows, 16-17
Origanum
heracleoticum, 172
majorana, 170-171
vulgare, 172-173
Ornamental plants. See also Annuals; Flowers; Perennials
difficult to divide, 199
easy to divide, 199
easy to start by cuttings, 200
edible, 123
for cool greenhouses, chart, 50
needing rooting hormone to start by cuttings, 200
species descriptions, 105-155
Orris root, 131
Osteospermum, 122-123
Oswego tea, 163-164. See also *Monarda*
Outdoor planting, schedule, 46-47
Outdoor seed-sowing, 46-47, 54
Oyster plant, 96-97. See also Salsify
Paeonia, 139
Painted daisy, 114
Painted tongue, 39, 138-139
Pansies, 46, 50, 218
Papaver, 141-142. See also Poppies

nudicaule, 141
orientale, 141
rhoeas, 141
somniferum, 141
Paper
    as mulch, 181
    in compost, 42
Parasitic wasp as beneficial insect, 186, 189
Parkinson, John, 167, 170
Parsley, 173
    Chinese, 167. See also Coriander
    container growing, 207, 210
    curled, 173
    fall sowing, 218
    French, 165, 173
    frost hardiness, 215
    Greek, 173
    Hamburg, 173
    in vegetable gardens, 159
    Italian, 173
    planting time, 46
    pollination, 203
    turnip-rooted, 173
    yield, 27
Parsley family and crop rotation, 39
Parsleyworm, 72, 74, 161, 173, 185, 189; photo, 188
Parsnips, 89-90
    and crop rotation, 39
    drying, 223
    frost hardiness, 215
    overwintering in the ground, 217, 224
    pollination, 203
    root-cellar storage, 225
    seed head, photo, 198
    seed-saving, 201-202
    yield, 27
Parthenocarpic, 193
Pasqueflower, 107
Pastinaca sativa, 89-90. See also Parsnips
Pattypan squash, 97-98; photo, 98. See also Squash, summer
Pe tsai, 75. See also Cabbage, Chinese
Pea family and crop rotation, 39
Peaches, root-cellar storage, 224
Peanuts, 39, 47, 91-92, 203
    Spanish, 91-92
    Valencia, 91-92
Pears, root-cellar storage, 224
Peas, 90-91
    and crop rotation, 39
    as green manure, 37
    'Blue Pod Capucijners,' photo, 90
    chick. See Beans, garbanzo
    container growing, 207
    drying, 223
    edible-podded, 91
    field, as green manure, 37

frost hardiness, 215
location in garden, 18
planting time, 46
pollination, 193, 203
pre-germination, 52
seed-saving, 200
snap, 90-91
snow, 90-91
soup, 90-91
space efficiency, 17
sweet. See Sweet pea
yield, 27
Peat moss, 50-51
    as remedy for alkaline soil, 36
Pelargonium, 207, 210, 214; photo, 207
    peltatum, 126
    x *hortorum*, 126-127
Pennsylvania Dutch tea thyme, 177
Pennyroyal, 171
Penstemon digitalis, 139
Peonies, 139
Pepper as insecticide, 186
Pepper maggots, 93
Peppergrass, 77. See also Cress
Peppermint, 171
Peppers, 92-93
    ancho, 165
    and crop rotation, 39
    banana, 166
    bell, photo, 92
    bringing indoors for winter, 216
    cayenne, 165
    chile, 159, 165-166, 202, 210
    container growing, 207, 210
    drying, 223
    freezing, 221
    frost tenderness, 214
    Hungarian wax, 166
    jalapeño, 165
    length of growing season, 19
    light preference, 16
    planting time, 46, 47
    pollination, 193, 203
    pre-germination, 52
    seed-saving, 202
    sowing and transplanting, 49
    space efficiency, 17
    tabasco, 165
    yield, 27
Perennials
    beds, mulching, 217
    cessation of growth in fall, 215
    characteristics, 105
    container growing, 205, 207-208, 210
    definition, 230
    fall sowing, 218
    fertilization in fall, 215
    long-blooming, chart, 23
    needing winter mulch, 215-216

overwintering in containers, 205
transplanting, 24
vegetative propagation, 199-200
Periwinkle, 139-140, 199, 210
    Madagascar, 113
Perlite, 50
Perovskia atriplicifolia, 145-146
Pesticides, 185-187, 230. See also Disease control; Insect control
    botanical, 186-187
Pesto, 160
Petroselinum crispum, 173. See also Parsley
Petunia, 140-141; photo, 207
    and crop rotation, 39
    container growing, 207, 211
    in cool environment, 50
    planting time, 46
    surfinia, 140
    x *hybrida*, 140-141
pH, 35, 230
Phaseolus
    angularis, 68
    coccineus, 66
    limensis, 66. See also Beans, lima
    lunatus, 66. See also Beans, lima
    vulgaris, 65-67. See also Beans, snap
Pheromone lures for insects, 186
Phlox, 141
    annual, 141
    container growing, 207
    drummondii, 141
    moss, 141
    paniculata, 23, 141
    perennial, 141
    subulata, 141
Phosphate
    colloidal, as fertilizer, composition, 34
    rock, as fertilizer, composition, 34
Physalis
    franchetii, 124. See also Chinese lantern
    ixocarpa, 101. See also Tomatillos
    peruviana, 80-81. See also Ground cherries
Pickles, 220-221
Pickling onions, 88
Pig manure as fertilizer, composition, 35
Pigweed, redroot, 101, 182
Pimpinella anisum, 161. See also Anise (*Pimpinella*)
Pincushion flower, 146-147
Pine cones, shredded, in planting mixes, 51
Pinks, 50, 121-122. See also *Dianthus*
Piperine in black pepper, 160
Pisum sativum, 90-91. See also Peas
Plant diseases, 190-192
Plant families and crop rotation, 37-39;

chart, 38-39
Plant names, botanical, 38
Plant protection
    fall, 216-217
    shelters, 54-59
    spring, 19, 58-59
Planters. See Container gardens;
    Containers
Planting seeds, 45-47. See also
    Transplanting
    depth, 51, 54
    fall, 217-218
    in containers, 209
    indoors, 46, 51-52
    outdoors, 46-47, 54
Plants
    bedding, definition, 227
    bedding, transplanting into
        containers, 209
    mail-order sources, 232-238
Plastic
    mulches, 59, 181
    plant protectors, 58-59
    row covers, 58-59; illustration, 58
Platycodon grandiflorus, 23, 109
Pliny the Elder, 161
Plums, root-cellar storage, 224
Pollination, 192-193, 230
    cross, 228
    hand, 192-193
    preventing, among different varieties,
        197
Popcorn, 76-77
Poppies, 46, 123, 141-142
    alpine, 141
    annual, sowing and transplanting,
        26, 49-50
    California, 141, 218; photo, 107
    carnation, 141
    corn, 141; photo, 140
    Flanders, 141
    Iceland, 141
    opium, 141
    Oriental, 141, 218; photo, 130
    peony, 141
    Shirley, 141, 218; photo, 140
Poppy-flowered anemone, 107
Portulaca, 26, 142, 207, 211
    grandiflora, 142
Potato beetle, Colorado, 94. See
    Colorado potato beetle
Potatoes, 93-95
    and Colorado potato beetle, 37
    and crop rotation, 39
    drying, 223
    frost hardiness, 215
    in single-row gardens, 20
    location in garden, 18
    nematodes and French marigolds,
        185

overwintering in the ground, 224
    planting time, 46
    pollination, 203
    root-cellar storage, 224, 225
    saving for propagation, 202
    sweet. See Sweet potatoes
    yield, 27
Potentilla for wind protection, 18
Poterium sanguisorba, 175. See also Salad
    burnet
Potpourri, definition, 230
Powdery mildew, 91, 99, 108, 121, 191,
    192
Prairie crocus, 107, 118
Praying mantid as beneficial insect,
    186, 189
Pre-germination, 52-53
Preparing garden beds, 29-32
Preservation methods for garden
    produce, 219-225
    canning, 219-220
    drying, 223
    freezing, 221-223
    jams, jellies and pickles, 220-221
    root-cellar storage, 223-225
Primroses, 142-143
    common, 50, 142
    drumstick, 142
    evening, 123
    fairy, 50
    German, 142
    polyanthus, 142
    showy, 123
Primula, 142-143
    auricula, 142-143
    bulleyana, 142
    chionantha, 142
    denticulata, 142
    malacoides, 50, 143
    obconica, 142, 143
    vulgaris, 50, 142
Prince's-feather, 107
Propagation, 195-203. See also Seeds,
    sowing
    cuttings, 200
    division, 199
    layering, 199-200
    seeds and seed-saving, 195-199
    vegetative, 199-200
Protecting plants from frost and cold, 19,
    216. See also Plant protection, shelters
Psophocarpus tetragonolobus, 68
Pulsatilla vulgaris, 107
Pumpkins, 98-99
    and crop rotation, 39
    base temperature, 19
    curing, 225
    drying, 223
    in vertical gardens, 25
    planting time, 46, 47

pollination, 203
    root-cellar storage, 225
    seed-saving, 202
    space efficiency, 17
    yield, 27
Purple climber, 119
Purple martins in insect control, 183
Purple Sensation, 106
Purslane as weed, 182
Puschkinia scilloides, hardiness, 225
Pyrethrin, 186
Pyrethroids, synthetic, 187
Pyrethrum (insecticide), 186-187
Pyrethrum roseum, 114. See also Daisies,
    painted
Quack grass, 30, 182
Quinine in plants, 160
Raab, broccoli, 69
Radichetta, 74, 75
Radicle, 52
Radishes, 95
    and crop rotation, 39
    fall sowing, 218
    planting time, 46
    pollination, 203
    space efficiency, 17
    winter, root-cellar storage, 225
    yield, 27
Rainwater, 180
Raised beds, 19, 22-23; photo, 18
Ranunculus, hardiness, 225
Raphanus sativus, 95. See also Radishes
Raspberries in single-row gardens, 20
Reemay, 59
Reproduction, 195-203. See also Seeds,
    sowing
    cuttings, 200
    division, 199
    layering, 199-200
    vegetative, 199-200
Rheum rhaponticum, 95-96. See also
    Rhubarb
Rhizobium, 37
Rhizome, definition, 230
Rhododendron and layering, 200
Rhubarb, 95-96
    fall planting, 218
    juice and syrup, processing time, 220
Ring rot, 190
Rocambole garlic, 80
Rock cress, 50, 108-109. See also
    Aubrieta
Rock phosphate as fertilizer,
    composition, 34
Rocket, 63
Romaine lettuce, 83
Root, Richard, 184
Root borer, 132
Root-cellar storage, 223-224
Root cellars, construction, 224;

illustration, 223
Root maggot, 70
Root vegetables
    curing, 225
    drying, 223
    harvesting, 217
Rooting hormone, 200
Roots, tap, definition, 231
Roquette, 63
Rosa, 143-144. See also Roses
    rugosa, 144
Rose, moss, 142. See also *Portulaca*
Rose campion, 144
Rose mallow, 129
Rosemary, 173-174, 207, 210; photo, 201
Roses, 25, 143-144, 215
Rosmarinus officinalis, 173-174. See also Rosemary
Rot
    black, 96, 121
    black root, 110, 127
    neck, 191. See also Botrytis
    ring, 190
    soft, 190
Rotation, crop, and plant families, 37-39
Rotenone, 186
Row covers, 58-59, 183; illustration, 58
Ruchetta, 63
Rudbeckia, 144-145; photo, 145
    and crop rotation, 39
    annual, planting time, 46
    container growing, 207
    direct sowing, 26
    fulgida 'Goldsturm,' 144
    hirta, 144, 145
    laciniata, 23, 145
    nitida 'Autumn Glory,' 23
Rumex, 176. See also Sorrel
    acetosa, 176
    scutatus, 176
Rust, 64, 67, 108, 144, 171-172, 191, 217
Rutabagas, 96
    and crop rotation, 39
    frost hardiness, 215
    pollination, 203
    root-cellar storage, 224
    yield, 27
Rye, fall, as green manure, 37; photo, 36
Ryegrass, Russian wild, as green manure, 37
Sage, 174-175; photo, 201
    'Aurea,' photo, 174
    common, 175; photo, 174
    container growing, 207, 210
    garden, 175
    in knot gardens, 158
    pineapple, 175
    'Purpurea,' photo, 174

Russian, 145-146
scarlet, 146
terpenoids in, 160
tricolor, 175
'Tricolor,' 175, photo, 174
Salad burnet, 158, 175
Salpiglossis sinuata, 138-139. See also Painted tongue
Salsify, 96-97
    and crop rotation, 39
    black, 97. See also *Scorzonera hispanica*
    frost hardiness, 215
    overwintering in the ground, 217
    pollination, 203
    root-cellar storage, 225
Salvia, 146, 157, 174-175. See also Sage
    'Aurea,' photo, 174
    elegans, 175
    farinacea, 146
    horminum, 146
    officinalis, 175
    'Purpurea,' photo, 174
    splendens, 146
    'Tricolor,' 175, photo, 174
    viridis, 175
    x *superba*, 23, 146
    x *sylvestris* 'May Night,' 23
Sand in soil mixes, 50
Sandy soil, 32
Sanguisorba minor, 175. See also Salad burnet
Santolina in knot gardens, 158
Sanvitalia, 39, 146
    procumbens, 146
Sapphire flower, 111-112. See also *Browallia*
Saskatoons for wind protection, 18
Satureja, 175-176. See also Savory
    hortensis, 175-176
    montana, 175
Sauerkraut, 220
Saving seeds. See Seeds, saving
Savory, 175-176, 210
    summer, 158-159, 175-176, 207, 214
    winter, 158, 175
Sawdust
    as fertilizer, composition, 34
    as mulch, 181
    in compost, 42
Scab, 69, 95, 191
Scabiosa, 146-147
    atropurpurea, 147
    caucasica, 23, 146
Scale insects, control, 186, 192
Scallions, 88, 207
Scallop squash, 97-98. See also Squash, summer
Scanmask, 190

Scarlet runner beans, 66; photo, 66
Schizanthus in hanging baskets, 210
Scilla, 147
    siberica, hardiness, 225
    tubergeniana, hardiness, 225
Scorzonera hispanica, 97, 225
Sea lavender, 123
Seasonal routines for container gardens, 208-210
Seaweed
    as mulch, 181
    in compost, 40, 42
Sedum, 147-148
    acre, 147
    'Autumn Joy,' 23, 148; photo, 147
    kamtschaticum, 148
    spectabile 'Brilliant,' 148
    spurium 'Dragon's Blood,' 148
Seedlings
    cold treatment, 53
    containers for, 48-50; photo, 49
    damping-off, 46, 53
    definition, 231
    hardening off, 53-54
    leggy, cause, 48
    transplanting, 52, 53, 54; photo, 52
Seeds
    amount to buy, 45
    containers for starting, 48-50; photo, 49
    exchanges, 196
    hybrid and nonhybrid, 196-197
    mail-order sources, 232-238
    maturity, 198
    organizing, 46
    saving, 195-196, 197-199
    saving, best vegetables for, 200-202
    sharing, 202
    sowing, 45-47
    sowing, depth, 51, 54
    sowing, fall, 217-218
    sowing in containers, 209
    sowing indoors, 46, 51-52
    sowing outdoors, 46-47, 54
    starting, easy plants, 15-16
    storage, 198-199
    treated and untreated, 45-46
    viability, checking, 199
    watering, 51
Self-sterile, definition, 231
Set, definition, 231
Sewage sludge as fertilizer, composition, 34
Shade and container gardens, 211
Shade-tolerant ornamental plants, 18
Shallots, 38, 89, 203
Sheep manure as fertilizer, composition, 35
Shellflower, Mexican, 150
Shelterbelts, 18-19

Shelters for plants, 54-59
Side-dressing, 38, 231
Silt soil, 32
Silver dollar, 124
Single flower, definition, 231
Single-row garden, 20
Site evaluation, 16-19
Size of beginners' gardens, 15-16
Slipperwort, 50. See also *Calceolaria*
Slugs, 78, 84, 102, 111, 121, 133, 135, 183, 186, 189
Smut, 191
Snails, 111, 121, 133, 135, 186, 189
Snakeroot, 148
Snake's-head, 125
Snap peas, 90-91
Snapdragons, 26, 46, 50, 148, 218
Snow-in-summer, 149, 205
Snow peas, 90-91
Snowdrops, 148-149. See also *Galanthus nivalis*
Soaps, insecticidal, 185
Sod, removal, 29-30; photo, 31
Soft rot, 190
Soil, 29-43
    acidic, 33-36, 227
    alkaline, 33-36, 227
    amendments, 31-43
    clay, 32
    fertilizers, 32-40
    loam, 32
    mixes for container gardens, 208
    mixes for starting seeds, 50-51
    sandy, 32
    silt, 32
    tests, 35, 36, 217; sources, 43
    thermometer, 26
    well-tended, advantages of, 16
Solanaceae and crop rotation, 39
Solanaceous, definition, 231
Solanum
    melanocerasum, 79-80. See also Huckleberries, garden
    melongena, 79. See also Eggplant
    nigrum, 79-80. See also Huckleberries, garden
    tuberosum, 93-95. See also Potatoes
Soldier bug as beneficial insect, 186
Sorrel, 176, 210
    French, 176
    garden, 176
Soup peas, 90-91
Sources
    of plants, seeds and supplies, 232-239
    of soil tests, 43
Sourgrass, 176. See also Sorrel
Sowing. See Seeds, sowing
Soybeans. See Beans, soy
Space efficiency

of single-row gardens, 20
of temporary wide-row gardens, 20
of vegetables, chart, 17
of vertical gardens, 24-25
of wide-row gardens, 21
Spaghetti squash, 98-99. See also Squash, winter
Spanish onions, 88
Spanish peanuts, 91-92
Sparaxis tricolor, hardiness, 225
Spearmint, 171
Species, definition, 231
Speedwell, 153-154. See also *Veronica*
Sphagnum moss, 51
Spider flower, 115-116. See also *Cleome*
Spider mites, 136, 185, 186
Spiderwort, 152
Spinach, 97
    and crop rotation, 39
    base temperature, 19
    blanching for freezing, 222
    cessation of growth in fall, 215
    Chinese, 100-101
    drying, 223
    fall sowing, 218
    frost hardiness, 215
    Malabar, 85
    New Zealand, 87-88; photo, 87
    perpetual, 85
    planting time, 46
    pollination, 203
    shade tolerance, 17
    sowing and transplanting, 49
    space efficiency, 17
    yield, 27
Spinacia oleracea, 97. See also Spinach
Spring
    activities, 45-59
    frost dates, last, 46; chart, 47
    plant protection, 19, 58-59
Spring onions, 88
Sprinkling, 179-180
    as frost protection, 216-217
Sprouting. See Germination
Squash. See also Pumpkins
    acorn, 98-99
    and crop rotation, 39
    blanching for freezing, 222
    buttercup, 98-99
    butternut, 98-99
    crookneck, 97-98
    curing, 225
    drying, 223
    frost tenderness, 214
    pattypan, 97-98; photo, 98
    planting time, 46, 47
    pollination, 192, 203
    pre-germination, 52
    scallop, 97-98
    seed-saving, 202

sowing and transplanting, 49-50
space efficiency, 17
spaghetti, 98-99
straightneck, 97-98
summer, 97-98, 207, 216
turban, 98-99
winter, 25, 98-99, 225
yield, 27
Squash bug, 78, 99, 186, 189
Squash vine borer, 78, 99
Squill, 147. See also *Scilla*
Stamen, definition, 231
Standard seeds, 196, 197
Star of the veldt, 122-123
Starters for compost, 42-43
Statice, 123; photo, 122
    perennial, 123
Sterilizing
    compost and topsoil, 51
    jars for preserves, 221
Sternbergia lutea, hardiness, 225
Steroids in herbs, 160
Stigma, definition, 231
Stocks, 149-150
    and crop rotation, 39
    annual, planting time, 46
    evening-scented, 149
    in cool environment, 50
    10-week, 149; photo, 149
    Virginia, 26, 149
Stokesia, 39, 150, 218
    cyanea, 150
    laevis, 23, 150
Stonecrop, 147-148. See also *Sedum*
Straightneck squash, 97-98. See also Squash, summer
Straw
    as fertilizer, composition, 34
    as mulch, 181
    in compost, 40, 42
Strawberries, 158, 199, 210
Strawflower, 23, 39, 123; photo, 122
Stunt virus and chrysanthemums, 115
Sucker, definition, 231
Suey choy, 75. See also Cabbage, Chinese
Sulfur
    as remedy for alkaline soil, 36
    for insect and fungal-disease control, 192
Summer activities, 179-193
Sunberries, 79-80. See also Huckleberries, garden
Sunchokes, 62-63. See also Artichokes, Jerusalem
Sundrops, 123
Sunflower family and crop rotation, 39
Sunflowers, 151-152; photo, 196
    and crop rotation, 39
    direct sowing, 26
    false, 151. See also *Heliopsis*

location in garden, 17
Mexican, 152
planting time, 46
pre-germination, 52
'Russian Giant,' 202
seed-saving, 202
Sunlight, need for, 16-18
Sunrooms, 55
Supplies, mail-order sources for,
238-239
Supports for vining and climbing plants,
25
Surfinia, 140. See also *Petunia*
Swallows in insect control, 183
Swallowtail butterfly, black, 72, 74, 189
Swedes, 96. See also Rutabagas
Sweet cicely, 176
Sweet pea, 23, 26, 39, 46, 52, 152
Sweet potatoes, 19, 47, 99-100
Sweet sultan, 117-118
Sweet William, 50, 121-122
Swiss chard, 100; photo, 100
and crop rotation, 39
frost hardiness, 215
pollination, 203
sowing and transplanting, 49
space efficiency, 17
Synthetic fertilizers, 32-33
Tabasco pepper, 165
Tagetes. See also Marigolds
erecta, 136
in cool environment, 50
minuta as companion plant, 185
patula, 102, 136, 185. See also
Marigolds, French
signata, 136
tenuifolia, 136
Tampala, 100-101. See also *Amaranthus
tricolor*
Tansy in insecticidal sprays, 186
Taproot, definition, 231
Taraxacum officinale, 78-79. See also
Dandelions
Tarragon, 39, 176-177
French, 176-177
Russian, 177
Temperature, base, 19
10-week stocks, 149; photo, 149
Tender plants, 19
Tendril, definition, 231
Tent caterpillars, control, 185
Terpenoids in herbs, 160
Tetragonia expansa, 87-88. See also
Spinach, New Zealand
Tetraploids, 196
Texas bluebonnet, 135
Thermometer, soil, 26
Thistle, globe, 39, 127; photo, 12
Thorn apple, 120
Thrips, 150, 186, 187

Thunbergia alata, 111, 210
Thyme, 177
and layering, 199
caraway, 177
common, 177
container growing, 207
garden, 177
in hanging baskets, 210
in knot gardens, 158
in vegetable gardens, 159
lemon, 177
lemon, creeping, 177
wild, 177
Thymus, 177. See also Thyme
herba-barona, 177
pulegioides, 177
serpyllum, 177
vulgaris, 177
x *citriodorus*, 177
Tickseed, 117
Tiger flower, 150
Tigridia, 150
Tillers, rotary, overuse of, 31
Timothy as green manure, 37
Tipburn and lettuce, 84
Tithonia rotundifolia, 152
Tobacco, flowering, 138. See also
Nicotiana
Tobacco mosaic, 102
Tomatillos, 39, 101
Tomato hornworm, 81, 102, 185, 189
Tomatoes, 101-102
and crop rotation, 39
base temperature, 19
canning, 219
cold tolerance, 19
container growing, 207, 210
drying, 223
ease of starting from seed, 15
freezing, 221
frost tenderness, 214
in vertical gardens, 25
indoor ripening, 216
juice, sauce and ketchup, processing
time, 220
location in garden, 18
nematodes and French marigolds,
185
planting time, 46, 47
pollination, 193, 203
pre-germination, 52
processing time, 220
root-cellar storage, 224
seed-saving, 202
sowing and transplanting, 49
space efficiency, 17
started by cuttings, 200
'Sweet 100' in hanging baskets, 210
transplanting seedlings, 53
yield, 27

Tools, 26-27
mail-order sources, 238-239
maintenance, 218-219
Top onions, 88
Topsoil
in seed-starting mixes, 51
sterilizing, 51
Torenia, 50
Tradescantia x *andersoniana*, 152
Tragopogon porrifolius, 96-97. See also
Salsify
Traill, Catharine Parr, 76, 195, 202
Transplanting
bedding plants into containers, 209
outdoors, 54
seedlings, 52, 53; photo, 52
Transplants, definition, 231
Traps for insects, 186
Treasure flower, 126
Tree onions, 88
Trenching, 30-31; illustration, 30
Treveris, Peter, *Grete Herball*, 173
Trickle irrigation, 180
Trinity flower, 152
Tropaeolum, 172
majus, 138. See also Nasturtium
(*Tropaeolum*)
majus nanum 'Alaska,' 138
peregrinum, 112. See also Canary
creeper
Tsukamoto, Joe, 218
Tubers, 217, 225, 231
Tulipa, 152-153
'Apeldoorn,' 153, 225
fosterana, 152-153, 225
kaufmanniana, hardiness, 225
tarda, 152
Tulips, 152-153. See also *Tulipa*
Turban squash, 98-99. See also Squash,
winter
Turner, William, 170, 175
Turnip mosaic in rutabagas, 96
Turnips, 37, 96, 102-103. See also
Rutabagas
and crop rotation, 39
frost hardiness, 215
planting time, 46
pollination, 203
stem, 81-82. See also Kohlrabi
summer, 102-103
white, 102-103
Twining plants, 24-25
Twitch grass, 30, 182
Umbel, definition, 231
Umbelliferae and crop rotation, 39
Urban microclimates, 209-210
Urine in compost, 42
Vaccinium ovatum, 79
Valencia peanuts, 91-92
Valerianella locusta, 77. See also

Corn salad
Variety, definition, 231
Vegetable amaranth, 100-101
Vegetable gardens, 61-103
 and herbs, 158-159
 and light, 16-18
 fall cleanup, 217
 types, 20-23
Vegetable marrow, 97-98. See also
 Squash, summer
Vegetable oyster, 96-97. See also Salsify
Vegetable soy beans, 67-68. See also
 Beans, soy
Vegetables. See also names of specific
 vegetables
 best for seed-saving, 200-202
 container growing, 207, 210
 definition, 61
 easy to divide, 199
 fall harvesting, 217
 fall sowing, 218
 freezing, 221-223
 pollination, chart, 203
 space efficiency, chart, 17
 species descriptions, 61-103
 yields, chart, 27
Vegetative propagation, 199-200
Verbena, 153, 211
 bonariensis, 23
 x *hybrida*, 153
Verbena, lemon (*Aloysia, Lippia*), 170,
 207
Vermiculite, 50
Veronica, 23, 153-154, 207
 incana, 153
 latifolia 'Crater Lake Blue,' 153
 teucrium, 153
Vertical gardens, 24-25
Verticillium wilt, 79, 102, 191-192
Vetch as green manure, 37
Vicia faba, 65. See also Beans, broad
Vigna
 radiata, 68
 unguiculata, 68
Vinca
 minor, 139-140. See also Periwinkle
 rosea, 113, 207, 211
Vinegars, herb, how to make, 160
Vining plants, 24-25
 in containers, 206-207, 210
Viola, 46, 50, 154, 218
 cornuta, 154
 cucullata, 154
Violet, 50, 154. See also *Viola*
Viral diseases, 190
 aspermy, 115
 mosaic, 78, 84, 115, 190
 mosaic, cucumber, 135
 mosaic, tobacco, 102
 mosaic, turnip, 96

stunt, 115
Virginia stocks, direct sowing, 26
Viscaria in hanging baskets, 210
Wallflowers, 39, 154
 Siberian, 154
Walnut trees as harmful to plants, 102,
 181
Warmth, 19
Wasp, parasitic, as beneficial insect,
 186, 189
Water, gray, definition, 229
Watercress, 39, 103, 172, 203
Watering, 179-180
 by hand, 180
 container plants, 206
 equipment, 26
 schedule, 180
 seeds, 51
 sprinkling, 179-180
 trickle irrigation, 180
 with gray water, 180
 with rainwater, 180
Watermelons, 103
 in vertical gardens, 25
 length of growing season, 19
 planting time, 47
 root-cellar storage, 225
 space efficiency, 17
 yield, 27
Weeding, 182
Weight considerations in container
 gardens, 208
Wheat, winter, as green manure, 37
Wheat celosia, 113
Wheatgrass, crested, as green manure, 37
Wheelbarrows, 26
White grubs, identification and control,
 190
Whiteflies, 185, 186
Wide-row gardens
 permanent, 21-23
 temporary, 20-21; photo, 21
Wilt
 bacterial, 78, 217
 clematis, 115
 fusarium, 64, 102
 verticillium, 79, 102, 191-192
Wind, 18-19, 206
Window boxes, 211
Window greenhouses, 55-56; photo, 55
Wireworms, 72, 87, 94, 185, 190
Wishbone flower, 50
Witloof chicory, 74, 75
Wonderberries, 79-80. See also
 Huckleberries, garden
Wong bok, 75. See also Cabbage,
 Chinese
Wood for raised beds, 22-23
Wood ashes
 as fertilizer, composition, 34

 as remedy for acidic soil, 35, 36
Wood chips as mulch, 181
Wood shavings as fertilizer, composition,
 34
Woodruff, sweet, and layering, 199
Woods, J.J., 41
Worms
 earth, 38-40
 wire, 72, 87, 94, 185, 190
Wormwood in knot gardens, 158
Xeranthemum, 123
Yarrow, 39, 154-155, 205, 207; photo,
 155
 woolly, 155
Yellow jackets, control, 186
Zantedeschia, 150
Zea mays, 75-76. See also Corn
Zinnia, 155
 angustifolia, 155
 as cutting flower, 23
 container growing, 207
 planting time, 47
Zinnia, creeping (*Sanvitalia*), 146
Zonalite, 50
Zones, climatic, 19-20; map, 226
Zucchini, 17, 97-98. See also Squash,
 summer

Credits

Photographs

Jennifer Bennett: pages 16, 31, 32, 33, 48, 51, 55, 59, 66, 92, 98, 110, 147, 149, 162, 163, 164, 185, 188, 196, 198 and 222.

Stephen Errington: page 216.

Turid Forsyth: pages 6, 10, 12, 13, 14, 18, 21, 22, 24, 28, 36, 44, 49, 52, 60, 63, 64, 69, 71, 72, 74, 80, 83, 87, 88, 90, 100, 104, 107, 109, 114, 116, 119, 122, 128, 130, 132, 134, 137, 140, 151, 155, 156, 160, 166, 168, 172, 174, 178, 180, 181, 183, 184, 187, 193, 194, 197, 199, 201, 204, 206, 207, 208, 209, 211, 212, 214, 218, 221 and 224.

John Ruskay: page 145.

Illustrations

Cover illustration by Heather Cooper.
All black-and-white illustrations by John Mardon.